GW00361497

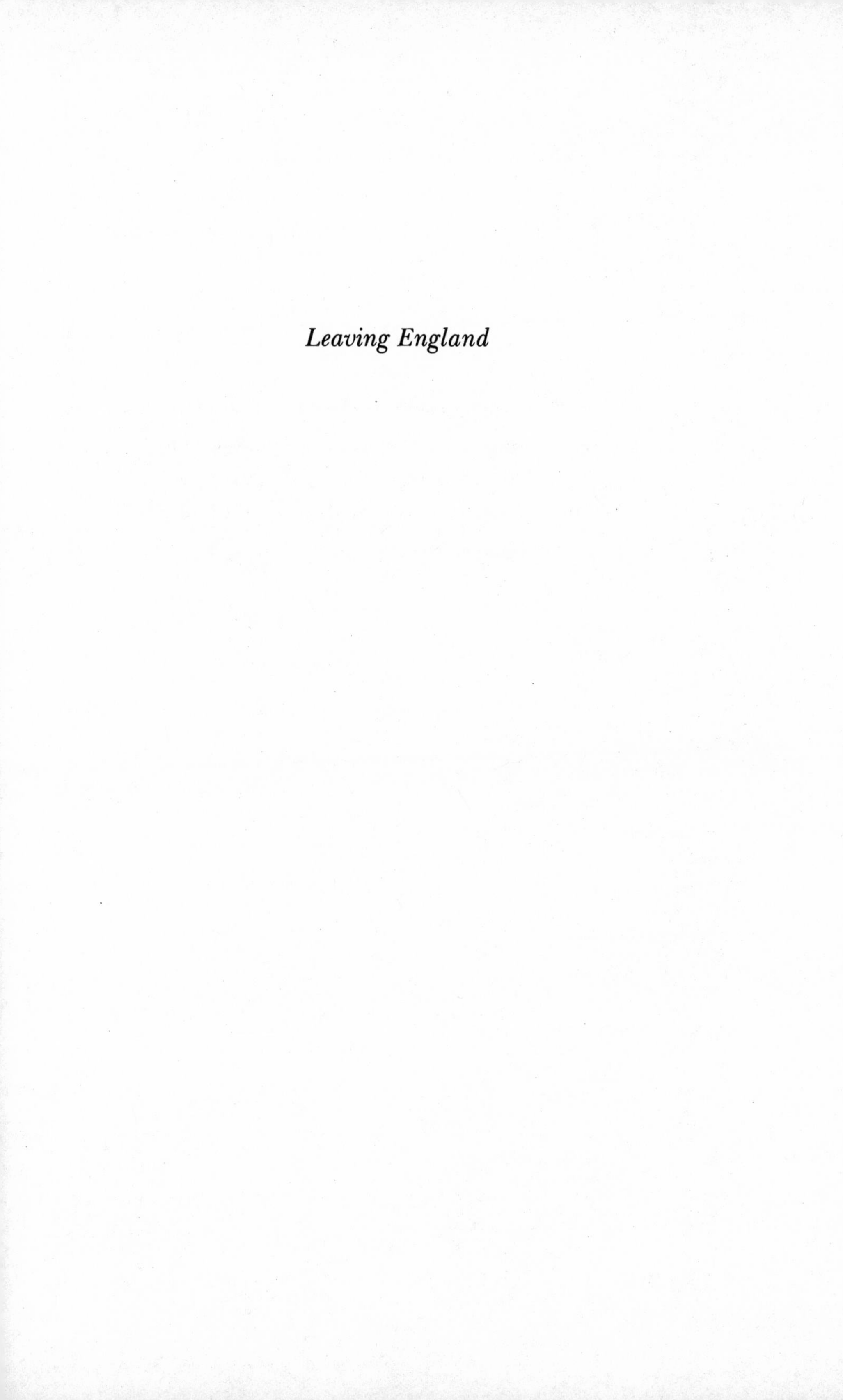

Leaving England

ALSO BY CHARLOTTE ERICKSON

American Industry and the European Immigrant, 1860–1885

British Industrialists, Steel and Hosiery, 1850–1950

Invisible Immigrants: The Adaptation of English and Scottish Immigrants in Nineteenth-Century America

Emigration from Europe, 1815–1914

Leaving England

Essays on British Emigration in the Nineteenth Century

Charlotte Erickson

Cornell University Press

ITHACA AND LONDON

First published 1994 by Cornell University Press.

Printed in the United States of America

♾ The paper in this book meets the minimum requirements of the American National Standard for Information Sciences—Permanence of Paper for Printed Library Materials, ANSI Z39.48-1984.

Library of Congress Cataloging-in-Publication Data

Erickson, Charlotte, 1923–
Leaving England: essays on British emigration in the nineteenth century / Charlotte Erickson.
p. cm.
Includes index.
ISBN 0-8014-2820-3
1. British Americans—History—19th century. 2. Immigrants—United States—History—19th century. 3. United States—Emigration and immigration—History—19th century. 4. Great Britain—Emigration and immigration—History—19th century. I. Title.
E184.B7E744 1994
304.8′0941′09034—dc20 93-40633

For Tom and David

Contents

Tables

Preface

The seven essays in this book were written over a period of thirty years, from 1960 to 1990. Presented in the order in which they were written, they follow the path of my exploration of new sources for the study of emigration from the British Isles and especially from England.

Thus the first essay on agrarian myths is based on early discoveries of immigrant letters. The bias in these letters toward immigrants in the Old Northwest led to the second piece, which makes some excursion into census manuscripts and county histories. Then follow three essays based mainly on passenger lists. The first of these, on the 1880s, sets the framework and definitions used in the other two and appears very largely in its original form. For the essay on the immigrants of 1831, I have done more work to try to improve on earlier comparisons with the British census of that year. The essay on 1841 is new to this volume. It represents my call for more analysis of migration differentials in English (and British) emigration to different destinations.

The sixth essay, on emigration from Lancashire, also appears here for the first time. In it I give some hint of the promise of county histories for the discovery of the elusive, "invisible" English immigrants to the United States. It will be evident that, early in my career, I paid little attention to immigrant women, partly because the sources were so scant and partial. When I was asked to say something about women, I found that there were more Englishwomen's voices than I had noticed. More have been found since that paper was first presented to the Fawcett

Society in 1981, and I have taken the opportunity to expand and revise it.

For the five essays that have been published previously, I am grateful to publishers and editors for permission to present somewhat revised versions here. "Agrarian Myths of English Immigrants" was originally published in 1964 in *In the Trek of the Immigrants: Essays Presented to Carl Wittke*, edited by O. Fritiof Ander, adapted by permission of the General Editor of Augustana Library Publications. "British Immigrants in the Old Northwest, 1815–1860" is reprinted from *The Frontier in American Development: Essays Presented to Paul W. Gates* (Cornell University Press, 1969), edited by David Ellis. "Who Were the English and Scots Emigrants to the United States in the Late Nineteenth Century?" is reprinted from *Population and Social Change* (London: Edward Arnold, 1972), edited by David Glass and Roger Revelle, by permission of Hodder and Stoughton. An earlier version of "Emigration from the British Isles to the United States of America in 1831" appeared in *Population Studies* 25 (1981) and is published with the permission of the editors. "Englishwomen in America in the Nineteenth Century" is based on a pamphlet published by the Fawcett Library, City of London Polytechnic, in Fawcett Library Papers, no. 7, 1983.

The John Simon Guggenheim Foundation, the Social Science Research Council (as it then was) in England, the California Institute of Technology, the Huntington Library, the Nuffield Foundation, and the John D. and Catherine T. MacArthur Foundation all provided funds, at various times, for research and writing.

Assistance that I received in the preparation of the original versions of these articles is acknowledged in the text. I single out the following individuals for calling my attention to particular letters and collections of letters or providing me with materials from their own research: Mary Blewett, Hugh Brogan, Michael Brook, Donald Coleman, Robin Craig, Bernard Crick, Roger Haydon, John Hoffman, David Jeremy, Kevin Schurer, and William Van Vugt.

Substantial help in research was provided by Nick Tiratsoo, Susan Ritter, Sheila Kerr, Peter Martland, Brian Ward, and Margaret Gilmour, for which I am grateful, particularly in that some of that research was fairly tedious but required careful concentration.

Carol Hewlett introduced me to computers and to the Statistical Package for Social Sciences. Joan Lynas typed the original versions of four of these essays and eased my work load in many ways when she was the administrative secretary of the Economic History Department at the London School of Economics. My thanks also to Martin Tilling for giving so generously of his time in recent months whenever I ran into a problem with my new personal computer.

For advice and encouragement through the years, I am indebted particularly to Oscar Handlin, the late David Glass, Dudley Baines, Jim Potter, John Thompson, Ira Glazier, and Tony Wrigley. More recently, my editor at Cornell University Press, Roger Haydon, has taught me much about English emigrants, in addition to reading and advising on the manuscript.

Without the love, faith, and help in myriads of ways of my sons, Thomas and David Watt, this book could not have been completed. I dedicate the volume to them.

For this volume, I have taken the opportunity to correct a few errors in earlier articles and hope that I have not introduced new ones. In all these papers I have called attention to some of the subsequent literature relevant to the material presented. At the same time, I think I have kept my original conclusions intact. I have tried not to display more wisdom after the event, as it were, than I had at the time.

CHARLOTTE ERICKSON

Cambridge, England

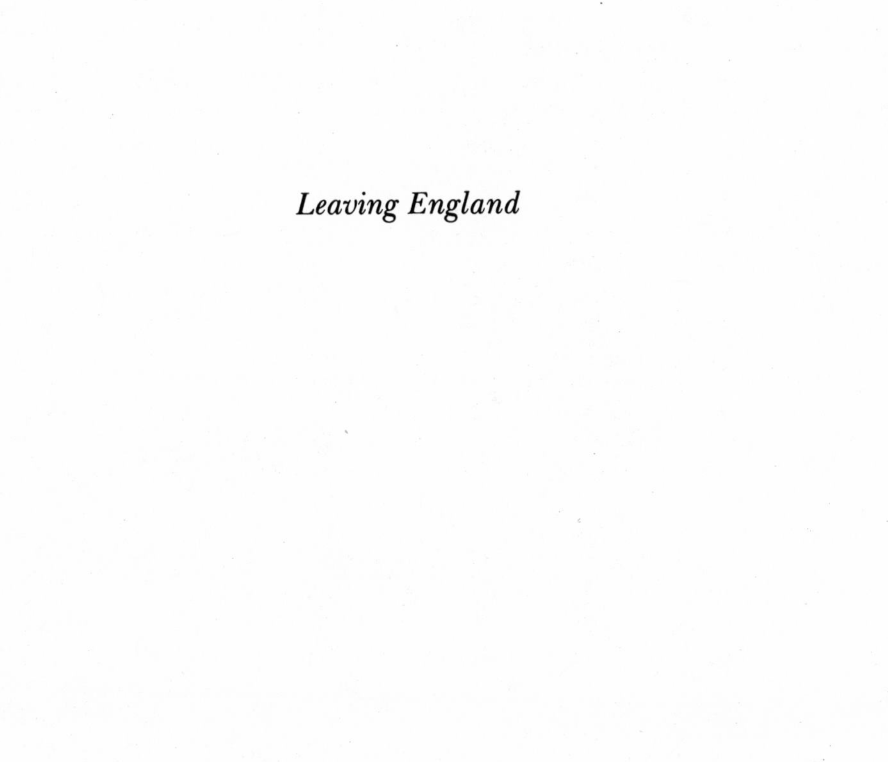

Leaving England

INTRODUCTION

Leaving England

During the last thirty years or so, the study of immigrants and emigrants—of internal, international, and intercontinental migration—has moved out of a somewhat obscure corner of academia to become a flourishing academic industry.[1] Students and scholars today bring to their researches a training in sophisticated methods and a range of disciplines compared to which mine was and remains a horse-and-buggy technology. In all this activity, very few scholars, particularly in the United States of America, have shown much interest in examining English-born people as immigrants. After all, even at the time of their peak numbers in the United States in 1890, the English-born did not constitute more than 1.5 percent of the population or more than 15 percent of the foreign-born inhabitants. They patently did not share many of the disabilities and problems faced by other immigrants. They were rarely hyphenated: the term Anglo-American refers as much to native-born Americans as to English immigrants.

Over the years I have tended to focus increasingly on English emigrants as distinct from the Celts—the Scottish, Welsh, and Irish inhabitants of the United Kingdom of the nineteenth century. Such a focus was very far from my thoughts when I began my research in the field of immigration history more than forty years ago.

[1] For a survey of the various ways in which the revival of interest among historians is manifested, see Rudolph Vecoli, "The Resurgence of American Immigration History," *American Studies International* 17 (1979): 44–66.

When, as a graduate student at Cornell University in 1947, I began to contemplate writing a dissertation on immigration, the idea of writing about a single national group did not attract me. Inspired as I was by the writings of Marcus Hansen on the Atlantic migration as a whole, I particularly rejected the thought of a dissertation on Swedish immigration because of Hansen's warnings of the hazards of filiopietism.[2] From his chapter on research prospects in *The Immigrant in American History* I obtained my subject, the recruitment of immigrant labor by American industry. This was just the sort of transnational subject I was seeking. At that time there were few historians working on immigration. Naturally, I turned to Oscar Handlin for advice. He encouraged and advised me but warned of the grave risk involved in so wide-ranging a project, for which there was no core of source material that might ensure that one actually ended up with a dissertation. In working on that dissertation, I pored over Hansen's notes in the Widener Library, notes made for a projected second volume of *The Atlantic Migration*, which his untimely death interrupted. It became my foolhardy youthful ambition to write a history of the European background to the Atlantic migration after 1860.

I confess to an astonishing naïveté. It would have taken all my life to master the languages that I would have needed, so little scholarly work had then been done on the background to emigration other than from northern and western Europe.[3] Yet from the standpoint of the 1950s, the lull in scholarly interest among American historians reflected, at least in part, the perception that history had come to an end so far as mass intercontinental migration was concerned. As late as 1960, it was possible to see the great cycle of European emigration as having ended.[4] Such a massive movement of people would never be repeated because the circumstances of the nineteenth century were unique. Insofar as the

[2] Marcus Lee Hansen, *The Immigrant in American History* (Cambridge: Harvard University Press, 1942), pp. 27–28. For an expression of confidence that historians of the period would now be able to avoid the bias of the "classical historians," see Edward Saveth, *American Historians and European Immigration, 1875–1925* (New York: Columbia University Studies in History, Economics, and Public Law, no. 540, 1948).

[3] Outstanding exceptions to this statement are the study by the economist Robert Foerster, *The Italian Emigration of Our Times* (Cambridge: Harvard University Press, 1919), and by the sociologists William Thomas and Florian Znaniecki, *The Polish Peasant in Europe and America*, 1st ed. (1918–20; New York: Dover, 1958), 2 vols.

[4] Frank Thistlethwaite, "Migration from Europe Overseas in the Nineteenth and Twentieth Centuries," 1960, reprinted in *A Century of European Migrations, 1830–1930*, ed. Rudolph Vecoli and Suzanne Sinke (Urbana: University of Illinois Press, 1991), p. 35.

relatively unstudied countries of southern and eastern Europe were concerned, the European background was seen as being similar, in all but timing, to that of immigrants from northern and western Europe. As a result of the past generation's researches, the picture is no longer so simple. Not only the scholarship of the intervening years but also world events discouraged me from trying to fulfill that early dream.[5]

It has become clearer that pressures for large-scale international and intercontinental migration did not end with the American Quota Acts, the Great Depression, and World War II. Today immigration is again as much a public issue in receiving countries as it was shortly before and after the First World War. Yet, differences between current population movements and those of the nineteenth century are striking. These have produced equally different responses from governments and people in both donor and host countries.

In the nineteenth century, a marked reciprocity existed between the interests of sending and receiving countries that is not so evident today. Donor countries gradually reduced and even eliminated restrictions on emigrants, and the receiving nations tended to welcome them. Then migration from Europe and the flow of capital to developing regions of the world assisted in raising the living standards in both. Migration was a means of dealing with structural dislocations in the early phases of industrialization in Europe and at the same time helped provide the donors with cheaper food and the raw materials for cheaper consumer goods. The movement out of agriculture in Europe helped furnish workers to develop the natural resources as well as to build the infrastructure and to staff growing industries in the receiving countries.

In some ways this position represents an unfashionably benign view of nineteenth century migrations and an impersonal attitude toward the participants. Marxist-oriented historians are less willing to regard the emigration from Europe in a favorable light. As Dirk Hoerder asks, "Would societally responsible rather than merely economically profitable investments have slowed down the process of out-migration?"[6]

[5] With a far greater knowledge of European languages than I acquired, Walter Nugent has produced such a volume that covers the principal countries in Europe which produced significant numbers of emigrants as well as four of those in the New World that received most of them (*Crossings: The Great Transatlantic Migrations, 1870–1914* [Bloomington: Indiana University Press, 1992]).

[6] Dirk Hoerder, ed., *Labor Migration in the Atlantic Economies: The European and North American Working Classes during the Period of Industrialization* (Westport, Conn.: Greenwood Press, 1985), p. 18.

And some of that movement of people in the nineteenth century was still involuntary or unfree. The British navy did not succeed in eradicating the slave trade to Brazil. Indentured servitude remained a principal means of recruiting immigrants to the Caribbean, Queensland, South Africa, and elsewhere.[7] Nevertheless, the far more numerous migrations from Europe to the United States, Canada, South America, and Australasia resulted from the voluntary decisions of people organized chiefly at the primary group level, in family and village networks. In the largest single transfer of population, from many parts of Europe to the United States, neither governments nor firms were directly involved, except very occasionally, in enabling or directing people to move long distances. Shipping merchants and their agents were meeting a demand from people who hoped and trusted that they would find more productive land or employment and thereby enhance their current or lifetime earnings.[8] If capital flowed along the same channels as the European emigrants, capitalists did not make the decisions, or organize the movement, except in providing the transport. People were not shot for trying to emigrate; nor did they leave in such utterly unseaworthy vessels as those of Vietnamese boat people and the Haitians in recent times. In fact, governments in that much-maligned age of laissez-faire took a decidedly interventionist position, sometimes raising costs for prospective emigrants, in attempting to safeguard the health and safety of ocean-going passengers.

Governments intervene in the late twentieth century far more directly. In the nineteenth century, at least until near the end of it, people who wanted to emigrate to better their economic circumstances were welcomed for the most part. Today, with restriction of immigration in place in the countries to which people want to move, economic motivation is suspect. Refugee status, enabling families and individuals to surmount the barriers, cannot be obtained except on political grounds. Neither a search for economic betterment nor a flight from subsistence crises yields automatic entitlement to immigrate. Population

[7] For recent studies, see Shula Marks and Peter Richardson, eds., *International Labour Migration: Historical Perspectives* (Hounslow, Middlesex: Maurice Temple Smith, 1984), and Kay Saunders, ed., *Indentured Labour in the British Empire, 1834–1920* (London: Croom Helm, 1984).

[8] Berit Brattne, "The Importance of the Transport Sector for Mass Emigration," in *From Sweden to America: A History of the Migration*, ed. Harald Runblom and Hans Norman (Minneapolis: University of Minnesota Press, 1976), pp. 176–200; Charlotte Erickson, *American Industry and the European Immigrant, 1860–1885* (Cambridge: Harvard University Press, 1957).

explosion, wars, famine, and political upheavals have brought, at the end of the twentieth century, a pent-up potential for migration that dwarfs the nineteenth-century "causes" in Europe. With the exception of the tragic Irish famine, the demographic and economic pressures of the nineteenth century seem relatively mild in retrospect. The variety of religions, races, and nationalities of those now seeking entry, and of those achieving it, make the nineteenth-century social, cultural, and political challenges pale in comparison. Since the Second World War, European countries (apart from the former Soviet Union and the Communist bloc) have become, on balance, receivers of immigrants from other parts of the world, as France was before 1914, though not all have offered eventual citizenship to those permitted to work within their borders.

A revival of historical writing on nineteenth-century (and earlier) migrations began before this potential for an even greater world migration in the late twentieth century became apparent. Insofar as events of the time influenced the concerns of historians, the civil rights movement of the 1960s, by highlighting issues of ethnic and minority rights, stimulated this surge in scholarship. The university-trained children and grandchildren of immigrants from southern and eastern Europe were stimulated to research the origins and experience of their forebears. But the flood of dissertations and monographs that began to appear had few of the filiopietist attributes of the early twentieth-century literature. The social sciences and quantitative methods were brought to bear in historical research, and scholars did not confine themselves to studies of their own ancestors.

An inspiration for a significant body of this historical scholarship was the seminal paper delivered by Frank Thistlethwaite to the international conference of historians in Stockholm in 1960. Some American historians heeded his call for serious examination of the European background to emigration. The influence of his paper was even more marked in Europe, where serious study of the mass migrations of the nineteenth century had been relatively limited. Thistlethwaite emphasized the complexity of this great movement of peoples, that the United States had not been the only destination, and that the movement overseas needed to be interpreted in conjunction with internal migration and other intra-European transfers of people. Even more provocative was his suggestion that European migrations were not so much national in scope, from Sweden to America, for example, as constituted by particular streams from one village or region to a particular county or city elsewhere. To my mind, some of the most innovating and illuminating work in recent years has followed this approach.[9]

Such work further undermined the myth of a melting pot in the United States in which immigrants learned to conform to an Anglo-American type. It led to comparative studies of the experience of different peoples in the light of the values, knowledge, and experience they brought with them from another culture.[10] The social structure of immigrant communities in particular places, the attitude of ethnic leaders, and interaction with other immigrant groups all came to be recognized as influencing the assessment of opportunities and the paths followed by immigrants.[11] Regional differences in the immigrant experience in the United States were analyzed not only in terms of the structure of the economy where migrants settled but also in terms of the

[9] Hans Norman, "Swedes in North America," in *From Sweden to America,* ed. Runblom and Norman, pp. 229–300; Robert Ostergren, *A Community Transplanted: The Trans-Atlantic Experience of a Swedish Immigrant Settlement in the Upper Middle West, 1835–1915* (Madison: University of Wisconsin Press, 1988); Odd Lovoll, "A Pioneer Chicago Colony from Voss, Norway: Its Impact on Overseas Migration, 1836–1860," and Juliana Puskas, "Hungarian Overseas Migration: A Microanalysis," both in *Century of European Migrations,* ed. Vecoli and Sinke, pp. 182–99, 221–39; Jon Gjerde, *From Peasants to Farmers: The Migration from Balestrand, Norway, to the Upper Middle West* (Cambridge: Cambridge University Press, 1985); Walter Kamphoefner, *The Westfalians: From Germany to Missouri* (Princeton: Princeton University Press, 1987); Donna Gabaccia, *From Sicily to Elizabeth Street* (Albany: State University of New York Press, 1984); Gabaccia, *Militants and Migrants: Rural Sicilians Become American Workers* (New Brunswick, N.J.: Rutgers University Press, 1988); John Briggs, "Fertility and Cultural Change among Families in Italy and America," *American Historical Review* 91 (1986): 1129–45; Briggs, *An Italian Passage: Immigrants to Three American Cities, 1890–1930* (New Haven: Yale University Press, 1978); Charles Price, *Southern Europeans in Australia* (Oxford: Oxford University Press, 1963).

[10] See, for example, John Bodnar, Roger Simon, and Michael Weber, *Lives of Their Own: Blacks, Italians, and Poles in Pittsburgh, 1900–60* (Urbana: University of Illinois Press, 1982); Josef Barton, *Peasants and Strangers: Italians, Rumanians, and Slovaks in an American City, 1890–1950* (Cambridge: Harvard University Press, 1975); Ronald Bayor, *Neighbors in Conflict: The Irish, Germans, Jews, and Italians of New York City, 1929–41* (Baltimore: Johns Hopkins University Press, 1978); Samuel Baily, "The Adjustment of Italian Immigrants in Buenos Aires and New York, 1870–1914," *American Historical Review* 88 (1983): 281–305; and Gary Mormino and George Pozzetta, *The Immigrant World of Ybor City: Italians and Their Latin Neighbors in Tampa, 1885–1985* (Urbana: University of Illinois Press, 1987).

[11] Victor Greene, *American Immigrant Leaders, 1800–1910: Marginality and Identity* (Baltimore: Johns Hopkins University Press, 1987); John Higham, ed., *Ethnic Leadership in America* (Baltimore: Johns Hopkins University Press, 1978); Kathleen Neil Conzen, *Immigrant Milwaukee, 1836–60: Accommodation and Community in a Frontier City* (Cambridge: Harvard University Press, 1976); Hartmut Keil, ed., *German Workers' Culture in the United States, 1850–1920* (Washington: Smithsonian Institution Press, 1988); Keil, "The German Working Class of Chicago, 1875–90: Workers, Labor Leaders, and the Labor Movement," in *American Labor and Immigrant History, 1877–1920s: Recent European Research,* ed. Dirk Hoerder (Urbana: University of Illinois Press, 1983), pp. 156–76.

selectivity of the immigrant population itself, the hopes, aspirations, and human and material resources of the people involved.[12]

Not all the scholars who wrote about immigrants linked the American experience with specific European backgrounds and sources. A multitude of monographs appeared on social mobility, the new labor history, and immigrant cities, studies that began and ended within the boundaries of the United States. It is not to deny the value and interest of much of this work to suggest that the research in European archives and cooperation between American and European scholars during the past thirty years have been more productive of understanding of the experience of migration and the intricacies of adaptation. Other previously neglected subjects have also come to the fore, such as the diffusion of technology, return migration, and the impact of emigration on the sending countries.[13]

Possibilities for advancing and deepening our knowledge about European migration have not been exhausted. The diversification of immigration to the United States in the wake of the Immigration Act of 1965, which abolished national quotas, has brought a flood of literature on non-European immigrants. Those from the Caribbean and Central America and from the Far East and the Middle East now figure largely as subjects of historical investigation. This new "new immigration" and the heightening of immigration as a contemporary issue actually enhance the value of pursuing new themes, methods, and sources in European migrations, especially in view of the greater accessibility and richness of sources for examining the background to migration, as compared with regions of more recent emigration.

[12] Robert Burchell, *The San Francisco Irish, 1848–80* (Berkeley: University of California Press, 1980); Jo Ellen Vinyard, *The Irish on the Urban Frontier: Nineteenth-Century Detroit* (New York: Arno Press, 1976); Nora Faires, "Occupational Patterns of German-Americans in Nineteenth-Century Cities," in *German Workers in Industrial Chicago, 1850–1910: A Comparative Perspective,* ed. Hartmut Keil and John Jentz (De Kalb: Northern Illinois University Press, 1983), pp. 39–41.

[13] For more detailed and critical discussions of the historiography of immigration studies in the United States, see Thomas Archdeacon, "Problems and Possibilities in the Study of American Immigrant and Ethnic History," *International Migration Review* 19 (1985): 112–34; John Higham, "From Process to Structure: Formulations of American Immigration History," in *American Immigrants and Their Generations*, ed. Peter Kivisto and Dag Blanck (Urbana: University of Illinois Press, 1990), pp. 11–41; Kathleen Neil Conzen, et al., "The Invention of Ethnicity: A Perspective from the U.S.A." and comments thereon, *Journal of American Ethnic History* 12 (1992): 3–63; and Dirk Hoerder, "International Labor Markets and Community Building by Migrant Workers in the Atlantic Economies," in *Century of European Migrations*, ed. Vecoli and Sinke, pp. 78–107.

Some of these themes and methods which have entered historical writing on migration derive from the social sciences. Economists, economic historians, demographers, geographers, anthropologists, sociologists, and students of literature have all contributed to the extraordinary richness apparent in the study of immigration in recent years. Indeed, as Thistlethwaite reminded historians in Stockholm in 1960, demographers and sociologists were writing about migration before American historians began to produce work in the field.[14]

Economists had participated in the debate about the restriction of immigration in the United States before the First World War. Harry Jerome's *Migration and the Business Cycle* appeared in 1926 after the Quota Acts were on the statute books. He then abandoned a projected study of migration and the labor market to work on *Mechanization in Industry*. Not until the 1960s were there signs of a renewed interest among American economists in the quantitative study of immigration. Although this upsurge in scholarship paralleled that of the historians, with economist-economic historians the inspiration was the growth of cliometrics. Economists went beyond the methods of quantification used by the pioneers Harry Jerome, Dorothy Swain Thomas, Simon Kuznets, and Brinley Thomas, to seek the causes of emigration through multiple regression analyses of available statistics and proxies for missing variables. The results of this considerable crop of studies at a national level, undertaken in the late sixties and seventies, were far from conclusive. In the long run they did contribute to a rejection of the hypothesis that emigration was to be explained *either* by the pull of overseas regions *or* the push of circumstances at home. When econometricians introduced a "friends and relatives" variable into their equations, they found it to be at least as significant as economic push or pull.[15]

More recently other econometricians have returned to the issue of the relationship between migration and economic growth that Brinley Thomas explored in the 1950s. Timothy Hatton and Jeffrey Williamson have submitted tentative and preliminary tests of the relative impor-

[14] Thistlethwaite, "Migration from Europe Overseas," pp. 22–23.

[15] For an excellent critical review of these studies, see J. D. Gould, "European Inter-Continental Emigration, 1815–1914: Patterns and Causes," *Journal of European Economic History* 8 (1979): 593–670. See also Dudley Baines, *Migration in a Mature Economy: Emigration and Internal Migration in England and Wales, 1861–1900* (Cambridge: Cambridge University Press, 1985), pp. 8–44; and Charlotte Erickson, "Explanatory Models in Immigration and Migration Research," in *Scando-Americana Papers on Scandinavian Emigration to the United States*, ed. Ingrid Semmingsen and Per Seyersted (Oslo: American Institute of the University of Oslo, 1980), pp. 7–26.

tance of commodity trade, capital flows, and migration in bringing about a trend to convergence of real wages in the Atlantic economy between 1870 and 1914 and since 1950.[16]

The lack of communication between econometricians employing ever more sophisticated models to assess the relative importance of specified influences on the causes and consequences of migration on the one hand and many social and cultural historians of migration on the other is legendary. Nevertheless, the latter generally assume that economic factors provide the most general explanation of the great migrations of the nineteenth century, be they the quest for subsistence and flight from distress or hopes and expectations of economic betterment. I shall return later to the issue of the importance or otherwise of economic factors in the British context. For the moment, it is sufficient to note that government officials today, in both sending and receiving countries, fear the consequences of unrestricted international migration because of assumptions about the overriding economic motivation of migrants and the economic effects of the loss of educated, skilled, and ambitious young people.

In this great outpouring of works on international migration from so many disciplines during the past thirty years, British and, more particularly, English immigrants have not received a great deal of attention. This cannot be said of the colonial period of American history, about which historians have published highly original, in-depth studies that very clearly distinguish the English from the Scots,[17] and other major monographs.[18] Much less has been done, however, on the diaspora of the nineteenth century and next to nothing on the smaller but distinc-

[16] Timothy Hatton and Jeffrey Williamson, "International Migration and World Economic Development: A Historical Perspective," National Bureau of Economic Research, Working Paper Series on Historical Factors in Long Run Growth, no. 41, September 1992; Larry Neal and Paul Uselding, "Immigration: A Neglected Source of American Economic Growth, 1790–1912," *Oxford Economic Papers*, n.s., 24 (1972): 68–98.

[17] Bernard Bailyn, *Voyagers to the West: A Passage in the Peopling of America on the Eve of the Revolution* (New York: Knopf, 1986); David Hackett Fischer, *Albion's Seed: Four British Folkways in America* (Oxford: Oxford University Press, 1990).

[18] David Cressy, *Coming Over: Migration and Communication between England and New England in the Seventeenth Century* (New York: Cambridge University Press, 1987); Stephen Foster, *The Long Argument: English Puritanism and the Shaping of New England Culture, 1570–1700* (Chapel Hill: University of North Carolina Press, 1991); David Grayson Allen, *In English Ways: The Movement of Societies and the Transferal of English Law and Custom to Massachusetts Bay in the Seventeenth Century* (Chapel Hill: University of North Carolina Press, 1981); David Galenson, *White Servitude in Colonial America: An Economic Analysis* (New York: Cambridge University Press, 1981); Roger Ekirch, *Bound for America: The Transportation of British Convicts to the Colonies, 1718–1775* (Oxford: Clarendon Press, 1987).

tive immigration from Britain during the period of the French Wars, the first generation of American nationhood. Neither American nor British historians have demonstrated much interest in nineteenth-century English emigration. Thistlethwaite conjectured that to English historians, "emigration appears to be an embarrassing subject, best ignored."[19] Nonetheless, there are reasons for arguing for more attention to the subject.

One reason why English emigration itself merits more attention is that, unlike that from other parts of northern Europe, emigration actually increased as the country's industrial base matured. More British (as distinct from Irish) people emigrated to North America after 1870 than had gone in 250 years before that date. The Irish-born population of the United States declined from 1.8 million in 1890 to just over a million in 1920, whereas the English-born recorded in the census fell only from 909, 092 to 813, 853 between those dates. English people continued to seek homes overseas in greater numbers with each succeeding wave of migration throughout the nineteenth century, and until 1907 most of the English continued to choose to go to the United States. After that, Canada's stunning economic growth and then the First World War and the Quota Acts diverted most of the continuing overseas movement to the Empire. With national quotas abolished, however, by the 1970s and 1980s, more immigrants from the United Kingdom were arriving in the United States than from any other European country.

Another distinguishing feature of this continued movement out of Britain was the variety of destinations—not only the United States and the Empire, but also wherever Britain traded, financed trade, or exported capital. The English residents of Latin America were not insignificant in number, though barely noticed by scholars. The *Economist* magazine recently described this phenomenon as the "single most widespread global dispersion of people from one small territory that the world had ever seen."[20] I suppose that only the Jewish and the Chinese people could rival it for the degree of dispersal around the world. The British had an extraordinary range of choice as to destination and rarely experienced discrimination or exclusion anywhere.

Among the emigrants from the British Isles, the Scots, the Irish, the Welsh, and the Cornish have all attracted more historical interest than the English, who are usually dealt with as a part of the British emigration by both American and British (though not so much by

[19] Thistlethwaite, "Migration from Europe Overseas," p. 21.
[20] *Economist*, December 26, 1992–January 8, 1993, p. 34.

Canadian and Australian) scholars. An obvious reason for this neglect is the want of the kind of solid body of source material that Oscar Handlin warned me was desirable. The English left very few newspapers or organizational records through which to study their experience in America. Except very sporadically, they did not organize politically, attach themselves to a single religious denomination, or cluster in a few communities. When they organized, or helped to organize, trade unions, cooperatives, friendly societies, churches, or communities, their institutions quickly became "Americanized."

Even more discouraging is the want of adequate and accessible evidence in England of their departure. No police, local government or provincial officials, or clergy recorded the exodus. It is difficult to discover whether there were significant chains from one point in England to another in the United States. No important ones have yet been identified for rural areas in either country. The chief opportunities lie in the study of the emigration of English industrial workers to particular cities in the United States: of framework knitters from the East Midlands to the Philadelphia region; of silk workers from Coventry and Macclesfield to Paterson; of cotton textile workers from Bolton and Oldham to Fall River; of Staffordshire potters to East Liverpool, Ohio, and Trenton, New Jersey; of skilled workers in special steels from Sheffield to Pittsburgh; and of brass workers from the Birmingham area to southern Connecticut.[21] The obstacles to discovering who the emigrants were, as compared with those who stayed behind, and the networks by which they moved to and adapted in their new homes are enormous. Was the emigration from the world's first industrial nation different from that from other European countries?

Most writers of general works and textbooks of English history and even agricultural, labor, and social historians continue to pay little attention to this long-term outflow of people as a part of English history.

[21] Geoffrey Tweedale, *Sheffield Steel and America: A Century of Commercial and Technological Interdependence* (Cambridge: Cambridge University Press, 1987); Frank Thistlethwaite, "The Atlantic Migration of the Pottery Industry," *Economic History Review*, 2d ser., 11 (1958): 264–78; Richard Margrave, *The Emigration of Silk Workers from England to the United States of America in the Nineteenth Century with Special Reference to Coventry, Macclesfield, Paterson, New Jersey, and South Manchester, Connecticut* (New York: Garland, 1986); Amy Zahl Gottlieb, "'British Coal Miners: A Demographic Study of Braidwood and Streator, Illinois," *Journal of the Illinois State Historical Society* 72 (1979): 179–92; Mary H. Blewett, "Traditions and Customs of Lancashire Popular Radicalism in Late Nineteenth-Century Industrial America," International Labor and Working-Class History/Mouvement Sociale Colloquium, Paris, October, 1991, copy kindly given to me by the author.

Emigration receives no mention,[22] or but passing reference, in many well-known surveys currently in use.[23] Not all major historians have so conspicuously neglected it, however; those of an earlier generation did devote some space to it. Assisted emigration and emigration to the Empire, the work of the Colonial Land and Emigration Commission, and the regulation of the passenger trade were the chief subjects mentioned.[24] Still, students reared on more recent surveys would not learn that the United States was the principal destination of English emigrants throughout the nineteenth century.

One can hardly blame historians for this oversight in general histories: the monographic literature specifically on English emigration is sparse. The priority for assessing the nature of emigration and its consequences for England must be to discover who went when and from what areas. Yet local historians rarely touch on the subject. It is notably absent from the Victorian county histories.[25] A few writers have

[22] For example, J. V. Beckett, *The Agricultural Revolution* (London: Blackwell, 1990); John D. Claire, *Agriculture since 1750* (London: Macmillan, 1988); Terence Gourvish, ed., *Later Victorian Britain, 1867–1901* (London: Macmillan, 1988); Peter Mathias, *The Transformation of England* (London: Methuen, 1979); Gordon Mingay, ed., *The Unquiet Countryside* (London: Routledge, 1989); John Belcham, *Industrialization and the Working Class: The English Experience, 1750–1900* (Aldershot, Hants.: Scolar, 1991).

[23] Malcolm Thomis, *Responses to Industrialization: The British Experience, 1780–1850* (Newton Abbot, Devon: David Charles, 1976); Sydney Pollard, *British Public Policy, 1776–1939* (Cambridge: Cambridge University Press, 1983); J. F. C. Harrison, *The Early Victorians, 1832–1851* (London: Weidenfeld and Nicolson, 1971); Eric Hobsbawm, *The Age of Empire, 1874–1914* (London: Weidenfeld and Nicolson, 1987); Peter Mathias, *The First Industrial Nation: An Economic History of Britain, 1700–1914* (London: Methuen, 1969); Harold Perkin, *The Origins of Modern English Society, 1780–1880* (London: Routledge and Kegan Paul, 1990); F. M. L. Thompson, ed., *The Cambridge Social History of Great Britain, 1750–1950,* 2 vols. (Cambridge: Cambridge University Press, 1990). In his chapter "Work," vol. 2, *People and Their Environment,* pp. 139–40, Patrick Joyce refers to Cornish and Scots miners and Lancashire cotton operatives "colonising the industry of the United States and further afield."

[24] Lillian Knowles, *The Industrial and Commercial Revolutions in Great Britain during the Nineteenth Century,* 4th ed. (London: George Routledge and Sons, 1924), pp. 324, 341, and elsewhere; J. H. Clapham, *An Economic History of Modern Britain,* 3 vols. (Cambridge: Cambridge University Press, 1926–38); G. M. Young, ed., *Early Victorian England, 1830–65* (Oxford: Oxford University Press, 1934), vol. 2, chap. 12; R. C. K. Ensor, *England, 1870–1914* (Oxford: Clarendon Press, 1936), pp. 271, 500; Jonathan David Chambers, *The Workshop of the World: British Economic History from 1820 to 1880* (Oxford: Oxford University Press, 1961), pp. 128–29; W. L. Burn, *The Age of Equipoise* (London: Allen and Unwin, 1964), p. 112; Sydney Checkland, *The Rise of Industrial Society in England, 1815–1885* (London: Longman, 1964), p. 335; Gordon Mingay, *The Transformation of Britain, 1830–1930* (London: Routledge and Kegan Paul, 1986), pp. 2, 99–105.

[25] Exceptions to this criticism that I have encountered are B. E. Harris, ed., *Victorian History of the Counties of England: A History of Cheshire* (London: University of London Institute of Historical Research, 1979–87), 2: 241; *Warwickshire* (1908; rpt., London:

characterized emigration as a safety valve or as evidence of rural discontent.[26] Asa Briggs went so far as to declare that without the safety valve afforded by emigration, one finds it difficult to imagine what would have happened to English, and certainly to Irish, society in the 1840s and 1850s.[27] It is therefore disappointing when studies of rural discontent in England in the first half of the century make no reference to emigration.[28] A recent study of the attachment of urban workers in England to ideas of land nationalization or of land reform by means of small private farms, and of the central importance of such ideas in movements of social protest in the period, dismisses the relevance of emigrants to the issue.[29]

A few economic historians have probed the relationship between structural change in England and the overseas movement. Arthur Redford, Brinley Thomas, and Alec Cairncross all considered the question of the possible links between internal and external migration.[30] Dudley Baines has cast serious doubt on Thomas's view

---

Institute of Historical Research, 1965), 2: 242; vol. 7, R. B. Pugh, *Birmingham* (London: Oxford University Press, 1965), p. 18; vol. 8, W. B. Stevens, ed., *Coventry* (1969), p. 170.

[26] Janet Roebuck, *The Making of Modern English Society from 1850* (London: Routledge and Kegan Paul, 1973), p. 64; Eric Hobsbawm and George Rudé, *Captain Swing* (London: Lawrence and Wishart, 1969); J. H. Clapham, *Machines and National Rivalries, 1887–1914* (Cambridge: Cambridge University Press, 1938), p. 547.

[27] Asa Briggs, *The Age of Improvement* (London: Longman, 1959), pp. 388–90.

[28] Roger Wells, "Rural Rebels in Southern England in the 1830s," in *Artisans, Peasants, and Proletarians, 1760–1860,* ed. Clive Emsley and James Walvin (London: Croom Helm, 1985), pp. 124–45; Wells, "The Development of the English Rural Proletariat and Social Protest, 1700–1850," *Journal of Peasant Studies* 6 (1979) 115–39; Andrew Charlesworth, "Social Protest in a Rural Society: The Spatial Diffusion of the Captain Swing Disturbances of 1830–31," *Historical Geography Research Series,* no. 1 (Norwich, Norfolk, 1979); Greg Finch, "Devonshire Farm Labourers in the Victorian Period," *Transactions of the Devonshire Association* 119 (1987): 87–100. Compare John Archer, *"By a Flash and a Scare": Arson, Animal Maiming, and Poaching in East Anglia, 1815–70* (Oxford: Clarendon Press, 1990), p. 40, for specific mention of emigration to Canada as relieving troubled spots such as Blything in North Suffolk in the 1830s. W. A. Armstrong also noted evidence of "local banding or clustering in the places of origins of emigrants," citing Benenden in Kent, a village with high unemployment when the parish assisted 56 people to emigrate between 1826 and 1831 ("Wages and Income" in *The Agrarian History of England, 1750–1850,* ed. Gordon Mingay [Cambridge: Cambridge University Press, 1989], 6: 712).

[29] Malcolm Chase, *The People's Farm: English Radical Agrarianism, 1775–1840* (Oxford: Clarendon Press, 1988).

[30] Arthur Redford, *Labour Migration in England, 1800–50,* 2d ed. (Manchester: Manchester University Press, 1964); Brinley Thomas, *Migration and Economic Growth* (Cambridge: Cambridge University Press, 1954), pp. 123–38; A. K. Cairncross, *Home and Foreign Investment, 1870–1913: Studies in Capital Accumulation* (Cambridge: Cambridge University Press, 1953), pp. 65–83, 209–22.

that English farm workers went to towns at home when conditions were good and overseas in the downswings of domestic cycles—that is, that internal migration and emigration were reciprocal means of reducing the farm labor force.[31] Edward Hunt emphasized the barriers to emigration for poor rural laborers: the cost of the voyage, the want of information, and the possible deterrent effects of the English poor law (in comparison with Scotland and Ireland).[32] Nonetheless, both contemporaries and students of British emigration during the first half of the nineteenth century have assumed that agricultural laborers formed a significant share of the overseas emigrants.[33]

Thus I would argue that emigration ought to be a part of English as well as Irish, Scottish, and Welsh history. Although there never was a mass emigration like that in the wake of the Irish famine, the dispersal of the English people to so many parts of the world over such a long period of time did not have its impact only on the rest of the world. Australian historians have access to records of both convicts and assisted immigrants that make possible the tracing of their lives both before and after emigration. Noting that Australian sources "are comparatively rich on questions such as origins, occupations, family, age and literacy," Eric Richards has suggested that "Australian sources could be used to help write British history."[34] Stephen Nicholas and Peter Shergold have demonstrated how they can be used, not only in the analysis of administration in early nineteenth-century England, but also for the study of internal migration and literacy within England during industrialization.[35] Thus it is refreshing to find an English historian of

[31] Baines, *Migration in a Mature Economy*, pp. 213–85.

[32] Edward Hunt, *Regional Wage Variations in Britain, 1850–1914* (London: Oxford University Press, 1973), pp. 279–80. Others now doubt that the settlement provisions of the poor laws had any significant deterrent effect on migration. See Ann Digby, *Pauper Palaces* (London: Routledge and Kegan Paul, 1978), p. 21, and George Boyer, "The Poor Law, Migration, and Economic Growth," *Journal of Economic History* 46 (1986): 419–30. The English poor laws did not apply to Scotland and Ireland.

[33] See "Emigration from the British Isles to the United States of America in 1831," below, p. 129. G. D. H. Cole and Raymond Postgate, in their classic volume *The Common People: 1746–1938* (London: Methuen, 1938), suggested: "[Agricultural] labourers near the growing industrial areas did better, for they had a way of escape. But from the purely rural areas escape was still very difficult indeed. It might often be easier to emigrate to Canada or the United States than to move over a long distance in Great Britain looking for work" (p. 339).

[34] Eric Richards, "Voices of British and Irish Migrants in Nineteenth-Century Australia," in *Migrants, Emigrants, and Immigrants: A Social History of Migration*, ed. Colin Pooley and Ian Whyte (London: Routledge, 1991), pp. 20, 22.

[35] Stephen Nicholas and Peter Shergold, "The Intercounty Labour Mobility during the Industrial Revolution: Evidence from Australian Transportation Records," *Oxford Eco-*

the "labouring poor" drawing on published emigrant letters from the 1830s and 1850s for evidence of their values and attitudes. K. D. M. Snell concluded that family ties, access to land, and the quality of social relations were more significant in English laborers' assessment of the quality of life than wages and the cost of living.[36]

In broaching the issues of return migration to England and the relationship between emigration and urban growth, Dudley Baines has made a major contribution to the understanding of industrialization in England.[37] As he has written elsewhere, to reduce explanations of the mass overseas movement of people in the nineteenth century to population growth and industrialization alone runs the risk of over-simplifying an intricate and complex process.[38] It is difficult to accept that Hatton and Williamson have come close to illuminating, as they claim, the "inner secrets" of the nineteenth-century migrations when, on the basis of data from 1860–1914, the same explanations can be made to apply to eleven countries in western Europe.[39] Industrialization and urbanization had gone further in England than in other countries by this time, and population growth began to slacken, with falling fertility rates, later in the process of industrialization. It is likely that more understanding of some aspects of English social and economic history can be achieved by delving deeper into the background of specific individuals and groups.

The essays in this volume represent an effort to probe the story of English emigration. Could one learn more about who the emigrants were, about their geographical and social origins in England, and about

---

nomic Papers 39 (1987): 624–40; Nicholas and Shergold, "Internal Migration in England, 1818–1839," *Journal of Historical Geography* 13 (1987): 155–68; Stephen Nicholas and Jacqueline Nicholas, "Male Literacy, 'Deskilling', and the Industrial Revolution," *Journal of Interdisciplinary History* 23 (1992): 1–18. See also Stephen Nicholas, ed., *Convict Workers: Reinterpreting Australia's Past* (Cambridge: Cambridge University Press, 1988), pp. 45–51. For an earlier study of the background of specific groups of emigrants that starts with Australian records, see Ross Duncan, "Case Studies in Emigration: Cornwall, Gloucestershire, and New South Wales, 1877–1886," *Economic History Review*, 2d ser., 16 (1963): 272–89.

[36] K. D. M. Snell, *Annals of the Labouring Poor: Social Change and Agrarian England, 1660–1900* (Cambridge: Cambridge University Press, 1985), pp. 9–14.

[37] Baines, *Migration in a Mature Economy*, pp. 126–40, 213–65.

[38] Dudley Baines, *Emigration from Europe, 1815–1930* (London: Macmillan, 1991), p. 74.

[39] Timothy Hatton and Jeffrey Williamson, "What Drove the Mass Migrations from Europe in the Late Nineteenth Century?" National Bureau of Economic Research, Working Paper Series on Historical Factors in Long Run Growth, no. 43, November, 1992.

the attitudes of those who chose to emigrate as well as of those who stayed behind? Finding an answer has involved the exploration of sources other than the government records and newspapers that have been used in the past. Before I specify some of the issues that might be investigated in the light of recent work by historians of continental emigration and by English and American labor and social historians, some discussion of these alternative sources is in order. Three types of source material open up new possibilities in the study of English emigration: emigrant letters, original passenger lists, and county histories. So I present some introduction to the sources that lie behind the essays in this volume, about their limitations and potential, before I consider further what we would like to discover and what chance there is of advancing knowledge through their use.

The first two essays in this volume, written in the 1960s, are based largely on immigrant letters. My search for private letters began in 1948 when Edith Fox, founder and first curator of the Collection of Regional History at Cornell University, made me a small grant—I think it was $250—to look for private letters when I first came to Britain as a graduate student. In my travels throughout the British Isles in 1948–49, I advertised in the local press and spoke to trade union and Labour Party groups in cities in Scotland and England. A few collections were given to me for deposit at Cornell; others that I was permitted to copy have subsequently been deposited in local archives in England. At that time it proved fruitless to look for any but published collections in libraries and archives. I well remember making inquiries for nineteenth-century emigrant letters in the Public Record Office (PRO) in Belfast to be told that their collecting policy did not extend to manuscripts after 1800. Later that policy was changed, and Belfast now has one of the finest collections of emigrant letters in the British Isles.[40] Many emigrant letters have also found their way into archives scattered throughout England and the United States. Any effort to locate them all, much less read and research the lives of all the writers, seems destined to fall short of completeness.

While I traveled as a graduate student to gain access to newspapers—local ones as well as trade and labor journals—or my dissertation, I found many published immigrant letters. On the whole they were characterized by consistent and blatant bias, whether for or against emigration. Some did contain useful material, especially in comparing

[40] Government of Northern Ireland, PRO, *Report of the Deputy Keeper of the Records for the Years 1954–59* (Belfast: HMSO, January. 1966), Cmnd. 490, and Report . . . 1960–65 (Belfast: HMSO, May 1968), Cmnd. 521.

working and living conditions, technology, and work methods in England and America. I became convinced that more could be learned about the experience of migrants from private letters, when series covered at least several years and offered the possibility of tracing reactions over time and discovering the writers' backgrounds in Britain. I have discussed elsewhere the particular biases of these private letters.[41] Recently, in his brilliant book, *Sea Changes*, Stephen Fender has challenged my defense of private letters. He argued that the texts of private and published letters, at least before 1840, form part of a common discourse, and he has persuasively demonstrated certain common patterns of assumptions, form, and language.[42] Our aims have been complementary rather than conflicting. My interest has been to trace the lives of emigrants, his to link a discourse with American literature.[43]

My concern with reconstructing lifetime careers of the letter writers led me to explore other sources. Occasionally I found one of my letter writers in a county history. These huge volumes, published in profusion in the midwestern and mid-Atlantic states and California, less frequently in New England, over a period of half a century from the 1870s to the 1920s, were expensive to purchase. (This probably accounts for the dearth of them in the South). It cost even more to get one's biography inserted in a volume. These life stories varied greatly in quality from one publisher to another. They were written by staff commissioned by the publisher but relied on the subjects for facts sought in a fixed format and embellished by the compilers with laudatory conventional comment.[44] Because the subjects of these biographies were so obviously selective, no random samples of immigrants can be drawn from them. (The selection of prominent persons was far more apparent in counties containing large cities than it was in counties

[41] Charlotte Erickson, *Invisible Immigrants: The Adaptation of English and Scottish Immigrants in Nineteenth-Century America* (1972; rpt., Ithaca: Cornell University Press, 1990), pp. 13–21.

[42] Stephen Fender, *Sea Changes: British Emigration and American Literature* (Cambridge: Cambridge University Press, 1992).

[43] The work of David Fitzpatrick on letters written from Australia by Irish immigrants carries the enterprise to a new high level of insight into both the writers' purposes and their backgrounds ("'Oceans of Consolation': Letters and Irish Immigration to Australia," in *Visible Immigrants: Neglected Sources for the History of Australian Immigration*, ed. David Fitzpatrick [Canberra: Australian National University, 1989], pp. 47–86).

[44] In Ohio, a volume cost $25, but securing a biography cost $150. See Archibald Hanna, "Every Man His Own Biographer," *Proceedings of the American Antiquarian Society* 80 (1970): 291–98. Correspondence with agents concerning the compilation of such a volume for Milwaukee County in the 1920s is to be found in the J. G. Gregory Correspondence, Wisconsin State Historical Society, Milwaukee, box 2, file 1930–33.

in the Middle West with only small towns and rural populations). Nonetheless, the facts afforded in them promised a bridge to the Old World for some immigrants whose original homeland failed to keep any account of their movements. County histories opened up other sources for some of my letter writers. They also encouraged me to try an experimental sample of about four hundred immigrants, to test whether the information provided was sufficiently accurate to be linked with other sources on both sides of the Atlantic, to provide something like lifetime careers of larger numbers of immigrants than the doubtless equally untypical letter writers afforded.

The results were decidedly mixed, but not altogether discouraging. The scope for verifying and augmenting information about careers after immigrants arrived in the United States seemed limited mainly to the United States census manuscripts of population and agriculture. When I began this work in the 1960s, one could still consult the enumerators' books themselves. Although we can now see only sometimes less legible film, the census returns have gradually become more accessible to such genealogical-type research through the proliferation of indexes, at first by state, and now for the nation for, 1900, 1910, and 1920. The soundex for 1880, which also covers the nation, includes only those households that contained children under ten years of age.[45]

The earliest census manuscripts usable for these purposes (1850–70) provided estimates of dubious reliability, but perhaps rough indications, of the value of an individual's property. More important in the quest for links with the Old World and filling gaps in the county histories were clues about age (again sometimes rounded), date of marriage, date of emigration, previous migrations within the United States, and literacy. Sadly, just as in some of the poorer county histories, the place of birth was almost always given simply as England. If a subject survived to 1900, the enumerators were required to ask about the month and year of birth, date of emigration, and date of marriage.

Both the biographies in county histories themselves and the additional information found in the census manuscripts provided links with

[45] Indexes to the 1880, 1900, 1910, and 1920 censuses are supplied on microfilm by the National Archives in Washington. They are in soundex, a phonetic form of indexing based upon surname consonants and Christian names that circumvents some of the problems of spelling of surnames in the sources. Soundex is also used in the partial indexes available for passenger lists from the National Archives. Indexes to the federal censuses of 1850, 1860, and 1870 have in large part been completed in most of the individual states, and are gradually being made available, along with indexes to state censuses, in both book and machine-readable form by Accelerated Indexing Systems International, Salt Lake City.

sources in England. Fortunately, the staff of the Registrar General's office in England provided national indexes of births and marriages from 1837 onward. Unfortunately, registration was far from complete in the first two or three decades and obtaining copies of the certificates is now very expensive. This source can be supplemented, especially for the years before 1837, by parish registers, frequently indexed, and by nonconformist registers in the PRO, which have been indexed for a few counties. If one has the exact place of birth and last residence of an immigrant from the American sources, the British census manuscripts (also now available only on film) can be used, though very few of the large towns and cities have been indexed. Local directories in England did not provide information on so large a proportion of the population as did American ones. Thus far I have rarely found an immigrant affluent enough to purchase a biography in a county history whose family appeared in a local directory in England. Taken together, these sources are capable of filling gaps about fathers' occupations, early careers, previous migrations, and dates of birth and marriage of English immigrants as well as other details about their lives before emigration. The essay on emigrants from Lancashire in this volume is based substantially on such research arising out of county histories.

Work on letter writers and county histories increased my frustration with the want of reasonably reliable statistics on the nationality of emigrants from the British Isles before 1854 and with the lack of any information on occupations, sex, age, place of birth, or family status of the mass of those emigrants.[46] It was in 1947 that I first saw the passenger lists of vessels carrying immigrants and others to American ports from 1819 onward. At that time I was shown some of the original manifests in the National Archives in Washington. I was not permitted to touch them, so fragile were they. These are now held, and have received modern conservation treatment, at the Balch Institute in Philadelphia. By the time I began to consult them, they were available on microfilm, partially indexed, and have since been used by many scholars.[47]

I first turned to the passenger lists back in the 1960s for further clues about the lives of letter writers and subjects of county histories. It then

[46] For discussions of the quality of published statistics on immigration and emigration from the British Isles, see Edward Hutchinson, "Notes on Immigration Statistics of the United States," *Journal of the American Statistical Association* 53 (1958): 963–1025, and Brinley Thomas, *Migration and Economic Growth*, pp. 35–55.

[47] Robert Swierenga, "List upon List: The Ship Passenger Records and Immigration Research," *Journal of American Ethnic History* 10 (1991): 42–53.

seemed possible that they might also be used to try to assess how representative these samples might be of the movement from Britain to the United States as a whole.

To seek clues as to individuals in the passenger lists requires that one knows in advance either the ship on which they traveled or a fairly accurate date of embarkation or landing. Even then, they rarely yield that invaluable information on place of birth or last residence. A single man traveling alone is almost impossible to trace, particularly if his age is rounded in the lists, unless he was blessed with fairly unusual Christian and surnames. Women, of course, are even more elusive. In the fairly rare cases of successful linkage, information about occupation and names and ages of family members of those traveling with wives or children can lead to sources in England. Sometimes it is possible to judge whether the emigrants reported their past occupations or their intended ones in America. In general, the passenger lists do not give much assistance in tracing individual lives.[48] If they are eventually transcribed into machine-readable form, as has been proposed, they will be far more useful for this type of research.

An effort to capture separately the demographic and economic features of immigrants from England, Scotland, Wales, and Ireland for the period from 1819 to 1875, when the United States authorities began publishing fuller analyses, seemed more promising. Here two major problems arose: the inadequacy of some lists because of the prolific use of ditto marks and the vast quantity of the data.

Insofar as I can judge, the lists were compiled before embarkation because such was required by both the British and the American authorities under the passenger laws. Some masters were very diligent. On the ship *John Dennison* bound for New York in 1833, a careful search was carried out to make sure that every passenger was recorded in the muster role. Before the end of the voyage the passengers were mustered twice more, the second time to collect the head tax to finance the care of passengers who were ill or became ill after arrival.[49] A Methodist preacher, Matthew Dinsdale, who emigrated from Yorkshire in 1844 on the packet ship *St. George* bound for New York from Liverpool, reported that "the passengers had their names called over two or three

[48] Juliana Gilheany traced individual British immigrants from the New York passenger lists for 1821–23 in subsequent years, so long as they remained in the city ("Subjects of History: English, Scottish, and Welsh Immigrants in New York City, 1820–1860," Ph.D. diss., New York University, 1990).

[49] Richard Weston, *A Visit to the United States and Canada in 1833* (Edinburgh, 1836), pp. 8–9, 11, 36.

times during the day."[50] The passenger lists are not the same documents as the register which immigration clerks in the ports were supposed to keep and which have been discredited by reports that overworked clerks sometimes took them home at night to fill up the columns.[51] There is also evidence that the passenger lists were more accurate than the observations of newspaper reporters as to the characteristics of the emigrants.[52]

Passenger lists provide the principal data for the third, fourth, and fifth essays presented in this volume. I stumbled on the lists used for the third essay (on the 1880s) while searching for individuals. At that point (1966) these lists had barely been touched by scholars. To find a series of lists that actually reported places of last residence in detail seemed to demand their analysis, and the late David Glass, then Britain's leading demographer, warmly encouraged me in that response. In retrospect, I now see that I might have done much more with them. I did not consider using any more advanced technology than a calculating machine, nor did the notion of sampling such prime new material seem appropriate. I failed to transcribe detailed information on ages of immigrants, women and children, and family composition. Needless to say, I would use different work methods today. My analysis of passenger lists is not based on a master plan conceived from the outset. Instead, one thing led to another, as will be seen.

By the time I tackled the 1841 lists, on which the fifth essay is based, with better funding and computer resources, the numbers of passengers were already so large that I had to use sampling. The method adopted—namely, to enter all passengers from every fifth ship arriving in New York and from all ships at the minor ports—very soon ran into the problem of poor lists that described origins as "Great Britain and Ireland" and occupations as "labourers" or, even worse, as "farmers, artisans and labourers." After examining and noting the quality of the list from every ship carrying more than six passengers, if that from the

[50] Matthew Dinsdale Journal, Wisconsin State Historical Society, Madison.

[51] Brinley Thomas quoted *Reports of the Industrial Commission* (Washington, 1901), 15: 179, which indicated that the few registry clerks who were supposed to take details on nationality, destination, and ages of immigrants when they arrived were often too busy to provide more than a list of names (*Migration and Economic Growth,* pp. 44–45n). See also James Macaulay, *Across the Ferry* (London, 1871), quoted in Rhoda Hoff, *America's Immigrants: Adventures in Eyewitness History* (New York: Henry A. Walck, 1967), p. 80: "On the arrival of a cargo of immigrants, the names and places of birth, embarkation, and so on, are entered in a registry."

[52] Charlotte Erickson, "Emigration from the British Isles to the U.S.A. in 1841," Part 2, "Who Were the English Emigrants?" *Population Studies* 44 (1990): 26.

first, sixth, and eleventh ship was poor, I substituted for it the list of the ship that arrived just before or just after it. Comparisons of all ships with the resulting sample as to date of arrival in port, number of passengers carried, and port of embarkation satisfied me that there was no obvious distortion in my sample, except, of course, that of the attitudes of masters about recording details.[53]

Although methods changed from one study to the next, with, I hope, richer results as time progressed, I tried to keep the findings comparable at the three dates—1831, 1841, and 1885–88—as did William Van Vugt in his analysis of a similar sample of the 1851 lists.[54] Why our results, especially with respect to the proportion of laborers aboard, should be markedly different from those of Raymond Cohn for a sample drawn over a longer period (1836–53) is not clear.[55] Analyzing lists that he had used for his study of shipboard mortality, Cohn found significantly more laborers among the English emigrants. Presumably those captains who bothered to record births and deaths at sea would also have been more likely to provide other details more carefully. Perhaps my method has underestimated the numbers of laborers; Cohn agrees that using both good and bad lists, as he did, may have overestimated them. The issue merits further investigation. Both methods of sampling, however, produce a higher proportion of general laborers in the emigration from England to the United States during and after the increased migration at mid-century than I had expected. The so-called labor migration (as distinct from family settlement) identified by the 1880s for so many countries appears to have begun earlier in England.[56]

[53] This analysis appears in Charlotte Erickson, "The Uses of Passenger Lists for the Study of British and Irish Emigration," in *Migration across Time and Nations: Population Mobility in Historical Contexts*, ed. Ira Glazier and Luigi de Rosa (New York: Holmes and Meier, 1986), pp. 318–35. The main results were published in two parts in *Population Studies* 43 (1989): 347–67, and 44 (1990): 21–40.

[54] William Van Vugt, "British Emigration during the Early 1850s, with Special Reference to Emigration to the U.S.A.," Ph.D. diss., University of London, 1985.

[55] Raymond Cohn, "The Occupations of English Immigrants to the United States, 1836–53," *Journal of Economic History* 52 (1992): 377–87.

[56] Alternatively, as in the case of Sweden, settler emigration and labor migration may have taken place concurrently, in differing proportions over time (Hans Norman and Harald Runblom, "Migration Patterns in Nordic Countries," in *Labor Migration in the Atlantic Economies*, ed. Hoerder, p. 55). Such labor migration extending over long distances had already become a tradition not only in the British Isles but in many parts of the Continent in early modern times. The participation of English laborers in the nineteenth-century overseas movement casts serious doubt on Thistlethwaite's contention that a growing percentage of British emigrants in the 1880s and 1890s were "skilled technicians moving from one industrial area to another" ("Migration from Europe Overseas," p. 38).

Most scholars who have worked with passenger lists have provided data for rather long periods of time. My work on single years obviously suffers from the fact that the social profile of immigrants in peak years of migration, such as I studied, differed from that in years of low migration. That the composition varied over short periods, as well as secularly over time, is clear from evidence from years after 1875, when better published data become available.[57]

For insight into the impact of cycles on the migrating population, annual data are essential. It is difficult to imagine that resources could be found, if anyone were sufficiently interested, to sample English immigrants every year from 1819 to 1875. It might be fruitful to examine a few carefully selected years, to explore the nature of cyclical fluctuations on the extent of family movement, occupations, and age of migrants. Alternatively, more years might be examined by analyzing selected months, say April, when the emigration of agriculturists and laborers was high, and September, when a minor surge in the emigration of industrial workers and artisans seems to have occurred.

County histories and immigrant letters are not the only sources that might be used to reconstruct lifetime careers of English immigrants in the United States. Dino Cinel has demonstrated the richness of naturalization records in his study of Italians in San Francisco.[58] Some naturalization records also make possible the kind of linkage with Old World records that I have discussed, which might be a means of including more urban immigrants, who are underrepresented in county histories.

This discussion of sources presupposes that emigrants from the country that gave birth to the industrial revolution are worth studying in their own right. The significant increases in knowledge about continental emigrants gained during the past thirty years make this endeavor more worthwhile today in that comparisons can be made that would have been impossible a generation ago. One can now compare English emigrants with internal migrants in England, with overseas emigrants from several continental countries, as well as with assisted immigrants to Australia. The social and demographic profiles obtained from passenger lists make possible cross-tabulations—for example, of age and occupation—that cannot be done with official published statistics. The value of life stories lies in the insights they may provide to strategies used by people confronted with structural change. Those who

[57] See the Appendix, Tables 3.12 and 3.13 below.

[58] Dino Cinel, *From Italy to San Francisco* (Stanford: Stanford University Press, 1982).

went overseas, as well as those who migrated to towns and cities at home, were making private decisions that also shaped those structural changes.

It has long been assumed that economic motives dominated both English and continental emigration of the nineteenth century. In a survey of the econometric studies of migration, which were produced during the 1960s and 1970s, that used economic and demographic variables, J. D. Gould concluded "that the array of explanations usually considered in econometric studies is far more capable of generating an acceptable 'explanation' of Swedish emigration to the [United States] than of British."[59]

Other recent research has undermined purely economic interpretations that fail to explain the selectivity of the process: why not all people in similar economic circumstances chose to emigrate. Some scholars emphasize social and cultural factors as determining why some people migrate while others stay behind.[60] Sune Åkerman summarized Swedish evidence that even in mass emigration districts, some villages resisted emigration while "early start" villages continued to produce emigrants for long periods of time.[61] Was Thistlethwaite right that religious dissenters were more likely than Anglicans to emigrate from England during the first half of the nineteenth century and that they were more concerned with status than with job opportunities?[62] Did economic motivation become more pronounced among English emigrants in the last half of the century? Is there any evidence of a tradition of emigration in parts of England (certainly there was in Cornwall), or was English emigration characterized by many sudden bursts of movement from a host of places which soon subsided?

Dirk Hoerder, who still favors a Marxian emphasis on overriding economic causes, finds room for personal factors on a secondary level.[63] A student of African migrations, Clyde Mitchell, considered that economic factors might be necessary conditions of migration but not

[59] Gould, "European Inter-Continental Emigration," p. 665.

[60] Cinel, *From Italy to San Francisco*, pp. 257–58. James Clyde Mitchell interpreted the normative system of a society as one level of motivation for migration ("Types of Urban Social Relationships" in *Present Interrelations in Central African Rural and Urban Life*, ed. Raymond Apthorpe [1958; rpt., Lusaka: Rhodes Livingstone Institute, 1968], p. 17).

[61] Sune Åkerman, "Towards an Understanding of the Emigrational Processes," in *Human Migration: Patterns and Policies*, ed. William McNeill and Ruth Adams (Bloomington: Indiana University Press, 1978), p. 300.

[62] Thistlethwaite, "Migration from Europe Overseas," pp. 41–42.

[63] Dirk Hoerder, "Labor Markets and Community Building by Migrant Workers," p. 82.

sufficient ones: an additional "last straw" cause is needed.[64] Marriage and the termination of marriage have been the "most significant demographic spurs" to migration, according to Charles Tilly.[65] In gradually piecing together life histories, I have been struck with the frequency with which the death of a wife, husband, or parent, a desire to end a marriage, a family scandal, or individual dissipation lay in the immediate background to the decision to emigrate. Possibly such events were more usual in the background to overseas movement than to internal migration.[66] Letters that survive in American archives, written from England to immigrants, shed light on the reasons for not emigrating and thereby enhance our understanding of why others chose to go.

Life histories can also throw light on how English emigrants, who had such an extraordinary choice of destinations (including the Continent), decided where to go and the networks in which they moved and settled. Cornish miners were not the only ones who actually tried more than one continent, as well as more than one state. The essay in this volume on the emigrants of 1841 to Canada, New South Wales, and the United States is a preliminary attempt to explore the possibilities of extending the analysis of migration differentials at the macrolevel among British and Irish emigrants to different destinations.

We simply do not know how relevant the now conventional concept of chain migration is to English emigration. The biographies and letters provide many instances of various patterns of previous family movement apparently determining destination: young men going out to older brothers or to fathers or uncles, as well as parents joining their children. Cases in which a wife or fiancée's family directed a man to a particular place are suggestive of the role of women in decision

[64] Mitchell, "Types of Urban Social Relationships," pp. 18–19; Clyde Kiser, *Sea Island to City: A Study of St. Helena Islanders in Harlem and Other Urban Centers* (New York: Columbia University Studies in History, Economics, and Public Law, no. 368, 1932), pp. 142–58.

[65] Charles Tilly, "Migration in Modern European History," in *Human Migration*, ed. McNeill and Adams, p. 66.

[66] For the continuing strength of family links with places of origin among internal migrants, see Michael Anderson, *Family Structure in Nineteenth Century Lancashire* (Cambridge: Cambridge University Press, 1971), and Kevin Schurer, "The Role of the Family in the Process of Migration," in *Migrants, Emigrants and Immigrants,* ed. Pooley and Whyte, pp. 106–42, 134–35n. For close family ties as a deterrence to migration, see R. J. Johnston, "Resistance to Migration and the Mover/Stayer Dichotomy: Aspects of Kinship and Population Stability in an English Rural Area," *Geografiska Annaler,* ser. B, *Human Geography* 53 (1971): 16–27.

making.[67] English people sometimes had relatives in different parts of the United States and of the world. Thus far it has not been possible to find chain migration among English emigrants as lasting more than a generation or leading to substantial settlements.

The English used networks other than those of family and village. As Donna Gabaccia found for Sicilian emigrants, in her work on Lancashire immigrants in Fall River, Massachusetts, Mary Blewett has suggested that occupation was more significant than family link in determining destination.[68] Among other emigrants from England to mining and manufacturing regions, occupation must have been paramount in choice of where to settle, though overlapping family networks are also likely. But English immigrants turned up in many communities where their compatriots were not strongly identified with a particular industry.

It may be possible to identify other networks—religious, fraternal, or masonic—that enabled prospective English emigrants without family or a friend in a trade in the United States to emigrate. The host of colonies of various kinds that the English attempted to found in the United States throughout the nineteenth century collapsed within a short time. Projectors of colonies, however, did offer assistance with travel arrangements and frequently other inducements, often unfulfilled, to people who wanted to emigrate but who lacked the confidence or the information on which they felt able to go it alone.[69] The Mormons provided the most outstanding case whereby people without contacts could emigrate in a remarkably organized network.

To my mind, the most engaging issue, and one to which reconstruction of immigrant lives may be able to make a contribution, is that of the role of emigration in structural change in employment in England. In comparison with twentieth-century experience, that change was slow in England. Many years ago, T. S. Ashton challenged the appropriateness of the term "industrial revolution" to describe economic development in England in the late eighteenth and early nineteenth centuries.[70]

[67] M. Estelle Smith, "Networks and Migration Resettlement: Cherchez la Femme," *Anthropological Quarterly* 49 (1976): 20–27.

[68] Gabaccia, *Militants and Migrants,* pp. 169–71; and Blewett, "Lancashire Popular Radicalism."

[69] For three young Yorkshiremen who emigrated with advice and assistance of the land agent of the Burlington Railway with no intention of purchasing land from the railway, see Charlotte Erickson, ed., "An Emigrant's Letter from Iowa, 1871," *Bulletin of the British Association for American Studies,* n.s., 12/13 (1966): 7, 9, 11–12, 18, 39.

[70] T. S. Ashton, *The Industrial-Revolution, 1760–1830* (London: Oxford University Press, 1948), p. 2. See also Donald Coleman, "Industrial Growth and Industrial Revolutions," *Economica,* n.s., 23 (1956): 1–20.

Although we continue to use the term, economic historians have now pretty well rejected the concept of a period of "take-off" into industrial growth.[71] The rate of overall urban growth in England was also slow in comparison with that of other countries and some twentieth-century rates.[72] Changes in the structure of employment often took place between generations, with sons not following the occupations of their fathers. The study of emigrant lives can reveal something of the anatomy of occupational change.

A number of questions can be addressed. Was emigration associated with change in occupation? What evidence is there of shifts in occupation before emigration, and what was the nature of the choices made? Were they made in conjunction with internal migration before emigration? How important was family in facilitating occupational diversification, through training in another job with an uncle, for example, or adopting that of one's father-in-law? The essay in this volume on Lancashire is an experiment in using life histories to explore such questions. My focus is not on social mobility but on occupational change and stability. Were the emigrants people who resisted occupational change or more adventurous people who sought new and different opportunities because of constraints, either social or economic, experienced in England?

In England the structural shift in employment away from agriculture was relative before the middle of the century. An absolute decline in the labor force in agriculture was not evident until the 1850s. Even in the eighteenth century, England did not have an ideal-type peasant society. Farmers normally rented their land and were not novices in commercial agriculture. Most of the people on the land were wage laborers. If one can trust the evidence of the passenger lists, it was those commercial farmers, rather than agricultural laborers, who were the most overrepresented class of emigrants in relation to their proportion of the labor force of the country. It is not easy, however, to assess how many of them were aspiring farmers rather than farm operators. We know very little about the background of English farmers who emigrated. Were they tenant farmers, and if so, did they operate small or large-scale farms?

[71] For the concept of take-off, see W. W. Rostow, "The Take-off into Self-sustained growth," *Economic Journal,* 66 (1956), pp. 25–48. N. F. R. Crafts, *British Economic Growth during the Industrial Revolution* (Oxford: Fontana Paperbacks, 1985); C. Nick Harley, "British Industrialization before 1841: Evidence of Slower Growth during the Industrial Revolution," *Journal of Economic History* 42 (1982): 267–89.

[72] Jeffrey Williamson, "Migration Selectivity, Urbanization, and Industrial Revolutions," *Population and Development Review* 14 (1988): 287–314.

Were they drawn more from the small sector of owner-operators? Or were they mainly farmers' sons? Intensive work on local sources in England to follow up the biographies in county histories and letters might begin to provide some answers. This effort would require searches for individuals in the 1851 census, local directories, and land tax records.[73] Were there certain villages in which farmers used overseas emigration as a means of adjusting to structural change? We need to get closer to a local level than estimates of net emigration by county afford to begin to get a picture of who the farmer-emigrants were.

Then there is the vexed question of who the increasing numbers of laborers found in the passenger lists were. It now seems clear that by the 1880s nearly all of them were emigrating from towns and cities. County histories in the midwestern and mid-Atlantic regions provide careers of people who emigrated before that time. They contain many entries of people were were sons of farm or general laborers and who began their own working lives in the same way. At least for some of them, it is possible to discover whether they changed occupation or migrated in search of work other than general laboring before leaving England.

In addition to evidence of stage migration, one would like to know whether laborers in some villages showed a clear tendency to include emigration in their repertoire of dealing with change, whereas others did not. The emigration schemes of Joseph Arch's Agricultural Labourers Union during the famous Revolt of the Fields in the early 1870s have received much attention; the possible links between rural unrest and emigration in the 1830s and 1840s have not. Did laborers in villages experiencing violence spurn emigration, even if assistance was offered, whereas those in less turbulent ones more often emigrated if they could? Alternatively, did a tradition of emigration from a village reduce the tendency to violent protest? It is possible from poor law reports and other sources to identify villages in which the parish, the guardians of the poor in the unions created in 1834, or landowners assisted laborers to emigrate. To find those villages from which young laborers somehow ventured overseas on their own resources is more difficult. Comments by census enumerators, along with evidence from county histories and a handful of passenger lists, can at least provide some clues.

Finally, did English farmers and farm laborers usually end up in agriculture in the United States? How did former laborers acquire land? Thus far the evidence is fairly thin of shifts to other sectors of

[73] Gordon Mingay, "The Land Tax Assessments and the Small Landowner," *Economic History Review*, 2d ser., 17 (1964): 381–88.

employment than agriculture in the United States. One would like to know whether English farmers and farm laborers who did end up in towns and cities in America entered tertiary employment rather than manufacturing industry.[74]

Throughout the century men trained in traditional crafts outnumbered male emigrants from agriculture among those who arrived in the United States. They also outnumbered those who were leaving modernizing industries. David Montgomery has speculated that it was neither "the daring innovator" nor the "veteran artisan, . . . but the mobile youth who spurned Briton's [*sic*] factories for the possibility of plying the [to him] family trade in a new location."[75] In my study of the 1841 passenger lists, I found two-fifths of the craftsmen to have been over thirty years of age, hardly "mobile youths." In 1831 and 1841 such artisans were somewhat more likely than emigrants from industries characterized by change in job content to be traveling with their families.[76] Were the emigrant craftsmen following their fathers' trades? Were some of them farmers' sons who had learned a trade before emigrating? And is there evidence of carpenters or blacksmiths, for example, seeking and obtaining work in American factories? The county histories record a considerable drift of craftsmen, including miners, into agriculture in America, temporarily or permanently.

Men working in modernizing industries appear to have traveled alone or without dependents more frequently than did craftsmen and farmers. Fewer of them can be found in county histories, and it would be more difficult to get significant numbers of lifetime careers. Among them, the most challenging group are the handloom weavers, whose numbers contracted so greatly, albeit over a period of thirty years or more. John Lyons has been able to demonstrate that not all weavers who remained in England depended on their children for support. Some did change occupation. He makes clear how difficult it was for adult male weavers to follow their children into cotton factories because managers could obtain an ample supply of adult male workers from among the boys and teenage males they employed without hiring older men.[77] Handloom weavers had good cause to emigrate and were

[74] Tilly, "Migration in Modern European History," p. 58.

[75] David Montgomery, "Working Classes of the Pre-Industrial American City," *Labor History* 9 (1968): 10–11.

[76] See Table 4.16 below, and Erickson, "Who Were the English Emigrants?" pp. 32–33.

[77] John Lyons, "Family Response to Economic Decline: Handloom Weavers in Early Nineteenth-Century Lancashire," Working Paper no. 87–05, Department of Economics, Miami University, Oxford, Ohio, 1987, pp. 45–46, 39–41.

overrepresented among emigrants during the 1820s, 1830s, and 1840s. What now intrigues me is whether they tended to be men with children too young to work. Were the former cotton millworkers who appear in county histories men who had been unable to secure permanent jobs in the mills where they had worked? I now wish that I had raised these questions specifically as I worked on passenger lists.

Some progress might also be made on the matter of quality of skills. As is so often the case in literary immigration history, writers generalize without specific evidence. Some emphasize the impact of skills in the receiving country, whereas others question whether highly skilled men, with long periods of training behind them, would be attracted by the possibility of work in a less developed industry. Did the more highly skilled people remain in the East and those who had merely picked up or acquired skills on the job go farther west?

Charles More's work on the ways in which skill was acquired in different industries in nineteenth-century England can be of use in considering the level of skill industrial immigrants brought with them.[78] In the fuller biographies, men who had been apprenticed appear to have mentioned that fact; others were simply introduced to their trades by working with fathers or other relatives. Some examples have been found of men who improved the scope of their knowledge by travel and work for various firms before emigration or who did so in the United States. Many young emigrants in their teens acquired what skills they had after emigration, though there is a suggestion in some of the data that males aged 15 to 19 may have been underrepresented among English immigrants. The letters reveal cases of teenage sons left behind in England when the rest of the family emigrated.

The issue of possible entrepreneurial failure in late nineteenth-century England has been endlessly debated. We have little evidence about a possible erosion of the quality of the labor force through the emigration of mature men whose human capital was high through training and work experience in England.[79] My present suspicion is that men who could not find an opportunity to acquire such training in England were those more likely to emigrate. I have been surprised by

[78] Charles More, *Skill and the English Working Class, 1870–1914* (London: Croom Helm, 1980).

[79] A very different suggestion arises from an analysis of the records of convicts in Australia. A decline in literacy among urban, rural, northern, and skilled workers in England during industrialization was found. The writers attributed "a long tradition of underinvestment in skills in the British economy" to disinvestment in human capital during early industrialization (Nicholas and Nicholas, "Industrial Revolution," pp. 16–17).

how many English emigrants to the United States did not sign the registers when they married or on the births of their children. Australian scholars have reported exceedingly high levels of literacy, both in reading and in writing, higher than estimates for England at the time, among assisted immigrants to Australia. I suspect that the level of literacy among English immigrants to the United States may not have been so high as the 85–95 percent reported for Australia.[80]

Immigrant letters also yield evidence about attitudes toward change of occupation and innovations in work methods. Were those who emigrated more willing to turn their hands to any work they could find than were those who stayed behind? Did English immigrants outside New York City share the shock at long hours or work intensity in America that Richard Stott found in letters written from the City?[81]

Despite all the qualifications that must be made about the representativeness of life histories constructed on the basis of county histories and letters, a few demographic questions that cannot otherwise be approached for English immigrants can at least be addressed from these data. Those who married Englishwomen before emigration can be considered apart from those who married after emigration. The extent to which intragroup marriage after emigration involved marriage to women from the same part of England or other parts of the British Isles can be examined. Were immigrants who married American-born women more likely to marry for the first time at a later age than did others? Second and third marriages appear very often to have been to American-born women. Expressions of a desire to find an English wife are far from absent in letters. Emigrants who ended up where there was no considerable settlement of other English people "assimilated" more rapidly by this convertional criterion.

The size of immigrant families in comparison with those in the old country has been considered by a number of historians as one index of cultural continuity. Some of the English immigrants in the Middle West had very large families. Were they as large or larger than those of their parents? An impressionistic perusal of the data still being collected suggests that those who married American-born women may have had smaller families than those with English-born wives, though it may turn

[80] Robin Haines, "Government-assisted Emigration from the United Kingdom to Australia, 1831–1860: Promotion, Recruitment, and the Labouring Poor," Ph.D. diss. Flinders University of South Australia, 1992, pp. 108–19; Eric Richards, "Annals of the Australian Immigrant," in *Visible Immigrants*, ed. Fitzpatrick, p. 20.

[81] Richard Stott, "British Immigrants and the American 'Work Ethic' in the Mid-Nineteenth Century," *Labor History* 26 (1985): 86–102.

out that this is explained by the age of brides. A decline in family size over time may also be observed. English immigrants in California, who on balance arrived later than those in the Middle West, appear to have had smaller families.

County histories, in conjunction with other sources, provide abundant data on the second generation. Children are usually named, and the occupations of sons and the place of residence of both sons and daughters given. Practices with respect to inheritance might be investigated. Did English-born farmers succeed in acquiring enough land to be able to endow their children with farms? Or did they demonstrate a willingness to educate their children for careers outside agriculture? What sorts of occupations did their children enter, not so much from the standpoint of simplistic social mobility as that of particular ones they favored? We know little about the persistence of English people in their choice of residence in the United States in comparison with the Scots. Analysis in terms of occupational background, regional origins, and urban-rural upbringing in England might conceivably yield results relevant to English history itself.

These questions are merely a sampling of some that might be raised in considering life histories. Such research unfortunately implies a massive amount of work, travel, and expense. It implies the acquisition of needed finance and also points in the direction of cooperation among scholars on both sides of the Atlantic such as has been achieved in some German and Scandinavian centers. In the end, the most informed and perceptive work may come out of studies of emigration from particular counties and regions in England, such as the attention Cornwall has received. This study must reach the village level. With the dearth of information on origins of emigrants within England, even this kind of research might have to begin with American sources that could be linked with English ones to make possible richer insight into the types of people and sorts of situations that actually lay behind English emigration, other than those famous ones of the Macclesfield silk workers in the 1880s or the Bradford worsted workers in the 1890s.

I have tried to develop a history from below free from preoccupations with the making of the working class and the congealing of class consciousness, social mobility in the raw, or old-fashioned demonstrations of the "contributions" of immigrants. Immigrants sought goals other than class solidarity or even national or religious solidarity in America. The history of those who left bears a relation to English history itself. Thus another way of advancing knowledge of emigrants from England to the levels now attained for emigrants from the Continent would be for more students of English labor, agricultural, and local history to be stimulated to consider emigration as potentially a part of their subjects.

This book contains the results of my efforts to date to take up some of the challenges to historians laid down by Frank Thistlethwaite in 1960, challenges that have been grasped so much more readily by historians on both sides of the water who write about emigration from countries on the Continent. Only after I had drafted this introduction did I encounter an article by James Jackson, Jr., and Leslie Moch that calls for the kind of research that is represented in my essays: the desirability of integrating migration studies with the social history of Europe in the specific context of national histories; the need for descriptive work and data on lifetime careers of migrants; and the dangers of falling into the trap of ideological assumptions such as those that have bedeviled the standard-of-living debate in England.[82] These are but faint beginnings. The obstacles to bringing the study of the English to the level of that done on parts of the Continent are enormous. Without the English, the history of the Atlantic migration of the nineteenth century is incomplete.

At the present time, English people are facing structural changes of a magnitude probably as great as those during the classic industrial revolution. A deeper understanding of how they responded to and contributed toward those changes in the nineteenth century, in ways other than by agrarian protest followed by political and trade union organization, lies in the history of emigration.

[82] James Jackson, Jr., and Leslie Moch, "Migration and the Social History of Modern Europe," *Historical Methods* 22 (1989): 12.

CHAPTER ONE

Agrarian Myths of English Immigrants

"Every immigration to America," wrote Carl Wittke, "has included men and women who dreamed of building a Utopia on the prairies of mid-America. In the spirit of Rousseau's 'free and noble savage' they entertained romantic but unrealistic notions about carving a home out of the primeval forest, where they might live according to their heart's desire."[1] Among English immigrants, such notions were not confined to the educated who had read Rousseau or James Fenimore Cooper. The lure of an idyllic existence on a pioneer farm penetrated deep into the social structure of this industrializing country in the early nineteenth century.

The evidence lies in the private letters of English immigrants in the United States. A large proportion of the slender remains of such correspondence came from settlers on the land who emigrated during the generation following the Napoleonic Wars. Although these immigrants came to the United States at a time when opportunities to enter agriculture on the basis of the family farm were still abundant and not so costly as they were later to become, one cannot fail to be impressed in reading these letters by the absence of superlatives for or against America or particular parts of America. Their tone was usually more cautious than that of emigrant letters, including English ones, which were printed in newspapers or pamphlets shortly after they were written. Although they subscribed to the universal view that an industrious man could not fail to

[1] Carl Wittke, *Refugees of Revolution: The German Forty-Eighters in America* (Philadelphia: University of Pennsylvania Press, 1952), p. 111.

make a living on an American farm, the letters do not fit into the usual stereotype of the emigrant letter as a golden description of utopia beckoning others to follow to the promised land.

Several factors may explain this reserve. One might argue that the most favorable descriptions of the United States had gone to America in the pockets of emigrants who responded to their invitation and for that reason did not turn up in private collections and libraries in England. Possibly private letters, not written for publication or to be read out at the public house, were always more careful accounts.[2] Yet the letters also seem to support the view of many travelers that, in spite of advantages such as familiarity with the language, the English did not have an easy economic and social adjustment to make in America.

Among those English who deliberately chose to go into agriculture in the United States, difficulties and disappointments were closely linked with the motives which led them to make that choice. "As the returns diminished," one emigrant later reminisced, "the glamor wore off and soon we awakened to a painful realization that our imagination had run away with our judgement, and that we were left with nothing but a piece of land from which nothing could be extracted save by the hardest of work and the most rigid economy, neither of which had been included in our promised bill of fare."[3]

Many English immigrants seem to have held certain ideas and preconceptions about farming in the United States that did not prove to correspond altogether with reality. Some revision of these ideas was essential to a successful adaptation in America, either in agriculture or in another sphere of activity. These ideas had the quality of myth, if myth is defined in Henry Nash Smith's words as "an intellectual construction that fuses concept and emotion into an image" and as a "collective representation rather than the work of a single mind."[4]

[2] Marcus Lee Hansen, *The Atlantic Migration* (Cambridge: Harvard University Press, 1940), pp. 146, 152–54; Carl Wittke, *We Who Built America* (Cleveland: Western Reserve University Press, 1939), p. 103; Merle Curti and Kendall Birr, "The Immigrant and the American Image in Europe, 1860–1914," *Mississippi Valley Historical Review* 37 (1950): 228.

[3] H. Harcourt Horn, *An English Colony in Iowa* (Boston: Christopher Publishing House, 1931), p. 24.

[4] Henry Nash Smith, *The Virgin Land* (Cambridge: Harvard University Press, 1950), preface. In a fascinating recent study based on many of the same private letters that I used as well as printed sources from the colonial period to 1840, Stephen Fender expresses a mild objection to "agrarian," whereas he agrees with the term "myth." "What the rhetorical history suggests is that the exploration of the New World owes something to the exploration of the human place in the world in general" (*Sea Changes: British Emigration and American Literature* [Cambridge: Cambridge University Press, 1992], p. 61).

No one would doubt that the agrarian myth Smith discussed as "the Garden of the World" had strong roots in European thought. Praise of agriculture for its importance in economic life and an insistence on the virtues of the country dweller as contrasted with the city dweller were classical themes rediscovered during the Renaissance. In England they did not lose currency in works on agriculture from the sixteenth century onward, and the vogue was considerably enhanced after about 1700.[5] The ideal of the small freehold farmer, as developed in America, was justified in terms of the natural rights argument of John Locke, with particular emphasis on his view that the labor of cultivation was the foundation of private property.[6] In short, because the ideal of the virtuous society of yeoman farmers stemmed from a tradition shared by England, one should not be surprised to find elements of it in the notions of English people who emigrated to America.

Yet, the agrarian myths that motivated these English emigrants differed in both emphasis and content from the tenets of the American version. Nor were the English aspirations, as expressed in these myths, identical with the images of America to which continental emigrants responded.[7] These preconceptions held by certain Englishmen about agriculture as it was carried on in the American West had more to do with their cultural traditions and experiences in England than with information or empirical data about the West. To identify these notions indicates an element of nonrational behavior in the emigrants' decision making. During this early period of English emigration, letters written about the time of departure suggest that for those emigrants who intended to go to the land, a very strong qualification must be made to the view that "among no group of migrants did material ambition bulk larger than among the nineteenth- and early twentieth-century British."[8] It is worth examining the views of these emigrants for the light they throw on problems of social and economic adjustment in America. Perhaps equally important is the insight one gains into the social attitudes of ordinary English people, although admittedly not

[5] Paul Johnstone, "In Praise of Husbandry," *Agricultural History* 2 (1937): 86–87, 93.

[6] Chester Eisinger, "The Influence of Natural Rights and Physiocratic Doctrines on American Agrarian Thought during the Revolutionary Period," *Agricultural History* 21 (1947): 17.

[7] Henry Steele Commager, ed., *Immigration and American History* (Minneapolis: University of Minnesota Press, 1961), pp. 36ff.; Hansen, *Atlantic Migration*, pp. 157–64; Curti and Birr, "The Immigrant and the American Image," pp. 214–24.

[8] Rowland Berthoff, *British Immigrants in Industrial America, 1790–1950* (Cambridge: Harvard University Press, 1953), p. 15.

from the very bottom of the social scale, during these years of unprecedented social and economic change.

Without presenting quantitative evidence, writers have generally agreed that most of the Englishmen who went overseas during the first half of the nineteenth century came from agriculture or rural crafts.[9] The strongest supporting data for this view, usually not cited, are to be found in the 1841 Census of Great Britain. During that year of intense hardship in many of the new industrial towns, the census authorities inquired about the number of overseas migrants from each county. Although Lancashire and the West Riding of Yorkshire sent out more emigrants than any other counties, a few agricultural counties in the south and southwest and on the northwest coast were providing most of the emigrants (see Table 1.1). Perhaps we should not be so certain as some writers have been in looking at the statistics of occupations of immigrants that even after the mid-nineteenth century the industrial worker was preeminent among English migrants. When Maldwyn Jones, a leading British historian, described the causes of emigration in the late nineteenth century, the period during which per capita rates of gross emigration from England to the United States reached their peak, he wrote about the so-called Great Depression in English agriculture.[10] Because of the inadequacy of the English and American statistics, we may never know the precise character of overseas migration from the world's then most industrialized country.

What does not seem to be recognized generally is the extent to which emigrants from this industrializing economy were choosing to enter agriculture when they arrived in the United States. As late as 1870, when the first occupational statistics for immigrant groups were published by the census authorities, the English and Welsh were nearly as well

[9] Wilbur Shepperson, *British Emigration to North America: Projects and Opinions in the Early Victorian Period* (Oxford: Basil Blackwell, 1957), p. 5; Maldwyn Jones, *American Immigration* (Chicago: Chicago University Press, 1960), p. 112; Dudley Kirk, *Europe's Population in the Interwar Years*, League of Nations, Economic and Financial Series, II, A.8 (Princeton: Princeton Office of Population Research, 1946), p. 82. Berthoff thought this was the case only until the late 1820s (*British Immigrants*, p. 107).

[10] Jones, *American Immigration*, p. 195. Jones later offered a far more cautious discussion of the relation between agricultural depression and emigration, a treatment that emphasized the migration of agricultural laborers to towns ("The Background to Emigration from Great Britain in the Nineteenth Century, *Perspectives in American History* 7 [1973]: 58–63). Here he is closer to the older, unsupported view of E. C. Snow that after the middle of the century the numbers of farmers and agricultural laborers leaving the country were relatively small ("Emigration from Great Britain" in *International Migrations,* ed. Imre Ferenczi and Walter Willcox [New York: National Bureau of Economic Research, 1931], 2: 250).

Table 1.1. Rank order of leading English counties by emigrants per 10,000 inhabitants during the five months ending June 4, 1841

County	Number of emigrants	Emigrants per 10,000	Percent of labor force in agriculture
Sussex	758	25	30.5
Cornwall	795	23	20.9
Cumberland	357	20	21.6
Monmouth	213	16	15.4
Somerset	671	15	25.0
Devon	736	14	24.8
Kent	652	12	21.7
Westmorland	61	11	27.8
Dorset	177	10	30.1
Hereford	111	10	34.8
Yorkshire, W.R.	944	8	10.7
Chester	328	8	15.1
Lancashire	1,362	8	6.7
Yorkshire, E.R.	162	8	29.0
Yorkshire, N.R.	153	8	34.5
Nottingham	175	7	20.2
Gloucester	291	7	17.4
All England	9,501	7	18.8

Sources: Census of Great Britain, 1841, Enumeration Abstracts, Pt. 1, *England and Wales*, British Parliamentary Papers, 1843 (496), XXII, pp. 399, 458, and *Occupation Abstracts*, Pt. 1, *England and Wales*, British Parliamentary Papers, 1844 (587), XXVII, p. 22.

represented in agriculture, in relation to their numbers, as were German immigrants and much better represented than Irish immigrants.[11] Although by 1870 only about 26 percent of the English and Welsh immigrants were still in agriculture, this proportion had undoubtedly been higher twenty years earlier. Of the English people who had settled in the United States by 1850, more than half were to be found in predominantly rural states: 45 percent of the immigrants were reported to be living in states in which agriculture employed more than half of the working population. No state had so high a proportion of English-born inhabitants in its population at that date as Wisconsin. In fact, Illinois, Michigan, and Iowa all had a higher proportion of English-born residents than did Massachusetts and Connecticut (see Table 1.2). During the fifties the states and territories whose English-born population increased most rapidly were Minnesota, Kansas, Nebraska, Utah, Oregon, Iowa, Michigan, and Illinois. By 1860 there were

[11] Edward Hutchinson, *Immigrants and Their Children, 1850–1950* (New York: John Wiley, 1956), pp. 81–82.

Table 1.2. English-born population, urbanization, occupations of people, and population density, 1850

	Percent of population English-born	Percent of population rural[a]	Percent of male workers over 15 engaged in agriculture[b]	Population density per square mile
Utah	9.3	100	50	0.1
Wisconsin	6.2	91	52	5.6
California	3.3	93	3	0.6
Rhode Island	3.0	44	20	136.0
Michigan	2.7	93	60	6.9
New York	2.7	72	35	65.0
New Jersey	2.3	82	26	65.7
Illinois	2.2	92	66	15.2
Iowa	2.0	95	67	3.5
Massachusetts	1.7	76	19	123.7

Source: Based on *Seventh Census of the United States*, 1850 (Washington, 1853), pp. 36–337.

[a] Population defined as residing in places of fewer than 2,500 inhabitants. Since there are serious difficulties in defining urban places in many eastern states in these early census returns, these figures should be taken as representing rough approximations. See *Sixteenth Census of the United States: 1940, Population* (Washington: G.P.O., 1942), 1: 11.

[b] Labor force figures in the 1850 census are not very reliable, particularly because slaves were not counted. But this defect does not distort the picture in the states considered here.

over 140,000 English people in the Old Northwest (Ohio, Michigan, Indiana, Illinois, and Wisconsin) as compared with only 45,680 in New England and 168,410 in the Middle Atlantic states.

The distribution of English immigrants in the United States before 1860 supports the inference from immigrant letters that the lure of agriculture as a way of life and of land ownership as a desirable goal were operating as inducements to emigration. Although it is true that many literary men and public figures in England were condemning industrial society, the deliberate choice of agriculture by English emigrants is still quite remarkable, more noteworthy than a similar choice by those from more agricultural and rural societies. One is even more surprised to discover that English people with industrial skills were attracted by the idea of farming in America. Historians did not regard this as curious, so long as the yeoman farmer myth so clouded their perspective that they thought it too obvious to require comment that urban workers in industrial occupations would try to become farmers if they could. But today, the choice of farming by urban workers in an industrializing economy seems to require explanation. Neil Smelser described the reaction of cotton textile workers to technological change in the industry during the 1820s and 1830s as disturbed and irrational.[12] Without attempting a rigorous application of the theory of social action to the whole of English society in this period, one might describe this movement of English emigrants into American agriculture as a disturbed reaction to economic and social change.

American agriculture attracted Englishmen of widely different backgrounds and experience. Four groups may be distinguished among the families whose letters we have. Such a classification forms a convenient basis for discussion of the ideas but is necessarily arbitrary. One can, in fact, find industrial and agricultural workers, factory hands and factory managers, and agricultural laborers and farmers within the same families. Indeed, a study of these letters illustrates the relative fluidity of the English social structure of this period.

The first two groups of families had gained their livelihood principally from agriculture before emigration. Among the farming families, the best-known emigrant was Morris Birkbeck, who left both public and private letters. Birkbeck had been farming about fifteen hundred acres at Wandsworth, Surrey, before he emigrated in 1817.[13] Other farming families to whom the letters introduce us also came from the agricultural, rather than the industrializing, counties of England.[14] They—or

[12] Neil Smelser, *Social Change in the Industrial Revolution, 1770–1840* (London: Routledge and Kegan Paul, 1959), pp. 278–79.

[13] Gladys Thomson, *A Pioneer Family: The Birkbecks in Illinois* (London: Jonathan Cape, 1953); Morris Birkbeck, *Letters from Illinois, 1818–1827*, 2d ed. (Philadelphia, 1818); and Edwin Sparks, ed., *The English Settlement in the Illinois* (London: Museum Book Store, 1907).

[14] Most of the manuscripts on which this essay draws are listed and annotated in Bernard Crick and Miriam Alman, eds., *A Guide to Manuscripts Relating to America in Great Britain and Ireland* (London: Oxford University Press, 1961), pp. 327–34. The collections that contain letters from members of farming families in England are the Corlett Letters, 1831–76*; the Fisher Letters, 1831–38*; the Birket Letters, 1833–59*; the Wozencraft Letters, 1843–49*; the Meatyard Letters, 1836–38; and the Needham Letter, 1834. Those marked with an asterisk here and below were later published in Charlotte Erickson, *Invisible Immigrants: The Adaptation of English and Scottish Immigrants in Nineteenth-Century America* (London: Weidenfeld and Nicolson, 1972: rpt., Ithaca: Cornell University Press, 1990). In addition to manuscripts listed in Crick and Alman, the following were also consulted: copies of letters from Robert Shedden, Elgin, Ill., 1845; and from John Muir, Lisbon, 1842, given to the British Library of Political and Economic Science (hereinafter BLPES) by the British Record Association; and the Robert Bowles Letters, 1823, Ohio Historical Society, Columbus. Since this essay was written, many more collections have been found in both British and American archives.

their fathers—farmed on a much smaller scale than Birkbeck, however, occupying farms of between one hundred and two hundred acres—not large by the standards of southeastern England, but in fact much closer to the American norm. Yet they had not managed these farms as family farms. John Fisher's elder brother, for example, employed ten laborers and three waggoners on their Norfolk farm of 210 acres in 1851. Moreover, these families did not occupy land that their fathers had farmed continuously from one generation to the next. Migration had already begun in these families, who came from a rural society that was by no means static.

As far as we know, no manuscript letters from the second group of agricultural emigrants—laborers—have survived from the period before the early 1840s. A few printed collections of laborers' letters date from the 1820s and 1830s, when poor law authorities and others were granting assisted passages.[15] Occasionally one gets earlier glimpses of laborers in the farmers' letters. The late appearance of letters from laborers whose emigration was not subsidized probably reflects quite accurately the period when emigration from the English countryside deepened, as fares became cheaper and literacy spread. The laborers who appear in printed collections or in the farmers' letters usually went out under some kind of patronage and came from those same nonindustrialized counties that produced farmer-emigrants. In contrast, the few laboring families who emigrated on their own initiative, as it were, about whom we have some information, usually came from parts of England in which opportunities for nonagricultural employment were expanding quite rapidly at the time they left.[16]

It has been said that the English agricultural laborer did not have the kind of experience to prepare him for adaptation to American

[15] The editors of the following collections claimed that they published both favorable and unfavorable reactions of emigrants, in spite of making cuts: G. Poulett Scrope, ed., *Extracts of Letters from Poor Persons Who Emigrated Last Year to Canada and the United States* (London: James Ridgeway, 1831); Benjamin Smith, ed., *Twenty-four Letters from Labourers in America to Their Friends in England,* 2d ed. (London: Edward Rainford, 1829); T. Sockett, ed., *Letters from Sussex Emigrants . . . for Upper Canada,* 2d ed. (London: Longman, 1833); *Counsel for Emigrants with Original Letters from Canada and the United States* (Aberdeen: John Mathison, 1834).

[16] Letters from emigrants from laboring families, cited in Crick and Alman, *Guide to Manuscripts,* include the Griffith Letters, 1848–65*; the Gilley Letter, 1845; the Fewins Letters, 1850–52; the Goodchild Letter, 1851; and the Bishop Letters, 1872–74*. See also the Bond-Greyston Series*, copies in the Collection of Regional History : Cornell University. The Fewins Letters were published in Charlotte Erickson, ed., *Emigration from Europe, 1815–1914* (London: Adam and Charles Black, 1976), pp. 127–30.

agriculture.[17] His work had been too specialized to enable him to fit into the family farm or to venture into independent farm management. This may have been true of the laborer from the southeast, but it did not apply so forcefully to a family such as the Griffiths, who came to Illinois in 1841 from a part of Shropshire where the average number of laborers per farm was only three.[18] In the more pastoral west and north of England, the family-managed farm was more common and labor not so specialized as it was in the arable southeast.

In any case, agricultural laborers were probably better equipped by experience for American farming than were the other immigrant groups to be considered. The element of myth was particularly strong in the emigration of people from urban areas and industrial occupations. How many such people went to American farms it is impossible to say. In certain places there were enough of them to lead to complaints that "too few English farmers come out; too many from the manufacturing districts."[19] It seems quite probable that the states of the Middle West gained a reservoir of diversified industrial skills from immigrants who failed as farmers.

Perhaps the emigrants least well prepared for a farmer's life in America were those who came from urban or industrial families of some education and means, immigrants who paralleled Wittke's Latin farmers to a limited extent. Richard Flower, who went with Morris Birkbeck to the English prairie in Illinois, had been the owner of a brewery in Hereford before he turned to farming.[20] One of the leaders of the English settlement in southern Indiana, founded about the same time, was Saunders Hornbrook, who had been a woolen manufacturer and iron founder in Devon.[21] Another similar figure, even less successful in

[17] Percy Bidwell and John Falconer, *Agriculture in the Northern United States, 1620–1860* (Washington: Carnegie Institution, 1925), p. 205; William Cobbett, *A Year's Residence in the United States of America*, 2d ed. (London, 1819), pp. 138, 323–34; Samuel Laing, *Observations on the Social and Political State of the European People in 1848 and 1849* (London: Longman, Brown, Green, and Longmans, 1850), p. 70.

[18] Both published and manuscript census materials have been used to identify the emigrants and establish their backgrounds in England. The Griffiths came from the village of Hindford in Whittington Parish, Shropshire. Mrs. Griffith's father and all her brothers were farm laborers (Census Manuscripts, England and Wales, 1851, HO 107, bdl. 1994, enumeration district 4, 1c: 4, London, PRO).

[19] Grant Foreman, "English Settlers in Illinois," *Journal of the Illinois State Historical Society* 34 (1941): 333.

[20] George Flower, *History of the English Settlement in Edwards County, Illinois* (Chicago: Chicago Historical Society Collections, 1882), 1: 26–27.

[21] John Inglehart, "The Coming of the English to Indiana in 1817 and Their Hoosier Neighbors," *Indiana Magazine of History* 15 (1919): 91–94.

American agriculture than Flower and Hornbrook, was George Courtauld, an Essex silk manufacturer and the father of Samuel Courtauld, who laid the foundations of the present-day firm. Courtauld had lived in New York State during the late 1780s, returned to England in 1794, and reemigrated in 1818, this time to the wilderness in southeastern Ohio, taking along as many of his children as he could persuade to go.[22]

Another emigrant from a manufacturing family with fewer social pretentions and less class consciousness was Edwin Bottomley, the son of a manager of a woolen factory in Huddersfield, whose letters from Wisconsin in the 1840s have also been published.[23] Most desperately unprepared for her life on an American farm was Rebecca Butterworth, the daughter of an estate agent in Rochdale, Lancashire, who found herself on a fever-ridden farm in Arkansas in the 1840s.[24]

The final group of emigrants—obscure industrial workers, village craftsmen, and provision dealers—could not be studied but for the manuscript letters. Their letters tell the story of individuals and families who acted on some of the same assumptions as produced the abortive potters' colony in Wisconsin and the land schemes of a branch of the Chartist movement.[25] More than the agriculturists, these urban and industrial people were seeking on an American farm a return to a mythical past.

These groups of emigrants did not all draw their ideas from the same sources. But because they were able to write letters, they were likely to be influenced by the written word. Not a great deal can be said about the specific sources from which they drew their ideas about the United States. Birkbeck and Flower seem to have become interested in the prairie regions of the West through reading the same radical literature that helped formulate the American confidence in a continental

[22] *Courtauld Family Letters, 1782–1900, 8 vols.*, (Cambridge: Bowes and Bowes, 1916).

[23] Milo Milton Quaife, ed., *An English Settler in Pioneer Wisconsin: The Letters of Edwin Bottomley, 1842–1850*, Publications of the State Historical Society of Wisconsin, Collections 25 (Madison, 1918).

[24] The Butterworth Letters were published in Erickson, *Invisible Immigrants*, pp. 175–78.

[25] Grant Foreman, "The Settlement of English Potters in Wisconsin," *Wisconsin Magazine of History* 21 (1938): 374–96. The manuscript collections representing this group include the Mearbeck Letters, 1815–21 (typescript copy in Central Reference Library, Sheffield); the Morris Letters, 1829–46*; the Whittaker Letters, 1849–56*; the Hirst Letter, 1829; and the Poulton Letters, 1834. All are listed in Crick and Alman, *Guide to Manuscripts*. See also the Smith Letters in the Fisher Letters, 1848–60, manuscripts in the Ipswich and East Suffolk Record Office, Ipswich, 2815/1–4.

destiny.[26] Certain passages in the writings of Gilbert Imlay, erstwhile lover of Mary Wollstonecraft, emphasized the beauty and abundance of the prairies: "Everything that a reasonable mind can desire, is to be found, or may with little pains be produced here."[27] In turn, George Courtauld and some of the early English settlers in southern Indiana were acquainted with Birkbeck's own *Letters from Illinois*. Aware of the controversy that they produced, Courtauld was still intent on founding his own American farm. Hopes shared with Birkbeck probably influenced Courtauld more than did the incidental information contained in *Letters from Illinois*.

Apart from this radical elite, few emigrants appear to have read widely in the travel literature of the early nineteenth century. Of the many guides for emigrants then on the market, that published by William Chambers of Edinburgh was the only one referred to in any of the manuscripts consulted for this paper. Robert Bowles, in what he called his "rural bower" in southern Ohio in the 1820s, was using broom stalks for thatching according to a "hint" he obtained "from Cobbett's book."[28] Although his was the only letter that specifically referred to Cobbett, the recurrent clichés against parsons, landlords, and tax collectors suggest the great influence of William Cobbett. His ideas and language struck a profoundly responsive chord in his generation, in spite of the fact that he set out to write a cottage economy for laborers, but most of his suggestions were more appropriate for the gentry. Many familiar phrases may have been gained secondhand from newspapers. The experience of emigration heightened the addiction of industrial and urban people in particular to newspapers. And emigrant letters themselves were also a source of an image of the United States.

Yet the early letters of emigrants, like those of the travelers, were very likely to reveal more about their preconceptions than about the objective reality of the country to which they came. This is patently clear in letters that gained publication in English newspapers, as well as

[26] For discussion of these writers, see Smith, *Virgin Land*, pp. 9, 130, and Fender, *Sea Changes*, pp. 27–63.

[27] Quotation from the 1776 edition of Thomas Hutchins, *Topographical Description of Virginia, Pennsylvania, Indiana, and North Carolina*, in Gilbert Imlay, *Topographical Description of the Western Territory* (London, 1797), pp. 503–4.

[28] William and Robert Chambers, *The Emigrant's Manual, British America and the United States* (Edinburgh: Chambers' Instructive and Entertaining Library, 1855). Robert Bowles, Harrison, Hamilton County, Ohio, October 19, 1823, to his brothers, Bowles Letters. William Cobbett, *Cottage Economy* (London: C. Clement, 1822). There were many editions of this work.

those of colony projectors Courtauld and Birkbeck, who sat in bleak inns and boardinghouses in Indiana and Ohio describing the utopias they were going to carve out of the American wilderness. In fact, it is from the implications of these remarks by the unadjusted and unassimilated immigrants that one can construct a picture of the views they held before they emigrated, views that had more relevance to their English culture than to their circumstances in America.

To probe the content of the agrarian myth for British immigrants, we can begin at the top of the emigrant social scale, for the elite had certain ideas, gained from their reading, that were not shared by more ordinary emigrants. In harmony with an important theme in romanticism, Birkbeck and Courtauld expected to find great natural beauty in the West. Although Birkbeck and Flower did find the Illinois prairies beautiful, Courtauld very soon became disenchanted in Ohio. He warned his children, whose imaginations he had previously kindled, "The face of the country you must all know presents one uniform view of a rugged wilderness with here & there patches of partial clearings & slovenly cultivation, very little of beautiful scenery."[29]

One of the most important elements in the classical and biblical praise of husbandry, which Americans adopted with unabashed enthusiasm, was the view that the farmer's life produced virtue whereas city life bred wickedness. It is perhaps not to be expected that immigrants would write that they themselves expected to be better people by joining the American peasantry. Yet, well-read English immigrants, as did so many travelers, professed to expect to find the American farmers themselves to be shining examples of the pure and simple virtues of men in intimate contact with nature. Courtauld was predisposed to this view, which he thought was based on his own experience in New York during the first years of independence. But he was to be disappointed in southern Ohio a generation later.

> As to the idea that America is in that happy state of civilization which is equally removed from a vicious & luxurious refinemt as from the inconvenc of an uncivilized state, that the manners & morals of the people are simple & virtuous & that a noble-minded public spirit is generally prevalent, which gives them a decided superiority of character to old corrupt countries, I think much less of this than I once thought.[30]

[29] *Courtauld Family Letters*, 2: 486; Flower, *English Settlement*, pp. 53, 143, 148, 156, 188–89.
[30] *Courtauld Family Letters*, 2: 474.

Edwin Bottomley anticipated that life on a Wisconsin farm would enable him to protect his children's morals from the contamination that he regarded as inevitable in a factory.[31] The farther one goes down the emigrant social scale, the less frequently does one encounter this aspect of the agrarian myth. The working-class emigrant was less inclined to be critical of the American farmer because he had not expected him to be a demigod.

Norwegian immigrants appealed to their compatriots to follow them to "a land where local self-government and democracy were carried to a greater perfection than at home."[32] Such an emphasis is rarely to be found in the private letters of English immigrants in the early nineteenth century. Their comparative indifference to American politics was reflected in the fact that they adopted United States citizenship less frequently than immigrants from some other regions.[33] The English immigrants who expressed some interest in American political institutions and who looked forward to participating in the government of a small community were again the educated elite. Unsatisfied political ambitions probably colored the views of men like Birkbeck and Courtauld about America. Much to the disadvantage of his own economic interests, Courtauld had as a young man plunged into the fight in New York for the ratification of the United States constitution.[34] Birkbeck was involved in the struggle over the Illinois Constitution within a very few years of his arrival at Wanborough, Illinois. In admiring America for its republicanism, not for its democracy, these men were not in sympathy with the democratic aspirations that were shattering the deferential society of eighteenth-century America.[35] The most politically minded of the English emigrants from rural areas seem to have been more interested, in the true Cobbett spirit, in escaping from government—from high taxes, informers, and tithes—than they were in participation in democratic government. Emigrants from industrial regions seem to have taken little notice of American politics, even when they came from a background of intense political excitement in England. There are few counterparts in the unpublished letters to this excerpt from a letter written for the press by an emigrant potter: "Here

[31] Quaife, *English Settler*, p. 44.

[32] Ingrid Semmingsen, "Emigration and the Image of America," in *Immigration and American History*, ed. Commager, p. 36.

[33] Berthoff, *British Immigrants*, pp. 139–40.

[34] *Courtauld Family Letters,* 1: xxxi.

[35] Ibid., 1: xlviii, 43. Cf. Jack Pole, "Historians and the Problem of Early American Democracy," *American Historical Review* 67 (1962): 626–46.

we can breathe the pure and wholesome atmosphere of REPUBLICANISM. Since I have been here, I have had the pleasure of voting at a general August election, and I went in for Pure Democracy."[36] Edwin Bottomley accepted the duties of a magistrate in his Wisconsin township as necessary but rather irksome. He rejoiced that "Politicks [sic] are a subject that we are never troubled with hear" and asked his father to "tell Brother Henry not to let me have quit[e] so much of Politics in his next."[37]

These letters suggest that expectations of natural beauty, of a uniquely virtuous people, and of beneficent republican institutions were confined to the highly literate minority among English immigrants. These ideas were found among those who had the most difficulty in adapting to the rigorous life of an American farm and to the easygoing atmosphere of American social democracy.

A belief common to most of the immigrants who came from farming families in southern and eastern England was that their knowledge of English methods of improved farming would give them an advantage over the native-born farmer in the United States.[38] This faith in improvement, which led them to criticize the slovenly methods of American farmers, may have been a disadvantage in their adjustment in the American West.[39]

Paul Gates concluded that English immigrants probably assisted in the development of the Illinois prairies by introducing advanced methods of drainage.[40] But Morris Birkbeck's son did not believe that his father's preoccupation with drainage would forward his agricultural enterprise: "My father has enclosed about 350 acres of most excellent land and has been ditching it most thoroughly, although it was scarcely wanted, except in a few places. Ditching, if you recollect, was my father's favourite operation, and he would never rest until he had completely secured any spot which appeared even likely to be ever

[36] Foreman, "English Settlers in Illinois," p. 321.

[37] Quaife, *English Settler*, p. 57. Stephen Fender argues that "the act of emigration itself, both objectively and subjectively, was always a political act when it concerned the British going to the United States" (*Sea Changes*, p. 45). Even the yearning for independence was "a political aspiration" (p. 44).

[38] Johnstone, "In Praise of Husbandry," p. 87.

[39] See, for example, Charles Barclay, ed., *Letters of Dorking Emigrants Who Went to Upper Canada . . .* (London: J. and A. Arch, 1833), p. 31; *Counsel for Emigrants*, pp. 38, 43; and Hubert G. Schmidt, "Some Post-Revolutionary Views of American Agriculture in the English Midlands," *Agricultural History* 32 (1958): 166–75.

[40] Paul Wallace Gates, *The Illinois Central Railroad and Its Colonization Work* (Cambridge: Harvard University Press, 1934), pp. 12–13; Flower, *English Settlement*, p. 165.

wet.[41] Living in New York State in the 1840s, Henry Petingale, son of a Norfolk farmer, had not learned what progressive American farmers had long since discovered: that the revered turnip was not so useful where winters were long and severe. Immigrants from other parts of England may not have shared his contempt for New York, where "the farms are all small and conducted on the milk, eggs and butter pedling system."[42]

English farmers were determined to farm in a better manner than their neighbors, by careful treatment of the soil, more thorough clearing, and improved livestock husbandry. Their faith in English methods was a kind of moral principle and as such was part of a myth that an inflexible immigrant was unlikely to find useful under the circumstances of factor supply in the West. One English farmer, who spent the years 1824 to 1830 in various parts of America, observed that many English who settled as farmers "are so fond of their own opinions as to attempt the introduction of English husbandry, and entail a heavy expense upon themselves for their folly."[43]

In addition to these views about American agriculture, which can be associated with particular groups of immigrants, another cluster of ideas can be identified that all groups shared. The first of these was the not unrealistic notion that land was cheap in America. It has been observed that the prospect of land ownership was attractive to English immigrants because of the prestige they attached to it.[44] In contrast, Norwegian immigrants are said to have been attracted by the obverse—the social equality that cheap land made possible.[45]

Neither the desire for status via land ownership nor the search for social equality among other yeoman farmers is a persistent theme in the private letters of English immigrants. George Courtauld did hope to achieve a respectability he felt he was losing in England as his daughters were forced to undergo the humiliations of the position of governess and as the family was forced to restrict its "visiting" for want of money. Like Birkbeck in Illinois and John Ingle in Indiana, Courtauld thought that as a paternalistic colonizer he could retrieve his status. These men were too well-informed to believe that in the United States the kind of

[41] Thomson, *Pioneer Family,* p. 64.

[42] Henry Petingale, Newburgh, N.Y., August 6, 1849, to his sister, in Erickson, *Invisible Immigrants,* pp. 446–47. Cf. Rodney Loehr, "The Influence of English Agriculture on American Agriculture, 1775–1825," *Agricultural History* 2 (1937): 3–15.

[43] Joseph Pickering, *Inquiries of an Emigrant* (London: Effingham Wilson, 1832), p. vi.

[44] Berthoff, *British Immigrants,* p. 109.

[45] Semmingsen, "Emigration and the Image of America," pp. 36, 46–47.

status they yearned for was an automatic by-product of land ownership. For this reason, Courtauld preferred to devote his energies to the affairs of a new township, which "will naturally, necessarily give me sufficient influence to be useful and respectable, which is in much less degree practicable where self important and ignorant men have already obtained power and influence."[46] The very occasional references to the "aristocratic" status of immigrant landowners found in the letters of agricultural and industrial workers were offered half in fun and lack the heavy seriousness of Courtauld's anxieties.

It is true that the idea that "workmen here are not afraid of their masters; they are all seen as equals" was common in the published letters of assisted emigrants.[47] Moreover, that key word in English aspirations—independence—occasionally carried a meaning allied to that of social equality, as when George Courtauld complained of the absurd independence of his neighbors in southern Ohio or when another immigrant praised the "independence from all supercilious and brow-beating superiors" he found in Michigan.[48] In the manuscript letters this theme of social equality is rarely to be found. If one relied on them for evidence, one would have to conclude that a longing for equality was no more important among most English immigrants than was the desire for democratic politics.

Nevertheless, cheap land was a magnet for English emigrants of all classes, whether they wanted land for a gentleman's estate, for commercial farming, for a subsistence farm, or simply as an investment. The lure of cheap land led to mistakes, hardship, and frequent disillusionment, as immigrants discovered that, although it was cheap in comparison with England, land was not cheap enough for them to carry out unrealistic plans.

Whether their savings for land purchase were large or small, farmers, industrial workers, and others who arrived in the United States with the intention of buying land found prices too high in the regions of older settlement. Marcus Hansen believed that Europeans found their place

[46] *Courtauld Family Letters*, 2: 469; see also Inglehart, "Coming of the English to Indiana," p. 100.

[47] Smith, *Twenty-four Letters*, pp. 31, 45; John Knight, *Important Extracts from Original and Recent Letters Written by Emigrants in the United States of America* (Manchester: Thomas Wilkinson, 1818), p. 43; Foreman, "English Settlers in Illinois," p. 304. The only clear statement of this kind found in the collections used was the following from weaver Andrew Morris: "For my part I could not live contented in England where there is so much distinction between the working class and the rich" (Andrew Morris, Aurelius, Ohio, February 5, 1844, to his brother, in Erickson, *Invisible Immigrants*, p. 171).

[48] *Courtauld Family Letters*, 2: 467; *Counsel for Emigrants*, p. 129.

in American agriculture as "fillers-in." Lacking the skills and endurance of the frontier farmer, they preferred to buy improved farms and leave to the native-born the tasks of clearing and breaking the land.[49] Cobbett and other writers strongly advised prospective emigrant farmers to do just that.[50]

It was therefore rather surprising to discover that most of these English immigrants actually did buy unimproved land. Few moved into quite such undeveloped territory as did John Fisher, who arrived in Lewanee County, Michigan, in 1831, when the population density was still less than two inhabitants per square mile. Yet most of these immigrants aimed at getting unimproved government land at the minimum price. In the large Morris family, most of whom had been industrial workers in Lancashire, the only one to purchase an improved farm was a son-in-law who had farmed in England. Sometimes when government land was purchased, a prior claim had to be bought out. Edwin Bottomley paid forty dollars to a man named Flint, who had readied some lumber for a small house on an eighty-acre claim.[51] Although some of the English picked up less desirable spots that had gone unsold behind the so-called frontier line, others moved out to become squatters in advance of sale. The Birkets, a Westmorland family, arrived in the neighborhood of Peoria in 1826, before the great trek from New England to Illinois began. None of the federal lands had been surveyed and put up for auction when they staked claims in Washington and Tazewell counties in 1832, claims they purchased under preemption privileges in 1835 and 1836. Industrial workers and urban people showed a remarkable proclivity for unbroken land.

This compulsion to get cheap land sometimes meant that immigrants did not choose their location or land very wisely. Few purchased quite so blindly as a Sheffield metal plater by the name of Samuel Mearbeck, who bought his land in an office in Washington, D.C., without even seeing it. It lay in what is now West Virginia, in a region to which there was not so much as a crude road and no market for commercial agriculture.[52] Coming from Huddersfield, Edwin Bottomley selected his land in Wisconsin within a month of landing at New York.[53] George Courtauld was equally precipitate in his choice of five thousand acres

[49] Marcus Lee Hansen, *The Immigrant in American History* (Cambridge: Harvard University Press, 1940), pp. 65–69.

[50] Cobbett, *Year's Residence*, pp. 83, 325, 562.

[51] Quaife, *English Settler*, p. 31.

[52] Erickson, *Invisible Immigrants*, p. 46.

[53] Quaife, *English Settler*, p. 31.

near Athens, Ohio, bought at a bargain price from a speculator. Others scouted their land in advance but were usually satisfied if there was some kind of road in the vicinity and if they liked the look of the land. Many found themselves in what came to be arrested frontiers. Arriving after the bottomlands had been taken, they settled, along with southerners, in the hill country of southern Ohio, Indiana, and Illinois, where land subject to erosion became gullied. Nearly all the industrial or urban people whose letters are analyzed here bought land in counties that were to experience a decline in population within twenty years of their arrival.

The most advantageous choices were made by people from farming families in England. Although they were among the very early settlers in these neighborhoods, John Fisher near Ann Arbor, the Birkets at Peoria, and the Corletts near Cleveland did well as farmers because of rapid town growth during the late forties and fifties. To a certain extent, at least, we might say that immigrant laborers who arrived in America without the means to buy land and who took laboring jobs in a farming region until they had the savings to become landowners, afterward stocking and improving those farms, also had a good chance of buying land wisely and of getting the necessary experience in American farming.[54] In contrast, those who worked in the East to accumulate savings for land purchase and immigrants who came to the United States with capital were more likely to make mistakes.

The mythical element in the attraction of cheap land led to other difficulties as well. In spite of the increasing volume of warnings in the literature about the problem of obtaining labor, sanguine immigrants simply refused to recognize its difficulty, especially where land was cheapest. One after another, they found their timetables for clearing and improving wrecked because of the shortage of labor. It was not simply a matter of high wages but also the impossibility of finding labor at all, at any wage, of labor that was too "independent," and of workers who were unreliable because they also had farms to clear or other commitments.[55]

The hope of reducing farm-making costs and heavy labor led many English immigrants to move from timbered lands to the prairies. Morris

[54] Examples of such people are to be found in the Fisher Letters; Flower, *English Settlement*, p. 45; and Merle Curti, *The Making of an American Community: A Case Study of Democracy in a Frontier County* (Stanford: Stanford University Press, 1959), pp. 208–9.

[55] Quaife, *English Settler*, pp. 114, 131, 155; Richard Flower, *Letters from the Illinois* (London: James Ridgeway, 1822), p. 12; Flower, *English Settlement*, p. 279.

Birkbeck and George Flower claimed to have considered buying prairie land before they left for the United States.[56] More commonly, English immigrants first attempted to create a farm out of uncleared woodland and, in discouragement when they realized the immensity of the task before them, looked about for oak openings or small prairies. After she had witnessed the struggle of her father and brothers with the timber and vines in Athens County, Eliza Courtauld Ash and her husband, who had been a cabinetmaker in England, settled on prairie land in southern Ohio.[57] Many instances of English immigrants who added eighty acres or so of prairie land to their original land purchase, not for the use of their animals but as the basis for their arable farming, support Paul Gates's contention that English immigrants helped break down the American prejudice against the prairies.[58] The English exhibited no fear of a want of fertility in the prairie lands. Coming from a land of cleared farms, they regarded the grass, and particularly the weeds, as evidence of fertility.

The belief that land was cheap in the United States influenced most ranks of English society. Although it could operate as the basis of a perfectly rational economic choice, in some instances at least it led to serious mistakes. A belief in subsistence farming as a way of life, common to many but not all of these immigrants, was an even greater obstacle to market-minded behavior. Particularly among industrial workers, urban dwellers, and even village craftsmen, one notes a marked absence of any notion of economic advance through land purchase in the States. Their desire for a farming life did not result from a weighing up of economic inducements. This craving for a pastoral life and for the opportunity to make their own consumer goods was in part the fruit of fears about what the future in England would bring. Writing in 1822, Ruth Courtauld feared "this country does not seem as tho' it could last long."[59] A decade later John Fisher wrote, "I have left the country cowring with Doubt and danger where the rich man trembels and the poor man frowns where all repine at the present and dread the future." And in the early forties, Edwin Bottomley confessed that "though I had a good situation my mind was fill'd with dark forbodings" about the future.[60]

[56] Flower, *English Settlement*, pp. 36, 352; Knight, *Important Extracts*, 2d ser., p. 27.

[57] *Courtauld Family Letters*, 2: 910.

[58] In addition to manuscript sources, see Quaife, *English Settler*, p. 34, and Foreman, "English Settlers in Illinois," p. 331.

[59] *Courtauld Family Letters*, 2: 899.

[60] In a remarkable coup of scholarship, Stephen Fender discovered that Fisher's remarks paraphrased almost exactly a speech of Washington Irving on his return from

The willingness to abandon a more advanced material standard of living in favor of subsistence farming may be interpreted in part as a disturbed reaction to changes, the outcome of which was unforeseen. As he set off on a journey by horseback and on foot to his Virginia land, Samuel Mearbeck reflected, "I shall be where neither affluence nor poverty is known where every man may procure by his own Industry everything that is necessary in the world to make him comfortable."[61] Here was a complete rejection of the advantages of economic specialization.

The view was mixed with a misunderstanding of what a farmer's life and prospects really were. One immigrant working as a country weaver in the Ohio Valley and earning $1.50 a day wrote, "I should like to have some land, for they live so comfortably who milk their own cows, live in their own houses, grow their own corn, make their own sugar and everything they want."[62] Even Ruth Courtauld, sensitive as she was to the comforts her daughters had known in England, could encourage them thus: "You become the sole owner of a nice piece of ground which is capable of supplying you with all the necessaries of life, and I think I may say, all its rational comforts in time. But you must work for them, and even that will make them the sweeter."[63]

Prospective emigrants believed that subsistence farming could provide an adequate standard of living partly because homemade articles had an inherent superiority over any that were purchased. Cobbett insisted that they retained this superiority so long as they were at least made by one's own servants. Such overtones were even more evident in remarks suggesting that making one's own consumer goods would be peculiarly pleasant in the United States because soap, candles, sugar, ale, and whiskey were not taxed.[64] An explicit disciple of Cobbett, Robert Bowles noted that in Ohio "we can make what we please without the dread of an Exciseman and informer."[65] So strong was the rejection

---

seventeen years in Europe, a speech that was reported in the press two days before Fisher wrote this letter (*Sea Changes*, pp. 43–44, 369). For Fisher's letter, see Erickson, *Invisible Immigrants*, pp. 117–18. See also Quaife, *English Settler*, p. 184.

[61] Samuel Mearbeck, Washington City, November 9, 1818, Mearbeck Letters.

[62] John Garside, Salem, January 17, 1818, to his father-in-law, in Knight, *Important Extracts*, 2d ser., p. 30.

[63] *Courtauld Family Letters*, 2: 865.

[64] *Counsel for Emigrants*, pp. 22, 48; Cobbett, Cottage Economy, p. 65; Knight, *Important Extracts*, 2d ser., pp. 42–43.

[65] Robert Bowles, Harrison, Hamilton County, Ohio, August 5, 1823, Robert Bowles Letters.

of industrial and even commercial civilization by one of the emigrant potters that he "rejoiced" to inform his friends "that we do not depend upon a monied currency for subsistence, as you do in England . . . . I have now been in this country near 12 months . . . and have not yet received a dollar in cash for my labor."[66]

The extreme left of the English agrarian myth favored not hard money but no money at all. The existence of this lunatic fringe does not detract from the main point that the image of a subsistence farm was attractive to many English people whose standard of life embraced goods and services that could not be obtained on an isolated farmstead. This appeal was largely a by-product of the immense value they attached to independence. The immigrant letters strongly support Neil Smelser's contention that the value of independence afforded one of the mainsprings of action in early nineteenth-century England, but they do not confirm his estimate of what the term conveyed. Basing his definition mainly on tracts written to advise the laboring classes, he concluded, "Applied to the laboring family . . . independence meant a man at the head of his family, self-supporting, seeking the best opportunity the market offered, and experiencing the pride of independence which arose from this condition. . . . The traditional relationships between master and man did not contradict the value of independence."[67]

This assessment of the meaning of independence in English society is not borne out by the emigrant letters. Impelled by a desire for independence, as they understood it, emigrants turned their backs on the best opportunities the market offered to try to escape from traditional relationships between master and man. In fact, so contrary to Smelser's assumptions was the use of this term by emigrants who hoped to attain it for themselves that one is reminded of Robert Webb's contention that the literature of moral uplift, on which Smelser based his definition, had little appeal for the growing literate public in the working classes.[68]

To the writers of these letters, independence meant, above all, freedom from an employer. Thus it struck at the very roots of "traditional relationships between master and man." An example of the meaning attached to the term is to be found in the autobiography of William Farish, a handloom weaver who did not emigrate: "I was very

[66] Foreman, "English Potters in Wisconsin," p. 322; Smith, *Twenty-four Letters*, p. 14.

[67] Smelser, *Social Change*, pp. 210–11.

[68] Robert Webb, *The British Working Class Reader*, 1790–1848 (London: George Allen and Unwin, 1955), pp. 160–61.

tired of leaving the bread of myself and wife in other men's hands, and as our little hotel was yielding more profit than the highest amount of my wages, I now, for the first time in my life, felt a real sense of independence."[69] In the same way, the only brother in the large Morris clan who did not go to the United States achieved his independence as a shopkeeper, leaving his job as a mechanic in a cotton factory.[70] More than half a century later, Ernest Bevin, a young emigrant from rural Devon to the city of Bristol, clung to his independence by working as a carter whose time was his own after he picked up his load at 6:00 in the morning, in preference to better-paid work in which he would be supervised continuously.[71]

The term was used in much the same sense by people from middle-class families. As a silk manufacturer in Essex with an income of about £900 in a good year, Samuel Courtauld cautioned his brother George in Ohio not to turn schoolmaster because then he could never be independent.[72] And one of Morris Birkbeck's sons, who went to Mexico after his father drowned, regretted that he had accepted a position as a district manager of mines worked by a joint-stock company: "I have . . . lost my independence and am subject to the whims and caprices of Italians and Germans who are preferred by the Directors of an English company to their own countrymen for the chief places of trust."[73]

A subsistence farm in America seemed to some Englishmen of this generation a means of achieving this goal of independence from an employer. Benjamin Franklin's phrase that farming is the most independent way of life occurred quite often in letters. Many who went to America hoped, like John Fisher, "to live as independent as your richest farmer though not in such great style."[74]

Among emigrants who came from agriculture in England, independence conveyed the idea of freedom from landlords as well. This concept was several degrees removed from the formal idea of freedom

[69] William Farish, *The Autobiography of William Farish: The Struggles of a Handloom Weaver* (pr. pr., 1889), p. 93.

[70] Census Manuscripts, England and Wales, 1851, HO 107, bdl. 2205, e.d. 3, 2: 17, London, PRO; *Slater's Classified Commercial Directory and Topography of . . . Lancashire* (London, 1851), p. 117.

[71] Alan Bullock, *The Life and Times of Ernest Bevin* (London: Heinemann, 1960), 1: 8, 11.

[72] *Courtauld Family Letters*, 3: 964.

[73] Thomson, *Pioneer Family*, p. 125.

[74] John Fisher, Franklin, Mich., June 11, 1832, to his brother, in Erickson, *Invisible Immigrants*, p. 117.

from feudalism cited by Henry Nash Smith as expressing the meaning of independence to an eighteenth-century Englishman.[75] There is also a suggestion that some English farmers had adopted the American concept of fee simple land ownership as constituting independence. Certainly some were attracted by Cobbett's idea that people who made their own consumer goods (or whose servants made them) were more independent than those who bought them. Because independence to these English people meant freedom from certain persons who formerly had some authority over them—employers, landlords, or parsons—its fulfillment was expected to bring a certain social freedom—equality, if you will. One farmer hoped to be "independent of the world, neither fearing its frowns nor counting its smiles."[76] Whatever the emphasis as to its ultimate felicities, subsistence farming in America clearly formed one avenue to independence in the thoughts of English emigrants of this generation.

For the industrial worker, one of the attractions of independence gained on a subsistence farm was freedom from trade fluctuations. Voicing the family decision, William Morris assured his brother that "we have no intention of entering into any kind of trade in this country; it is attended with many changes and fluctuations."[77] Another immigrant who received regular subsidies from his father for his Wisconsin farm still retained the view that "such a home as this would be a hard matter to gain and Especially in England where theire are so many fluctuations of trade which you are aware will affect cottage property [which was his father's kind of independent means] in greater or lesser Degree."[78] The desire to have a farm that would be insulated from trade fluctuations was part of the rejection of economic advance so persistent in the dreams of many of these immigrants.

Another mythical element in the image of a subsistence farm was the belief that it would provide great leisure. This object was one that led men such as Birkbeck and Courtauld, who were nearly sixty years of age, to the American wilderness.[79] It induced others to try to let their

[75] Smith, *Virgin Land*, p. 136; Chester Eisinger, "The Freehold Concept in Eighteenth-Century American Letters," *William and Mary Quarterly* 4 (1947): 49–50.

[76] John Fisher, Franklin, Mich., July 23, 1833, to his brother-in-law, Robert Smith, and his sister, in Erickson, *Invisible Immigrants*, p. 120.

[77] William Morris, Providence, June 4, 1837, to his brother, in Erickson, *Invisible Immigrants*, p. 164.

[78] Quaife, *English Settler*, p. 186.

[79] Thomson, *Pioneer Family*, p. 58; *Courtauld Family Letters*, 2: 894.

small unimproved farms on shares at an early stage.[80] Before he realized the enormity of his task and found himself responding to the high price of provisions in a rapidly growing settlement, John Fisher simply looked forward to the day when he could devote most of his time to his books. The Morrises thought they would very soon have to work only half or two-thirds of the year. Such underemployment was perhaps more characteristic of the eighteenth-century English countryside than it was of the United States in the nineteenth century.

One other motive operating among people who chose American agriculture was the desire to keep the family together. Although they often mentioned the opportunities offered by America for the "rising generation," they visualized a farm as affording such opportunities without making necessary the dispersal of the family. In a number of instances, the fear of physical disruption of the family and the loss of authority and control over children operated as inducements to emigration. Jonathan Morris's children were having to scatter to find jobs. George Courtauld liked neither the family separation nor the situation of his daughters as governesses in other families. Many times he carried on in the face of difficulties with the image of social and improving evenings to be spent with his sons and daughters around him, once they had arrived on their American farm: "Whatever we may gain or lose of worldly Pelf or distinction, we may . . . expect a continual encrease of Social Love, of parental & filial Affection."[81] Although he had not succeeded in gaining a subsistence from his farm, Edwin Bottomley thought his step had been justified because "thank god I have not to rouse my children at the sound of a bell from their beds and Drag them through the pelting storm of a Dark winters morning to earn a small pitance at a factory[.] [N]o thank god such is not the case with us[.] [T]he sun is our guid and when the storm pelts against our windows and [it is] not fit to labour I can sit comfortably with my family and employ my time in improveing thire minds."[82] Needless to say, this part of the myth was also challenged as immigrants discovered that in America "your child will take their own way."[83]

[80] Instances of share-renting were to be found in nearly every collection of letters from immigrants in agriculture.

[81] *Courtauld Family Letters*, 2: 489, 917, and 3: 1002, 1022; Eisinger, "Freehold Concept," p. 51.

[82] Quaife, *English Settler*, p. 185.

[83] Hugh John Needham, Monroe Township, Adams County, Ohio, February 9, 1834, to W. Barns, Staplehurst, Kent, copy made from original in private possession. For an autobiographical work in which family cohesion is given as a principal reason for

The core of this agrarian myth held by English emigrants consisted of the combination of cheap land and subsistence farming. Here was a current of immigration that reinforced the peasant attitudes ascribed by William Parker to many native-born American farmers. Immigrants who were not preoccupied with security often showed highly speculative instincts, "the other extreme of the spectrum of rational economic behaviour."[84] Obviously, not all the English immigrants to American agriculture—even among the handful represented in these letters—can be so categorized. In some individuals the two extremes of the spectrum merged. George Courtauld bought a large tract of land speculatively in the hopes of financing his ideal retreat on a portion of it. He was thus both a gambler and a peasant. Although he railed against the "specula-tion and Peculation" he saw about him, he was, like many Jacksonians, himself both judge and judged.[85] There are other examples of reactions that the challenge of the American environment made to the austere myths these people brought to America. Edwin Bottomley's concern with morality did not prevent him from joining his neighbors in helping themselves to timber from federal lands.[86] A Scottish immigrant on the Gull Prairie in Michigan in 1833 showed the same ambivalence when he wrote, "Now you know I am not a speculator, but the temptation is so great that I wish you to send me all the money I can spare, as I hope, at least to double it soon."[87]

Nor is this the only paradox in the views of these people. Some of them combined social and political radicalism with economic conservatism. They were kindred spirits to M. K. Ashby's father, a late nineteenth-century agrarian radical, who like "all true revolutionaries . . . looked backward for his main motion."[88] The inducement of high wages was not enough to attract such people into American industry in the first instance. They were rejecting what they knew of industrial civilization in the act of emigration. In its most developed form the myth was encountered among

---

emigration, see Sarah Mytton Maury, *An English Woman in America* (London: Thomas Richardson, 1848), p. cxvii.

[84] William Parker, "The Slave Plantation in American Agriculture," in *Conference Internationale d'Histoire Economique, Stockholm* (Paris, 1960), p. 321.

[85] *Courtauld Family Letters*, 2: 427–29, 435, 465, 467, 485; Marvin Meyers, *The Jacksonian Persuasion: Politics and Belief* (Stanford: Stanford University Press, 1957).

[86] Quaife, *English Settler*, p. 40.

[87] *Counsel for Emigrants*, p. 31.

[88] M. K. Ashby, *Joseph Ashby of Tysoe, 1859–1919* (Cambridge: Cambridge University Press, 1961), p. 255.

urban dwellers in the rapidly developing parts of England and in the industrial sector of the population. Among the people who wrote these letters, the longing for a farm in America was not the product of economic hardship, even in terms of the relatively wealthy English economy. The letters suggest that emigration carried off not only, as is usually said, the most alert and ambitious sector of the population but also many people who were unwilling to make the social and psychological adaptations that pervasive changes in the English economy were demanding. The criticism of commercial and industrial values and the idealization of the peasant and artisan were by no means drained away by emigration. They became persistent themes in English thought.

CHAPTER TWO

British Immigrants in the Old Northwest, 1815–1860

By no means the largest group among the Europeans who migrated to the United States in the nineteenth century, English immigrants nevertheless made a modest impact on the composition of the American population. Apart from the years 1852–62, when the Australia gold rush, depression in the United States, and the outbreak of the Civil War discouraged British emigration thence, the United States remained the principal destination of passengers going overseas from England and Wales from 1850 to 1890, as it had been since the end of the Napoleonic Wars. During the last half of the century the English-born constituted about 10 percent of the foreign-born population recorded in each census and a little less than 1.5 percent of the entire population. The English were not sufficiently concentrated in any single state to influence greatly the size of the state's population or its labor force. Only in the Mormon territory of Utah, where they made up 18.5 percent of the population in 1870, were the English statistically significant. The highest concentration of English-born inhabitants in any other state or territory was recorded in 1850 in Wisconsin, where the English formed 6.2 percent of the population.

This mid-century concentration of English immigrants in Wisconsin is noteworthy. At that time, commercial agriculture was still in its infancy in the state. According to census estimates, the proportion of the male labor force engaged in agricultural occupations actually increased from 52 percent in 1850 to 86 percent in 1860. In mid-century a mere 8 percent of Wisconsin's people lived in towns of more than eight thousand inhabitants, and the density of its population was 5.6 persons per square mile. In England, on the other hand, the census of 1851 reported only about a fifth of the labor force engaged in agricultural work, and half of the people were living in towns and cities of more than eight thousand inhabitants.

In such contrasts lies the peculiar interest of the study of English overseas migration. Although the incidence of emigration was never so high as in certain other European countries, thousands of English emigrants were leaving a country with a developing economy, in which agriculture was highly commercialized and opportunities for industrial work were expanding. The English migration to America provides an outstanding case of economic growth acting as an inducement to emigration—of heightened economic ambitions or social dissatisfaction—rather than extremely low or depressed living standards.[1] In fact, emigration from England was higher in relation to total population during some of the years of confidence and rising real wages after 1846 than it had been during the troubled years of social unrest in the first part of the century.[2]

English emigrants have not proved easy for the historian to study because no authorities collected information at the time about the parts of England from which people were emigrating and because the English as a distinctive group tended to "disappear" in the United States. Nevertheless, scholars have examined some aspects of the subject. The standard works, based on official documents, probably place undue emphasis on assisted emigration, the plans under which mainly colonial governments, landlords, and local governments provided subsidies to persons going to the dominions or colonies.[3] Later, scholars turned their attention to the contributions that skilled British immigrants made to American industrial technology.[4] English agricultural colonies in the

[1] This emphasis on growth as a background to migration is to be found in United Nations, Department of Social Studies, Population Division, *The Determinants and Consequences of Population Trends*, Population Studies, no. 17, 1953, pp. 111–14.

[2] N. H. Carrier and J. R. Jeffery, *External Migration: A Study of the Available Statistics, 1815–1950*, General Register Office, Studies on Medical and Population Subjects, no. 6 (London: HMSO, 1953), p. 14. See also, "Who Were the English and Scots Emigrants to the United States in the Late Nineteenth Century?" in this volume, below.

[3] William A. Carrothers, *Emigration from the British Isles* (London: P. S. King, 1929); Stanley Johnson, *A History of Emigration from the United Kingdom to North America, 1763–1912* (London: George Routledge and Sons, 1913).

[4] Rowland Berthoff, *British Immigrants in Industrial America, 1790–1950* (Cambridge: Harvard University Press, 1953); Frank Thistlethwaite, "The Atlantic Migration of the Pottery Industry," *Economic History Review*, 2d ser. 11 (1958): 264–78. Other such works,

States, which almost invariably failed to achieve their goals, have also received attention.[5] In contrast, the English and Scottish immigrants who entered American agriculture as individuals and in family groups have nearly escaped the historian's notice. Yet, until the panic of 1857, the prospect of engaging in agriculture was probably the strongest single force attracting the English to the United States. Even after that date, a substantial minority continued to seek out the newer agricultural states as places of settlement.

Some indication of the strength of agriculture as an attractive force can be obtained indirectly from an examination of the distribution of English immigrants in the United States. The five states of the Old Northwest, (Ohio, Michigan, Indiana, Illinois, and Wisconsin) all of which were still predominantly rural and agricultural in 1850, the first year for which we have any figures, contained two and two-thirds times as many English immigrants as the New England states. Compared with England, the Old Northwest was still economically underdeveloped in 1850. The English who settled there between 1817 and 1850 found themselves in a region of lower per capita incomes, a poorer standard of housing than in most parts of Britain, more expensive manufactured consumer goods, and inferior public facilities such as roads and water supplies, as well as churches, schools, and banks.

From 1850 onward, it is possible to trace very roughly the destinations of newly arrived immigrants in each decade by looking at net changes in the number of English-born people in each state and territory. The movement of English immigrants into the midwestern states continued unabated during the expansive fifties. Illinois made the greatest net gain in English settlers between 1850 and 1860; and Michigan, Wisconsin, Ohio, and even Iowa were among the ten leading destinations of English immigrants.

The decade of the sixties brought a decided shift in the distribution of

---

published more recently, are noted in the essay entitled "Was the American West a Safety Valve for Lancashire?" in this volume, below.

[5] Wilbur Shepperson, *British Emigration to North America: Projects and Opinions in the Early Victorian Period* (Oxford: Basil Blackwell, 1957); Grant Foreman, "English Settlers in Illinois," *Journal of the Illinois State Historical Society* 34 (1941): 303–33; Foreman, "The Settlement of English Potters in Wisconsin," *Wisconsin Magazine of History* 21 (1938): 374–96; Foreman, "English Emigrants in Iowa," *Iowa Journal of History and Politics* 43 (1946): 385–420; H. Harcourt Horn, *An English Colony in Iowa* (Boston: Christopher Publishing House, 1931); John Inglehart, "The Coming of the English to Indiana in 1817 and Their Hoosier Neighbors," *Indiana Magazine of History* 15 (1919): 90–177; Jacob Van der Zee, *The British in Iowa* (Iowa City: State Historical Society of Iowa, 1922). This is merely a note of some of the earlier works in this field; many more have been published since this essay was first written.

the English. After 1860 the Old Northwest lost ground as a destination. Instead, southern New England, Pennsylvania, New Jersey, and the mining territories of the Rocky Mountain region began to increase their share of the total number of English-born inhabitants of the United States. Even after 1860, however, a subsidiary stream of English immigrants continued to push into new agricultural areas. The plains states also increased their share of the English-born population between 1860 and 1890 (see Table 2.1).

The 1870 census was the first to classify the foreign-born by occupation, combining the English with the small number of Welsh immigrants. As can be seen from Table 2.2, the English and the Welsh who had settled recently in Iowa, Minnesota, and Kansas were strongly represented in agriculture in 1870. They were farmers in about the same proportion as the total employed population of these states. Even in Wisconsin and Michigan, which had received their largest increase in number of English-born in the fifties, the concentration of these immigrants in agriculture was still pronounced as late as 1870. The representation of the English in agriculture was lower in the states that had attracted potential farmers from England before 1850. Many of these farmers, who had settled in New York State and in the river counties of Ohio, Indiana, Illinois, and Missouri, had left farming before 1870. Further evidence that destination and intended occupation were closely linked is the very low concentration in agriculture of the new English and Welsh immigrants in the industrial states of the East in 1870.

Table 2.1. Distribution of English immigrants by region, 1850–1890

Region	1850	1860	1870	1880	1890
Mid-Atlantic	48.2%	39.0%	37.5%	34.3%	34.4%
East north-central	28.5	32.4	29.7	26.7	23.3
New England	11.2	10.6	11.7	12.8	14.7
South and Southwest	7.2	6.6	5.0	5.3	5.1
West north-central	3.3	6.5	8.5	10.8	11.1
Mountain and Pacific	1.6	4.9	7.6	10.1	11.4
Total	100.0%	100.0%	100.0%	100.0%	100.0%
Total English enumerated	278,675	431,692	550,924	662,676	908,741

Sources: Calculated from figures for English-born inhabitants in *Seventh Census of the United States, 1850* (Washington, 1853), pp. xxxvi–xxxvii; *Population of the United States in 1860 . . . from the . . . 8th Census* (Washington, 1864), pp. 620–21; *Ninth Census, 1870*, vol. 1, *The Statistics of the Population of the United States* (Washington, 1872), pp. 340–41; *Statistics of the Population of the United States at the 10th Census, 1880* (Washington, 1883), p. 493; *Compendium of the Eleventh Census: 1890*, pt. 2, *Vital and Social Statistics* (Washington, 1894), pp. 600–601.

Table 2.2. Shifts in destination of English immigrants to the United States, 1850–1870, with proportion of English and Welsh labor force engaged in agriculture

States	No. of English (000's) 1850 (1)	Net increase of English (000's) 1850–1860 (2)	1860–1870 (3)	English and Welsh in agriculture 1870 (4)	Total labor force in agriculture 1870 (5)	Index of representation 4/5 × 100 (6)
STATES OF ENGLISH AGRICULTURAL SETTLEMENT, 1815–1850						
New York	84.8	21.2	4.1	21.2%	25.1%	85
Ohio	25.7	7.0	3.9	26.7	47.2	57
Illinois	18.7	23.1	12.1	39.8	50.7	79
Indiana	5.6	3.8	.6	37.6	58.1	65
Missouri	5.4	4.6	4.3	28.0	52.2	54
AGRICULTURAL STATES AND TERRITORIES WITH LARGE ENGLISH IMMIGRATION, 1850–1860						
Wisconsin	19.0	11.6	- 2.4	62.2%	54.5%	114
Michigan	10.6	15.1	9.3	45.2	46.3	98
Iowa	3.8	7.7	5.1	60.3	61.2	99
Utah	1.1	6.0	9.0	46.8	48.6	97
Minnesota	.1	3.4	2.2	62.1	56.7	110
Kansas	—	1.4	4.8	50.5	59.1	86
INDUSTRIAL STATES WITH LARGE ENGLISH IMMIGRATION, 1860–1870						
Pennsylvania	38.0	8.5	23.1	6.9%	25.5%	27
Massachusetts	16.7	7.2	10.3	3.5	12.6	28
New Jersey	11.4	4.5	10.8	6.7	21.3	32
Connecticut	5.1	3.8	4.1	12.3	22.6	54

Sources: For columns 1–3, see Table 2.1. For columns 4 and 5, see *Ninth Census of the United States, 1870*, vol. 1, *The Statistics of the Population of the United States* (Washington: G.P.O., 1872), pp. 340, 698–99.

Note: Although scholars have adjusted upward estimates of the numbers of people engaged in agriculture in 1870, I have used those reported at the time in the census because similar upward revisions have not been made by country of birth. It seems likely that the numbers of English in agriculture were also underestimated. The figures used may be deemed valid for purposes of comparison. For the revised labor force estimates, see Harvey Perloff et al., *Regions, Resources, and Economic Growth* (Baltimore: Johns Hopkins University Press, 1960), pp. 622, 624.

A study of the private letters of English and Scottish immigrants in the United States to friends and relatives in Britain stimulated my interest in these migrants, so many of whom appeared to be moving counter to the mainstream of overseas migration in the nineteenth century insofar as they were leaving a developed, industrialized country and industrial occupations to enter primary production in new regions. Letters from immigrant farmers have survived in far greater numbers than those from industrial workers.[6] It would, of course, be dangerous to regard the immigrants whose letters have survived as representative of the migration movement as a whole. Moreover, letter writers were probably a select group. One element of selection may have been that farmers in relatively isolated areas felt a particular loneliness that encouraged them to retain contacts with home more than did immigrants who settled in cities. They were also capital-hungry people who did not want to lose contact with any possible source of funds.

The letters enable us to examine in some depth the experience of thirty four English and Scottish families who settled in Ohio, Michigan, Wisconsin, and Illinois between 1820 and 1850.[7] The purpose of this essay is to consider the economic adjustment of these few families, whose stories have been reconstructed from their letters and from local records in Britain and America. In certain respects, the method is inferior to the study of agricultural populations in entire counties, such as Merle Curti and Allan Bogue produced.[8] These writers did not distinguish the English and Scots from other English-speaking foreign-born, except to give examples of outstandingly successful immigrants. The sample of cases used here, infinitely smaller and drawn from the period before English emigration reached its peak, has the one important advantage that it permits us to examine the economic adjustment of a few families in the light of their origins and backgrounds in Britain.

It is often assumed that because they could understand the language of their adopted country, immigrants from England made an easy adjustment. They did not, however, escape all the difficulties faced by other immigrant groups. The vicissitudes of English immigrants in American agriculture frequently arose from a divergence between their motives for emigration and the realities of farming in America. The letters suggest that they were fortified in their economic and social adaptation not so

[6] Note also the high proportion of letters from agriculturists in Alan Conway, ed., *The Welsh in America* (Cardiff: University of Wales Press, 1961).

[7] I have consulted many more such letters in the historical societies of the Middle West since I first wrote this essay. The essay as presented here still relies chiefly on my collecting in the late 1940s for the Collection of Regional History at Cornell University and that carried out for Bernard Crick and Miriam Alman, eds., *Guide to Manuscripts Relating to America in Great Britain and Ireland* (London: Oxford University Press, 1961).

[8] Merle Curti, *The Making of an American Community: A Case Study of Democracy in a Frontier County* (Stanford: Stanford University Press, 1959); Allan Bogue, *From Prairie to Corn Belt: Farming on the Illinois and Iowa Prairies in the Nineteenth Century* (Chicago: University of Chicago Press, 1963).

much by the common language and legal institutions or by occasional familiarity with advanced farming techniques as by attitudes of family loyalty and religious faith. Their new situation required adaptability and responsiveness to a changed and changing environment. Yet many of these people emigrated precisely to avoid change, to escape from the uncertainties they associated with industrialization at home.

Immigrants who came from industrial occupations and cities faced the greatest challenge. Such people often thought of farming as a way of life rather than a commercial undertaking. They hoped to escape from price fluctuations and from taxes, to gain independence from employers, to live a more leisurely life, and to keep their families from dispersing.[9] Some agricultural laborers shared these hopes. In contrast to assisted emigrants from agricultural counties in southern England with high poor rates, the laborers who used only their own savings and credit to emigrate probably came largely from the hinterland of developing industrial areas, where opportunities for alternative employment were expanding and agricultural wages were higher than in the less industrialized parts of the country. In emigrating, they were attempting, like the industrial workers, to recapture an idealized older way of life, to escape from the changes they saw as inevitable in England. The more venturesome and commercially minded of the immigrants whose letters survive came from farming families in outlying regions some distance from the new industrial centers—from parishes in Hereford, Westmorland, and Dorset, for example, which were losing population.

Both farmers and industrial workers who were settling in the Ohio River Valley and along its tributaries between 1817 and 1837 wrote some of these letters. The settlements near the Wabash in Edwards County, Illinois, and in Vanderburgh County, Indiana, made before 1820, are well known. Through the immigrant letters one can follow the story of other families who purchased uncleared woodlands on the ridges beyond the river valleys: in Athens County, Ohio, in 1818; in Columbiana County, farther up the Ohio River, in 1821; in Hamilton, Gallia, Washington, Adams, and Jefferson counties—all Ohio River counties—later in the twenties and during the thirties. One Scottish immigrant in 1820 took the canal and lake route to Cleveland but then turned southeast to join relatives near the great bend in the upper reaches of the Ohio River. The letters also tell us about immigrants who settled near the Illinois River, in Tazewell, Peoria and Pike counties, between 1826 and 1831, and on the

[9] See the essay "Agrarian Myths of English Immigrants," above.

Ohio River in Gallatin County, Illinois, in 1829. The latest examples of such settlers in wooded upcountry near the great river valleys were immigrants of the early forties who began farming in Hancock and Monroe counties in Illinois.

Before the forties, the canal and lake transport system was carrying pioneers into northern Ohio and Michigan. Families of emigrants from the Isle of Man began settling in Cuyahoga County, near the village of Cleveland, as early as 1826. We also have a case of a bachelor immigrant from a farming family in Norfolk who followed his uncle's trail from Palmyra, New York, to Lenawee County, in southern Michigan, as early as 1830.

By the 1840s, Wisconsin had become the source of most of the letters used. Immigrants who arrived in 1841 and 1843 settled in Racine County, near Lake Michigan, and also farther inland in Rock County, as well as in the lead-mining region of Grant County, on the Mississippi River in the western part of the state. By the late forties the letter writers were settling nearer the interior of the state, in Jefferson and Dane counties, and also farther north in Manitowac. We also have letters from Scottish farmers on the prairies of northern Illinois, in Kane County.

Most of the immigrant letters and memoirs were written by people who settled on uncleared, unbroken land and who were engaged in farm making. Even those who had to purchase prior claims, or tracts previously settled, were not "fillers-in" in the sense of taking over farms ready for commercial exploitation. For example, the improvements on the claim that Edwin Bottomley purchased consisted of some lumber prepared for building a cabin. Only two of these collections of letters concern immigrants who bought farms already cleared and cultivated.[10]

The search for cheap land led the English into the Old Northwest in the early decades of its settlement. Morris Birkbeck and George Courtauld, men who had substantial amounts of capital, went west to acquire large estates. Farmers who brought more modest savings with them or who left money in England until they decided where to settle also found that they had to go beyond the mountains to align their savings with the amount of land they hoped to acquire. Even more

[10] In a survey of the biographies of 421 English and Scottish farmers whose careers were described in county histories of Lenawee County, Michigan; Washington County, Ohio; Hancock, Monroe, and Tazewell counties, Illinois; and Lafayette, Dane, Rock, Green, and Jefferson counties in Wisconsin, 105 subjects were specifically described as having cleared wild prairie or timbered land for a farm and only 17 as having bought improved farms. Many bought partially improved farms that still required much clearing, breaking, fencing, and barn and house building.

urgently, industrial workers and farm servants, who hoped to buy a farm for the three hundred or five hundred dollars they had saved, were tempted to regions where government land was still available in large quantities. Before they migrated to one of the states where they hoped to get cheap land, many lived, worked, and saved for several years in the East. New York State was the principal staging point for would-be farmers, though many also stopped in states of the Old Northwest before they finally bought land.[11]

Among the migrants stopping for a time in the East were industrial workers who wanted to become farmers but lacked funds. Using the jobs as stepping-stones to farming, handloom weavers, who had left England rather than change occupation, worked on power looms and even as spinners in the United States. The members of the Morris family from Chorley, Lancashire, are particularly interesting. Sending one brother to an uncle in western Virginia, who helped him buy land in Ohio, the others settled in the Philadelphia region and followed their trades—two as weavers and one as a blacksmith. In 1837 they all decided to take what savings they had accumulated and follow their brother, Thomas, to Ohio, not because they were unable to find employment, but because they saw other workers put on short time and wage rates weakening. They thought savings of three hundred dollars enough to begin farming. Their sojourn in Philadelphia had merely been a stop at a way station on the road to their ultimate goal of acquiring subsistence farms.[12]

Occasionally immigrants advised relatives to emigrate precisely at times when land prices were low because savings would go farther in land purchase.[13] The low price of land attracted some of these potential farmers more than the low price of crops deterred them because they regarded land as a basis for subsistence, not because they hoped to make capital gains from rising land prices.

[11] In the above sample of English and Scottish farmers from county histories, 369 biographies gave details about the early careers of the subjects. Just over a third of them had lived in at least one other state before they came to the state in the Old Northwest in which they finally settled.

[12] Morris Letters, Houghton Muniments, DDHt 12, Lancashire Record Office, Preston, largely published in Charlotte Erickson, *Invisible Immigrants: The Adaptation of English and Scottish Immigrants in Nineteenth-Century America* (1972; rpt., Ithaca: Cornell University Press, 1990), pp. 139–74.

[13] See, for example, a letter from Charles Rose, Scotch Settlement, near Lisbon, Ohio, October 15, 1822, to John Rose, his nephew in Inverness, Rose Letters in private possession; John Birket, Mount Pleasant, Ill., December 25, 1841, to his brother in Lancashire, Birket Letters, DP/265–78, Lancashire Record Office, published in Erickson, *Invisible Immigrants*, p. 90.

Few instances have been found of Englishmen who worked on the transport projects or in the lumber camps of the Great Lakes region to get capital for purchasing land. Some of the immigrants from the Isle of Man who settled in northern Ohio in the late twenties worked on the canal that was to connect Cleveland with the Ohio. A Scots immigrant who arrived late in the season in 1830 was disappointed that canal work had already stopped.[14] One of the tenants on the Courtauld lands, near Athens, Ohio, considered canal employment but rejected it on the grounds of dangers to health and the uncertainty of obtaining cash wages.[15]

Most English immigrants who had neither capital nor industrial skills tried to get work on a farm because a newcomer could learn to farm according to American methods while saving for land purchase.[16] About a sixth of a sample of 421 immigrant farmers whose biographies were analyzed worked as farm laborers before they bought land. One catches glimpses of these immigrant farm laborers in the letters, as well as in census manuscripts. At least two who worked for John Fisher in Michigan during the thirties bought land for farms from their savings. Immigrant farmers who could afford help were eager to hire their own compatriots, but on longer contracts or at lower wages than were customary where they had settled. They tried to persuade relatives to send out their young sons to work for board and lodging or to hire a "hind" for them at one

[14] H. Rose, Scotch Settlement, Ohio, February 2, 1830, to his brother in Inverness, Rose Letters; W. T. Corlett, *The People of Orrisdale and Others* (Cleveland: Lakeside Press, 1918), p. 52. More references to canal work were made by assisted immigrants in New York State around 1820 (Benjamin Smith, ed., *Twenty-four Letters from Labourers in America to Their Friends in England* [London: Edward Rainford, 1829], pp. 18, 24; Conway, *Welsh in America*, pp. 60, 61). In the survey of 421 English and Scots farmers who settled in the Old Northwest, only 33 men (8 percent) bought farms after having begun their careers in America in nonfarm laboring occupations. Of these, only 9 individuals worked on transport projects and 2 in the Wisconsin pineries. In contrast, 81 (20 percent) had begun in skilled industrial occupations, including mining.

[15] *Courtauld Family Letters* (Cambridge: Bowes and Bowes, 1916), 3: 1482. For cases of Scots immigrants working in lumber camps in order to buy farms, see Curti, *Making of an American Community*, p. 21; Archibald McKellar, Taylors Falls, Minn., August 11, 1852, to his father in Iowa, Peter McKellar Papers, 1830–97, Minnesota Historical Society Archives, St. Paul. The sample drawn from county histories indicates that at least the more successful British farmers rarely chose work in lumber camps or in canal or railway construction as a means to achieve farm ownership.

[16] *Courtauld Family Letters*, 5: 2047; John Knight, *Important Extracts from Original and Recent Letters Written by Emigrants in the United States of America* (Manchester: Thomas Williamson, 1818), p. 25; Richard Hails, Lincoln, Mass., July 31, 1849, to his brother in Northumberland, Hails Letters, 865, Collection of Regional History, Cornell University, and also in Erickson, *Invisible Immigrants*, pp. 316–17. The same advice was often given to emigrants to the plains in a later period. See, for example, Percy Ebbutt, *Emigrant Life in Kansas* (London: Swan Sonnenschein, 1886), pp. 231–32.

of the surviving agricultural fairs in England.[17] The inability or unwillingness of other immigrants to pay prevailing wages may also have encouraged newcomers to seek jobs on American-owned farms.[18] If immigrants had worked in an English factory, they were likely to find farm labor both unremunerative and exhausting, whoever the employer might be. This was the reaction of a Huddersfield-born cloth finisher who came to Wisconsin in 1855 hoping to get land through farm labor:

> I think I shall have to come back to Philadelphia and work right steady for about three years and then get a steady Wife and come west again. Any body with three Hundred dollars out here may live independent of any body helping them. Been a Farmer's Man out here is as bad as Been a Slave. They wont hire any one if they can help it for no less than Six Months and more than Eight. Wages for good men 15 to 18 Dollars a month and to pay it to you at fall. I have had the offer of 12 Dollars a month. You must bear in mind they work all the Daylight God sends and a little more sometimes, except Sunday.[19]

Partly because of their attitudes, including their cherished independence, English immigrants sometimes rented land immediately. Employ-

[17] John Birket, Mount Pleasant, Ill., May 19, 1843, to his brother, Birket Letters, in Erickson, *Invisible Immigrants*, p. 97; John Fisher, Franklin, Mich., October 7, 1835, and November 30, 1836, to his brother in Norfolk, Fisher Letters, 2815/104, Ipswich and East Suffolk Record Office, Ipswich, published in Erickson, *Invisible Immigrants*, pp. 121, 123. A version of these letters edited by Louis Tucker appeared in Michigan History 45 (1961): 219–36. Robert Pollock, Cambridge, Wis., April 16, 1858, to his niece in Ayrshire, Pollock Letters, 805, Collection of Regional History, Cornell University; Milo Milton Quaife, ed., *An English Settler in Pioneer Wisconsin: The Letters of Edwin Bottomley,* Publications of the State Historical Society of Wisconsin, Collections 25 (Madison, 1918), p. 59.

[18] Though the numbers are small, these are the results of a count of British immigrant employees in four of the Wisconsin townships in which these letter writers settled.

	Employers		
Employees	Natives	Foreign-born	percent working for natives
English	36	17	68
Scots	5	7	42
Irish	24	21	53
Average	65	45	59

The townships examined in the population schedules of the census of 1850 and 1860 were Porter and Union, Rock County; Lake Mills, Jefferson County; and Christiana, Dane County. Immigrants obviously working for relatives were not counted.

[19] Titus Crawshaw, Porter, Rock County, Wis., April 16, 1855, to his family, Crawshaw Letters, British Library of Economic and Political Science (hereinafter cited as BLPES), in Erickson, *Invisible Immigrants*, p. 338.

ers who could not pay cash were willing to rent out land in exchange for labor.[20] In particular, workers with industrial skills found that they could rent a bit of land in return for work they did for the owner. A brickmaker might undertake to deliver a certain quantity of bricks, or a carpenter to provide rails cut for fencing or a specified amount of work on a house.[21] John Birket went so far as to give a man some land as payment for plastering his house.[22] Sharecropping was another option for immigrants without capital. In return for half the produce of the land, the immigrant might be provided with land, livestock, a team, and farm implements. One finds sharecropping mentioned in connection with English and Welsh immigrants in New York before 1830 and in parts of Ohio, Indiana, Illinois, and Wisconsin throughout the period from 1820 to 1860.[23]

The private letters consulted do not afford examples of immigrants who acquired land from the profits of sharecropping. Through the letters one learns more about the supply aspect of share-tenancy than about the demand aspect. The Courtauld family became absentee landlords after they returned to England in 1825, as they rented their American lands through an immigrant storekeeper. This agent arranged tenants for them on the basis of one-half shares, one-third shares, and sometimes fixed shares, and complained constantly about the tenants' carelessness. One tenant to whom the Courtaulds rented land they had themselves cleared expected to be given the farm after five years' cultivation and decided to give up farming when the Courtaulds refused to deed it to him.[24] Other immigrant landlords were near enough to keep an eye on their tenants themselves. John Birket leased his Peoria land on shares during the mid-1830s because poor health (he was only thirty five) made it difficult for him to continue

[20] Quaife, *English Settler*, p. 110; *Courtauld Family Letters*, 3: 1365; William Morris, Providence, R.I., June 4, 1837, to his brother in Lancashire, Morris Letters, in Erickson, *Invisible Immigrants*, p. 164.

[21] *Courtauld Family Letters*, 3: 1310, and 5: 2331–32.

[22] *Portrait and Biographical Album of Peoria County, Illinois* (Chicago: Biographical Publishing Company, 1890), 3: 278.

[23] See, for example, *Flint's Letters from America, 1818–1820*, in *Early Western Travels, 1748–1846*, ed. Reuben Thwaites (Cleveland, 1904), 9: 39, 293; Conway, *Welsh in America*, pp. 59, 101, 123; Smith, *Twenty-four Letters*, pp. 7, 11, 12, 23, 38; William Chambers and Robert Chambers, *Information for the People* (Edinburgh, 1842), p. 383; Elizabeth Cawley, ed., *The American Diaries of Richard Cobden* (Princeton: Princeton University Press, 1952), p. 187; Paul Wallace Gates, *The Farmers' Age: Agriculture, 1815–1860* (New York: Rinehart, 1960), p. 44. In the survey of 421 farmers' biographies, 26 (6 percent) reported that they had rented land before purchasing farms.

[24] *Courtauld Family Letters*, 3: 1315, and 5: 2042–44, 2336–37.

to cultivate it.[25] A former silk manufacturer in southwestern Ohio, finding farming too onerous, decided to let his land for shares of corn, which he planned to convert into whiskey.[26]

Many immigrants came to the United States with the idea that as landowners they would soon gain an independent income that would free them from work. Most were clearly disappointed in this aim; but a few took a step in this direction by leasing out their land on shares and occasionally for cash rents.[27] The only share-tenants among our immigrant letter writers were men who added to their original land purchase a bit of cleared land, rented on shares, which they could cultivate while they worked at improving their own land.[28]

In fact, nearly all the immigrant letter writers brought capital with them for land purchase, either directly from Britain or from the East. Some of them were also able to obtain funds from Britain to add to their own savings. We have, however, no cases in which immigrants were as regularly provided with funds as were the remittance men who flocked to northwestern Iowa in the early eighties.[29] Nor did these immigrants have access to capital that was being invested in American farming and livestock raising at that time by banks and other financial institutions. The flow of funds in the early period was in the form of loans, gifts, and subsidies, obtained almost exclusively through the immigrants' own families. Earnings from industry, from investment in government bonds, and from rents were sent to midwestern farmers. For example, Edwin Bottomley's father, the manager of a woolen factory in Huddersfield, persistently subsidized his son's Wisconsin farming enterprise in the 1840s, partly with the idea that it might one day provide the father with a comfortable home.[30] For the few years during which they struggled to make farms in the wilderness of southeastern Ohio, the

[25] John Birket, Peoria, Ill., May 7, 1835, to his brother, Birket Letters, in Erickson, *Invisible Immigrants*, p. 88.

[26] Robert Bowles, Harrison, Hamilton County, Ohio, August 10, 1823, to his brothers, John and Richard Bowles, Bowles Letters, Ohio Historical Society, Columbus. I wish to thank the Ohio Historical Society for permission to quote from the Bowles Letters.

[27] Milo Milton Quaife, ed., *A True Picture of Emigration* (Chicago: Lakeside Press, 1936), p. 152; Thomas Corlett, Granville, Ohio, December 7, 1853, to his uncle in the Isle of Man, Corlett Letters, Manx Museum, Douglas, Isle of Man.

[28] Quaife, *English Settler*, p. 48. See also Bogue, *From Prairie to Corn Belt*, pp. 266–67.

[29] Van der Zee, *British in Iowa*, p. 75; Cowan Letters, microfilm, BLPES.

[30] Quaife, *English Settler*, pp. 67, 73, 111, 133, 145, 149, 155, 163, 189. For the same reason, James Steel, a Scottish-born excise officer in London in the 1840s, subsidized the farm operations and land purchases of his son Thomas, a frontier doctor, in Wisconsin (Steel Letters, Wisconsin State Historical Society Library, Madison).

members of the Courtauld family expected and received gifts of money from Samuel Courtauld's income as a silk manufacturer in Essex.[31] Other immigrants tried to borrow from their families at lower rates of interest than they had to pay locally, or they asked for gifts outright to meet a particular need.[32] Legacies were claimed vigorously.[33]

The ability of some immigrants to obtain money from England was not an unmixed blessing. They used such aid from their families for living expenses as often as for investment. A few neglected to make their farm enterprises self-sufficient at the earliest possible date, and others purchased more land than they could manage profitably. One of the more successful immigrant farmers confessed that he was able to make money borrowed at 30 percent in Michigan in the early thirties "answer my purpose."[34] Low-interest loans from England might act as a disincentive to profitable farm management, whereas high-interest loans obtained in the West could stimulate effective management.

A few immigrants tried to extend the base for the flow of capital beyond their immediate families. One means of doing this was to stress the returns to be made from industrial development in a region. John Birket tried to raise capital for a sawmill, the Courtaulds for a silk factory, but little came of these attempts.[35] Appeals to England for charitable aid for schools and churches met with more response. Kenyon College, in Gambier, Ohio, may be the only survivor among these schools started with money raised in England. Jubilee College, in Peoria, is today only a historical monument. Edwin Bottomley did manage to get some money for a chapel, and John Birket received some for a school; but they did not earmark the money for special purposes.[36]

[31] *Courtauld Family Letters*, 2: 850, and 3: 1049.

[32] John Fisher, Tecumseh, Mich., July 12, 1831, to his mother, in Erickson, *Invisible Immigrants*, p. 116; Robert Smith, Franklin, Mich., July 12, 1851, to Francis Fisher, Fisher Letters; Reuben Carpenter, Jefferson County, Ohio, February 16, 1842, to his father in Gloucestershire, BLPES; *Courtauld Family Letters*, 3: 1369, and 4: 1899.

[33] Robert Smith, Franklin, Mich., July 12, 1851, October 18, 1858, October 22, 1860, Fisher Letters; Alfred Jones, Mo., July 30, and September 7, 1864, January 17, 1880, to a Shropshire solicitor, BLPES; Edward Phillips, Greenville, Ill., December 10, 1842, Vandalia, Ill., May 7, 1845, to his father, Phillips Letters, Shropshire Record Office, Shrewsbury, in Erickson, *Invisible Immigrants*, p. 273.

[34] John Fisher, Franklin, Mich., July 18, 1833, to his mother, Fisher Letters, in Erickson, *Invisible Immigrants*, p. 119.

[35] John Birket, Mount Pleasant, Ill., December 25, 1841, to his brother, Birket Letters, in Erickson, *Invisible Immigrants*, p. 90; Quaife, *English Settler*, pp. 58, 62; *Courtauld Family Letters*, 1: 639.

[36] Francis Weisenburger, *The Passing of the Frontier, 1825–1850*, vol. 3 of *History of the State of Ohio*, ed. Carl Wittke (Columbus: Ohio State Archeological and Historical Society,

Most of these immigrants could not hope to get financial assistance from Britain. They were able instead to borrow locally, even in remote areas, the local immigrant network being wider than that of the family. When the Burlends were in great difficulty, they appealed to a neighbor from Yorkshire. At first he refused to lend to them but changed his mind because he could not sleep after his refusal.[37] Fourteen years after he arrived in America, Andrew Morris finally repaid a loan from another immigrant from his neighborhood in Lancashire, who had settled eighty miles away from him.[38] Some immigrants with capital chose to put money out at interest at the high western rates rather than reinvest all their earnings in farm improvement or land.[39] One Scottish immigrant named William Richardson, who by 1860 had been in Wisconsin for nineteen years, owned four hundred acres of land, with only thirty improved and only ten dollars' worth of farm implements. Though at that time he called himself a farmer, in a later census he simply referred to himself as a money lender.[40]

The English and Scots emigrants in this capital-hungry region did not send money home. Before he had to purchase his preemption claim, John Birket did, however, offer to pay the rent on his father's Lancashire farm in a roundabout way. He proposed to give the amount of the rent to another emigrant from Lancashire, whose relatives would pay Birket's father.[41] An immigrant farmer in Wisconsin offered the proceeds of the sale of his house in Scotland to his brother who had not emigrated.[42] These were exceptional cases, and in neither one did any

---

1941), pp. 175–76; Thomas Ford, *A History of Illinois from Its Commencement as a State in 1818 to 1847* (Chicago: S. C. Griggs, 1854), pp. 228–29; Quaife, *English Settler,* pp. 108, 111, 125, 230; John Birket, Peoria, Ill., December 7, 1834, and Mount Pleasant, Ill., December 15, 1841, November 28 and December 14, 1842, to his brother, Birket Letters, in Erickson, *Invisible Immigrants,* pp. 87, 91, 92–94.

[37] Quaife, *Picture of Emigration,* pp. 118–19. See also *Courtauld Family Letters,* 3: 1245–46.

[38] Andrew Morris, Aurelius, Ohio, February 21, 1846, to his brother, Morris Letters, in Erickson, *Invisible Immigrants,* p. 174.

[39] John Birket, Mount Pleasant, Ill., December 25, 1841, to his brother, Birket Letters, in Erickson, *Invisible Immigrants,* p. 90; Robert Pollock, Cambridge, Wis., April 16, 1858, to his niece, Pollock Letters, BLPES; Quaife, *Picture of Emigration,* p. 148.

[40] United States Census Manuscripts, Population Schedules, Cambridge, Dane County, Wis., 1860, p. 14, and 1880, p. 274, and Agriculture Schedules, Cambridge, Dane County, 1860, p. 171a.

[41] John Birket, Peoria, Ill., December 7, 1834, and May 7, 1835, to his father, Birket Letters, in Erickson, *Invisible Immigrants,* p. 86.

[42] John and Mary Thompson, Wingville, Grant County, Wis., January 24, 1850, to his brother in Fifeshire, Wisconsin State Historical Society Library, Madison.

cash actually flow out of the region in which the immigrants were living. Although they were often willing to receive relatives on their farms and to give them work and food while they established themselves, the farmers did not offer to pay passages or send cash to England.

Their farm enterprises required that profits be plowed back continuously. Even those immigrants who bought so-called improved farms found that clearing and breaking the soil formed a significant part of farm work in this region before the Civil War. If there was not enough capital to contract it out (the Burlends once had a field broken in return for a watch), clearing was a skill that the immigrant had to learn. It was a formidable task for the inexperienced. Indeed, one Welsh immigrant in Utica, New York, commented in 1818, "The land is a desolate wilderness of uncleared timber so that it is not worth the Welsh buying it."[43] Yet probably thousands of English and Scots immigrants tried clearing land. In the early 1820s, the Courtauld family, in the neighborhood of Athens, Ohio, worked, became discouraged, set to work again, but finally gave up a desperate attempt to get a farm going. The clearing of ten acres a year was never more than an elusive goal to immigrants in wooded regions.[44] Few approached the five acres a year later suggested as a more realistic norm for a family in timbered country before 1850.[45] It took Andrew Morris, a weaver from Lancashire, three years to clear thirteen acres. An English immigrant in Stark County, Ohio, boasted that he had cleared twenty acres of woodland in five years. The Burlends managed to clear between three and four acres their first year in Pike County but found that this acreage was not a measure of the land they could add to production because it still had to be fenced and plowed. One former handloom weaver in Iowa broke, cleared, and fenced a mere forty acres between 1845 and 1858.[46]

[43] Conway, *Welsh in America*, p. 61.

[44] Ten acres a year was the average used for calculations of farm output by Wayne Rasmussen and Marvin Towne "Farm Gross Product and Farm Investment in the Nineteenth Century," in National Bureau of Economic Research, *Trends in the American Economy in the Nineteenth Century*, vol. 24 in *Studies in Income and Wealth* (Princeton: Princeton University Press, 1960), p. 270. For statements of this as a goal, see Quaife, *English Settler*, p. 66; *Extracts from Various Writers on Emigration* (Norwich, 1834), p. 12, photostat, BLPES.

[45] Martin Primack, "Land Clearing under Nineteenth-Century Techniques," *Journal of Economic History* 22 (1962): 484.

[46] Petition of Richard Stephenson, Fairfield, Iowa, March 28, 1858, Stephenson Papers, in private possession; Knight, *Important Extracts*, p. 21; Quaife, *Picture of Emigration*, p. 86; William Morris, Aurelius, Ohio, December 30, 1838, and Barnsville, Ohio, July 14, 1841, to his brother, Morris Letters, in Erickson, *Invisible Immigrants*, pp. 166, 167.

Immigrants who had enough capital to hire labor for clearing were often disappointed to find the supply inelastic.[47] Some English settlers in the river counties of Ohio and Illinois in the late twenties and early thirties complained of the indolence of the native-born. As James Knight put it, "Few work from principle . . . , not enough from necessity."[48] Immigrant farmers also found the plows they had bought or brought with them unsuitable for breaking new land, though travelers continued to laud the Scottish plows.[49] Another impediment to rapid clearing for some farmers from England was the high standard of clearing they visualized. "George and I have grubbed up stubbs out of number," wrote Robert Bowles, "and I intend to continue clearing for I hate to see them, and I wish my farm to look like an English one."[50]

Hopes of reducing farm-making costs and heavy-labor requirements induced many English immigrants who could not pay the price of an improved farm to purchase prairie land and oak openings. George Flower maintained that he and Birkbeck had bought prairie land for these reasons, so that every individual who came to their colony would be saved "a generation of hard and unprofitable labour."[51] Two years after he arrived in Michigan, John Fisher wrote home, "I bought one farm 80 acres and went to work on it but finding it had too much timber on it and I could not chop very well I bought 80 acres more clear openings similar to a pasture."[52] Many instances have been found of immigrants who added some grassland to their original land purchase or who bought prairie land in the first instance and used it not for their livestock as did the Americans, but as arable land for farming.[53] The

[47] William Faux, *Memorable Days in America: Being a Journal of a Tour to the United States* (London: Simkins and Marshall, 1823), p. 232; Morris Birkbeck, *Letters from Illinois* (Philadelphia: M. Carey and Son, 1818), pp. 83–87.

[48] *Courtauld Family Letters,* 2: 910, and 5: 2227, 2332; Quaife, *Picture of Emigration,* p. 131.

[49] Quaife, *English Settler,* p. 96; Robert Shedden, Kane County, Ill., 1842, to Andrew Foulds, photostat, BLPES; William Oliver, *Eight Months in Illinois* (Newcastle-on-Tyne: William Andrew Mitchell, 1843), pp. 97–98.

[50] Harrison, Hamilton County, Ohio, April 20, 1823, Bowles Letters. See also Smith, *Twenty-four Letters,* pp. 17–18; Gladys Thomson, *A Pioneer Family: The Birkbecks in Illinois, 1818–1827* (London: Jonathan Cape, 1953), p. 70.

[51] George Flower, *History of the English Settlement in Edwards County, Illinois* (Chicago: Chicago Historical Society Collections, 1882), p. 352.

[52] John Fisher, Franklin, Mich., June 11, 1836, to his brothers, Fisher Letters, in Erickson, *Invisible Immigrants,* p. 118.

[53] Robert Meatyard, Alton, Ill., March 22, 1846, to his mother, Meatyard Letters, Dorset Record Office, Dorchester; Robert Shedden, Kane County, Ill., 1842, to Andrew Foulds, BLPES; Knight, *Important Extracts,* p. 27; Foreman, "English Settlers in Illinois," p. 311; Quaife, *English Settler,* p. 34.

Birkets wrote to their family in Lancashire to ask them to find out what prairie soil was; but most of the immigrants seem to have trusted in its fertility in the early days of their settlement.[54]

On prairie land an English farmer who had the necessary livestock, equipment, and labor could come closer to clearing ten acres a year. An inexperienced man like Eliza Courtauld's husband, a cabinetmaker by trade who had little equipment and unreliable labor, found that two acres were all that he could clear and break in a year, even on a patch of prairie near Gallipolis, in southern Ohio.[55] Edwin Bottomley, formerly a pattern designer in a woolen mill, also discovered that he could not reach his goal of ten acres a year on his prairie land, because his plow was useless and he simply could not provide the fencing for the land he did manage to break. By the time of his death, nine years after his arrival in Wisconsin, he had succeeded in clearing and improving only thirty five acres.[56] In contrast, a Norfolk-born farmer's son, John Fisher, cleared twenty acres of prairie land in a single year with the aid of ten bullocks and at least two hired hands. Five years after he arrived in Michigan, he had cleared and improved 75 acres,[57] far and away the best achievement of any of these immigrants on prairie land.

Thus the immigrant letters support the view expressed by Paul Gates many years ago that English immigrants helped dispel the American prejudice against prairie soils.[58] Before 1840, while prairie cultivation was still in its infancy, British immigrants were already acquiring prairie land as a means of saving labor.

Apart from this readiness to believe in the fertility of grassland soils, one seeks in vain in the immigrant letters for differences in innovations

[54] John Birket, Peoria, Ill., May 6, 1833, to his brother, Birket Letters, in Erickson, *Invisible Immigrants* , p. 86. The Burlends seem to have assimilated the American suspicion of the prairies after fifteen years in the States (Quaife, *Picture of Emigration,* p. 84).

[55] *Courtauld Family Letters,* 3: 910.

[56] Quaife, *English Settler,* p. 81.

[57] John Fisher, Franklin, Mich., October 7, 1835, and September 5, 1837, to his mother, Fisher Letters, in Erickson, *Invisible Immigrants,* pp. 121, 124.

[58] Paul Wallace Gates, *The Illinois Central Railroad and Its Colonization Work* (Cambridge: Harvard University Press, 1934), pp. 12–13n, 36. Other writers later challenged his conclusion. Douglas McManis held that the reputation of prairies among the native-born was not so uniformly bad as Gates thought and that New England immigrants were also settling on prairies at the edge of woodland in parts of Illinois before 1840 ("The Initial Evaluation and Utilization of the Illinois Prairies, 1815–1840," University of Chicago Department of Geography, Research Paper, no. 94, 1964, pp. 32–34, 50, 56, 83–85, 92–93). In discussing the selection of land in Wisconsin, Eric Lampard maintained that the choice of timbered or prairie land was simply a matter of time of arrival and circumstance and followed no "ethnic principles" (*The Rise of the Dairy Industry in Wisconsin* [Madison: State Historical Society of Wisconsin, 1963], pp. 17–20, 365n).

in farming techniques. Allan Bogue was right in suggesting that the contribution of immigrant groups to the development of agricultural methods in the incipient corn belt was marginal. What else could one expect?[59] The English came from a country whose reputation for advanced agriculture was largely due to methods that were labor-intensive and thus quite unsuitable for American conditions. Even immigrants from the English pastoral regions were accustomed to a higher ratio of labor to land than was profitable in the Old Northwest in this period.

Immigrants, especially nonfarmers, tended to criticize American farming methods for the lack of manuring, the poor standard of livestock care, the untidy and wasteful harvesting, the strange farm implements in use, and the absence of turnip cultivation.[60] Those who actually took up farming began to change their ideas about good farming, as English farmers on the East Coast had already done by 1820.[61] We find immigrants telling their compatriots that in America manure was likely to injure the soil, cattle were "inured" to fending for themselves, crop rotation was unnecessary on American soils, and they had not yet had time to turn their attention to turnip cultivation.[62] After five years in Michigan, John Fisher was ready to confess that he could not farm in the English fashion. His brother-in-law, formerly a shoemaker, who had less success as a commercial farmer in Michigan, wrote after twenty five years in America that he was still trying to get into the English way of farming but that it did not seem to work.[63] Some immigrants became suspicious of newcomers with experimental ideas. When he had been in Athens County, Ohio, for thirteen years, James Knight hesitated to lease land to an English market gardener because the man "had too many new views—too many notions—which I knew he must have time to wear of."[64]

A few of the British immigrants were inclined to speculate in land and hoped to gain more from rising land values and high interest rates than from farming operations. Among them was John Birket. Son of a small

[59] Bogue, *From Prairie to Cornbelt*, p. 211.

[60] Jonas Booth, New Hartford, N.Y., March 20, 1829, to his brother and sister, typed copy, BLPES; H. Rose, near Lisbon, Ohio, February 2, 1830, to his brother, Rose Letters; Henry Petingale, Newburgh, N.Y., August 6, 1849, to his sister in Norfolk, Petingale Letters, BLPES, in Erickson, *Invisible Immigrants*, pp. 446–47.

[61] Rodney Loehr, "The Influence of English Agriculture on American Agriculture, 1775–1825," *Agricultural History* 2 (1937): 3–15.

[62] Quaife, *Picture of Emigration*, pp. 63, 106, 112; Corlett, *People of Orrisdale*, p. 54.

[63] John Fisher, Franklin, Mich., October 7, 1835, to his mother, in Erickson, *Invisible Immigrants*, p. 121, and Robert Smith, Franklin, Mich., October 22, 1860, to his brother-in-law, both in Fisher Letters.

[64] *Courtauld Family Letters*, 4: 1648–49, and 5: 2193.

tenant farmer of about a hundred acres in Westmorland, Birket emigrated to Vermont in 1819 to join two uncles who had already settled there. In 1824 he set out alone for the West, paying his way by peddling tea, coffee, and calicoes. After a short stay in Ohio, he arrived in Peoria, Illinois, then a village of six log cabins, in January 1826. There he claimed land ten years before it was possible to buy it under preemption privileges. During his early years in Peoria, he engaged variously in farming, orchard planting, carpentering, money lending, and digging coal from surface outcroppings on his land. John Birket was always more interested in diversified development than in farming. But as Peoria's growth slackened in the late thirties, he moved out to Tazewell County, where his two brothers and his uncles had settled in 1831. His interest in industrial development and land prices continued unabated. Not until the 1850s did his town property in Peoria (once the location of his farm) begin to sell profitably. Thus it took twenty five years before his land investments began to pay. Birket did not simply sell his town lands. He himself built residential additions to Peoria and sold land at more favorable prices to buyers who would undertake to build factories within a given period of time.[65]

Most of the immigrants intended from the outset to farm, either for a subsistence livelihood or as commercial farmers. Though they did not arrive quite so long in advance of settlement and the sale of government lands as did John Birket, they were likely to appear in thinly populated regions where much government land was still unsold. There can be little doubt that those who came with some experience in farming, either as farmers or laborers, were more likely to succeed in wresting farms from the wilderness. Experienced farmers did buy improved farms if they had the capital.[66] When their means permitted them to buy only unimproved or slightly improved land, those with experience in farming were more inclined to keep some of their capital for purchasing livestock.[67] For

[65] A letter from John Birket and his son John C. Birket, July 31, 1856, to the former's brother describes terms of the sale, Birket Letters. Information on John Birket has also been obtained from United States Census Manuscripts 1850, Peoria County Ill., p. 215; from Aaron Wilson Oakford, *The Peoria Story* (Peoria, 1949–57), 1: 35–36; and from *Album of Peoria County,* 3: 278. For similar, though less successful, speculators, see Joseph Hirst, Equality, Gallatin County, Ill., August 29, 1829, to his son, BLPES; James Knight letters, in *Courtauld Family Letters,* 3–4: passim. Merle Curti found a few British immigrants of this type in Trempeleau County (*Making of an American Community,* p. 418).

[66] Hugh Needham, William Corlett, and John Birchal (Morris Letters) fall into this category.

[67] John Fisher, Tecumseh, Mich., July 12, 1831, to his mother, Fisher Letters, Erickson, *Invisible Immigrants,* p. 114; Edward Gilley, Union, Rock County, Wis., September 28, 1845, to his sister in Northumberland, BLPES.

example, John Griffiths, who came from a laboring family in Shropshire to Hancock County, Illinois, in 1840, had by 1860 added 80 acres to his original purchase of eighty acres. In that year he reported that all his land had been improved. He was growing very little wheat but estimated his livestock, including cattle and pigs, to be worth eleven hundred dollars. Not many miles away to the south, in Monroe County, lived Thomas Whittaker and his family. They had been petty provision dealers in Leeds before they arrived in Illinois at about the same time as Griffiths. Thomas Whittaker had acquired 280 acres of land by 1860 but had succeeded in improving only seventy acres of it. He had six hundred dollars' worth of livestock, as many horses as swine, and was still devoting much more of his land to wheat than to corn and other animal foods.[68]

John Fisher, the Norfolk farmer's son, was also more inclined to continue to grow wheat than was a man reared in the more pastoral farming of Western England. Yet Fisher was careful to treat his land with manure, though he did not practice rotation. In contrast, in southeastern Ohio, the Morris brothers and their brothers-in-law, most of whom had been weavers in Lancashire, noted that they did not use manure from their scant livestock. Instead of treating the soil when their yields declined, the Morrises imitated some of their neighbors by turning to another soil-exhausting crop—tobacco.[69] Robert Pollock, an immigrant from the town of Ayr in Scotland, who was farm making in Dane County, Wisconsin, in the 1850s, remarked that the chinch bugs had been reducing his wheat yields since 1856. Yet four years later he was still planting wheat as his main grain crop.[70]

These few case histories suggest that the most successful farmers among the British immigrants not only had experience in farming but were also empirically minded, not wedded to a particular scheme of farming. When these qualities were reinforced by a location near a growing town or by fortunate timing of emigration, success was

[68] Based on the Griffiths and Whittaker Letters, in Erickson, *Invisible Immigrants* pp. 195–202, 179–88, and on United States Census Manuscripts, Agriculture Schedules, 1860, Monroe County, Ill., p. 65, and Appanoose Township, Hancock County, Ill., p. 70.

[69] Andrew Morris, Aurelius, Ohio, February 5, 1844, and February 21, 1846, to his brother, Morris Letters, in Erickson, *Invisible Immigrants,* pp. 172, 173; Paul Henlein, *Cattle Kingdom in the Ohio Valley* (Lexington: University of Kentucky Press, 1959), p. 73; Weisenburger, *Passing of the Frontier*, p. 65.

[70] Robert Pollock, Cambridge, Wis., April 16, 1858, to his brother, Collection of Regional History, Cornell University; United States Census Manuscripts, Population Schedules, 1860, Cambridge, Dane County, Wis., p. 7 and Agriculture Schedules, 1860, Cambridge, Dane County, p. 171a.

probable and the family likely to be firmly established on the land. Some of the children of John Griffiths, Walter and William Birket, and William Corlett remained on farms close to their fathers' land.

Those who did not succeed in commercial farming or who found their image of a subsistence idyll dissolving after they had struggled for a time with farm making are equally interesting. Industrial workers and other urban people often purchased land in the southern counties of Illinois, Indiana, and Ohio—rolling country affected by water erosion. Within twenty years of settlement, most of them found themselves in counties or townships that were losing population. Even immigrants who had for a time profited from a market of new settlers as population swelled in their neighborhood now found many of their neighbors leaving for new areas. This experience, as Bogue has pointed out, was a common one because most counties attracted more farmers during their early burst of settlement than could possibly continue to make a living there in farming. Thus at some point immigrants who had settled in the uplands adjoining river valleys, in particular, found local markets weakening and their lands declining in fertility.[71]

What did the English immigrant do on meeting such reverses? Curti and Bogue found that the English-speaking foreign-born were slightly more persistent in Trempeleau County, Wisconsin, and Bureau County, Illinois, between 1850 and 1860 than were the native-born and considerably more so than immigrants from the Continent.[72] The statistical

[71] Bogue, *From Prairie to Corn Belt,* p. 20.

[72] In a sample of seven townships to which these letter writers came (Union and Porter, Rock County, Lake Mills, Jefferson County, and Christiana, Dane County, Wis.; Aurelius,

	Trempeleau County 1860 base		Seven townships (males only) 1850 and 1860 base		
	All	ESF	English	Scottish	Irish
Farm operators leaving in less than 10 years	68%	66%	49%	29%	34%
All gainfully employed leaving in less than 10 years	73%	75%	74%	57%	75%
Numbers	662	160	174	84	233

ESF = English-speaking foreign-born. Curti, *Making of an American Community,* pp. 69–71; Bogue, *From Prairie to Corn Belt,* pp. 25–26; National Archives, microfilm, *Seventh Census of the United States, 1850,* no. M432, Wisconsin, rolls 95, 1000, 1005; Ohio, Roll 738; Illinois, rolls 109, 129; *Eighth Census of the United States, 1860,* no. M653. Wisconsin, rolls 1403–4, 1413, 1430, 1431; Ohio, rolls 1048–49; Illinois, rolls 184, 232.

differences were so slight, however, as to be insignificant. Yet an attitude of persistence was expressed in most of the letters. Restless John Birket wrote of his brother, "I thought for us all to sell here and buy again near Bishop Chase, but Walter thinks it so much trouble to begin again that he will die where he now lives."[73] The common feeling against mobility was also expressed by a farmer from Kent: "[Mr. Pound] is quite a Yankee in respect to moving. I hope, my dear friend, if you come here you will not catch the disease."[74] He wrote with particular feeling because his own son had "caught" it.

Mobility continued until the immigrant actually bought land.[75] Only one instance arises in these letters of a British family who, having once bought land, sold out to move farther west. Edward Gilley, who had been a farm servant in Northumberland, emigrated with his brother George in 1843 to Rock County, Wisconsin. Edward had a hundred sovereigns, his brother less. They both married and began farm making. Edward married an English-born woman who died childless, whereas George soon acquired a large family by his Michigan-born wife. When Edward remarried in 1853, George sold his eighty-acre farm to him in order to move to Minnesota. After twenty five years on a farm there, George Gilley eventually returned with his four youngest children to spend his last years on his brother's flourishing farm in Wisconsin.[76]

These British immigrants seem to have hesitated to repeat the process of farm making because many of them looked on farming, rather than on rising land values, as their source of improved living standards. If they could not achieve their social and economic aims on one farm, they

---

Washington County, Ohio; Appanoose, Hancock County, and Washington, Tazewell County, Ill.), the rate of departure from the township of English, Scottish, and even Irish-born farm operators was significantly lower than Curti found in Trempeleau County and Bogue in Bureau County.

[73] John Birket, Mount Pleasant, Ill., December 25, 1841, to his brother, Birket Letters, in Erickson, *Invisible Immigrants*, p. 91.

[74] Hugh Needham, Monroe Township, Adams County, Ohio, February 15, 1834, to a friend in Staplehurst, Kent, BLPES.

[75] *Courtauld Family Letters*, 5: 2042, 2230–31; Smith, *Twenty-four Letters*, p. 27; Conway, *Welsh in America*, p. 98; Quaife, *English Settler*, p. 169; John Fisher, Franklin, Mich., November 30, 1836, to his mother, Fisher Letters, in Erickson, *Invisible Immigrants*, p. 123; Clarence Paine, ed., "Edward Hawkes: The Diaries of a Nebraska Farmer, 1876–1877," *Agricultural History* 22 (1948): 1–3.

[76] Edward Gilley, Union, Wis., September 28, 1845, to his sister, BLPES; *Portrait and Biographical Album of Rock County, Wisconsin* (Chicago: Acme Publishing, 1889), p. 1900.

were unlikely to realize them on another. Living in the hinterland of Cincinnati in the early 1820s, Robert Bowles considered looking for some prairie land in Indiana; but his wife, who had suffered through the process of farm making and had just found some suitable English friends, firmly vetoed the project.[77] Similarly, the Morris brothers in Washington County, Ohio, watched their neighbors sell out in the early forties but decided not to follow the trek to the Illinois prairies.[78] After 1860 the English and Scots on the plains were probably recruited, not so much from immigrants who had failed as farmers in the Great Lakes states, as from new arrivals who had not yet bought land and from immigrants' British-born children who were unable to buy land in the neighborhood of their fathers' farms.[79]

Once having bought land, the English and Scots immigrants tried first to adjust to the difficulties of farm making or low incomes where they were. Rural areas in the Old Northwest acquired many artisans in these Britons who had been attracted originally by the prospect of farming. Thus Robert Smith, in Lenawee County, Michigan, found that he could earn thirty shillings a week at his craft of shoemaking in 1836 and hire a man to run his farm.[80] A blacksmith from Lancashire discovered that he could do better at his trade than by tilling his soil in Washington County, Ohio.[81] A Cornish carpenter in Racine County, Wisconsin, at first leased his prairie land for three years in return for breaking and fencing; but by the end of that time he was doing so well as a carpenter and undertaker in the village of Yorkville that he continued to hire someone to run his farm.[82]

Others diversified their activities to supplement their incomes from farming. Thomas Morris erected a horse-drawn flour mill when after six years of effort he still had only about eight acres of his timbered land

[77] Robert Bowles, Harrison, Hamilton County, Ohio, August 10, 1823, to his brothers, Bowles Letters.

[78] Andrew Morris, Aurelius, Ohio, February 5, 1844, to his brother, Morris Letters, in Erickson, *Invisible Immigrants,* p. 172.

[79] This can be no more than conjecture at this point. A larger sampling of immigrant biographies now in progress (1993) provides many more instances of British immigrants who sold a farm to buy another, often in the same neighborhood, however.

[80] John Fisher, Franklin, Mich., November 30, 1836, to his mother, Fisher Letters, in Erickson, *Invisble Immigrants*, p. 122.

[81] William Morris, Aurelius, Ohio, December 30, 1838, to his brother, Morris Letters, in Erickson *Invisible Immigrants*, p. 166

[82] "Autobiography of Hannibal Lugg, as told to Frances Green," c. 1909, typescript, pp. 7–8, Wisconsin State Historical Society Library, Madison.

under cultivation.[83] Some immigrants used skills acquired before they emigrated in the struggle to keep their original farms. None of these individuals had distinctive skills born of the industrial revolution. Their skills—in the making of clothes, the building trades, weaving, blacksmithing, and flour milling—were preindustrial ones that could still be found in most country villages in England. During the early industrial revolution, England had drawn on this diversity of skills in its rural population to make engineers of carpenters and other craftsmen. The society of the Old Northwest, in its early development, gained a great variety of knowledge of industrial crafts from British immigrants, as well as from Germans and New Englanders.

The immigrants in the Old Northwest before 1850 did not apply these skills there at anything like the level of specialization common in their homeland. Robert Bowles, who had been a farmer in England, found that he had other rudimentary skills he could employ in a new territory. "I now find," he wrote, "my mechanical knowledge of great use to me, and it often enables me to earn many dollars in an easy way. . . . I am now a tolerable proficient in the smith way. . . . I have likewise made several vessels in the cooper's line."[84] A Lancashire weaver, who had saved from his earnings in Fall River, Massachusetts, to buy land, found that he could do better by using his elementary knowledge of coopering in Manitowac, Wisconsin, as a by-occupation to farming.[85]

To English immigrants, including those from rural communities, the lack of specialization among crafts workers in the United States stood out as a remarkable fact relevant to their adaptation. Thus many immigrants who were not artisans in the British sense of the word saw opportunities to practice rudimentary skills in developing regions of the West. One immigrant advised a young relative to pick up a little information on the tanning business before emigrating; others counseled women to "get a sketch of the tailoring trade" if they did not already have it. A tailor from North Shields told his brother to keep his eyes open around the potteries. John Rochester asked George Courtauld to send some surveyor's instruments and a book on surveying. A

[83] William Morris, Aurelius, Ohio, December 30, 1838, Morris Letters, in Erickson, *Invisible Immigrants,* p. 166; Quaife, *English Settler*, pp. 58, 63, 69; R. H. Kinvig, "Manx Settlement in the U.S.A.," *Isle of Man Natural History and Antiquarian Society Proceedings* 5 (1955): 7; William Savage Diary, Iowa State Historical Society Library, Des Moines.

[84] Robert Bowles, Harrison, Hamilton County, Ohio, April 20, 1823, to his brothers, Bowles Letters.

[85] Mabel Kalmach Spencer, "Sketch of John Spencer," typescript, n.d., Wisconsin State Historical Society Library, Madison.

family asked for a "recipe for making fire bricks."[86] In the early days of settlement, skills could be bartered; later they could make a contribution toward keeping a farm enterprise afloat.[87] Probably more English and Scots immigrants adapted to reverses by diversifying their occupations than by moving to new farming regions.

The impetus toward diversification of the midwestern economy came also from immigrants who gave up their farms altogether. The only unmarried member of the Morris family finally sold his unimproved land in eastern Ohio to seek full-time work as a weaver. Like many others, he drifted into western towns.[88] After a few years of experience of American farming, many immigrants warned relatives in industrial occupations in England against contemplating farming as a way of life. "If you come to this country," wrote William Morris to his brother, a carpenter turned mechanic in a cotton mill, "I think you would not like to go to the back countrey and go to clearing land and farming but you might do well in or near some of the Eastern Cittyes working at your trade. Or you could start a macheene shop of your own in some of the western towns."[89] By 1870 the English and Welsh inhabitants of the midwestern states were concentrated largely in mechanical occupations.

Immigrants who did not have a trade were not quite so easily absorbed into the economy. Schoolteaching, as Morris Birkbeck noted with reference to his son, was "only too often the refuge of the indigent and the failures." The sons and daughters of George Courtauld found it a poorly paid alternative to farming.[90] Even storekeeping and innkeeping were hazardous in the constantly changing environment of weakening local monopolies and a sudden melting away of population.[91] An immigrant farmer with a good education but no

[86] John Muir, Lisbon, Ohio, October 3, 1842, to David Moore, BLPES; Quaife, "English Settler," p. 87; Foreman, "English Settlers in Illinois," pp. 311, 318; *Courtauld Family Letters*, 2: 844; Samuel Mearbeck, Beverley, Randolph County, Va., February 6, 1820, to his sister in Sheffield, typed copy, Mearbeck Letters, Central Reference Library, Sheffield.

[87] Bogue, *From Prairie to Corn Belt*, p. 266.

[88] John Hale, ed., *Settlers: Being Extracts from the Journals and Letters of Early Colonists in Canada, Australia, South Africa, and New Zealand* (London: Faber and Faber, 1950), pp. 97–98; Foreman, "English Settlers in Illinois," p. 308; Foreman, "English Emigrants in Iowa," p. 413n; Inglehart, "Coming of the English to Indiana," p. 176; Horn, *English Colony in Iowa*, p. 31; Quaife, *English Settler*, p. 163; *Courtauld Family Letters*, 2: 914, and 3: 931–34, 1020–22; Flower, *English Settlement*, p. 135.

[89] William Morris, Barnsville, Ohio, July 14, 1841, Morris Letters, in Erickson, *Invisible Immigrants*, p. 168.

[90] Thomson, *Pioneer Family*, p. 84; *Courtauld Family Letters*, 3: 1019.

[91] Flower, *English Settlement*, pp. 123, 359. This was also the experience of James Knight (in the Courtauld series) and of Robert Pollock.

mechanical skills or aptitude was likely to give up and return to the East or to England if he failed to make a livelihood from farming commensurate with his expectations. To succeed at farming, he had to have resources of his own or from his family if he was unable to realize a return from his investment in land and improvements.[92] The ordinary immigrant could not so easily change his occupation once he had made the investment. While he was trying to establish himself on a western farm, he was unlikely to earn enough cash to return home. Because of his predicament, the states of the Old Northwest gained industrial skills and commercially minded people from among British immigrants who had failed as farmers but who were flexible enough in the face of adversity to turn to industrial occupations, either on the land or in the growing towns of the region. For many who hoped to escape from the uncertain results of industrialization in England, a period on the land in the Middle West was simply a detour back into industrial occupations, though probably, in their generation, with more of the independence they valued so highly.

Whether they came from agriculture or from industry and commerce in England, these immigrants had to change their ways of gaining a livelihood as well as their standards of living if they sought to enter either commercial or subsistence agriculture in the Old Northwest before 1860. The adaptability of individuals and isolated families to a different environment is a fascinating part of nineteenth-century history, especially when we think of the unwillingness of many twentieth-century people, in more affluent societies, to take such risks. In making their adaptation, the immigrants made little impact on American farming methods. Yet indirectly, despite their initial goals in farming, these English and Scots immigrants probably did make a contribution to the economic development of the region because of their drive toward diversification, for which their experience helped prepare them. Coming with preconceived ideas about the nature of good farming or about farming as a way of life, they sometimes revived those skills and attitudes they thought they had discarded by emigrating.

[92] See, for example, Rebecca Butterworth, Outland Grove, Ark, July 5, 1846, to her father in Rochdale, Lancashire, BLPES, in Erickson, *Invisible Immigrants,* pp. 175–78; Thomson, *Pioneer Family,* p. 71; *Courtauld Family Letters,* 2: 844; Flower, *English Settlement,* p. 150.

CHAPTER THREE

Who Were the English and Scots Emigrants to the United States in the Late Nineteenth Century?

The great migration of European peoples in the nineteenth century has been interpreted as a movement in which economic influences dominated both underlying causes and timing. Through overseas migration and intracontinental movements, people were redistributed from regions of lower to regions of higher labor productivity, from the countryside and rural occupations to urban areas and industrial occupations. Except in the case of the disaster of the Irish famine, emigration was more a means of escaping from relative rural poverty in regions touched by economic growth and structural change than a flight from pure Malthusian crisis. As the writer of a report for the United Nations put it, emigrants came from areas "first in contact with urban and commercial influences." The inhabitants of the poorest and most isolated rural areas in Europe either did not participate in mass emigration at all or joined it late as that isolation was infringed.[1]

The author thanks Gwenda Moseley Williams, for valuable assistance in research, and Dudley Baines, for reading and commenting on an earlier version.

[1] United Nations Department of Social Studies, Population Division, *The Determinants and Consequences of Population Trends,* Population Studies, no. 17, 1953, p. 111. See also Dudley Kirk, *Europe's Population in the Interwar Years,* League of Nations, Economic and Financial Series, II, A.8 (Princeton: Princeton Office of Population Research, 1946), p. 81. "Emigration began to achieve importance just at the point at which industrialization was making real strides in the Swedish economy" (Dorothy Swain Thomas, *Economic Aspects of Swedish Population Movements, 1750–1933* [New York: Macmillan, 1941], p. 166); Ingrid Semmingsen, "Norwegian Emigration in the Nineteenth Century," *Scandinavian Economic History Review* 8 (1960): 152–53; Theodore Saloutos, *The Greeks in the United States* (Cambridge: Harvard University Press, 1964), pp. 2–3, 24.

If mass emigration usually accompanied a reorganization of agriculture with the beginnings of industrialization, the maturing of an industrial economy tended in the long run to stem the overseas flow. This is the standard explanation of the decline of emigration from some of the older regions of emigration in northwestern Europe in the early twentieth century. The gross rate of emigration from Germany, for example, declined from 49 per 10,000 of population in 1881 to a mere 3.9 per 10,000 in 1901.[2] Even in the short run, cyclical upswings in the industrial sector at home could discourage emigration, despite the stronger impact of conditions overseas on the timing of the migration movement.[3] Moreover, the inhabitants of a few European countries that gained relatively high per capita incomes—like Belgium, France, and the Netherlands—participated as little in the great nineteenth-century migrations as did people from the most underdeveloped parts of the Continent.

Overseas emigration from England and Scotland does not seem to have conformed to the pattern of these generalizations. Per capita incomes were almost certainly higher in Great Britain than they were on the Continent of Europe. By this criterion England and Scotland should have been as unimportant as sources of overseas emigrants as were France and Belgium. Yet average rates of gross emigration from Great Britain during the entire period from 1861 to 1910 exceeded those of Sweden, Germany, Switzerland, and Austria-Hungary as well as Belgium, France, and the Netherlands. According to Gustav Sundbärg's estimates of gross annual rates of emigration from various European countries, only Sweden, Norway, and Ireland experienced higher rates of emigration during the 1880s than did England and Scotland. Emigration from England itself never reached the high annual rates attained in certain decades by regions of truly mass emigration, such as Ireland, Norway, Baden, Württemberg, and Alsace, though Scotland's loss of population in the eighties approached the Scandinavian rates.[4]

[2] W. D. Forsyth, *The Myth of the Open Spaces* (Melbourne: Melbourne University Press, 1942), p. 68; J. D. Gould, "European Inter-Continental Emigration, 1815–1914: Patterns and Causes," *Journal of European Economic History 8* (1979): 667–68; and Semmingsen, "Norwegian Emigration," pp. 155–56. For a more complete set of estimates of comparative rates of gross emigration from European countries, see Gustav Sundbärg, *Aperçus Statistiques Internationaux,* 11e Année (Stockholm, 1908), pp. 103, 105.

[3] "Prosperity in America was highly important as a stimulus to emigration from Sweden, but . . . cyclical upswings in Sweden were a far more powerful counter-stimulant than is generally recognised" (Dorothy Swain Thomas, *Swedish Population Movements,* p. 169).

[4] Richard Easterlin, "Influences in European Overseas Emigration before World War I," *Economic Development and Cultural Change* 9 (1961): 335; Sundbärg, *Aperçus Statistiques Internationaux,* p. 105.

Indeed, the assumption that maturing industrialization ought to stem the flow of population overseas was so strong among some early students of British emigration that they stated flatly that the peak of emigration from England, relative to population size, had been reached by the mid-nineteenth century, after which the expansion of industrial employment and the growth of towns at home absorbed migration from the countryside.[5] Implied in such a statement is the counterfactual proposition, which cannot be tested, that emigration from England would have been higher than it was in the last part of the nineteenth century had that country not become the workshop of the world. The statement that emigration declined is patently false. Emigration was greater in the last half of the century than it had been in the first half. Gross rates of emigration from England and Scotland were higher in the prosperous fifties than they had been in the early forties. The next bulge in emigration in the late sixties and early seventies produced a greater absolute volume of emigrants from England and Scotland than ever before, though the incidence in the population was probably slightly less than in the fifties. The rates of emigration during the eighties, however, when 67 percent of passengers going overseas from the United Kingdom still gave the United States as their destination, were higher than those of the fifties. Again in the decade after 1900, by which time only 44 percent of the emigrants from the United Kingdom were bound for the United States, the relative rates of emigration were again nearly as high as they had been in the eighties. The evidence suggests that some English and Scottish people responded to the American business cycle as well as to the "Kuznets cycles" during the last third of the nineteenth century (see Table 3.1).

An obvious reason for some of the confusion about emigration from industrial Britain is the relatively poor quality of its migration statistics. Before the Passenger Act of 1852, the statistics of the United Kingdom related only to the total number of passengers sailing from its ports in

[5] "After the first half of the century, however, industrial developments in Great Britain had a depressing effect on emigration" (E. C. Snow, "Emigration from Great Britain," in *International Migrations*, ed. Imre Ferenczi and Walter Willcox [New York: National Bureau of Economic Research, 1932], 2: 251–52). This statement formed the basis for similar remarks by Maurice R. Davie, *World Migration* (New York: Macmillan, 1949), pp. 58–59; United Nations, *Population Trends*, p. 99; Kirk, *Europe's Population*, p. 81. Kirk made the entirely incorrect statement that in relation to population size the peak of emigration from England had been passed before the middle of the nineteenth century. See also Stanley Johnson, *Emigration from the United Kingdom to North America, 1763–1912* (London: George Routledge and Sons, 1913), p. 39.

Table 3.1. Passengers going overseas from Great Britain in peak years of emigration, 1832–1912

Year	England and Wales	Scotland
1832	50,700	11,112
1842	74,683	13,108
1854	90,966	26,872
1873	123,343	21,310
1883	183,236	31,139
1888	170,822	35,873
1907	265,229	66,355
1912	314,522	72,626

Sources: N. H. Carrier and J. R. Jeffery, *External Migration: A Study of the Available Statistics, 1815–1950*, General Register Office, Studies on Medical and Population Subjects, no. 6 (London: HMSO, 1953), pp. 93–94. Figures for 1832 and 1842 calculated from British Parliamentary Papers, 1831–32 (724), XXXII, p. 209, and 1842 (231) XXXI, p. 33.

Note: Figures for 1832 and 1842 refer to passengers leaving from English, Welsh, and Scottish ports in vessels covered by the Passenger Acts. The figures for 1854 onward refer to passengers of English, Welsh, or Scottish nationality.

certain types of vessels.[6] Not until 1853 were the various nationalities within the British Isles distinguished in the port records. From that date onward, the official statistics separated English, Welsh, Scottish, and Irish passengers according to destination, age, and sex. No distinction was made between prospective settlers and transient visitors. In 1863, cabin passengers were included for the first time in the published records, but no count was taken by nationality of the return of people from overseas places until 1895.

With all their limitations, these published statistics attest to the strength of the emigration movement from England and Scotland in the late nineteenth century and form the basis for hypotheses as to its responsiveness to economic conditions in receiving countries.[7] The only other means of estimating the magnitude of the emigration movement

[6] The most convenient summary of statistics of emigration from the United Kingdom is to be found in N. H. Carrier and J. R. Jeffery, *External Migration: A Study of the Available Statistics, 1815–1950,* General Register Office, Studies on Medical and Population Subjects, no. 6 (London: HMSO, 1953). See also Ferenczi and Willcox, *International Migrations,* 1: 619–58.

[7] Brinley Thomas, *Migration and Economic Growth* (Cambridge: Cambridge University Press, 1954), pp. 83–122; Harry Jerome, Migration and the Business Cycle (New York: National Bureau of Economic Research, 1926), pp. 156–58; Allen C. Kelley, "International Migration and Economic Growth: Australia, 1865–1935," *Journal of Economic History* 25 (1965): 333–54.

from England and Scotland, a method that provides no guide to annual fluctuations, is to estimate the net outward movement from one census to the next by projecting the probable increase in population from birth and death records and then comparing this figure with the actual population recorded in the census. Underregistration of births may explain, in part, the wide gap between estimates of net and gross emigration from England in the 1850s, but it is doubtful that the explanation applies to the even wider gap shown in the 1880s. Although there is good reason to believe that some of the gross emigration of the eighties was offset by the return of former emigrants and of visitors from abroad, the disparity between the two estimates suggests that nearly twice as many English people returned as remained overseas, a conclusion that is barely credible.[8] Thus although we can be certain that the permanent outward movement from England and Scotland was higher in many years after 1850 than it had ever been before, the precise absolute levels are not known (see Table 3.2).

Apart from providing information on annual fluctuations in emigration and the age and sex of migrants, British statistics reveal little about emigrants from England and Scotland in the last half of the nineteenth century. Occupations of outward-bound passengers were recorded after 1854 by destination rather than by place of origin. The only possibility of separating the British from the Irish by occupation is to use the separate series on the occupations of Irish emigrants provided after 1877 and to subtract.[9] Instead, scholars have turned to the records of immigrant-receiving countries for data on occupations of migrants from various parts of the British Isles. The most important of these, the United States, did not make a satisfactory effort to disaggregate the British immigrants according to occupation until 1875.[10] These much-used

[8] Since the above was written, Dudley Baines, using more sophisticated techniques than I envisaged, has provided upper- and lower-level estimates of net internal migration and overseas emigration for England and Wales by sex for each county, for the decades from 1861 to 1900 (*Migration in a Mature Economy: Emigration and Internal Migration in England and Wales*, 1861–1900 [Cambridge: Cambridge University Press, 1985]).

[9] Separate series of statistics of emigration from Ireland were begun in 1851 by the census commissioners. They included information about sex, age, occupation, county of origin in Ireland, destination abroad, and intended length of residence abroad. Thus they constitute a much more satisfactory guide to Irish emigration than exists for the English or Scots. For further details, see Carrier and Jeffery, *External Migration*, p. 145.

[10] These were the figures used by Brinley Thomas. The American census also gave information on occupations of English- and Scots-born inhabitants of the United States from 1870 to 1910. For discussion, see Edward Hutchinson, *Immigrants and Their Children, 1850–1950* (New York: John Wiley, 1956).

Table 3.2. Estimated gross and net emigration from England and Wales and from Scotland per 10,000 population, 1841–1910

Year	Gross emigration		Year	Net emigration	
	England and Wales	Scotland		England	Scotland
1841	-14	n.a	1841–1850	-5[a]	n.a.
1853–1860	-32	-50	1851–1860	-16	-101
1861–1870	-28	-46	1861–1870	-7	-44
1871–1880	-40	-47	1871–1880	-5	-28
1881–1890	-59	-71	1881–1890	-23	-58
1891–1900	-36	-44	1891–1900	-2	-13
1901–1910	-55	-99	1901–1910	-19	-57

[a] Refers to England and Wales.

Sources: Net emigration: Brinley Thomas "Wales and the Atlantic Economy," in *The Welsh Economy: Studies in Expansion*, ed. Brinlely Thomas (Cardiff: University of Wales Press, 1962), p. 7. Gross emigration from England and Wales, 1853–1910: N. H. Carrier and J. R. Jeffery, *External Migration: A Study of the Available Statistics, 1815–1950*, General Register Office, Studies in Medical and Population Subjects, no. 6 (London: H.M.S.O., 1953), pp. 92–93. 1841: *Census of Great Britain, 1841, Enumeration Abstracts, pt. 1, England and Wales,* British Parliamentary Papers, 1843 (496), XXII, pp. 399, 458. An estimate of the share of the year's emigrants who departed during the first five months of 1841 (included in the census of emigrants) was calculated from British Parliamentary Papers, 1841, 2d sess. (61), III, pp. 4–7, and used to gain an estimate of the total emigration of English and Welsh people for the entire year. This method gave an estimate of 20,484 English emigrants and 22,487 English and Welsh emigrants for the year 1841. If one assumes that the proportion of English and Welsh people in the total emigration from English and Welsh ports in 1841 was the same as that recorded in 1853, one gets a lower figure for total emigration because, almost certainly, more Irish were emigrating by way of English ports in 1853 than in 1841.

American statistics form the basis of the common generalization that skilled workers constituted a higher proportion of the immigrants America received from England and Scotland than of any other immigrant group in the last quarter of the nineteenth century. They also reveal a pronounced shift in the composition of the English and Scottish immigrants by occupation between the peak inflow of the 1880s and the next great secular upswing after 1900. As America slumped dramatically as a destination for British emigrants in the latter decade, those who did enter the States included an even higher proportion of skilled workers than formerly.[11]

If our knowledge of the occupations of British emigrants is thus seriously limited, we have no comprehensive information at all about certain other characteristics of the emigrants from England and Scot-

[11] Brinley Thomas, *Migration and Economic Growth*, pp. 60–65; Carrier and Jeffery, *External Migration*, p. 115.

land. We know little about the particular counties or the size of the communities from which they departed for places overseas after 1851. Arthur Redford's account of the geographical origins of English overseas emigrants in the 1830s and 1840s was based on comments by census enumerators and the emigration census of 1841.[12] After 1851, as the public debate about emigration subsided, the census authorities stopped publishing comments on the subject. For the last part of the century, the only analyses of the composition of emigrant populations are those by Philip Taylor of the Mormons and by Ross Duncan of a group of emigrants assisted to go to New South Wales.[13] Clearly these groups may not have been typical of the much larger voluntary, unassisted emigration.

Not all writers have ignored the increasing emigration after 1850. Because of the want of contemporary statistical data, however, those who have sought to explain the continued emigration have relied on literary evidence and supposition as to which groups might have been induced by hardship to leave the country. Maldwyn Jones assumed that because there was distress in certain branches of English agriculture at the time of the Great Depression, "tens of thousands of farmers and agricultural laborers were driven to emigrate."[14] Convinced that rising real wages in the towns in the eighties deprived town workers of an incentive to emigrate, A. K. Cairncross also thought that the "combined force of depression in British agriculture and expansion abroad resulted in a tremendous rural exodus, not so much to the towns as to America and the colonies."[15] Other writers, on equally slender evidence, tended

[12] Arthur Redford, *Labour Migration in England, 1750–1850,* 2d ed. (Manchester: Manchester University Press, 1964), pp. 124, 173–76.

[13] Philip Taylor, *Expectations Westward: The Mormons and the Emigration of Their British Converts in the Nineteenth Century* (Edinburgh: Oliver and Boyd, 1965), pp. 147–51; Ross Duncan, "Case Studies in Emigration: Cornwall, Gloucestershire, and New South Wales, 1877–86," *Economic History Review*, 2d ser., 16 (1963): 272–89. To these must now be added Robin Haines's analysis, "Government-assisted Emigration from the United Kingdom to Australia, 1831–1860: Promotion, Recruitment, and the Labouring Poor," Ph.D. diss., Flinders University of South Australia, 1992.

[14] Maldwyn Jones, *American Immigration* (Chicago: Chicago University Press, 1960), p. 194. Dr. William Farr, in the 39th Report of the Registrar General, 1877, "took the case of an agricultural labourer as being synonymous with that of the emigrant" (Johnson, *Emigration from the United Kingdom,* p. 306). Those writers at least examined the course of emigration. A contrary view was expressed by those who followed the interpretations of the National Bureau of Economic Research. Maurice Davie stated that farmers and laborers went to towns rather than abroad after 1850 (*World Migration*, p. 58). See also Kirk, *Europe's Population*, p. 82; Ferenczi and Willcox, *International Migrations*, 2: 250.

[15] A. K. Cairncross, *Home and Foreign Investment, 1870–1913: Studies in Capital Accumulation* (Cambridge: Cambridge University Press, 1953), p. 211.

to emphasize the difficulties of specific groups of industrial workers during the so-called Great Depression in explaining the relatively large emigration of the eighties.[16] In fact, we are still very much in the dark about the main characteristics of emigrants from England and Scotland as well as about any changes in the composition of the movement as it swelled in certain years in the latter half of the century.

The historical data available on these questions are so sparse that a hypothesis might be entertained that English emigration was entirely an individualistic movement, drawing off persons from all occupations and regions of the country at times when opportunities abroad looked promising. Because it is clear that parts of the countryside were losing population, however, what one would most like to know is the relationship between the rural exodus and overseas emigration. Were the rural laborers and handicrafts workers going overseas, as suggested by Jones and Cairncross, or were they attracted in the first instance by the possibility of employment in English towns? In her study of Norwegian port records, Ingrid Semmingsen found that as industrial development matured, more and more rural migrants went first to Norwegian towns for a period of time before emigrating and towns became more common as the last place of residence before emigration. She also discovered that skilled workers came to constitute a higher proportion of emigrants toward the end of the nineteenth century but that these skilled workers were more likely to be handicrafts than factory workers.[17] In England and Scotland as well, it is plausible that the movement overseas reflected the so-called rural exodus only indirectly and that towns and industries at home became the favored destination of the emigrant from agricultural areas in the last part of the century.

A certain amount of information about some of these elusive English and Scottish emigrants does survive on microfilms of ship lists in the National Archives in Washington.[18] Most of these lists give a bare

[16] William A. Carrothers, *Emigration from the British Isles* (London: P. S. King, 1929), pp. 216, 218, 227–28; H. Leak and T. Priday, "Migration from and to the United Kingdom," *Journal of the Royal Statistical Society* 46 (1933): 188–89; Jones, *American Immigration*, p. 195.

[17] Semmingsen, "Norwegian Emigration," pp. 156–57. More recently, Jon Gjerde has discovered that residents on the Norwegian coast, who had a long tradition of seasonal migration, moved south to Bergen, whereas agriculturists from the hinterland went overseas ("Chain Migrations from the West Coast of Norway," in *A Century of European Migrations, 1830–1930*, eds. Rudolph Vecoli and Suzanne Sinke [Urbana: University of Illinois Press, 1991], pp. 158–78).

[18] The original lists, now lodged at the Balch Institute in Philadelphia, are too fragile to permit unrestricted use.

minimum of information. Occasionally the captains of ships carrying immigrants to New York took the trouble to fill out carefully the official forms for describing their passengers. Some lists contain not only the names and ages of the passengers, but also occupation, county of birth, and place of last residence. A few captains even provided information about the destinations of the passengers within the United States or Canada and whether they intended to settle permanently in the New World. For the mid-century period of heavy immigration from 1846 to 1854, I found twenty seven ships that arrived at New York from Liverpool, Bristol, London, and Glasgow with lists that provided satisfactory details about the English and Scottish passengers they carried (see Appendix Table 3.10). Roughly 850 adult men from England and Scotland were on these ships, about 9 percent of the total number of English and Scottish males reported as entering the United States during these years.[19] Dipping into the ship lists in the next immigration peak in the early seventies produced no "good" lists. After the federal government took over the regulation of immigration in the eighties, a new effort was made to get full details about passengers arriving in American ports. From 1885 through 1888, most captains conscientiously filled in the new form in the early part of each year, until the seasonal flood of migrants seemingly overwhelmed them sometime in April or May. For the first few months of these four years, it was possible to analyze the returns of English and Scottish immigrants arriving from London, Liverpool, and Glasgow on 129 ships (see Appendix Table 3.10). The ten-thousand-odd adult males on these ships who had been born in England or Scotland constituted about 5 percent of the total males reported in the American immigration records as coming from England or Scotland during these years.[20]

The contrast between the "good" lists and the usual passenger list submitted adds to any suspicions one might already have as to the reliability of published immigration statistics. The lazier or busier captain was likely to fill in the blank for occupation at the top of the form with the word "labourer" or "mechanic" and use ditto marks for

[19] The United States records clearly underestimated the numbers of immigrants from England and Scotland during this period because the largest category of immigrants from the British Isles were returned as "Great Britain, not stated" until the 1870s. See Appendix Table 3.10 for ships analyzed.

[20] It is quite possible that satisfactory lists exist for some of the years of low immigration. Limitations of time enabled me to search for clues as to the migrants of peak years of emigration only. Not until 1891 were federal immigration officials required to check the manifests provided by the ship captains by interviewing immigrants to ascertain whether details were correct. It is quite clear that even after this date, harassed officials were unable to carry out the requirements of the law in peak months and years of immigration.

the rest of the page. This liberal use of ditto marks accounts for the large numbers of immigrants to the United States recorded as coming from "Great Britain, not stated" until the mid-1870s. Because published records were based on such carelessly compiled lists, the documents that were completed carefully become the more interesting. Yet, as sources, they have drawbacks that make it unwise to treat them formally as random samples of the entire emigration from England and Scotland. They yield information about migrants who went to North America but not about the rest of the overseas movement. They are biased toward certain years and the migration of the first few months of those years. One's confidence is perhaps enhanced by the fact that both small vessels and large ships carrying hundreds of steerage passengers are included. Nevertheless, I have not ventured to assign tests of significance to the data because the criteria for randomness could not be applied.[21]

In this article the "good" ship lists have been exploited for three types of information: the occupations of male immigrants arriving in New York from England and Scotland; the counties from which they emigrated; and the size of the communities they reported as their place of last residence.[22] The viewpoint of the analysis is that of the sending rather than the receiving country. Instead of comparing the structure of the emigrant population with that of the receiving country or of other immigrant groups, as writers concerned with the impact of British immigrants on the American economy have done, I have compared the emigrant groups with the English and Scottish populations as recorded in the nearest census. The question to be answered was whether this evidence suggested that certain occupations and regions were losing an excessive share of their population through emigration to the United States. In an attempt to find an answer, I carried out experiments to compare the characteristics of adult male emigrants with those of all adult males in the censuses of England and Scotland in 1851 and 1881.

The samples from ship lists seemed too small to presume to say anything about emigration from particular counties. Instead, the En-

[21] More recently, Raymond Cohn has criticized the use of "good" lists as a basis for analyzing the occupations of immigrants. He is inclined to trust the designation "labourer," even when pages are filled with ditto remarks. Basing his sample on ship lists that he used for his study of mortality on immigrant ships, regardless of the quality of the information about occupations, he estimated 53 percent of English immigrants from 1846 to 1853 to have been laborers, significantly more than the 23 percent I obtained from a few good lists for that period ("The Occupations of English Immigrants to the United States, 1836–1853," *Journal of Economic History* 52 [1992]: 378–79).

[22] On some lists this column was headed "Starting point" or "Hailing from."

glish counties were grouped into four classes according to the share of the labor force in agriculture and the level of nominal weekly wages in agriculture reported by Sir Arthur Bowley. If more than a third of the male labor force was employed in agriculture, the county was ranked as an agricultural county; and if the weekly wages in agriculture in 1851 were lower than ten shillings, the county was ranked as a low-wage county. For 1881, the cutoff point for a low-wage county was raised to fifteen shillings. The Scottish labor force was divided into two classes: the counties in the Highlands and Lowlands in which agriculture was the principal employment and those Lowland counties in which agriculture employed less than a third of the labor force.[23]

To discover whether the men on these particular ships were coming from the countryside in excessive numbers, I made an effort to find all the towns of twenty thousand or more inhabitants in the 1851 and 1881 censuses. These communities were designated as urban. The question was whether the male emigrants from Britain were more or less urbanized than was the entire population of the country at the time they went overseas.[24]

The most complex comparison with the census related to occupations. I rejected, perhaps somewhat perversely, the occupational classifications suggested by the census authorities themselves and those employed by the American immigration officials,[25] because the conventional distinction between skilled and unskilled manual workers, which has formed the basis of so many summaries of migrant occupations, reveals less about the skilled men who emigrated than one would like to know. The fact that men were skilled was of significance to the American economy; but in attempting to explain why people emigrated, one would like to know whether the factory workers in the forefront of the industrial revolution emigrated in excessive numbers or whether the emigration of skilled men was primarily a movement from

[23] The counties in each class in 1851 and 1881 are listed in Appendix Table 3.11; sources appear in Table 3.5.

[24] These towns are not all included in the table in Brian Mitchell and Phyllis Deane, *Abstract of British Historical Statistics* (Cambridge: Cambridge University Press, 1962), pp. 24–27.

[25] W. Alan Armstong has urged all researchers to apply the census classes of 1951 for social classification and Charles Booth's scheme for industrial classification to nineteenth-century census materials ("The Use of Information about Occupation," in *Nineteenth-Century Society: Essays on the Use of Quantitative Methods for the Study of Social Data,* ed. E. Anthony Wrigley [Cambridge: Cambridge University Press, 1972], pp. 191–310). Charles Booth, *Scotland, and Ireland, 1841–1881 Occupations of the People: England* (London: Edward Stanford 1886).

the countryside of handicraftsmen whose skills were undermined as much from declining local populations as from the competition of factory production. The census occupations and the emigrant occupations were grouped into six classes:[26]

(1) Agricultural Workers.

(2) Laborers. This group includes all nonagricultural laborers listed in the census under whatever industrial classification. If this class was returned in small numbers because respondents did not like to describe themselves as simply laborers to census enumerators, the same considerations might be assumed to arise when such people were asked their occupation by a ship's captain or mate.

(3) Servants and the like (preindustrial tertiary workers). This class was made up very largely of servants, one of the subdivisions used in the American immigration statistics. Because those statistics did not always distinguish between males and females by occupation, they provided no indication of the numbers of male servants among English and Scottish immigrants. This class also includes such occupations as messengers, road and barge workers, grooms and coachmen, soldiers, and seamen.

(4) Craftsmen (preindustrial skilled workers). Here an attempt has been made to single out occupations and industries that did not undergo significant technological change before 1880. The group contains building trades workers; miners; clothing workers, such as tailors and shoemakers; food processors, such as millers, butchers, and grocers; metalworkers, such as blacksmiths; and woodworkers, such as cabinetmakers, coopers, and wheelwrights. These were occupations in which the job description was probably not very different in 1880 from what it had been in 1800. Thus these workers did not experience a sharp leap forward in productivity in the course of the nineteenth century, though some increase was possible. In emigrating to less developed regions overseas, they might expect to follow their traditional jobs with only minor modifications. These occupations were fairly widely dispersed in England and Scotland in both cities and villages, agricultural and industrial regions. These people probably did not face direct technological unemployment by the substitution of machinery for their labor in the community in which they worked, though some of their activities might be displaced indirectly by concentrated manufacturing

[26] For a more detailed listing of occupations in each group, see Appendix Table 3.12. My occupational code is given in full in my final report to the Social Science Research Council, "Estimates of The Social Composition of British Emigrants to the U.S.A., 1831 and 1841," in the British Lending Library, Boston Spa.

activities elsewhere. If they emigrated because of lack of opportunity, that factor might be connected with declining population in the area where they practiced their trades. This, then, is an attempt to distinguish handicrafts workers whose methods of work changed little, many of whom, like building trades workers and miners, found expanding opportunities to practice old trades with the advance of industrialization. These people were more likely to suffer cyclical than technological unemployment. Their opportunities might change with internal population movements, for most of them (apart from miners) served primarily local markets. The one common feature was the limited advance in productivity that established some kind of ceiling on earnings and might make higher wages paid in more labor-scarce regions seem the only means to obtain substantially higher earnings for roughly the same work.

(5) Industrial workers. This group contains workers in new and changing industries in which job classifications changed markedly sometime during the nineteenth century and the productivity of many jobs increased with the introduction of improved technology and reorganization of production. The semiskilled and skilled workers placed in this category were engaged in these changing industries—both those displaced by new machinery and those gaining from it. Into this industrial class went all workers attached to the great nineteenth-century industries of textiles, iron and steel, engineering, and most of the secondary branches of metal manufacture. Thus, because of the difficulties of interpreting census classifications, this group includes both the workers in new occupations specifically created by industrialization as well as those suffering at some point from technological unemployment, such as handloom weavers and framework knitters. In the 1850s the class clearly contains both workers in collapsing occupations and those in more modern sectors of industry. By the 1880s the class can be taken to represent primarily the skilled and semiskilled workers in the industrialized sectors of the economy.

(6) Modern tertiary workers. This class includes service workers in the distinctly nineteenth-century railway industry as well as workers in commercial, clerical, and professional occupations that can be distinguished in the census from producers. Where a class was returned as "maker and dealer," the occupation was placed in a skilled industrial group.

Obviously this classification is in part a compromise forced on one by the categories singled out by the census authorities. It does, however, form some basis for estimating whether the men on these ships came primarily from more traditional industries and occupations or from new and changing industries produced by nineteenth-century technology.

The passenger lists give some information about emigrants during two periods of peak emigration. After declining between 1842 and 1843, emigration from British ports began a long upward movement not significantly interrupted until 1855. In spite of the growing confidence and prosperity in the British economy, this mid-century emigration generated rates of gross emigration higher than those of the thirties and forties. The published statistics, however, afford no possibility of estimating the exact number of English and Scottish people who emigrated between 1846 and 1854. This movement was probably the largest one from England and Scotland during the whole nineteenth century, with the exception of the decade of the 1880s, which stands out as the most important, whether one looks at estimates of gross or net emigration. The year 1885, the first for which we have good ship lists, was the second of two years of falling emigration after the huge upswing that had begun in 1879. Emigration to America then rose in 1886 and 1887, to decline very slightly in 1888. Approximately 130,000 English, Welsh, and Scottish passengers left for the United States in 1887 and in 1888, which were the peak years for movement into America for the entire century.

These "samples" of emigrants based on port lists relate to passengers entering the United States in the years of heaviest emigration there from England and Scotland. The characteristics of the migrant population in those years may have been quite different from the migrant stream in troughs of emigration. Moreover, the structure of the migrant population may have changed from one emigration peak to another. Thus the data to be examined here cannot be generalized for years other than those specifically treated and cannot be interpreted as a cross section of English and Scottish emigration, even to the United States, throughout the last half of the nineteenth century. Only a tentative comparison can be made between the emigrants of the two peak periods. That in itself is some advance in knowledge, because we presently know practically nothing.

The ship lists cast doubt on the idea that emigration from England and Scotland to the United States in the eighties could be characterized by the term "rural exodus." Almost four out of five men who came to New York on these ships in the late eighties gave a principal town as his last place of residence. Because not quite half the population of England and Scotland was concentrated in towns of twenty thousand or more inhabitants in 1881 (53 percent in 1891), town dwellers were over represented among emigrants. This urban overrepresentation was greater during the three years of rising immigration from 1885 to 1887 and waned in 1888 at the crest of the migration wave. It was also slightly more pronounced among the Scottish emigrants than it was among the English (see Tables 3.3 and 3.4).

According to the ship lists, town dwellers had not been overrepresented among the emigrants of the mid-century. At that time, relatively more men were leaving for America directly from agricultural villages and small towns, and the inhabitants of larger towns were underrepresented among emigrants. The switch in origins between the two periods was much greater than could be accounted for simply by rising urbanization in England and Scotland during the intervening years. As urban growth advanced in the United States (by 40 percent in the 1880), urban rather than rural workers were attracted there from Britain. Many of these emigrants may previously have come into British towns from the countryside, later to set off for the United States, but our data do not enable us to see these previous migrations. It is also quite possible that the English and Scottish emigrants to Canada and Australia at this time were proceeding more frequently directly from rural communi-

Table 3.3. Adult male emigrants from England and Wales with principal towns as places of last residence, by date of emigration to the United States

	1846–1854	1885–1888
1. Total number in group	838	10,074
2. Percent from principal towns	26.8	78.0
3. Percent living in towns, 1851 and 1881 censuses	35.0	49.4
4. Index of representation: 2/3 × 100	77	158

Sources: Principal towns with populations of 20,000 or more in 1851 taken from *Census of Great Britain, 1851, Population Tables,* Pt. 1, *Numbers of the Inhabitants,* vol. 1, *England and Wales,* British Parliamentary Papers (hereinafter B.P.P.), 1852–53 (163.1) Summary Tables, pp. cxxvi, ccvi, ccxvii. In most instances the boundaries used were those of municipal boroughs. The following towns were also included, with boundaries as designated: Birkenhead, Burnley, and Stalybridge (local registrar's districts); Brighton (parish); Dudley and Cheltenham (parliamentary borough and parish); Huddersfield (parliamentary borough and township); Leicester and Stockport (municipal and parliamentary borough); Stoke-on-Trent (township); and Bury, Chatham, and Rochdale (parliamentary borough). Principal towns with population of 20,000 or more in 1881 were taken from the *Census of England and Wales,* 1891, *Preliminary Report,* p. 18, and vol. 2, *Area, Houses, and Population,* B.P.P., 1892 (C.6948–1), XCIV, p. vi; *Ninth Decennial Census of the Population of Scotland, 1891,* vol. 1, *Report and Tables,* B.P.P., 1892 (C.3320), XCIV, p. 123. Definition of towns was in all cases urban sanitary districts. Ship lists as in Appendix Table 3.10.

Table 3.4. English and Scottish adult male immigrants on New York ship lists, by size of place of last residence, 1885–1891

	1885	1886	1887	1888	Census 1881	Census 1891
England						
From towns	1,113	2,024	1,704	1,154		
Total male immigrants	1,478	2,591	2,098	1,492		
Percent from towns	75.3	78.1	81.2	77.3	50.9	55.3
Scotland						
From towns	361	697	413	398		
Total male immigrants	461	857	500	610		
Percent from towns	78.3	81.3	82.6	65.2	39.7	43.5

Sources: See Table 3.3.

ties. In the late eighties, it appears that the United States was attracting, selectively, urban workers from Britain and that the character of English and Scottish emigration was very different in this respect from what it had been in the middle of the century.

Analysis of the types of counties from which emigrants were departing for the United States also suggests a marked change in the composition of the emigrants between the fifties and the eighties. In the middle of the century, agricultural counties were still fairly well represented as places of last residence of emigrants to America. Yet the migrants of these years were not going overseas mainly from the least industrialized counties with the lowest agricultural wages. The most pronounced movement to America was coming from low-wage industrial counties—Cornwall and the Midlands (Worcestershire, Leicestershire, Staffordshire, Warwickshire, and Gloucestershire). The poorer agricultural counties produced as many emigrants for these ships, nearly a quarter of the total, but they contained almost a third of the adult male labor force of the country (see Table 3.5 and the Appendix Table 3.11).[27]

[27] Since the above was written, William Van Vugt has carried out a study of the lists for 1851. He found more ships with good lists in 1851 than had I, and his findings for the single year differed in some respects from mine for 1846–54. He found a higher proportion of emigrants coming from agricultural counties, 39 percent as compared with my 33 percent. The difference was accounted for by a higher proportion of his sample emigrating from high wage agricultural counties (17 percent as compared with my 9 percent). The low-wage agricultural counties were thus slightly less well represented among his 1851 emigrants (22 percent). See William Van Vugt, "British Emigration during the Early 1850s, with Special Reference to Emigration to the U.S.A.," Ph.D. diss., University of London, 1985, pp. 298–99.

Table 3.5. Adult male emigrants from England and Scotland on New York ship lists according to type of county in which they last resided before emigration, 1846–1888

	Ship lists		Census		Index	
Type of county	1846–1854 (1)	1885–1888 (2)	1851 (3)	1881 (4)	1851 1/3 × 100	1881 2/4 × 100
England						
Agricultural low-wage	24.3%	4.6	32.2%	14.0%	75	33
Agricultural high-wage	8.6	—	9.5	—	91	—
Industrial low-wage	23.8	20.9	16.3	29.3	146	71
Industrial high-wage	43.3	74.5	42.0	56.7	103	131
All English counties	100.0%	100.0%	100.0%	100.0%		
Numbers	608	7,238	4,788,000	7,231,000		
Scotland						
Agricultural	41.1%	20.1%	40.4%	24.8%	102	81
Industrial	58.9	79.9	59.6	75.2	99	106
All Scottish counties	100.0%	100.0%	100.0%	100.0%		
Numbers	68	2,421	873,000	1,109,000		
Unknown[a]	172	415				

Sources: Census of Great Britain, 1851, Population Tables, Pt. 2, *Ages, Civil Condition, Occupations, and Birth-places of the People,* vol. 1, *England and Wales,* B.P.P., 1852–53 (169-1), LXXXVIII, pp. ccxviii–ccxx, ccxxviii–ccxx; *Census of England and Wales, 1881,* vol. 3, *Ages, . . . Marriage, Occupations, and Birth-places of the People,* B.P.P., 1882 (C. 3722), LXXX, sec. 6, p. 24, and sec. 4, p. 7; *Ninth Decennial Census of the Population of Scotland, 1881,* vol. 2, B.P.P., 1883 (C. 3657), LXXXI, pp. 406–13; Sir Arthur Bowley, *Wages in the United Kingdom in the Nineteenth Century* (Cambridge: Cambridge University Press, 1900), table at the back of the book; ship lists, as in Appendix Table 3.10.

[a] Yorkshire had to be omitted from the 1846–54 analysis because too many migrants did not identify the part of Yorkshire from which they came and the Ridings of Yorkshire fell into different classes of counties. Most unknowns were migrants whose place of last residence could not be ascertained or who named a village but not a county when villages of the same name were to be found in more than one county.

The ship lists of the 1880s cast doubt on the idea of the depression in agriculture as the explanation for the swelling overseas emigration of the decade. Only four percent of the migrants studied came from agricultural counties, in which 14 percent of England's male labor force still lived in 1881. At this time, the older and richer industrial counties were supplying proportionately more emigrants to the States; indeed, 77 percent of those studied came from the counties classified as high-wage industrial counties. Because opportunities to emigrate had by this time been enhanced, as compared with the fifties, with respect to both the information available to prospective emigrants and the predictable cost of the journey and loss of earnings, the shift in the origins of migrants toward the industrial counties suggests that most young men who were leaving rural communities in England were seeking opportunities in English industrial areas first. The overrepresentation of Lowland industrial counties in the Scottish movement overseas in the late eighties was not so pronounced, but one Highland city, Aberdeen, was sending quite extraordinary numbers of building trades workers to New York in 1887 and 1888, though its county has been ranked as agricultural.[28]

The evidence that emigrants of the late eighties were departing not so much from the countryside and agricultural regions as from the principal towns and leading industrial counties might seem to suggest that the bulge in emigration was related, after all, to industrial unemployment in Britain's major industries, despite rising real wages in the towns. A look at the occupations of the emigrants dispels this impression (see Table 3.6).[29]

[28] "After a particularly dull winter in the Scottish trade, nearly every stonemason who could scrape together the passage money emigrated to recoup his fortunes. Two thousand landed in New York during six weeks of the spring of 1887." *Scottish American,* May 25, 1887, quoted in Rowland Berthoff, *British Immigrants in Industrial America, 1790–1950* (Cambridge: Harvard University Press 1953), p. 82.

[29] In his sample of one in every ten ships arriving in the States in 1851 with British passengers, William Van Vugt found a significantly higher proportion of adult males coming from agriculture, as well as from agricultural counties. As against my 15 percent for 1846–54, he estimated that 23 percent of the adult males in 1851 were recorded as farmers or farm laborers. Conversely, skilled workers were more poorly represented, particularly skilled workers from the modern sector, at only 9 percent as compared with my 17 percent ("British Emigration during the Early 1850s," p. 72). See also Van Vugt, "Running from Ruin: The Emigration of British Farmers to the U.S.A. in the Wake of the Repeal of the Corn Laws," *Economic History Review*, 2d ser., 41 (1988): 411–28. If one can place any confidence in these estimates, they would seem to suggest that 1851 was a year of especially high agricultural emigration from Britain, even as compared with the rest of the cycle of which it was a part.

Skilled industrial workers were fairly well represented in the mid-century emigration from England and Scotland according to the ship lists. Apart from building trades workers, who will be discussed shortly, two groups of industrial workers were somewhat overrepresented in the migration of this period: first, workers associated with preparing and distributing food, such as millers, grocers, and butchers; and second, metalworkers of all kinds and engineers. The analysis does not suggest that the men classified as preindustrial metalworkers showed a greater tendency to emigrate at this time than did workers in the more modern branches of the iron and machinery industries. Members of the two most numerous occupations, blacksmiths and engineers, appeared in approximately equal numbers in the ship lists. Very few practiced trades that were particularly depressed in the fifties: two nailers, one caster, one stamper, and a shuttle maker were identified. But six coach makers and eight molders as well as a patternmaker, an engine smith, a boilermaker, and two steel rollers were also there. Textile workers were not well represented, neither the prosperous cotton workers nor the depressed handloom weavers of the woolen industry. The impression that emigration was not at this time serving as a safety valve against technological unemployment to any significant degree is further enhanced by noting that so many of these skilled workers were leaving from principal towns, not small communities (see Table 3.7).

The attraction that the American economy exercised upon Britain's skilled workers seems to have diminished by the late 1880s. With the exception of building trades workers and miners, men following handicrafts were far less well represented in the emigrant labor force than they had been in the 1850s. When they did emigrate, they were as likely to go to the Empire as to the United States (see Table 3.8). Similarly, workers in the industrialized sector of the economy formed a smaller proportion of the emigrant labor force than they had in the fifties. The textile workers who did emigrate at this time went almost exclusively to the United States, but their underrepresentation in the emigrant labor force suggests that they were not choosing emigration as a means of adapting to the difficulties of that decade in a manner suggestive of a social movement.[30] Workers in heavy industry—such as iron- and steelworkers, engineers, shipbuilders, and boilermakers—did not show

[30] There is contrary evidence. For example, a contemporary, Thomas Ellison, referred to the large numbers of impoverished textile workers emigrating to the United States in the 1880s (*The Cotton Trade of Great Britain* [1886], p. 103, cited in J. Parry Lewis, *Building Cycles and Britain's Growth* [London: Macmillan, 1965], p. 124).

Table 3.6. Occupations of adult male emigrants from England and Scotland on certain ships arriving in New York

	Ship lists		Census		Index	
	1846–1854 (1)	1885–1888 (2)	1851 (3)	1881 (4)	1846–1854 1/3 × 100	1885–1885 2/4 × 100
Farmers	14.2%	8.4%	6.5%	4.1%	219	205
Farm laborers	0.5	1.1	20.4	11.4	2	10
All agricultural workers	14.7%	9.5%	27.3%[a]	15.6%[a]	54	61
Laborers	22.6	29.5	6.9	8.2	328	360
Servants, etc.	3.1	3.2	9.3	12.8	33	25
Building trades	10.1	18.1	7.4	9.1	136	199
Mining	5.2	8.0	5.2	6.4	100	125
Food trades	5.9	2.1	4.2	4.2	140	50
Metal trades	4.4	1.7	2.8	2.6	157	65
Clothing trades	6.7	1.5	6.4	4.4	105	34
Woodworking trades	2.1	0.5	2.2	2.0	95	25
Miscellaneous	1.8	0.9	2.0	1.2	90	75
Mechanics not otherwise designated	0.6	1.5	—	0.4	—	375
All craftsmen	36.7[b]	34.3%	30.2%	30.3%	122	113
Textiles	7.4	2.0	8.9	5.4	83	37
Steel and engineering	7.3	4.0	4.8	7.9	152	51
Miscellaneous	2.6	1.8	2.0	3.8	130	47
All industrial workers	17.3%	7.8%	15.7%	17.0%[b]	110	46
Railway workers	—	0.1	0.3	2.1	—	5
Clerical workers	1.2	5.6	2.1	3.7	57	151
Commercial workers	3.9	8.0	5.9	7.1	66	113
Professionals	0.5	1.9	2.5	3.3	20	58
All modern tertiary workers	5.6%	15.7%[b]	10.7%[b]	16.1%[b]	52	98

All occupations	100.0%	100.0%	100.1%	100.0%
Number stating occupation	838	8,698	6,625,000	8,893,000
Omissions[c]	—	753	26,593	626
Unknown[c]	—	632		

Sources: *Census of Great Britain*, 1851, *Population Tables*, Pt. 2, *Ages, Civil Condition, Occupations, and Birth-places of the People*, vol. 1, *England and Wales*, B.P.P., 1852–53 (1691–1), LXXXVII, pp. cxviii–cxxi and ccxviii–ccxxi; *Census of England and Wales, 1881*, vol. 3, *Ages, . . . Marriage, Occupations and Birth-places of the People*, B.P.P., 1882 (C. 3722), LXXVIII, pp. x–xvii; *Ninth Decennial Census of the Population of Scotland*, vol. 2, B.P.P., 1883 (C. 3657), LXXXI, pp. 406–13; ship lists as in Appendix Table 3.10.

[a] A few miscellaneous agricultural workers, not classifiable as farmer or farm laborers, were returned in the census, yielding a slightly larger proportion for agricultural workers as a whole.

[b] Subtotal does not add up to units within it because of rounding.

[c] The only adult male migrants omitted from this table were gentlemen, of whom 753 were found on the 129 ship lists. Unknown included illegible occupations and men listed with "none" in the occupation column. Totals do not always equal 100 percent because of rounding.

Table 3.7. English and Scottish male immigrants on ships arriving in New York between 1828 and 1854 who gave principal towns as places of last residence

	Number from towns	Total on ships	Percent from towns
Laborers	29	198	14.6
Building trades workers	39	111	35.1
Miners	2	42	4.8
Other handicraft workers	85	128	66.4
Textile workers	30	94	31.9
Ironworkers, engineers	36	63	57.1
Other industrial workers	11	28	39.2
All males on ships	316	1,163	27.2
Census, 1851			35.0

Sources: For ships included, 1846–54, see Appendix A, Table 3.10; for ships, 1827–32, see Table 4.19 below.

Table 3.8. Occupations of adult male passengers leaving United Kingdom ports for the United States, 1885–1888 and 1895–1898 (percent)

	1885–1888	1895–1898
All occupied males giving United States as destination	68.5	56.1
Occupations with a high preference for United States, 1880s		
Farm laborers	66.9	93.4
Laborers	77.8	75.0
Building trades workers	70.7	44.1
Miners	72.9	22.4
Mechanics not otherwise designated	83.9	88.1
Textile workers	86.6	96.4
Occupations with low preference for United States, 1880s		
Farmers	60.3	51.8
Handicraftsmen	52.7	61.1
Iron, steel, engineering workers	55.0	37.0
Clerks	55.7	51.7
Commercial workers	52.9	48.3
Professional occupations[a]	43.9	21.5
Servants, etc.	59.4	63.8

Sources: Statistical Tables Relating to Emigration from and into United Kingdom in the Year 1885, British Parliamentary Papers (hereinafter B.P.P.), 1886 (3) LXXI, pp. 14–15; *in 1886,* B.P.P., 1887 (32), LXXXIX, pp. 16–17; *in 1887,* B.P.P., 1888 (2), CVII, pp. 16–17; *in 1888,* B.P.P., 1889 (10) LXXXIV, pp. 16–17; *in 1895,* B. P.P., 1896, Pt. 1 (vi), XCIII, pp. 22–23; *in 1896,* B.P.P., 1897, Pt. 1 (vi) XCIX, pp. 22–23; *in 1897,* B.P.P., 1898 (154), CIII, pp. 22–23; *in 1898,* B.P.P., 1899 (188), CVII, pp. 24–25.

Note: Because these figures are based on official emigration statistics of the United Kingdom, the Irish are included with the British.

[a] Includes merchants, students, and gentlemen who cannot be separated in the original data.

a similar preference for the United States as a destination, and they, too, were underrepresented among emigrants to New York. Clearly, in the great migration of these years, many skilled industrial workers did emigrate, both to the United States and to other parts of the world, but they did not leave in such large numbers than one can explain the heavy emigration in terms of skilled workers who sought this means of escape from uncertain employment.[31] Even in 1886 and 1887, when trade unions in Britain reported relatively high rates of unemployment and the upward movement in real wages abated, skilled industrial workers were not flocking to America.

Two groups of skilled workers in Britain did demonstrate a responsiveness to the American boom of the eighties, however: miners and building trades workers. These occupations were fairly well represented among the emigrants of the mid-century, but both groups were overrepresented in the emigration of the late eighties. In the 1880s, miners formed 8 percent and building trades workers no less than 18 percent of the passengers analyzed. The striking mobility of these workers, who might hope to practice their trades with little modification in many parts of the world, is indicated in Table 3.8. At this time when the United States was undergoing rapid industrial expansion combined with a building boom, both groups clearly preferred the States as a destination. No other occupational groups among those studied changed the direction of their migration so conspicuously during the nineties, when American building slumped and new mines were being opened in Australia and South Africa.

This remarkable prominence of building trades workers among emigrants of the late eighties (they formed 36 percent of the male emigrants from Scotland alone) coincided with a period of low building activity in most English and Scottish towns.[32] Four out of five of these building craftsmen found on the ships arriving in New York came from principal towns, a slightly higher percentage than that for all male

[31] "In most American industries—iron and steel by 1870, coal and iron mining by 1880, most textile processes by 1900, and even upstarts like tinplating by 1905—the original English, Welsh and Scottish skilled hands lost their place to peasant greenhorns, Irish or French Canadians before 1880, southern and eastern Europeans thereafter. Many were able to move up into managerial jobs or even ownership, but, for their countrymen who might have followed them to America, opportunities were drying up" (Berthoff, *British Immigrants,* p. 87). The evidence of port records suggests that Berthoff may have antedated the decline of opportunities in the United States for coal miners and postdated that for textile workers.

[32] Lewis, *Building Cycles and Britain's Growth*, pp. 316–17; Cairncross, *Home and Foreign Investment*, pp. 16–17, 213; Brinley Thomas, *Migration and Economic Growth*, p. 297.

immigrants studied.[33] Writers who have investigated fluctuations in building activity in Britain, which (depending on which index one uses) reached a peak about 1877 and a trough in the late eighties, have also called attention to links between British overseas emigration and capital movements and domestic building activity. Cairncross noted the emigration of building trades workers to Canada after 1907, when domestic building activity was again at a low.[34] The port records indicate that these workers were behaving as though the Atlantic formed a single economy for building activity in the eighties as well. A very large number of these English and Scottish emigrants went back and forth each season in the 1880s, working during the peak of activity in the United States and spending the winter in England or Scotland.[35] Cairncross and J. Parry Lewis have provided persuasive evidence that the decline in building activity in most English and Scottish towns in the eighties was itself a consequence of the huge emigration that began its upswing in 1879. The movement of young people—those people who, as Lewis suggested, might shortly have been marrying and demanding housing had they remained in Britain—was one factor in the weak market for housing during this period.[36] The published occupational statistics of the United Kingdom and the United States indicate that this emigration of building trades workers was relatively weaker in the early eighties, as a share of total emigrants, and reached its peak during the latter half of the decade[37] (see Table 3.9 and Appendix Tables 3.13, 3.14 and 3.15). The building trades workers did not initiate the emigration movement of the eighties, but they found emigration, permanent or seasonal, a means of adapting to one of its consequences—the decline in house building.

The origins of the great emigration of the eighties are found instead in the sharp rise in the numbers of unskilled laborers going overseas,

[33] The percentages of building trades workers on New York ships coming from principal towns are 1885, 82.1 percent; 1886, 84.8 percent; 1887, 83.2 percent; 1888, 70.2 percent; and 1885–88, 80.7 percent.

[34] Cairncross, *Home and Foreign Investment*, p. 210; Lewis, *Building Cycles and Britain's Growth*, pp. 164–85; Brinley Thomas, *Migration and Economic Growth*, pp. 175–89.

[35] Berthoff, *British Immigrants*, p. 82; Charlotte Erickson, *American Industry and the European Immigrant, 1860–1885* (Cambridge: Harvard University Press, 1957), pp. 49–50; Roger Simon, "Birds of Passage," M.A. thesis, University of Wisconsin, 1966, pp. 3–4. Of course, this seasonal migration was partially responsible for the large numbers of building trades workers reported on the ships because each entry of an individual was counted. Although there is no way of allowing for this factor, it does not negate the analysis.

[36] Lewis, *Building Cycles and Britain's Growth*, pp. 179–80; Cairncross, *Home and Foreign Investment*, pp. 215–16.

[37] The proportion of building trades workers recorded in the ship lists rose from 10 percent of the immigrants of 1885 to 20 percent in 1888.

Table 3.9. Male passengers leaving the United Kingdom for all places, 1878–1897, by occupation (percent)

Occupation	1878	1882	1888	1897
Farmers	9.6	2.4	7.5	5.9
Farm laborers	20.9	7.0	28.1	10.5
Laborers	2.9	50.2	13.0	8.6
Servants, etc.	0.3	0.3	1.0	2.1
Building trades	6.0	4.4	6.0	5.4
Miners	3.6	4.1	5.9	8.6
Mechanics not otherwise designated	10.6	7.6	12.5	8.7
Other handicraft workers	1.5	1.4	2.8	3.2
Textile workers	—	0.3	0.7	1.5
Other industrial workers	1.3	0.7	2.0	3.1
Railway workers	0.3	0.2	0.5	1.2
Clerical workers	3.3	1.2	3.4	6.9
Commercial workers	1.3	1.3	1.5	3.8
Other tertiary occupations[a]	38.4	18.9	15.1	30.5
All occupations	100.0	100.0	100.0	100.0
Number stating occupation	28,931	73,276	79,720	43,026

Sources: Statistical Tables Relating to Emigration and Immigration from and into the United Kingdom in the Year 1878, B.P.P., 1878–79 (32), LXXV, pp. 12–13; and *Ireland, Emigration; Statistics for the Year*, (C.2221), pp. 10–11; *in 1882*, B.P.P., 1883 (89), LXXVI, pp. 16–17, and Ireland (C.3489), pp. 10–11; *in 1888*, B.P.P., 1889 (10), LXXXIV, pp. 16–17, and Ireland (C.5647), pp. 10–11; *in 1897*, B.P.P., 1898 (154), CIII, pp. 22–23; and Ireland (C.8748), pp. 10–11.

Note: Irish are excluded.

[a] Gentlemen, professional men, merchants, and students.

especially from England, after 1879. The responsiveness of laborers to conditions in the American economy is indicated by the seven-and-a-half-fold increase in the numbers reported by the American authorities as arriving from England between the trough of 1878 and the peak of 1882. The number of skilled workers arriving in the States from England rose only four times during those years. Both the American and the British statistics imply that laborers formed a higher proportion of total emigrants from England to the United States in the early eighties than they did in the latter half of the decade. Yet the analysis of the ship lists for 1885–88 indicated 33 percent of the English and 20 percent of the Scotsmen arriving in New York as general laborers.[38]

[38] These percentages are slightly lower than those recorded in the published American statistics of immigration for these years, when peaks of 48 percent of English immigrants in 1885 and 29 percent of Scots in 1887 were reported (Brinley Thomas, *Migration and Economic Growth*, pp. 269, 271). The ship lists probably bias the proportion of laborers downward by their concentration in the early months of the year. A breakdown of

Unskilled labor had also been the most overrepresented occupation among the emigrants of the mid-nineteenth century. In that period, the laborers had been going out directly from the countryside and smaller towns (see Table 3.7). Only 15 percent of the laborers came from principal towns. The laborers who emigrated in the late eighties had been, like the rest of the emigrants, highly urbanized.[39] The proportion of laborers from the countryside was highest—30 percent in 1885, the year of lowest emigration in the four years analyzed in the eighties. As prosperity seemed to be returning to the towns in 1887 and 1888, the share of emigrant laborers coming from principal towns actually appears to have risen.[40]

The chief feature, then, of the large emigration of the late nineteenth century was the exodus of some of the least qualified members of the urban labor force in England and Scotland, of the disadvantaged, for whom the continued high rate of population increase and entries to the labor force narrowed the range of opportunities, particularly in a decade when building activity was low. The port records suggest that farm laborers and preindustrial tertiary workers were the least well represented among the emigrants to the United States at this time. Farmers themselves were still emigrating in larger numbers than their share in the labor force might warrant, as they had been in the fifties. The poorer people from the countryside were being drawn first to English towns, though some of them may have proceeded overseas from those towns in the eighties. Contemporary accounts of the emigration of farm laborers in the seventies and eighties mentioned migration to the towns with greater frequency than they did overseas migration. Only one of the assistant commissioners for the Richmond Commission mentioned the United States as a destination for young men leaving the countryside. W.C. Little, in the report on Devonshire, quoted a landowner and M.P. who reported that "hundreds of labourers have

occupations of immigrants by months of immigration for the four years shows the proportion of laborers to have been higher in April than in earlier months.

[39] The percentages of laborers from principal towns are 1885, 71.2 percent; 1886, 80.3 percent; 1887, 87.9 percent; 1888, 80.3 percent; and 1885–88, 80.3 percent.

[40] On the beginning of a slight improvement in the home economy in 1887 and recovery in 1888, see Lewis, *Building Cycles and Britain's Growth,* p. 202 and H. Lance Beales, "The Great Depression in Industry and Trade," *Economic History Review* 5 (1934), reprinted in *Essays in Economic History,* ed. Eleanora Carus-Wilson (London: Macmillan, 1954), 1: 413. Unemployment reported by trade unions peaked in 1886 and was falling in 1887 and 1888 (Mitchell and Deane, *British Historical Statistics,* p. 64).

gone ... [to the Welsh coalfields.] Many too have emigrated to America, and no parish is without its representative in Canada and the United States."[41] More typical were reports of young men going to the towns to become porters, policemen, or postmen or seeking employment in mines or on the railways.[42] Thus the evidence does not support Brinley Thomas's suggestion that during periods—such as the seventies—of low emigration, high internal mobility, and building investment in England, the ambitious young people from the countryside left for British towns but that in the succeeding decade such people chose to go overseas.[43] The towns continued to attract the better educated, ambitious young men from the countryside in the eighties.

In contrast to farmers, industrial workers, and laborers, men in service occupations had been weakly represented on the ship lists used for the mid-nineteenth century. Although the traditional tertiary occupations, such as domestic service, continued to trail far behind others as a source of male emigrants to the United States in the eighties, modern tertiary workers such as white-collar workers and professional and commercial people tended to be somewhat better represented in the 1880s. Yet the ship lists do not suggest any overrepresentation of them in the flow to America. These classes were not so responsive as building trades workers, miners, and laborers to economic conditions in the United States. Railway workers were not significant in the emigration of

[41] Royal Commission on Agriculture, *Reports of the Assistant Commissioners,* British Parliamentary Papers (hereinafter B.P.P., 1882, (C.3375-I) XV, p. 21.

[42] Ibid. C.3375-II, p. 42. W.C. Little's summary for the ten counties he investigated, including Devon, Cornwall, and Somerset, mentioned young men drifting away into the towns or railway service (ibid. p. 54). S.B.L. Druce made roughly the same remark about Bedfordshire and reported from Essex that the best and youngest workers left villages to seek employment in London, on the railways, or in the manufacturing districts (ibid., C.3375-II, pp. 9, 30). For similar reports from Lincolnshire, Norfolk, Suffolk, Lancashire, Yorkshire, Buckinghamshire, and Hertfordshire, see ibid., pp. 56, 67, 94 and C.3375-V, p. 43. *Digest and Appendix to Part I of Evidence,* B.P.P., 1881 (C.2278-II) XVI, pp. 141, 364, 368. For similar reports from Forfar, Clackmannan, and Fife, see George J. Walker's report in *Digest and Appendix* pp. 544, 547, 549. Frederick Ernest Green remarked that by the late seventies, emigration had gone out of fashion among the men of Norfolk: "It began to be considered derogatory to be an exile." The young men went into navvying, into the police force, or to the railway lines, the mines, or the contractor's yard (Green, *A History of the English Agricultural Labourers* [London: P. S. King, 1920], pp. 89, 150). See also Arthur Clayden, *The Revolt of the Fields* (London: Hodder and Stoughton, 1874), p. 160.

[43] Brinley Thomas, "Wales and the Atlantic Economy," in *The Welsh Economy: Studies in Expansion,* ed. Brinley Thomas (Cardiff: University of Wales Press, 1962), p. 6. Dudley Baines also took issue with Brinley Thomas's interpretation on this point (*Migration in a Mature Economy,* pp. 220–27).

either the fifties or the eighties. As Table 3.8 indicates, none of these groups showed a high preference for the United States as a field for emigration during the 1880s.

Frank Musgrove suggested that the brain drain from Britain abroad—and particularly to America—began in the 1860s.[44] In support of this view, he used the percentages of United Kingdom passengers, by occupation, calculated by N. H. Carrier and J. R. Jeffery.[45] In comparing a period of high emigration in the late sixties with a period of low emigration in the nineties, Musgrove misinterpreted a cyclical fluctuation as a trend. As can be seen in Table 3.9 and Appendix Tables 3.13 and 3.14, for example, in years of relatively low emigration, men in occupations that might be called relatively insensitive to the short-term forces governing migration, such as farmers, skilled industrial workers, and the class designated by Carrier and Jeffery as "commerce, finance, insurance, professions," formed a higher proportion of the reduced number of emigrants. Another source of confusion is that the class entitled "commerce, finance, insurance and professions" included gentlemen in the original published data on which Carrier and Jeffery's percentages are based. The inclusion of more and more gentlemen travelers in the original data distorted the picture to give the illusion of an increasing exodus of professionally trained people. The ship lists of the eighties recorded the arrival of 753 gentlemen in New York from England and Scotland, or 8 percent of the adult males. Omitting from the analysis these gentlemen, who may not have had the specialized training implied in the term "brain drain," gives a better indication of the migrant stream, as is evident in Table 3.6. The ship lists suggest only a slight increase in the proportion of professional people among the immigrants of the eighties as compared with the fifties; professional people were still markedly underrepresented among the people emigrating to the States. The increase in modern tertiary workers was accounted for mainly by clerical workers. It would seem that the American economy and society were no more attractive to specialized and trained tertiary workers in the eighties than to skilled secondary workers.

The appearance of so many commercial men and gentlemen in the data of the eighties is related to another feature of the emigration of that period. A higher proportion of the Britons who embarked for the United States in this decade were transient visitors who steamed across the Atlantic with no intention of remaining abroad. These data are not

[44] Frank Musgrove, *The Migratory Elite* (London: Macmillan, 1963), pp. 18–19.
[45] Carrier and Jeffery, *External Migration*, p. 102.

so complete, because some ship captains who gave other useful information failed to ask this question of their passengers. But of 503 passengers clearly marked as temporary visitors, 70 percent came from modern tertiary workers, commercial men and gentlemen accounting for most of them. Another 7 percent of the transients were building trades workers, and an equal number represented the modern sectors of industry, especially iron, steel, and engineering.

One other feature of the migration of the eighties highlights the changed character of emigration from England and Scotland in the eighties as compared with the fifties. Most of the migrants of the later decade went out as young men who were either unmarried or had left their families behind. On any single ship there was a complement of English and Scots women and children, but they were not legally attached to the men on the same ships. Most of them were undoubtedly going out to join husbands and fathers already in America. The sex ratios in published migration data that suggest that one Englishwoman emigrated to America for every two men in the 1880s are misleading in that they greatly underestimate the extent to which this was a movement of young unattached males rather than a family migration. On ships arriving in New York before 1854, single men outnumbered men traveling with families and dependents by less than two to one. In the eighties, the ratio was eight to one.

In conclusion, three points may be made. First, the similarities between the conclusions drawn from data from ship lists about English and Scots migrants of the eighties and those of Ingrid Semmingsen about the nature of Norwegian emigration in the last decades of the nineteenth century are striking. In this period, she wrote, "those who wanted to find open land and conformed to the old pattern of emigration turned North, to the prairie provinces of Canada; the rest, to a much larger extent than before, found work in various industries and trades in the towns—a particularly large number in the building trades." Among Norwegian migrants on the eve of World War I, "there was a growing proportion of men to women, of young people to older people and of single persons to married persons." By World War I "there was little left of the family character of Norwegian emigration."[46] Our data on the eighties suggest that most of these remarks

[46] Semmingsen, "Norwegian Emigration," pp. 157–58. Dirk Hoerder distinguished between settlement migration and labor migration to describe these changes ("International Labor Markets and Community Building by Migrant Workers in the

might have been made of English and Scottish emigrants. In only one respect do the findings differ. No significant trend towards younger males was evident in the eighties.[47]

As Richard Easterlin has pointed out, Norway and Britain were two regions of emigration in which the rate of population growth remained high—by European standards—as industrialization progressed.[48] In the conventional accounts of American immigration, both these groups ranked as "old immigration," and their character was contrasted with that of the newer immigrants from southern and eastern Europe from the nineties onward. The tentative conclusion to be drawn from this analysis of ship lists and from Semmingsen's study of the superior Norwegian records is that the character of the migration from England, Scotland, and Norway also changed as America became more industrialized and opportunities in agriculture waned. One can speak of an "old

---

Atlantic Economies," in *Century of European Migrations,* eds. Vecoli and Sinke, p. 79, and "The European and North American Working Classes during the Period of Industrialization" in *Labor Migration in the Atlantic Economies: The European and North American Working Classes during the Period of Industrialization,* ed. Dirk Hoerder [Westport, Conn.: Greenwood, Press, 1985], pp. 8–9). Hans Norman and Harald Runblom emphasized that when "gradual family emigration" is taken into account, however, bonds of family and kin continued to be important through the last part of the century ("Migration Patterns in Nordic Countries," in Hoerder, *Labor Migration,* pp. 51–52.)

[47] Unfortunately, I do not have the microfilms of the ship lists of 1846–54 with me in London to make possible a breakdown of all male emigrants from England and Scotland by age group so as to compare my findings with those of Ingrid Semmingsen. She found 30.6 percent of male emigrants in 1866–70 in the age group of fifteen to thirty years and 89 percent in 1911–15. In abstracts from the microfilms I took details just of males over the age of 15, so I can conclude only that there was no trend toward younger age groups as compared with the older. The inclusion of children would change the ratios.

Adult male passengers on New York ships (percent):

	15–30 years of age	Above 30 years
1841	60%	40%
1845–1849	65	35
1850–1854	78	22
1885	65	35
1886	67	33
1887	67	33
1888	71	29

Data from ships listed in Appendix, Table 3.10.

[48] Richard Easterlin, "Influences on European Overseas Emigration before World War I," *Economic Development and Cultural Change* 9 (1961): 334–35.

immigration" from England and Scotland before 1854 of farmers and skilled industrial workers, many of whom hoped to establish themselves on the land or in towns in developing regions.[49] Many of the migrants of the eighties were "new immigrants," like the migrants who were soon to start going to the United States in large numbers from Italy, Hungary, and elsewhere: young unattached males, without industrial skills.

The laborers from England and Scotland of the eighties clearly differed from the new immigrants from southern and eastern Europe in one respect: they came from the towns of Britain, not the countryside. One cannot judge from the data available whether these town laborers who left England and Scotland in the eighties had themselves recently come into towns from the countryside.[50] The available evidence indicates that by the eighties, general laborers from agricultural regions in Britain tended to go first not to American but to British towns, unlike the Italians a couple of decades later. The slump in building in many British towns from the late seventies onward may have been one of the factors dislodging marginal urban workers and causing them to be the most responsive group to the return of prosperity in America after 1879. They were departing from towns in England and did not remain in the 1880s to see whether they could find employment or opportunities that might enable them to marry and possibly even to demand houseroom. Thus their migration, beginning in the early eighties, may partly explain the quite extraordinary flow, both seasonal and permanent, of building trades workers from England and Scotland to the United States late in the decade.

[49] See the above essay, "Agrarian Myths of English Immigrants."

[50] In a bold attempt to measure the degree of stage migration, Dudley Baines estimated an upper limit of a quarter of all emigrants from urban areas as stage migrants in the years from 1861 to 1900 (*Migration in a Mature Economy,* pp. 253–68).

Appendix

Table 3.10. Ships arriving in New York whose English and Scottish adult male passengers were analyzed

Roll number	Ship number	Date	Number of English and Scottish males aged 15 or older
61	321	1846	54
71	328	1848	45
72	397	1848	37
77	63, 71, 156, 178	1849	54
78	237, 250, 403	1849	87
79	560, 636	1849	66
81	878	1849	115
82	1066	1849	28
83	1264, 1302, 1304	1849	79
86	52	1850	33
88	349	1850	41
101	854	1851	74
109	127	1852	11
135	24	1854	10
137	347	1854	19
144	1032	1854	7
145	1275	1854	64
146	1365	1854	14
All adult males, 1846–1854			838
483	42, 50, 65, 66, 72, 78, 88, 89, 97,110, 111, 120, 127, 133, 166, 169 178, 180, 187, 200, 209, 221, 234, 236, 237, 247, 273, 282	1885	1,253
484	296, 319, 327, 336, 339, 369, 370, 374, 383, 396, 405	1885	767
493	269, 273, 286, 290, 304, 306, 322, 324, 330, 337, 343, 349, 360, 364, 374, 378, 379, 396, 397, 413, 415,	1886	1,760
494	426, 434, 455, 456, 460, 477, 485, 487, 491, 502, 507, 526, 530, 542, 543	1886	1,570
503	10, 13, 23, 38, 42, 48, 60, 62, 66, 75, 89, 94, 102, 108, 113, 130, 139, 150, 153, 153a, 166, 170, 177, 179a,193, 197, 204	1887	1,359
504	214, 217, 237, 243, 255, 265, 285, 319, 375	1887	1,344
516	196, 214, 230, 239, 242, 257, 258,279, 288, 292, 302, 312, 319, 334,350, 354, 357	1888	2,021
All adult males, 1885–1888			10,074

Source: National Archives, Microfilm Series 237.

Table 3.11. English and Scottish counties by share of labor force in agriculture, and average weekly earnings in agriculture for English counties

1851	Percent of male labor force in agriculture	Average weekly wages in agriculture
England		
1. LOW-WAGE AGRICULTURAL COUNTIES		
Bedfordshire	52	9s.
Berkshire	47	7s. 6d.
Buckinghamshire	50	8s. 6d.
Cambridgeshire	53	7s. 6d.
Devonshire	39	8s. 6d.
Dorset	44	7s. 6d.
Essex	50	8s.
Hampshire	34	9s.
Herefordshire	55	8s. 5d.
Hertfordshire	49	7s. 6d.
Huntingdonshire	56	8s. 6d.
Norfolk	45	8s. 6d.
Northamptonshire	44	9s.
Oxfordshire	48	9s.
Rutland	52	not returned
Shropshire	43	7s. 3d.
Somerset	38	8s. 7d.
Suffolk	52	7s.
Surrey (ex-metropolitan)	41	9s. 6d.
Wiltshire	50	7s. 3d.
2. HIGH-WAGE AGRICULTURAL COUNTIES		
Cumberland	34	13s.
Kent	37	11s. 6d.
Lincolnshire	52	10s.
Sussex	43	11s.
Westmorland	46	not returned
(North Riding, Yorkshire, omitted)	48	11s.
3. LOW-WAGE INDUSTRIAL COUNTIES		
Cornwall	31	8s. 8d.
Gloucestershire	28	7s.
Leicestershire	30	9s. 6d.
Warwickshire	19	8s. 6d.
Worcestershire	26	7s. 8d.
4. HIGH-WAGE INDUSTRIAL COUNTIES		
Cheshire	25	12s.
Derbyshire	23	11s.
Durham	13	11s.
Lancashire	10	13s. 6d.
London	2	13s. 6d.
Middlesex (ex-metropolitan)	29	11s.
Northumberland	22	11s.

Table 3.11. continued

1851	Percent of male labor force in agriculture	Average weekly wages in agriculture
4. High-wage industrial counties (continued)		
Nottinghamshire	27	10s.
(East Riding, Yorkshire, omitted)	32	12s.
(West Riding, Yorkshire, omitted)	14	14s.

1881	Percent of male labor force in agriculture	Average weekly wages in agriculture
1. Agricultural counties		
Bedfordshire	40	12s. 6d.
Berkshire	33	12s. 3d.
Buckinghamshire	36	12s. 9d.
Cambridgeshire	47	13s. 6d.
Dorset	35	10s. 9d.
Herefordshire	45	11s. 9d.
Hertfordshire	35	13s. 9d.
Huntingdonshire	51	12s. 6d.
Lincolnshire	40	13s. 6d.–15s.
Norfolk	38	12s. 6d.
Oxfordshire	39	12s. 9d.
Rutland	48	not returned
Shropshire	33	13s. 3d.
Suffolk	42	12s. 6d.
Westmorland	36	18s.
Wiltshire	38	11s. 9d.
2. Low-wage industrial counties		
Cheshire	15	12s. 6d.
Cornwall	29	13s. 9d.
Devon	27	13s.
Essex	28	12s. 6d.
Gloucester	19	13s. 3d.
Hampshire	21	12s.
Leicestershire	18	13s.
Northamptonshire	28	13s. 6d.
Nottinghamshire	15	14s.
Somerset	29	12s. 6d.
Staffordshire	8	14s. 6d.
Sussex	28	13s. 6d.
Warwick	11	14s. 3d.
Worcester	18	13s.
3. High-wage industrial counties		
Cumberland	22	18s.
Derby	13	16s. 6d.
Durham	5	17s. 9d.
Lancashire	11	17s. 6d.
Kent	24	15s. 9d.
London	1	—

Table 3.11. continued

1851	Percent of male labor force in agriculture	Average weekly wages in agriculture
3. HIGH-WAGE INDUSTRIAL COUNTIES (CONTINUED)		
Middlesex	9	15s. 6d.
Northumberland	11	17s.
Surrey	17	15s. 6d.
East Riding, Yorkshire	20	15s.
North Riding, Yorkshire	25	16s. 6d.
West Riding, Yorkshire	8	16s. 6d.

Scotland

1881 Agricultural counties	Percent of male labor force in agriculture	1881 Industrial counties	Percent of male labor force in agriculture
Aberdeenshire	33	Ayrshire	13
Argyllshire	35	Bute	26
Banffshire	42	Clackmannan	7
Berwickshire	43	Dumfriesshire	31
Caithness	36	Dunbartonshire	8
Elgin	35	Edinburgh	4
Haddington	36	Fifeshire	15
Inverness-shire	39	Forfar	12
Kincardine	44	Lanarkshire	3
Kinross-shire	35	Linlithgow	12
Kirkcudbright	37	Peeblesshire	31
Nairnshire	36	Perthshire	29
Orkney and Shetland	56	Renfrewshire	5
Ross and Cromarty	41	Roxburghshire	30
Sutherland	43	Selkirkshire	12
Wigtownshire	44	Stirlingshire	11

Sources: See Table 3.5.

Table 3.12. Classification of male occupations

Major occupations included in each class:
AGRICULTURAL WORKERS
A. Farmers, graziers, bailiffs, working relatives of farmers
B. Agricultural laborers, shepherds, woodsmen, gardeners
LABORERS
All laborers other than agricultural
SERVANTS, ETC.: *Tertiary preindustrial occupations*
Domestic servants, soldiers and seamen, messengers, police, workers on roads and waterways, gamekeepers, grooms, fishermen, chimney sweeps, crossing sweepers, scavengers
CRAFTSMEN: *Preindustrial (relatively unchanging) skilled occupations*
Building trades: bricklayers, carpenters, masons, painters, thatchers, plasterers, plumbers, slaters, brickmakers
Mining: all kinds of miners and quarrymen
Food trades: bakers, grocers, butchers, confectioners, millers, brewers, maltsters
Metal trades: blacksmiths; whitesmiths; lead, copper, and zinc manufacturers; tinsmiths, goldsmiths
Clothing trades: glovers, hatters, milliners, tailors, shoemakers
Woodworking trades: cabinetmakers, coopers, sawyers, wheelwrights, wood-carvers
Miscellaneous: curriers; saddlers; tanners; soapmakers; tallow chandlers; makers of willow, cane, and rush; carvers; brush makers
Mechanics not otherwise designated
INDUSTRIAL WORKERS: *Industrial (new and changing) skilled and semi-skilled occupations*
Textiles: Woolen, silk, cotton, linen, hemp, and jute workers of all kinds and finishers; hosiery manufacturers, including framework knitters and lacemakers
Iron, steel, and engineering: toolmakers, engineers, coach and railway carriage makers, shipbuilders, gunsmith and ordnance makers, cutlers, tin manufacturers, watchmakers and instrumentmakers
Miscellaneous: printers, chemical workers, cement manufacturers, earthenware and glass manufacturers, gasworkers, papermakers, machinists and machine workers, toy- and gamemakers, oil- and colormen, bookbinders and publishers
MODERN TERTIARY WORKERS : *Tertiary industrial occupations*
Railway workers: railway drivers, pointsmen, platelayers, guards, engine drivers, stokers
Clerical workers: civil servants, telegraph and telephone workers, railway officials and servants, warehousemen, commercial clerks
Commercial workers: all merchants and dealers distinguished only as such, contractors, and keepers of inns, lodging houses, and coffeehouses
Professionals: accountants, army and navy officers, musicians, artists, teachers, and veterinary surgeons in addition to the learned professions distinguished as such; gentlemen, not otherwise distinguished; students

Table 3.13. Occupations of British and Irish male passengers leaving the United Kingdom for the United States, 1878–1897 (percent)

	1878	1882	1888	1897
Farmers	9.7	4.7	5.6	5.4
Farm laborers	0.5	0.4	20.1	14.6
All agricultural workers	10.2	5.1	25.7	20.0
Laborers	43.3	68.8	39.6	35.7
Servants, etc.	0.8	0.3	0.8	2.0
Building trades	4.6	2.7	5.3	3.1
Mining	3.7	3.4	4.0	3.0
Other crafts	2.0	1.3	2.4	2.2
Mechanics not otherwise designated	9.3	5.4	10.4	11.5
All craftsmen	19.6	12.8	22.1	19.8
Textiles	0.0	0.4	0.6	2.0
Iron, steel, engineering and other	0.9	0.4	1.3	1.4
All industrial workers	0.9	0.8	1.9	3.4
Modern tertiary workers	25.2	12.2	9.9	19.0
All occupations	100.0	100.0	100.0	99.9
Number stating occupation	20,669	75,736	81,470	29,072

Sources: See Table 3.9.

Table 3.14. Occupations of male and female English and Scottish passengers arriving in the United States, 1878–1897 (percent)

	1878	1882	1888	1897
Farmers	12.6	7.9	5.9	5.9
Farm laborers	2.7	0.6	0.8	1.7
All agricultural workers	15.3	8.5	6.6	7.6
Laborers	26.7	47.1	35.1	14.0
Servants, etc.[a]	9.3	7.1	11.0	19.2
Building trades	5.9	5.2	10.2	6.1
Mining	7.6	7.8	7.8	10.2
Food trades	2.2	1.8	2.0	4.8
Metal trades	1.4	1.1	2.0	1.7
Clothing trades	2.9	1.5	2.2	5.1
Woodworking trades	0.3	0.3	0.6	0.6
Miscellaneous	0.4	0.3	0.5	0.4
Mechanics not otherwise designated	1.7	4.3	4.1	1.5
All craft workers	22.6	22.3	29.2	30.4
Textiles	2.6	2.5	2.7	9.5
Iron, steel, engineering	5.4	3.2	4.7	6.0
Miscellaneous	1.0	0.7	1.0	1.0
All industrial workers	9.0	6.3	8.4	16.6
Railway workers	0.1	0.1	0.4	—
Clerical workers	4.7	2.5	3.1	5.8
Commercial workers	9.1	4.3	3.8	3.4
Professionals	2.9	1.6	2.3	3.0
Gentlemen	0.2	0.2	—	—
Modern tertiary workers	17.1	8.8	9.7	12.2
All occupations	100.0	101.0	100.0	100.0
Number stating occupation	10,117	47,851	54,269	5,977
Errors	—	—	10	6

Sources: United States Department of the Treasury, Bureau of Statistics, *Annual Report on the Commerce and Navigation of The United States for The Fiscal Year Ended June 30, 1878*, Pt. 2 (Washington, 1879), pp. 752–91; 1882 (Washington, 1883), pp. 698–725; 1888 (Washington, 1888), pp. 744–95; 1887, pp. 25–31.

[a] Eighty-five percent of the English- and Scotswomen identified by occupation in ship lists, 1885–88, were servants. This fact explains the very much higher share of preindustrial tertiary workers in the published statistics, which did not distinguish females from males by occupation during these years.

Table 3.15. Occupational distribution of British immigrants to the United States according to United Kingdom and United States official records and selected ship lists, 1885–1888 (percent)

Occupations	United Kingdom records (Irish included)	United States records (women included)	Ship lists (British males only
Farmers	5.9	6.2	8.4
Farm laborers	16.3	0.6	1.1
All agricultural workers	22.2	6.8	9.5
Laborers	42.6	38.9	29.5
Servants, etc.	0.8	11.1	3.1
Building trades	5.1	8.2	18.1
Mining	4.9	6.8	8.0
Food trades	2.1 (Food, metal, clothing, woodworking trades, and miscellaneous combined)	1.9	2.1
Metal trades		1.4	1.7
Clothing trades		2.1	1.5
Woodworking trades		0.5	0.5
Miscellaneous		0.3	0.9
Mechanics not otherwise designated	9.1	3.4	1.5
All craftworkers	21.2	24.8	34.3
Textiles	0.6	2.9	2.0
Iron, steel, and engineering	1.6	4.2	4.0
Miscellaneous	—	1.0	1.8
All industrial workers	2.2	8.1	7.8
Railway workers	—	0.3	0.1
Clerical workers	2.5	3.7	5.6
Commercial workers	1.2	4.3	8.0
Professionals[a]	7.2	2.1	1.9
All modern tertiary workers	10.9	10.3	15.7
All occupations	99.9	100.0	99.9
Number stating occupation	281,514	163,098	8,698
Omissions, errors		17	1,385

[a] Includes gentlemen.

Sources: United States Department of the Treasury, Bureau of Statistics, *Annual Report on Foreign Commerce and Navigation for the Fiscal Year Ended June 30, 1885* (Washington, 1885), pp. 726–49; *1886* (Washington, 1887), pp. 720–41; *1887* (Washington, 1887), pp. 735–55; and *1888* (Washington, 1888), pp. 744 –97; see also Table 3.8.

CHAPTER FOUR

Emigration from the British Isles to the United States of America in 1831

Two scholars who pioneered the quantitative analysis of the timing of the great European migrations of the nineteenth century were Harry Jerome, in 1926, and Brinley Thomas, a generation later.[1] Although it has used increasingly sophisticated models, most of the work subsequent to these pioneering studies has been concerned with the era since 1870, when much-improved statistics of migration and economic indicators become available. Studying differently timed cycles of economic activity, Jerome and Thomas both found the American pull to have been significant in the timing of the movement into the United States after the Civil War. Perhaps because indicators of the business cycles or the longer-swing building cycle were not so relevant when land was the chief attraction to emigrants, they could not establish such a relationship in the period before 1860 or 1870.

Their work left both the timing and the causation of the emigration of the first part of the century up in the air. The great scholar of the Atlantic migration of these years, Marcus Hansen, who was not overly

I thank the California Institute of Technology for the opportunity to undertake the research on which this article is based while I was a Sherman Fairchild Scholar in 1976–77. I am also grateful to David Erickson Watt for unpaid research assistance on ship lists and the New Orleans data. The article was completed with the help of a grant from the Social Science Research Council (SSRC) and with the careful and cheerful help of Nick Tiratsoo as research assistant.

[1] Harry Jerome, *Migration and the Business Cycle* (New York: National Bureau of Economic Research, 1926); Brinley Thomas, *Migration and Economic Growth* (Cambridge: Cambridge University Press, 1954).

concerned with systematic quantification, assumed throughout that European conditions were uppermost in explaining the movement.[2] No one would deny that the potato famine increased the volume of emigration from Ireland and Germany during the late 1840s. We know much less about the secularly rising emigration from Britain and Ireland before those years because the statistical record is meager and probably inaccurate. Hansen paid remarkably little attention to the English emigration of these years. Yet there is obviously a great inherent interest in the question of who was leaving—and in what numbers—from the world's first industrial nation. Until we have a clearer picture of the groups who were emigrating in comparison with the population from which they selected themselves, statements about push and pull or long- and short-term causes of the movement must remain largely conjectural.

In this essay I explore what can be learned from the original passenger manifests submitted in the various American ports of immigration as required by the Passenger Act of 1819 about British and Irish, but especially English, immigrants to the United States. Having used such lists to describe the English and Scots immigrants of the late 1880s, I have been examining their usefulness in this earlier period.

Passenger lists from the years 1885–88 revealed that the migrants of that peak decade for English and Scottish emigration to the United States were not in the main either unemployed industrial workers or displaced farm laborers as was once thought. Building trades workers, miners, and unskilled laborers were overrepresented in comparison with the labor force at work in Britain.[3] Four out of five of the immigrants to the United States from Britain gave a principal town of twenty thousand or more inhabitants as place of last residence, and the proportion among laborers was slightly higher. Adult men among the English emigrants to the United States traveled without family, frequently as seasonal or temporary migrants.

These features of British emigration during the late nineteenth century are similar to those which students of Scandinavian and

[2] Marcus Lee Hansen, *The Atlantic Migration* (Cambridge: Harvard University Press, 1940).

[3] Maldwyn Jones has questioned the finding from the ship lists that laborers made up a significant portion of English emigrants to the United States. He based his doubts on reports from American consuls living in Britain as to the characteristics of emigrants ("The Background to Emigration from Great Britain in the Nineteenth Century," *Perspectives in American History* 7 (1973): 69–71.

German emigration have discovered for that period. By the First World War the Norwegian migration was no longer a family migration.[4] Swedish scholars have found that emigrants came increasingly from urban and industrial areas, though emigrants from Stockholm in the 1880s often had left the countryside some years earlier.[5] Emigration in stages—first to a town or city and then overseas—appears to have become increasingly common in the migration from both Sweden and Norway.

Continental writers have been able to demonstrate quite conclusively that the character of German and Scandinavian emigration changed over time. This change has been depicted as "labor migration" following on a "folk migration" in the earlier part of the century: a change from a migration of families to one of young, unattached adults.[6] The Dutch migration, at least as late as the 1870s, did not conform to this pattern. According to Robert Swierenga's comprehensive results from passenger lists, Dutch emigration became even more markedly a family movement over time.[7] These writers are inclined to interpret a mass migration of whole families as a consequence of serious social or economic stresses and strains in the society the migrants leave.

So far we have no firm evidence as to whether the English emigration began as a family and rural movement during the first half of the nineteenth century and changed over time—in common with other migrating peoples from northern Europe—as transport improved and opportunities for industrial work expanded in America or, alternatively, changed as stresses postulated to have induced whole families to emigrate overseas diminished.

There are other related questions about the emigration from England in this period. Because of the dearth of statistical information about who the migrants were and where they came from, even about the absolute size of the movement (we are not so much in the dark as to its fluctuations), historians have produced conflicting interpretations

[4] Ingrid Semmingsen, "Norwegian Emigration in the Nineteenth Century," *Scandinavian Economic History Review* 8 (1960): 158.

[5] Fred Nilsson, *Emigrationen från Stockholm till Nordamerika, 1880–1893: En Studie i Urban Utvandring* (Stockholm: Studia Historica Upsaliensia, 1970), p. 75; Wolfgang Köllman and Peter Marschalk, "German Emigration to the United States," *Perspectives in American History* 7 (1973): 531–53.

[6] Harald Runblom and Hans Norman, eds., *From Sweden to America: A History of the Migration* (Minneapolis: University of Minnesota Press, 1976), p. 132. Köllman and Marschalk, "German Emigration," pp. 525–29.

[7] Robert Swierenga, "Dutch Immigrant Demography, 1820–1880," *Journal of Family History* 5 (1980): 396–401.

based on quotations from contemporary sources such as parliamentary Blue Books and newspapers.

Some have seen the emigration of this period as an exodus of industrial workers suffering from technological or cyclical unemployment or low wages. Of all the examples that might be cited, it is enough to mention Rowland Berthoff's conclusion that British emigration to the United States was primarily industrial from the late 1820s onward. The movement of labor out of agriculture, even before the American Civil War, he maintained, was directed either to the Empire or to mines and factories in Britain.[8]

Perhaps more writers have viewed the emigrants of this period as drawn chiefly from rural areas and agricultural occupations. In his classic study of internal migration movements, Arthur Redford maintained that industrial workers were not tempted abroad because of the rudimentary state of industry there: emigration, he believed, was most attractive to agricultural laborers.[9] Similar views were expressed by Wilbur Shepperson, who wrote that "considering the perplexing urban discontent [1815–50] it is somewhat surprising to find that rural departures generally exceeded . . . metropolitan" and that "farmer withdrawals . . . exceeded those of any other class of agriculturists."[10]

Others have hedged their bets. Helen Cowan depicted emigration to British North America in these years as both urban and rural, industrial and agricultural. More recently, Maldwyn Jones has suggested that rural emigration was continuous and constant. When cyclical peaks in emigration occurred, these rural migrants were being joined not by rural crafts workers but by skilled workers from the manufacturing cities who were victims of cyclical unemployment. Except in periods of extreme industrial depression, he asserted, a majority of English emigrants during the first half of the nineteenth century were drawn from rural rather than urban areas. After contemplating the solitary

[8] Rowland Berthoff, *British Immigrants in Industrial America, 1790–1950* (Cambridge: Harvard University Press, 1953), pp. 117, 118. See also William A. Carrothers, *Emigration from the British Isles* (London: P. S. King, 1929), pp. 79, 181; Stanley Johnson, *A History of Emigration from the United Kingdom to North America, 1763–1912* (London: George Routledge and Sons, 1913), pp. 39–59; Imre Ferenczi and Walter Willcox, eds., *International Migrations* (New York: National Bureau of Economic Research, 1932), 2: 251–52.

[9] Arthur Redford, *Labour Migration in England, 1800–1850,* 2d ed. (Manchester: Manchester University Press, 1964), pp. 106–110.

[10] Wilbur Shepperson, *British Emigration to North America: Projects and Opinions in the Early Victorian Period* (Oxford: Basil Blackwell, 1957), pp. 5, 28, 32, 67–68.

emigration census of the century, which was taken during the first five months of 1841, Jones hazarded the implicit quantification that industrial emigrants "could not have" accounted for more than a bare majority.[11]

Equally contradictory and confusing are the speculations of historians as to which end of the economic and social spectrum within these sectors produced most emigrants. Even leaving aside the emigrants assisted to go to the colonies by poor law authorities, landowners, or colonial bounties, we find no agreement as to who the self-financing migrants were. It is a hardy tradition of immigrant historiography to cite groups in the population with particular problems and to infer that these were the emigrants. So the handloom weavers and the framework knitters are almost invariably mentioned in discussions of emigration in this period. The background to rural emigration is sketched by reference to enclosures, to displacement of rural populations, to agricultural depression and the unprofitability of stiff clay lands in the face of falling prices after the Napoleonic Wars. The links between these problem groups and emigrants are often tenuous, episodic, or impressionistic. Jones quoted a businessman who traveled between Liverpool and New York in 1829 to the effect that the majority of steerage passengers were poor farm laborers and their families. According to Berthoff, America did not draw emigrants so much in this period as Britain forced them to flee. And so on.

Maldwyn Jones took account of recent scholarship on handloom weavers and enclosures. In his view, handloom weavers did not have the means to emigrate because of their distressed circumstances. The movement from agriculture consisted of small farmers and the better class of laborers in husbandry, not the poor rural and agricultural laborers.[12] Consistent with this view is the writing about Lancashire labor of John D. Marshall, who pointed to education and the spur of ambition as operating on young people to induce them to migrate.[13] In contrast, Barbara Kerr depicted the Dorset farm laborer as uneducated, as considering migration "fearful" and regard-

[11] Helen Cowan, *British Emigration to British North America,* rev. ed. (Toronto: University of Toronto Press, 1961), pp. 29–30, 172–74; Maldwyn Jones, "Background to Emigration," pp. 45–46.

[12] Maldwyn Jones, "Background to Emigration," pp. 7, 9, 38, 43.

[13] John D. Marshall, "Some Aspects of the Social History of 19th Century Cumbria: Migration and Literacy," *Transactions of the Cumberland and Westmorland Antiquarian and Archeological Society* 69 (1969): 294.

ing assisted migration as "an intolerable persecution of the unfortunate."[14]

The field for speculation seems infinite. I can by no means dispel the uncertainties about the role of emigration during these decades of industrialization, urbanization, and unrest from the 1820s to the 1840s. My aims are more modest: to illustrate the ways in which passenger lists may help with some of these questions.

Because there was no way of sampling this vast body of material before more work had been done on it, I chose the year 1831 for a preliminary investigation.[15] One reason I did so was that the census taken in Britain in 1831 made some comparisons possible. No single year can be taken as representative, however. Emigration fluctuated from year to year in numbers and destination, as we know; and there is no reason to believe that the composition of the emigrating population with respect to age, sex, occupation, and nationality did not also change, if less remarkably, from year to year. To make any sense of this experiment, one must take at least a brief look at the English background.

The year 1831 witnessed a rise in emigration from the British Isles, an upward swing that had begun in 1829 and peaked in 1832 (see Table 4.1). Contemporary accounts suggested that the rural and agrarian element

[14] Barbara Kerr, "The Dorset Agricultural Labourer, 1750–1850," *Proceedings of the Dorset Natural History and Archeological Society* 84 (1962): 175; Edward Hunt, *Regional Wage Variations in Britain, 1850–1914* (Oxford: Clarendon Press, 1973), pp. 252–54.

[15] The very large numbers of British and Irish immigrants seemed to call for sampling. The quality of the lists was not established when I began my work, so all lists at one period of time had to be examined because I could not be certain of continuity or completeness. As it turned out, the 1831 lists lacked two months of New York arrivals. The quality of the lists varies from month to month, from year to year, and from vessel to vessel. One cannot sample within ships because households are not delineated as they are in the census, and to take individuals would mean to forgo the unique picture of migrating units that the lists reveal when examined in detail. For my work on the 1841 lists, which appeared to be complete, I sampled every fifth ship. When a five-month sample, such as was used for New York City in 1831, was compared with the sample of one in every five ships, variations were remarkably small. The greatest differences arose from the fact that a seasonal peak of Irish immigration occurred in May, a month that had to be excluded from the 1831 study because the records were missing. In 1841, the Irish were found to have been underrepresented by about 2 percent of the total British and Irish immigration in a sample based on the same five months that formed the basis of this study of 1831. For a fuller comparison of these samples, see Charlotte Erickson, "The Uses of Passenger Lists for the Study of British and Irish Emigration," in *Migration across Time and Nations: Population Mobility in Historical Contexts,* ed. Ira Glazier and Luigi de Rosa (New York: Holmes and Meier, 1986), pp. 318–35. On the use of passenger lists, see also Robert Swierenga, "List upon List: The Ship Passenger Records and Immigration Research," *Journal of American Ethnic History* 10 (1991): 42–53.

Table 4.1. Outward movement from the British Isles to the United States and Canada, 1827–1832

Year	To United States			To British North America			Total
	England and Wales	Scotland	Ireland	England and Wales	Scotland	Ireland	
1827	9,291	1,221	4,014	1,306	2,208	9,134	27,174
1828	8,855	1,085	2,877	1,468	3,921	6,695	24,901
1829	10,764	781	4,133	2,564	3,033	7,710	28,985
1830	20,260	1,646	2,981	6,992	4,242	19,340	55,461
1831	18,263	1,572	3,583	9,860	7,230	40,977	81,485
1832	26,433	2,267	4,172	20,554	8,717	37,068	99,211
1833	22,392	1,953	4,764	5,785	5,952	17,431	58,277
Total	116,258	10,525	26,524	48,529	35,303	138,355	375,494

Source: These figures are adapted from those in N. H. Carrier and J. R. Jeffery, *External Migration: A Study of the Available Statistics, 1815–1950,* General Register Office, Studies on Medical and Population Subjects, no. 6 (London: HMSO, 1953), p. 95.

Note: These figures represent passengers departing from ports in the respective parts of the British Isles, not the nationality of passengers. The total outward movement to Australia during these years was only 10,323. These official counts are generally considered to have underestimated the migration because ships carrying fewer than twenty passengers were not included and some ships are thought to have carried more passengers than was permitted under the Passenger Acts. On the other hand, returning migrants and visitors are included, which would tend to swell the number of emigrants.

in the outward movement of this year was particularly large, especially in comparison with the previous peak in 1827. This hypothesis is strengthened by the recorded increased importance of ports other than Liverpool in the emigration of the early 1830s.[16]

From the standpoint of short-term influences, the year 1831 was not one in which pressure for agriculturists to emigrate because of adverse economic circumstances was intense. The years 1827–32 were generally favorable for farmers, with prices exceptionally high in 1830 and 1831, turning downward only in 1832. The farmers on arable land were better off between 1829 and 1831 than at any time since the Napoleonic Wars. Nevertheless, the bad harvests that forced up wheat prices may have been difficult for farmers on poorer soils, especially those on the stiff clay lands. The year 1831 also saw a slight upward pressure on farm laborers' wages. If the Swing Riots of 1830 to some extent account for this increase, they also reflected a fear among farm workers that mechanization might be sought as a means of raising productivity while reducing agricultural employment.[17] Thus, in 1831, farmers and farm laborers who may have emigrated were probably influenced more by long-term than short-term considerations.

In contrast, industrial workers in both modernizing and traditional sectors may be said to have experienced a short-term push to emigration in this year. The years 1827–32 have been depicted as a period of "stagnant stability," with a slight downward drift of some wages, though not those of cotton factory workers. The fall in prices may have kept real wages constant or rising slightly for most industrial workers through the cycle. The most depressed year of the period was 1829. An upturn in 1830 was followed by a minor slump in 1831–32 in cotton, iron, and coal mining associated at least in part with the reform agitation of those years. High food prices made 1831 a relatively poor year in the movement of real wages and also brought some unemployment. One can postulate some short-term push to industrial emigration during this unsettled period. For manufacturers, the period 1827–32 has been

[16] See below, p. 159.

[17] Eric Hobsbawm and George Rudé, *Captain Swing* (London: Lawrence and Wishart, 1969), pp. 74–75, 233–36. For data on economic indicators in particular years, see Arthur D. Gayer, Walter W. Rostow, and Anna J. Schwartz, *The Growth and Fluctuation of the British Economy,* 1790–1850 (Oxford: Clarendon Press, 1953), 1: 234, 239. The miserable plight of the laboring population in arable parts of southern and eastern England has been discussed in detail by many writers and must be considered to have been in theory a sufficient cause for emigration. See, for example, Eric Jones, *Agriculture and the Industrial Revolution* (Oxford: Basil Blackwell, 1974), pp. 215–17, and W. Alan Armstrong, *Farm Workers: A Social and Economic History, 1770–1880* (London: Batsford, 1988), pp. 62–63.

described as "extremely difficult," with bankruptcies exceptionally high in 1831.[18] Thus, if short-term factors in the English economy were of significance in the outward movement, one would expect the overrepresentation of industrial workers, which Maldwyn Jones suggested for years of rising emigration, to appear in 1831.

The following description of the emigrants of 1831 is based on a sample of five months for the port of New York. Details on immigrants during the entire year were taken for the other most important immigrant-receiving ports—Boston, Philadelphia, and New Orleans—although, when appropriate, data from only five months were used.[19] The vast majority of British and Irish immigrants who entered the United States by way of its Atlantic and Gulf ports arrived in those included in the study. The sample of 9,629 British and Irish immigrants covers about 60 percent of the recorded inward movement to the United States from the British Isles. Many others, as is well known, crossed the border from Canada unrecorded.[20] A few lists provided additional details about place of last residence in addition to occupation, nationality, sex, and age, which were normally given. These "good lists" drawn from the years 1827 to 1832 constitute a smaller sample of 1,275 English immigrants, which must be used with even greater care because the number is so small.

These passenger lists make abundantly clear what has long been suspected: that United States officials, whether from indolence or overwork, did not include in their published statistics all the immigrants for whose arrival they had documentary evidence. Taking only five months of arrivals yields a larger number of immigrants from the British Isles than were recorded for the entire year ending September 30, 1831 (see Table 4.2).

Of even greater interest than this undercount is the fact that the original documents point to a much higher proportion of English

[18] This paragraph is based largely on data in Gayer, Rostow, and Schwartz, *British Economy,* 1: 211, 222, 225, 228, 232.

[19] The months of March, June, July, September, and October were used. Figures for May and August were missing entirely. The lists for the port of Baltimore for 1830 and 1831 are missing. Passenger vessels arriving in Baltimore during the mid-1830s came principally from Amsterdam, Bremen, and Le Havre, not from British ports, thus verifying contemporary comment about the predominance of Germans among immigrants landing at Baltimore (National Archives, microfilm, no. 255, roll 1; *Niles Weekly Register,* August 9, 1834, p. 398, October 4, 1834, p. 67, and August 21, 1839, p. 14). See also Hansen, *Atlantic Migration,* p. 258.

[20] Of the total number of passengers recorded as arriving during the year ending September 30, 1831 (22,633), only 1,016, or 4.5 percent, came in by way of a port other than New York, Boston, Philadelphia, New Orleans, or Baltimore.

Table 4.2. Immigrant arrivals by nationality, 1831

Nationality	Ship lists[a]		United States passenger arrivals[b]		United Kingdom passengers to United States		United Kingdom passengers to all places	
	No.	Percent	No.	Percent	No.	Percent	No.	Percent
English and Welsh	6,229	64.7	2,475	30.0	18,263	78.0	11,779	17.3
Scots	589	6.1	n.a.	n.a.	1,572	6.7	7,637	11.2
Irish	2,811	29.2	5,772	70.0	3,583	15.3	48,573	71.4
Total	9,629	100.0	8,247	100.0	23,418	100.0	67,989	99.9

Sources: Ship lists (National Archives, microfilm, No. 237, rolls 14, 15, no. 425, roll 46, and no. 277, roll 5, no. 259, rolls 9, 10). United States Bureau of the Census, *Historical Statistics of the United States: Colonial Times to 1970*, bicentennial ed. (Washington, 1975), pt. 1, p. 106; N. H. Carrier and J. R. Jeffery, *External Migration: A Study of the Available Statistics, 1815–1950*, General Register Office, Studies on Medical and Population Subjects, no. 6 (London: HMSO, 1953), p. 95.

[a]Five months only (March, June, July, September, and October) for arrivals at New York, Boston, Philadelphia, and New Orleans.

[b]For the year ending September 30, 1831.

immigrants among the arrivals from the British Isles than official clerks reported.[21] Historians have long assumed that, at least by the late 1820s, the majority of immigrants arriving from Liverpool were Irish.[22] As can be seen in Table 4.3, the sample gave an estimate of only 20 percent of the passengers arriving from ports in England and Wales as having been Irish. An estimate based on twelve good lists of Liverpool ships arriving in 1826 and 1827 yielded a figure of 16 percent Irish passengers.[23] How the American authorities hit upon a figure of exactly 70 percent of the immigrants from the British Isles in 1831 as originating in Ireland remains a mystery.

These lists from American ports tell us about that portion of emigrants from the British Isles who went directly to the United States. According to British records of passenger departures, only 28 percent of those leaving during 1831 gave the United States as their destination. Fifty-eight thousand were bound for British North America (see Table 4.4). Most of these appear to have been the poorer emigrants departing from Scottish and Irish ports, frequently on timber ships. The British authorities recorded only 8 percent of the passengers from Irish ports and 18 percent of those from Scottish ports as destined for the United States. Even among the minority of Irish emigrants who did sail on ships bound for the United States, a smaller share than among the English and Scottish entered by way of New York. At least in 1831, the Irish showed a greater

[21] According to William J. Bromwell of the State Department, only 382 of 8,247 immigrants arriving from the British Isles in 1831 were English and Welsh (*History of Immigration to the United States* [New York: Redfield, 1856], pp. 65–68). The British demographers N. H. Carrier and J. R. Jefferey prorated the huge class "Great Britain and Ireland not distinguished" to estimate 494 English and Welsh immigrants for that year (*External Migration: A Study of the Available Statistics, 1815–1950,* General Register Office, Studies on Medical and Population Subjects, no. 6 [London: HMSO, 1953], p. 94). The figure of 2,475 given in the most recent edition of *Historical Statistics of the United States* (U.S. Department of Commerce, Bureau of the Census [Washington: 900, 1975], p. 106) comes out suspiciously at exactly 30 percent of the recorded immigration from Britain and Ireland. On the shortfall in recording Dutch immigrants to the United States, see Robert Swierenga, "Dutch International Migration Statistics, 1820–1860: An Analysis of Linked Multinational Nominal Files," *International Migration Review* 115 (1981): 445–70.

[22] Marcus Hansen thought that from at least 1832 onward, nine-tenths of the emigrants from Liverpool were Irish; and Maldwyn Jones accepted a statement made in the late 1850s that the majority of passengers from Liverpool were Irish by the late twenties, rising to two-thirds or five-sixths by the thirties (Hansen, *Atlantic Migration,* p. 183; Jones, "Background to Emigration," p. 26).

[23] Some inferences were made about nationality from distinctive surnames on the ship lists, though most passengers were identified by nationality. For a fuller discussion of the methods used, see my final report on the SSRC project, "Estimates of the Social Composition of British Emigrants to the U.S.A., 1831 and 1841," available from the British National Lending Library, Boston Spa.

Table 4.3. Estimates of Irish among passengers from English and Welsh ports, 1831

Port of arrival	Arrivals from English and Welsh ports	Estimated number of Irish on board	Percent Irish
New York City	5,753	831	14
Boston	117	37	32
Philadelphia	766	337	44
New Orleans	270	195	72
Total	6,906	1,400	20

Source: 1831 ship lists (see Table 4.2).

preference for the all-water route to the interior via New Orleans than did the English. Among the small number of Irish entering by way of Boston, most had gone first to Nova Scotia or New Brunswick and then taken another ship down the coast (see Table 4.5). Not until 1848 and 1850 did a majority of passengers from Scottish and Irish ports go first to the United States.

In contrast to the Scots and Irish, 62 percent of the passengers leaving from English ports were going to ports in the United States. If the estimates of the proportion of the Irish on ships from Liverpool is near the mark, the sample used for this study includes about one-third of the total number of emigrants for all places from England and Wales in that year, but a much smaller proportion of the Scots and Irish.

The evidence about the proportion of each nationality among immigrants to American ports suggests that the English migrants could more frequently afford to travel by the more expensive route than could the Irish or Scots, who showed such an overwhelming preference for British North America, at least as an initial destination. It also seems likely that among the one-third of passengers from England and Wales bound for Canada were many of the poorer English emigrants, as well as assisted ones. As Charles Hicks, a farmer of great Holland, Essex, recorded in his diary in 1830: "This Spring Wm. Smith and family, a wheelwright, John Green and family, Isaac Duffield, Wm. Morris, labourers, and James Scarfe from the Red Lion Inn left Gt. Holland and embarked for Canada. Having so many out of work it was thought advisable to assist such as were disposed to emigrate. The passage out of Green, Duffield, and Morris was paid out of the Poor Rates."[24] Because the passage to

[24] A. F. J. Brown, *Essex People, 1750–1900, from Their Diaries, Memoirs, and Letters* (Chelmsford: Essex County Council, 1973), p. 75. See also Wilbur Shepperson's remark that "the two extremes of society, the lower class laboring groups and the sons of the

Table 4.4. Destination of passengers embarking from British and Irish ports, 1831

	English and Welsh ports		Scottish ports		Irish ports		Total	
Destination	Number	Percent	Number	Percent	Number	Percent	Number	Percent
To United States	18,263	62.0	1,572	17.6	3,583	8.0	23,418	28.2
To Canada	9,860	33.5	7,230	81.1	40,977	91.7	58,067	69.9
To Australasia	1,331	4.5	115	1.3	135	0.3	1,581	1.9
Total	29,454	100.0	8,917	100.0	44,695	100.0	83,066	100.0

Source: Calculated from figures in N. H. Carrier and J. R. Jeffery, *External Migration: A Study of the Available Statistics, 1815–1950*, General Register Office, Studies on Medical and Population Subjects, no. 6 (London: HMSO, 1953), p. 95.

Table 4.5. Distribution of British, Irish, and all immigrants by selected ports of arrival, 1831

Port	English and Welsh		Scottish		Irish		Total passengers arriving in the four ports[a]	
	Number	Percent	Number	Percent	Number	Percent	Number	Percent
New York City[b]	4,856	78.0	520	88.3	1,666	59.3	10,737	56.0
Boston	203	3.3	6	1.0	106	3.8	1,417	7.4
Philadelphia[c]	1,092	17.5	58	9.9	588	20.9	3,808	19.9
New Orleans	78	1.2	5	0.8	451	16.0	3,191	16.7
Total	6,229	100.0	589	100.0	2,811	100.0	19,153	100.0

Sources: Ship lists (see Table 4.2). *Immigration into the United States Showing Number, Nationality, Sex, Occupation, Destination, etc., from 1820–1903*, 57th Cong., 2d sess., H. Doc. 15, pt. 2, ser. 1902–03, Monthly Summary of Finance and Commerce of the United States (Washington: Treasury Department, Bureau of Statistics, May 1903), p. 4366.

[a]Fiscal year ending September 30, 1831.

[b]Data are for five months only, or an estimated 56 percent of all U.K. immigrants arriving at New York during the year.

[c]Estimated 62 percent of all U.K. immigrants arriving at Philadelphia during the year.

New York cost more, especially for children, owing to stricter regulations as to space for passengers, than on ships to Canada, one might expect the sort of description that appeared in one contemporary newspaper to be more typical of the English rural emigration to the United States: the ship *Hudson* was reported as sailing for New York with 170 passengers, principally mechanics, with wives and children, several tradesmen with small capital, and farmers who had sold their farms.[25]

These projected differentials in the relative means of migrants according to travel arrangements do not take account of the leakage of migrants from Canada into the United States. Some of the poorer emigrants to Canada may eventually have reached the United States and settled there. But these perplexing questions cannot be answered from the sources being appraised here. What the ship lists can do is give a profile of those emigrants from the British Isles who were able to afford the route via United States ports and chose to emigrate to the States rather than to the Empire.

The age structure of the immigrants sampled in 1831 is shown in Table 4.6. Perhaps the most striking finding is that English emigrants were taking with them the same proportion of children under the age of fifteen (35 percent) as were reported in the population of England and Wales in 1841. The Scots were accompanied by fewer children in proportion to their numbers, whereas only a fifth of the Irish emigrants were children.

In all, scarcely more than half (53 percent) of the English and Welsh emigrants were in the main productive age groups from fifteen to thirty nine. These ages were slightly overrepresented in comparison with those recorded in the 1841 census of population, chiefly at the expense of people over the age of fifty. Persons in their forties were fully represented. The concentration of English immigrants in the age group from fifteen to twenty four was significantly lower than among the Irish. It was also very much lower than it had been among the English emigrants on the eve of the Revolution analyzed by Bernard Bailyn. The contrast between Scots emigrants of the late eighteenth century and those of 1831 was not so marked, partly because fewer than a fifth of the Scottish emigrants of 1773–75 were bound as indentured servants, whereas more than two-thirds of the English went as indentured labor.[26] The age structure of

---

gentry, preferred the North American Colonies" (*British Emigration,* p. 32). Maldwyn Jones, "Background to Emigration," p. 41.

[25] *Hampshire Telegraph and Sussex Chronicle,* July 16, 1832, p. 3, col. 3.

[26] Bernard Bailyn, *Voyagers to the West: A Passage in the Peopling of America on the Eve of*

Table 4.6. Immigrants classified by age and nationality, 1831 (percent)

Age	English and Welsh	Scottish	Irish	Census of Population, 1841[a] England and Wales	Census of Population, 1841[a] Scotland	Male indentured servants from London, 1773–1775[b]
0–14	35	30	21	36	36	5
15–19	9	7	13	11	10	18
20–24	16	20	29	10	10	44
25–29	12	18	16	8	8	17
30–39	16	15	11	13	13	13
40–49	8	5	6	8	9	3
50 +	5	6	4	14	14	—
Total	101%	101%	100%	100%	100%	100%
Number	6,229	589	2,811	15,914,100	2,620,200	3,359

Sources: Ship lists (see Table 4.2); Brian Mitchell and Phyllis Deane, *Abstract of British Historical Statistics* (Cambridge: Cambridge University Press, 1962), pp. 12–13; David Galenson, *White Servitude in Colonial America: An Economic Analysis* (Cambridge: Cambridge University Press, 1981), p. 27.

Note: Arrival data are for five months at New York and for the entire year at Boston, Philadelphia, and New Orleans. Totals do not all add to 100 percent because of rounding.

[a]Figures are described in the census as being approximate only.

[b]Age groupings are slightly different in Galenson.

the English emigrants of 1831 had come to resemble that of the Scots. More of the English had apparently tried to adapt at home and begun their families before they took the step of permanent settlement overseas. The proportion of children among all three nationalities was higher in 1831 than it was in the last quarter of the nineteenth century, and the share in the main working-age groups was lower (see Table 4.7).

In fact, the British emigration of 1831 was to an astonishing degree a

the Revolution (New York: Alfred A. Knopf, 1986), p. 171. The smaller sample from good lists (1827–31) that stipulated place of last residence does not suggest that the dual migration discovered by Bailyn—families from northern England and Scotland and single migrants from southern England—continued after the Napoleonic Wars, when indentured service was no longer providing a means for impecunious young men from the South to emigrate. Bailyn found the percentage of males among emigrants from the countries of the Midlands and southern England to have ranged between 86 and 99 percent in the years 1773–75, whereas the good lists of 1827–31 reported between 58 and 81 percent males, depending on the region, and did not show the contrast between the Thames Valley and northern England that Bailyn found. If anything, the balance may have shifted toward a larger percentage of women from the South and a smaller proportion from the North.

Table 4.7. Immigrants by age and nationality, 1831, compared with the late nineteenth century (percent)

	English and Welsh,	English,	Scots		Irish		Danes
Age groups	1831	1873–1898	1831	1873–1898	1831	1873–1898	1868–1900
0–14	35	21	30	21	21	13	20
15–39	53	67	60	67	69	80	68
40 +	13	12	10	11	10	7	10
Not stated							2
Total	101%	100%	100%	99%	100%	100%	100%
Number	6,229	1,206,833	589	268,070	2,811	1,302,266	172,073

Sources: Ship lists (see Table 4.2); *Immigration into the United States Showing Number, Nationality, Sex, Occupation, Destination, etc., from 1820–1903*, 57th Cong., 2d sess., H. Doc. 15, pt. 2, ser. 1902–3, Monthly Summary of Finance and Commerce of the United States (Washington: Treasury Department, Bureau of Statistics, May 1903), p. 4360; Kristian Hvidt, *Flight to America: The Social Background of 300,000 Danish Emigrants* (New York: Academic Press, 1975), p. 73.

Note: Data on arrivals are for five months at New York and for the entire year at Boston, Philadelphia, and New Orleans.

movement of family groups.[27] More than three in four of the English and Welsh migrants traveled with other members of their families. We can compare this 77 percent of English migrants traveling with their families with a number of other estimates from the same period: 66 percent of the Swedes in the 1850s; 72 percent of emigrants from Baden, 1840–55; 64 percent of emigrants from Osnabrück, 1832–46; and 69 percent of Dutch immigrants between 1830 and 1839.[28] None of these other estimates is quite as high as that for the English. Not only did a larger proportion of the British travel with other family members, but they also went out in larger family groups on average than did the Irish (see Table 4.8).

Another way of looking at this question is to examine the way in which adult male emigrants traveled. Such an analysis makes it possible to compare the figures with my estimates for the late 1880s. In 1831 the number of males aged fifteen or older going out alone was nearly the same as the number traveling with family. In the late 1880s men traveling alone outnumbered those going with other family members by eight to one. Here was a vast change in the character of English emigration. The English migration seems to have changed in the same direction as did that of Scandinavia and Germany, from a family movement to one dominated by single persons.

English and Welsh immigrants aged 15 or older according to traveling companions, 1831

	Females	Males
Traveling alone	166	1,112
Traveling with families	942	1,070
Total	1,108	2,182

Half the English and Welsh migrants traveled as husband and wife or as married couples with children. Children with single parents, most of whom were mothers probably rejoining their husbands, accounted for 16 percent of the migrants. Another 10 percent went out in extended family groups, a few with three generations, a few with married siblings and their families, and 2 percent in other groups, which included servants,

[27] For a discussion of rules of inference used in grouping migrants in families, see my final report to the SSRC, "British Emigrants." It should be noted that numbers attached to family parties are likely to be underestimated because women with different surnames cannot always be linked with the family groups of which they were members.

[28] Kristian Hvidt, *Flight to America: The Social Background of 300,000 Danish Emigrants* (New York: Academic Press, 1975), p. 92; Köllman and Marschalk, "German Emigration," p. 530; Swierenga, "Dutch Immigrant Demography," p. 397.

Table 4.8. Immigrants to four ports, 1831, according to traveling companions, by nationality

	English and Welsh[a]	Scots	Irish	Dutch, 1830–1839	Dutch, 1871–1880	Swedish, 1871–1880	Danish, 1871–1880
Number traveling in family groups	4,483	384	1,718	672	12,392		
Number traveling alone	1,367	202	1,121	305	3,829		
Percent traveling in families	76.6	65.5	60.5	68.8	76.4	42	43
Mean size of families	4.40	4.26	3.52				

Sources: Ship lists (see Table 4.2); Kristian Hvidt, *Flight to America: The Social Background of 300,000 Danish Emigrants* (New York: Academic Press, 1975), p. 93; Robert Swierenga, "Dutch Immigrant Demography, 1820–1880," *Journal of Family History* 5 (1980): 397.

[a]British and Irish figures do not include children who could not be placed with families (unaccompanied children). See Table 4.9.

apprentices, children with different surnames, or grandparents with grandchildren. A smaller proportion of the Irish traveled in nuclear families, more of them alone or with unmarried siblings (see Table 4.9).

In spite of the large number of children and the pronounced tendency to travel in family groups, men outnumbered women among the adult immigrants over the age of 15. In this respect, differences between the four nationalities were insignificant. Sixty-five percent of the English and Welsh aged 15 or older were male, 67 percent of the Scots, and 64 percent of the Irish.[29] As one would expect, the ratio of females to males was considerably lower than in the British population in 1831. By the last three decades of the century, the female share had risen among all three groups, and the Irish had gained equality of the sexes in their overseas movement (see Table 4.10). This larger proportion of females among emigrants appeared when the overseas movement was no longer predominantly one of family groups traveling together as they did in 1831.

What the 1831 ship lists tell us about the occupations of British and Irish male immigrants is summarized in Tables 4.11–4.16. Scandinavian writers are inclined to associate the high incidence of family migration in the early stage of the overseas movement with agriculture. Most migrants came from agriculture and intended to enter farming, for which large families were an advantage.

Farm laborers, the most numerous class in British agriculture, simply do not appear in the passenger lists. I am inclined to think that those who were described as laborers had already sought work outside agriculture before they emigrated, which seems very likely in the case of laborers who came from large towns. In this period, however, many of the laborers indicated on the good lists as emigrating from smaller towns or villages and agricultural counties may have been farm laborers. On good lists for 1827–31, 58 percent of the male laborers came from small towns and villages, and just about half of them from agricultural counties (see Tables 4.19 and 4.20 below). On all the good lists located between 1827 and 1854, only 15 percent of the laborers emigrated from principal towns. Even before the new Poor Law of 1834 sought to reduce outrelief to underemployed farm laborers, many of them found other laboring work locally to supplement harvest earnings. Keith D. M. Snell writes of the "high degree of movement between purely agricultural

[29] Nearly three-quarters of the German emigrants between 1820 and 1855 were men, according to Köllman and Marschalk, "German Emigration," pp. 528–29.

Table 4.9. Immigrants arriving in four ports, 1831, by type of family group

How traveling	English and Welsh		Scots		Irish		Dutch, 1830–1839	
	Number	Percent	Number	Percent	Number	Percent	Number	Percent
Alone	1,367	23.4	202	34.5	1,121	39.5	305	31.2
Married couples	344	5.9	30	5.1	226	8.0		
Married couples with children	2,573	44.0	218	37.2	723	25.4		
							541	55.4
Males with children	208	3.5	6	1.0	65	2.3		
Females with children	704	12.0	71	12.1	235	8.3		
Siblings	144	2.5	32	5.5	226	8.0	42	4.3
Extended families	405	6.9	26	4.4	212	7.4	6	0.6
Other[a]	105	1.8	1	0.2	31	1.1	83	8.5
Total	5,850	100.0	586	100.0	2,839	100.0	977	100.0
Unaccompanied children	13		1		21			

Sources: See those for Table 4.8.
Note: Arrival data are for five months at New York, for the entire year at Boston, Philadelphia, and New Orleans.
[a]Families including servants, apprentices, children with different surnames, or a missing generation.

Table 4.10. Females per 1,000 males aged 15 or older among immigrants arriving in four ports, 1831, by nationality

Nationality	Immigrants, 1831[a]	U.K. population, all ages, 1831	Immigrants, 1871–1898
English and Welsh	537	1,040	641[b]
Scots	482	1,114	647
Irish	559	1,046	1,007
Danish emigrants, 1868–1900			560

Sources: Ship lists (see Table 4.2); Brian Mitchell and Phyllis Deane, *Abstract of British Historical Statistics* (Cambridge: Cambridge University Press, 1962), p. 8; *Immigration into the United States Showing Number, Nationality, Sex, Occupation, Destination, etc., from 1820–1903*, 57th Cong., 2d sess., H. Doc. 15, pt. 2, ser. 1902–03, Monthly Summary of Finance and Commerce of the United States (Washington: Treasury Department, Bureau of Statistics, May 1903), pp. 4349–50.

[a]Data from ship lists are for five months at New York City, for entire year at Boston, Philadelphia, and New Orleans.

[b]English only (no Welsh included).

Table 4.11. Occupations by nationality of immigrant men aged 20 or older arriving in four ports, 1831 (percent)

Occupational class[a]	English and Welsh	Scots	Irish
Agriculture	24.6	15.3	20.2
Labor	9.5	17.3	39.1
Service	2.1	0.5	1.8
Crafts	34.9	33.2	17.6
Industry	16.5	15.8	12.6
Commerce/professions	12.4	17.8	8.7
	100.0%	100.0%	100.0%
Number	1,794	202	959

Source: Ship lists from four ports for five months, 1831 (see Table 4.2).

[a]Classification of occupations as in Table 3.12, above.

employment and employment in small market town and village occupations," and the superintendent of the census of 1831, William Rickman, referred to the "many industrious labourers . . . employed in mines, or in road-making, and otherwise during the larger proportion of the twelve-month, but were occasionally employed in harvest." In rural areas of Lancashire in 1831, farm laborers were outnumbered three to one by nonagricultural laborers. Nonfarm laboring work in farming areas was expanding much faster than full-time employment in farm labor.[30] There is at least a probability, barring evidence to the contrary, that most of the 10 percent of men described as laborers in ship lists had already sought laboring work outside agriculture, at least for a good part of the year.

If we proceed on this assumption, only one-fourth of the men aged twenty or older among English and Welsh immigrants came directly from farms, and the proportions were even smaller among the mobile Scots and Irish (see Table 4.11). Agricultural workers appearing in the ship lists were almost all described as farmers, though in a few instances the terms "husbandman," "yeoman," or "agriculturist" were used. About fifteen gardeners have also been included as agricultural workers in the tables, as are farmers' sons who gave no other occupation. If we accept as bona fide farmers—that is, men who probably were actually managing farms before they emigrated—only those men listed as farmers who were twenty-five years of age or more, at least one-third of the men in the agricultural class were either relatives of farmers or young men who might better have been described as agricultural laborers (see Table 4.12).

The agricultural sector as a whole was not overrepresented among the English emigrants of 1831, a year when contemporaries commented on the increasing numbers of farmers departing from England (see Table 4.13). Farmers themselves, however, were overrepresented: they formed 19 percent of the adult male emigrants from England to the United States (omitting the younger men), whereas the census of 1831 reported only 8.6 percent of the male labor force aged 20 or more as occupiers of land in agriculture. It is only in this sense that one can speak of an exodus from British agriculture. The passenger lists do not tell us who the emigrating farmers were—whether they were landowners or tenants, occupied large or small farms, were affected by enclosure or increased rents, farming poor soils or not.[31] One must turn to other

[30] Keith D. M. Snell, *Annals of the Labouring Poor: Social Change and Agrarian England, 1660–1900* (Cambridge: Cambridge University Press, 1985), pp. 23, 263; E. Anthony Wrigley, "Men on the Land and Men in the Countryside: Employment in Agriculture in Early-Nineteenth-Century England," in *The World We Have Gained: Histories of Population and Social Structure,* ed. Lloyd Bonfield, Richard Smith, and Keith Wrightson (Oxford: Basil Blackwell, 1986), p. 319, citing William Rickman from the 1831 census, *Enumeration Abstracts,* vol. I, British Parliamentary Papers, 1833 (149), XXXVI, preface, p. xii; John D. Marshall, "The Lancashire Rural Labourer in the Early Nineteenth Century," *Transactions of the Lancashire and Cheshire Antiquarian Society* 71 (1961): 91–93.

[31] For a summary of the literary evidence, see Maldwyn Jones, "Background to Emigration," pp. 39–40. From just such a local study starting with passenger lists, Mildred Campbell emphasized enclosure and increased rents in the background to the emigration of farmers from the North and East Ridings of Yorkshire in the 1770s ("English

Table 4.12. Ages of English and Welsh farmers in ship lists, 1831

	Number	Percent
Farmers under 25 years of age	117	22
Farmers' sons	63	12
Farmers aged 15 or older	345	66
Total	525	100

Source: Ship lists (see Table 4.2).

sources to try to answer these questions. At least it seems clear that the familial character of English emigration in this period cannot be explained simply by its agricultural origins. These limited findings lend substance to the remark of a British immigrant in Canton, Illinois, in 1851: "Some of the Americans have often complained to me that so few of the regular stout English farmers come out to this country. They complain that too many come from the manufacturing districts . . . . It is very rare that I come across an Englishman who follows farming here that followed the same occupation in England."[32]

Farm laborers and nonagricultural laborers were underrepresented in the migrating work force. So also were tertiary workers such as domestic servants, soldiers, seamen, messengers, and road and waterway workers, who formed a negligible proportion of male emigrants, very much lower than they did of the British labor force in 1831. Servants and laborers may have formed a higher proportion of the English emigrants to Canada, but the United States was not acquiring the poorest and least skilled of the English labor force. In view of the 39 percent of Irish immigrants to the United States recorded as laborers in 1831, one must hesitate to attribute the poor showing of English servants and laborers entirely to the want of means. We know that they were

---

Emigration on the Eve of the Revolution," *American Historical Review* 56 [1955]: 11–12). In a regression analysis of the relationship between enclosure and population movement in England from 1700 to 1830, Lawrence White obtained his only significant results—which suggested a positive relationship—in fifteen agricultural counties between 1801 and 1831 ("Enclosures and Population Movements in England, 1700–1830," *Explorations in Economic History,* 2d ser., 6 [1969]: 175–86).

[32] Letter to the *Examiner and Times* (Manchester), quoted in Grant Foreman, "English Settlers in Illinois," *Journal of the Illinois State Historical Society* 34 (1941): 333. See also Charlotte Erickson, *Invisible Immigrants: The Adaptation of English and Scottish Immigrants in Ninteenth-Century America,* (1972; rpt., Ithaca: Cornell University Press, 1990), pp. 17–20, 22–31. In contrast stand the emigrants from Baden, Württemberg, and Hesse in the 1840s, among whom half came from agriculture (Köllman and Marschalk, "German Emigration," p. 530).

Table 4.13. Occupations of English and Welsh male immigrants to four ports in 1831 compared with the British census and all arrivals in United States ports (percent)

Occupations	English and Welsh immigrants	Census of England and Wales, 1831[a]	All United States arrivals, 1831
Agriculture	24.6	33.8	31.1
Labor, including mining	11.3	16.7	10.8
Service	2.1	4.0	6.7
Crafts, without mining	33.1	21.6	18.7
Industry	16.5	13.2	2.3
Modern tertiary workers	12.4	10.7	30.4
	100.0	100.0	100.0
Number	1,794	3,179,271	8,617
Males aged 20 or older returned in census without occupation		200,569	
	Total	3,379,840	
Census total of males aged 20 or older in population		3,394,690	
Omissions		14,850	

Sources: Ship lists for four United States ports for five months only, 1831 (see Table 4.2); *Population of Great Britain, 1831, Enumeration Abstracts, Pt. 1, England and Wales*, British Parliamentary Papers, 1833, (149), XXXVI, pp. xiii-xiv; *Census of Great Britain, 1841, Pt. 1, England and Wales: Occupation Abstract,* British Parliamentary Papers, 1844 (587), XXVII, pp. 27–30; *Immigration into the United States Showing Number, Nationality, Sex, Occupation, Destination . . . from 1820–1903*, 57th Cong., 2d sess., H. Doc. 15, pt. 2, ser. 1902–03, Monthly Summary of Finance and Commerce of the United States (Washington: Treasury Department, Bureau of Statistics, May 1903), p. 4406.

[a]The 1831 census provided a detailed breakdown of occupations in only one of the larger classes into which it grouped the occupations of males aged 20 or older: "Employed in Retail Trade, or in Handicraft as Masters or Workmen." I have classified these detailed occupations into my respective classes of service (preindustrial tertiary) occupations, preindustrial crafts, and industry according to the classifications described in Appendix, Table 3.12, above. Those assigned to service occupations have been added to the larger census class of male servants 20 years of age or older. Those occupations that I have classified as industrial because of significant changes in technology during the nineteenth century have been added to the census class of "Employed in Manufacture, or in making Manufacturing Machinery." The rest are entered in the table as preindustrial crafts. Miners were returned in the census under "Labourers employed in Labour not Agriculture." Because the two could not be separated from the information in the census, I have withdrawn miners from preindustrial craftsmen for the purposes of this table and added them to the labor class. As can be seen, the error resulting from this manipulation of the data is not large.

reluctant to take jobs in the industrializing north of England: they appear to have been equally hesitant to emigrate to the United States. Sixty-five laborers have been identified on ships with good lists between 1827 and 1831. Thirty-three of these men came from industrial counties where agricultural laborers' wages were higher than average, mainly from Lancashire and the West Riding of Yorkshire. Only fifteen of them came from the agricultural counties where wages were low.

The work of Josef Barton and John MacDonald suggests that emigration was weakest in those villages in Hungary and Italy whose main features were large-scale commercial farms, laborers not "living in," and where rural society was marked by deep class cleavages.[33] These features of English agriculture in many of the counties where wages were low hint at similar barriers to emigration. It is also possible that emigration had not established itself as a tradition in so many English villages among the laboring class as in Ireland, another factor that has been observed in countries from Scandinavia to Italy as one which led people from certain places to seek emigration as a means of coping with stress and hardship.

Farmers and laborers were outnumbered by those whom I have classified as preindustrial craftworkers, those whose methods of work had not changed since before industrialization and whose skills remained substantially unchanged in England throughout the century. As opportunities for employment shrank in some villages, they increased in the towns. If one compares the English- and Welshmen on the ship lists with the occupied males in the census of 1831, it appears that industrial workers of all kinds were overrepresented among the emigrants of 1831 (see Tables 4.13 and 4.14). Fifty percent of the males arriving in the United States in 1831 with recorded occupations were either craftsmen or industrial workers, as compared with my estimate from the 1831 census of 35 percent. The Scottish immigrants reported a similar figure (49 percent).

The hypothesis that English emigration during the early nineteenth century was less industrial than later in the century, when industrial workers formed a larger share of the British labor force, is not confirmed by these estimates from 1831. The good lists from 1827–28 indicate an even higher proportion of workers from Britain's newer industries during that depression in the cotton industry, with farmers forming only 15 percent and men working in modernizing industries as

[33] Josef Barton, *Peasants and Strangers: Italians, Rumanians and Slovaks in an American City, 1890–1950* (Cambridge: Harvard University Press, 1975), pp. 27, 32, 34; John MacDonald, "Cultural Organization, Migration, and Labour Militancy," *Economic History Review,* 2d ser., 16 (1963): 61–75. Their view was challenged with evidence from Sicily by Donna Gabaccia, *Militants and Migrants: Rural Sicilians Become American Workers* (New Brunswick, N.J.: Rutgers University Press, 1988), pp. 38–78.

Table 4.14. Occupational classification of craftworkers among English and Welsh male immigrants aged 15 or older, 1831

Occupational class	Number	Percent of class	Percent of all male immigrants aged 15 or older with occupation	Percent of labor force in England and Wales, 1831	Percent of U.S. passenger arrival all nationalities, 1831
Building trades workers	205	28.6	9.3	6.6	0.8
Food processors	118	16.4	5.3	3.4	0.7
Metalworkers	71	9.9	3.2	2.2	not listed
Clothing workers	162	22.6	7.3	6.1	2.4
Woodworkers	52	7.2	2.4	2.1	not listed
Miscellaneous	43	6.0	1.9	1.2	not listed
Mechanics not otherwise designated	67	9.3	3.0	not listed	14.4
Total	718	100	32.4	21.6	18.3
Number		718	2,207	3,179,729	8,617

Sources: See those for Table 4.13.

Note: Data are for those among arrivals during five months at New York and for the entire year at Philadelphia, Boston, and New Orleans. Including males 15 to 19 years of age in the immigrant labor force slightly reduces the percentage of craftsmen, as one would expect. Craftsmen are still very much overrepresented as a class as compared with the English and Welsh male labor force aged 20 or older. For additional notes, see those for Table 4.13.

much as 28 percent of the migrants and preindustrial craftsmen constituting about the same proportion as they did in 1831.[34]

Even early in the century, the men emigrating from Britain were mainly crafts and industrial workers of varying degrees of skill.[35] Men from new and changing industries were outnumbered by more than two to one in 1831 by craftsmen from traditional occupations with the same sorts of skills as were fairly abundant in the eastern part of the United States, though not in the West in the early years. To assess whether particular occupations were contributing more than their share of emigrants, one must look at these classes in more detail (see Tables 4.14 and 4.15).

This more detailed breakdown of occupations from the 1831 ship lists reveals no significant overrepresentation of any particular class of workers. Building trades workers may have demonstrated a slight proneness to emigrate, as did other providers of the necessities of life, workers in food and clothing. Those groups postulated earlier to have experienced a short-term spur to emigration from the perverse elasticity of wages during a period of rising food prices, such as miners, showed less inclination to go to the United States.[36]

Men employed in textile industries do appear to have been emigrating in larger numbers than they formed of the entire labor force. In 1827 (when the total emigration was lower), the sample yielded more than twice as large a proportion (26 percent) of textile workers. Weavers and calico printers, faced with change of occupation or work methods and some substitution of female labor in the cotton industry at this time, were conspicuous among the emigrating textile workers at both dates. A diversity of other industrial workers was to be found among the emigrants, to the advantage of the receiving nation; but no others showed any particular propensity to emigrate.

[34] The proportion of preindustrial craftsmen among the British immigrants of the 1880s was virtually the same—34 percent—as found in 1827 and 1831. At 2 percent, the proportion of textile workers among the males was significantly lower.

[35] This was suggested by Berthoff, *British Immigrants*, pp. 15–87.

[36] Only forty English or Welsh miners, 1.8 percent of the emigrant male labor force, appeared on the ship lists analyzed. As explained in the note to Table 4.13, miners were not distinguished from laborers in the 1831 census. In 1841 they formed 3.7 percent of the English and Welsh labor force, according to the census. Christopher Hunt found that before the mid-nineteenth century, when railways came into the lead mining region of Northumberland and Durham, miners migrated to the collieries and ironworks of Northumberland and Durham or to West Cumberland, not overseas (*The Lead Miners of the Northern Pennines in the Eighteenth and Nineteenth Centuries* [Manchester: Manchester University Press, 1971], p. 202).

Table 4.15. Occupations of industrial workers among English and Welsh male immigrants to the United States aged 15 or older, 1831

Occupation	Total	Percent of class	Percent of total English and Welsh male immigrants with occupations	Percent of male labor in England, 1841
Weavers	103	28.6	4.7	1.43
Spinners	37	10.3	1.7	0.07
Calico printers	53	14.7	2.4	0.20
Other textile workers	34	9.4	1.5	6.57
All textile workers	227	63.1	10.3	8.27
Iron- and steelworkers	32	8.9	1.4	0.69
Engineers and millwrights	18	5.0	0.8	2.76
Watch- and instrumentmakers	10	2.8	0.5	0.37
Other metalworkers	16	4.4	0.7	1.21
All engineers, etc.	76	21.1	3.4	5.03
Printers	20	5.6	0.9	0.36
Chemists/druggists	11	3.1	0.5	0.26
Glassworkers	11	3.1	0.5	0.15
Paperworkers	8	2.2	0.4	0.15
Other miscellaneous	7	1.9	0.3	1.08
All miscellaneous	57	15.8	2.6	2.00
Total		100.0	16.3	15.30
Number of immigrants	360		2,207	3,449,359
Percent of male labor force in England and Wales, 1831				13.2
Percent of passenger arrivals in United States with occupations, 1831				2.3

Sources: See those for Table 4.13; Charlotte Erickson, "Emigration from the British Isles to the U.S.A. in 1841," Part 2, "Who Were the English Emigrants?" *Population Studies* 44 (1990): 29.

Notes: Data are for arrivals during five months at New York, for the entire year at Philadelphia, Boston, and New Orleans. Because the industrial occupations were not given in the 1831 census or, if listed, the numbers appeared to be quite unreliable, I have provided estimates from the 1841 census for reference. Obviously, as can be seen at the bottom of the table, industrial workers constituted a smaller proportion of the 1831 work force than they did in 1841. Subtotals do not always add up because of rounding.

Tables 4.14–4.16 also expose the incompleteness and errors in the statistics that federal authorities published from the customs returns. Many industrial occupations specified in the passenger lists, such as weavers, did not appear at all in published statistics of occupations in which the vague category "mechanic" was used as a catchall, quite unnecessarily, had ship lists been properly tabulated for the returns. The flimsiness of published occupational figures is particularly evident in the summary of the white-collar, business, and professional sector in Table 4.16. Partly because I have omitted all merchants stating their

Table 4.16. Occupations of modern tertiary workers among English and Welsh male immigrants to the United States aged 15 or older, 1831

Occupational type	Number	Percent of class	Percent of all English and Welsh male immigrants with occupations	Percent of male labor in England, 1841
Clerical workers	24	8.3	1.1	0.1
Commercial workers	166	57.6	7.5	2.2
Professionals	53	18.4	2.4	4.9
Gentlemen, students	45	15.6	2.0	2.5
Total	288	99.9	13.0	9.7
Number			2,207	3,449,359
Percent of male labor force in England and Wales, 1831		11.0		
Percent of United States passenger arrivals stating occupations, 1831		32.1		

Sources: See those for Table 4.13.
Note: Data for arrivals are for five months at New York City, for the entire year at Boston, Philadelphia, and New Orleans. See also Table 4.13 notes.

intention to return to Britain, as well as American citizens and residents returning home, the commercial class is very much reduced in these estimates made directly from the ship lists. Nevertheless, men in commercial occupations were overrepresented among immigrants, in contrast with clerical and professional workers.

Some additional hints as to the class of migrants leaving with particular skills can be gleaned from examining their traveling companions. Comparisons with the Irish lead one to postulate that better-off migrants would travel in larger family groups because of their ability to raise fares and forgo earnings. This inference is not confirmed by the figures in Table 4.17. Here we see that farmers were somewhat more likely than most other selected groups to be traveling with other family members and in larger family groups than was typical for British immigrants of these months. Skilled craftworkers were a little more likely than farmers to be traveling alone and, if not, to be taking a smaller family along with them. In the case of both farmers and craftsmen, two-thirds of the migrating units included no dependent children under the age of fifteen, which suggests that the majority were able to choose a favorable moment in the family cycle for emigration.

The contrast between farmers and craftsmen on the one hand and laborers on the other is not so great as one would expect on the

Table 4.17. Traveling companions by occupation among English and Welsh immigrants to four ports in 1831

	Farmers	Laborers	Crafts without building	Building trades	Weavers	Other textile workers	Other industrial workers
Males of given occupation and their families as share of total immigrants	85%	79%	78%	75%	67%	58%	67%
Males of given occupation traveling alone as share of total migrating units	46%	57%	55%	60%	67%	74%	63%
Average size of emigrating families	4.80	4.82	4.27	4.58	4.15	3.57	3.49
Share of migrating units headed by male with given occupation traveling without dependent children	66%	69%	67%	74%	79%	85%	74%
Ratio of adults to dependent children	1.72	1.69	2.01	2.34	2.52	3.48	2.95
Number of units	441	196	411	204	101	117	123
Number of persons	1,345	520	1,013	494	205	206	235

Source: Ship lists (see Table 4.2).

hypothesis that finance determined travel arrangements and ability to emigrate. Among laborers who did emigrate to the United States, the proportion traveling alone was not significantly higher than that for craftsmen, nor was the share traveling without dependent children in the group. Laborers' families tended to be slightly larger on average and the ratio of adults to children lower than among either farmers or craftsmen. This result is rather startling.

Industrial workers from the modernizing sector, including men such as weavers who may have left because of restricted opportunities, boarded ship somewhat less encumbered by large families and dependent children and more frequently alone than did farmers, craftsmen, and laborers. Yet among the industrial workers, the weavers took larger families and showed a lower ratio of adults to children. Again, there seems to be little suggestion that absolute need was sending poorer groups like laborers and weavers off to America. Or, put another way, it is by no means clear that the poorer families among these disadvantaged groups were those going. Those most likely to travel as single men and with higher ratios of adults to children in family groups were other industrial workers and other textile workers not faced with secular decline of their occupations at home, indeed those whose situation both at home and in the American labor market would seem to have been most favorable. The English who chose to emigrate to the United States were probably not people expelled by need or absolute hardship but people able to make rational and conscious choices.

This rationality is also illustrated in Table 4.18. More than half of the English adult men who entered the country via Boston were industrial workers who reported occupations in the modernizing sectors of industry. Of those who chose Philadelphia as a destination, two-fifths were in traditional crafts, including mining, a much larger proportion than among those coming to Boston. Only 6 percent of the English immigrants to Boston were farmers as compared with 26 percent in New York on the main route to the West. A consideration of the ports of arrival of the Irish suggests a somewhat less calculated and informed distribution, though the amazing 58 percent of farmers among those landing at New Orleans is noteworthy.

The good lists to which I referred earlier can tell us a little more about the English immigrants of 1827–31. But the sample is far smaller and not systematically drawn. How much confidence can one have in the results? As I have already indicated, in these good lists a significantly

Table 4.18. Occupations of men aged 20 or older by nationality and port of arrival, 1831

Occupational class	English and Welsh				Scots				Irish			
	New York City[a]	Philadelphia	Boston	New Orleans	New York City[a]	Philadelphia	Boston	New Orleans	New York City[a]	Philadelphia	Boston	New Orleans
1. Agriculture	25.5%	19.2%	6.3%	14.3%	17.4%	0%			15.3%	9.1%	14.3%	57.7%
2. Labor	10.0	4.6	15.0	—	15.7	22.2	(2)		38.6	54.8	44.6	29.4
3. Service	1.9	2.7	3.8	—	0.6	3.7			2.2	0.5	3.6	—
4. Crafts	35.4	40.4	18.7	14.3	33.2	33.3		(1)	20.3	14.5	10.7	4.3
5. Industry	14.7	19.9	52.4	2.8	16.9	11.1	(2)		15.2	12.0	5.4	2.7
6. Commerce/ Professions	12.5	13.3	3.8	68.6	16.2	29.7		(2)	8.4	9.1	21.4	5.9
Total	100.0%	100.1%	100.0%	100.0%	100.0%	100.0%			100.0%	100.0%	100.0%	100.0%
Number	1,596	302	80	35	178	27	(4)	(3)	692	208	56	187

Source: Ship lists (see Table 4.2).
Note: For occupations included in classes 4–6, see Tables 4.14–4.16.
[a]Data are for five months only.

lower proportion of farmers and higher one of textile and other industrial workers was recorded in the migration of 1827 than in 1830 or 1831. Yet when the occupations on all the good lists are averaged together, they do not differ much from the large sample for 1831 because good lists of 1830–31 included a higher proportion of farmers than was evident in the larger sample.

This result is easily explained when one looks at the ports from which the immigrants had embarked. Most of the emigrants via Liverpool came from Lancashire and the West Riding of Yorkshire. Those who left from Hull came in greatest numbers from Lincolnshire and the East Riding of Yorkshire. The Bristol list reveals Gloucestershire and Somerset as the chief sources of emigrants, and London includes immigrants from Kent and Norfolk. Thus, the fact that all good lists surviving for 1827 happen to be Liverpool lists may raise the share of Lancashire workers in the results for that year; and the fact that more outport lists happen to be good in 1830 and 1831 increases the share of agricultural immigrants in the smaller samples for those years. This change in ports, however, was not a matter of chance alone. From British passenger returns we know that 87 percent of those recorded as sailing from English ports in 1827 left from Liverpool. In 1831, Liverpool's share was less than 70 percent and was below 60 percent in 1832. The increased agricultural element in this early peak in nineteenth-century emigration was accompanied by an increasing use of outports near the migrants. The good lists for 1830 and 1831 included more rural emigrants than would a stratified sample that gave Liverpool passengers their full weight.

Table 4.19, in which are summarized the origins of immigrants on ships whose captains were generous with information, must be interpreted in the light of these facts about the ports represented. The ships that sailed from Liverpool in 1827 carried almost exclusively emigrants from industrial counties where wages were higher than average and who may very well have been typical of that year's emigrants to the States. Those industrial counties were not so well represented among the immigrants of 1830 and 1831 by way of Hull, Bristol, and London. Nevertheless, one outstanding feature of the distribution of those years is that agricultural counties where wages were higher than average, such as Kent and Lincolnshire, were conspicuous as last places of residence among emigrants from rural areas. Agricultural and industrial counties, in which wages were below average, did not produce a fair share of migrants for these ships.

Table 4.19. Type of county from which English emigrants left on ships with good lists, 1827–1831

Class of county[a]	1827		1830–1831		Average (percent)	Population distribution, 1831 census (percent)
	Number	Percent	Number	Percent		
1. Agricultural low-wage	25	6	207	31	21	30
2. Agricultural high-wage	31	7	166	25	18	11
3. Industrial low-wage	7	2	65	9	6	14
4. Industrial high-wage	372	85	240	35	55	45
Total	435	100	678	100	100	100

Sources: The following ship lists were used: Boston, National Archives, microfilm 277, roll 3, nos. 121 and 127 in 1826 and 54 in 1827; New York, National Avchives, microfilm 237, roll 9, nos. 220, 240, 268, 329, 369, 399, 548, and 690 for 1827, microfilm 237, roll 11, nos. 250, 254, and 264 for 1830, and microfilm 237, roll 14, nos. 99, 109, 153, and 381 for 1831; Philadelphia, National Archives, microfilm 425, roll 46, nos. 3 and 10 for 1831; New Orleans microfilm 259, roll 9, no. 46; see also Table 3.5.

[a]Counties are ranked as in Table 3.11, above.

Table 4.20. County of origin of English immigrants on ships with good lists, 1831

Type of county	Farmers	Laborers	Craftworkers	Building trades workers	Weavers	Other textile workers
By occupation of male heads of family, 1827–1831 (families)						
1.	25%	45%	16%	30%	0%	0%
2.	18	22	20	19	7	16
3.	11	2	7	9	0	0
4.	46	31	57	43	93	84
Number	324	161	179	101	70	45
By occupations of males aged 15 or older (individuals)						
1.	26%	24%	17%	19%	0%	0%
2.	23	25	19	17	2	16
3.	12	4	8	12	0	0
4.	39	47	56	52	98	84
Number	153	67	96	58	41	19
Ratio of total immigrants to males aged 15 or older						
1.	2.08	4.50	1.75	2.73	—	—
2.	1.66	2.05	2.00	1.90	5.00	2.33
3.	1.89	2.00	1.63	1.29	—	—
4.	2.48	1.56	1.89	1.45	1.63	2.38
Average for all immigrants	2.12	2.32	1.87	1.74	1.71	2.37

Source: Good ship lists (see Table 4.19).
Note: Counties are classified as in Table 3.11, above.

Even if the good lists tend to exaggerate slightly the numbers of industrial workers among the immigrants of 1827 and the agricultural workers in 1830 and 1831, they can be used to establish the type of county and size of community from which emigrants with particular occupations and their families proceeded. Male immigrants from selected occupations by county of last residence are summarized in Table 4.20. Farmers and craftsmen were leaving from both agricultural and industrial counties. In absolute numbers, those most frequently mentioned as sources of emigrating farmers were the industrial counties of Lancashire and Cheshire and the East and West Ridings of Yorkshire where wages were high, the low-wage industrial county of Gloucestershire, the high-wage agricultural county of Lincolnshire, and the low-wage agricultural county of Shropshire. Farmers showed no particular tendency to leave the low-wage agricultural counties. Again, one is inclined to suspect that here were people who could afford to emigrate and who made positive choices about where they wanted to live.

The small sample of laborers is particularly interesting. The tendency to travel in large families, noted in the 1831 data, reappears in these samples. Forty-four percent of the people attached to a laborer as breadwinner came from the low-wage agricultural counties, a higher proportion than among any of the other occupations. The village of Headcorn in Kent turned up on these few good lists of 1831. This village was one of ten in the entire county that assisted paupers to emigrate, experienced self-financed emigration as well, and was also the location of Swing Riots in 1830.[37] Its population had not grown at all between 1821 and 1831. These few laborers from a poor village with a stationary population in the interior of Kent seem to indicate that emigration was possible, if sought, for the poorest in the English labor force with assistance from the Overseers of the Poor or landowners, if not without such help.

Weavers and other textile workers who appear on the good lists came almost exclusively from Lancashire and the West Riding, not from areas with declining preindustrial clothmaking industries. A closer look at the origins of the weavers turns up the towns of Bolton, Blackburn, Stockport, Bury, Rochdale, and Manchester in Lancashire, and Huddersfield and Halifax in the West Riding as their places of last residence. Not more than one or two of them came from the weaving villages of northeastern Lancashire, where, as Duncan Bythell has emphasized, power looms were not spreading and alternative sources of livelihood were scarcer than in the towns. Bythell wrote that "for nearly twenty years after 1826, commentators on the weavers' position frequently stressed the particular problems facing the country weaver, whose children might still have to be put to the loom long after it ceased to offer a prospect of remunerative employment."[38] These do not appear to have been the weavers who were setting off to the United States during the years of crisis in cotton handloom weaving. Those few who did emigrate came from areas where power looms were spreading, population increasing, and other jobs becoming more plentiful over time, though there is always the possibility that some country weavers had first migrated to one of the larger Lancashire towns.

According to the good lists, the emigrants of 1827–31 were just about as likely to come from principal towns with populations of twenty

[37] This statement is based on unpublished research on the relationship between emigration and rural unrest in the period. The research was sponsored by the Nuffield Foundation and carried out by Nick Tiratsoo and the author.

[38] Duncan Bythell, *The Handloom Weavers: A Study in the English Cotton Industry during the Industrial Revolution* (Cambridge: Cambridge University Press, 1969), p. 255.

thousand or more as was the population of England and Wales to reside in them (see Table 4.21). The high degree of urbanization among weavers and other textile workers who emigrated is apparent.

More than once the editor of *Niles Weekly Register* commented during these years, as English immigration through New York City rose sharply, that paupers were being sent or were expected shortly.[39] The ship lists do not provide evidence that such fears were well-founded, except for those few large laboring families that arrived from places like Headcorn in Kent. On the whole, those classes in the English population which experienced the greatest hardship during these years of expanding industrialization, whether because of the low productivity of their work methods, competition by machinery, or overpopulation in the agricultural villages, are hard to find on the passenger lists. Nailers, framework knitters, handloom weavers from the villages, and agricultural laborers appear to have been seriously underrepresented among emigrants to the United States. Of course, the skilled workers and farmers may have been marginal ones or at least people who feared a loss of income or status during these challenging times.

Of all the preindustrial craftmen, building trades workers appeared most frequently as coming from low-wage agricultural counties and smaller places. Of all workers, they experienced the least competition from new methods and possessed the most readily transferable skills—both to English towns and to the United States—though like most workers they uncountered fluctuations in the demand for their labor. Emigration rose in depressed years like 1827 and 1831 at least in part

[39] *Niles Weekly Register,* April 21, 1832, p. 125, June 10, 1837, p. 226, June 17, 1837, p. 242, and September 15, 1838, p. 45. Before the Poor Law Amendment Act of 1834, parishes that assisted emigrants were under no compulsion to send them to British colonies. See, for example, *Norfolk Chronicle,* April 3, 1830: "Last month a number of persons left North and South Lopham in waggons on their way to embark at Liverpool for the United States of America. Between 100 and 200 persons are emigrating from these parts, a considerable sum of money having been borrowed on the security of the rates to defray the expenses of their passage (about £6 10s. per head) and to furnish each family with the clear sum of £5 on their landing at New York." Short of a search in parish records in county archives throughout England, it would be impossible to estimate the number so assisted before 1834. For letters published to encourage the emigration of laborers at this time, see also S. H. Collins, *The Emigrant's Guide to and Description of the U.S.A.,* 4th ed. (Hull, 1830); G. Poulett Scrope, ed., *Extracts of Letters from Poor Persons Who Emigrated Last Year to Canada and the United States* (London: James Ridgeway, 1831); and Benjamin Smith, ed., *Twenty-four Letters from Labourers in America to Their Friends in England* (London: Edward Rainford, 1829). William Cobbett cited the Smith volume as evidence "of fitness of America for English labourers" in *The Emigrants Guide in 10 Letters Addressed to the Taxpayers of England* (London, 1929).

Table 4.21. English immigrants on good lists by numbers residing in principal towns before emigration, 1827–1831

Date of emigration and occupation	Total immigrants from towns		Males ages 15 or more from towns		Population of England in towns, 1831 (percent)
	Number	Percent	Number	Percent	
1827, all migrants	211	39	109	40	
1830–1831, all migrants	97	13	32	11	
Total, 1827–1831	308	24	141	25	28.5
Weavers, 1827–1831	50	78	29	74	
Other textile workers	20	49	10	56	
Building trades workers	25	28	20	21	
Craftsmen	67	40	34	40	
Laborers	22	42	12	39	

Source: Good ship lists, as given in Table 4.19.

Note: The definition of principal town was 20,000 or more inhabitants. The figures, however, include Huddersfield and Carlisle, with only 19,000 inhabitants, among the sources of urban migrants. Revision to conform with the definition of 20,000 would slightly reduce the percentage of emigrants from principal towns.

because those less than impoverished could get away at such times. The bulk of the English emigrants seem to have been the sort of people who would have had some assets to sell to finance emigration and to have been in a position to choose one risk as against another, trying a new country versus adapting at home. If it was not the "talented tenth" who were leaving England during its industrialization, it was at least people whose skills gave them the means to acquire land even when they had not previously accumulated the necessary capital. They were as easily absorbed economically as were the New Englanders who were also moving west during these years, and they made similar contributions to farm making and town building.[40]

The many craftsmen and weavers who took families indicates that theirs was not a speculative migration for personal reasons, not a labor migration pure and simple. As noted earlier, continental writers are inclined to interpret such family migration as evidence of social and economic stress and strain of a high order. If one is to seek socioeconomic reasons for this family or folk migration, no crude explanations drawn from the supposed adverse effects of industrialization or agricultural depression will do. If one wants to give the English emigrants a class location in society, the farmers and preindustrial craftsmen could be designated as lower middle class, what Gibbon Wakefield called "the uneasy class." Unhappiness with their status in a changing economy and fears for their children's position in society may have propelled them to emigrate more than did economic hardship, even in a relative sense. Such categories could also encompass the not insignificant numbers of commercial and professional people among them. These results seem to support the findings based on immigrant letters that an agrarian myth lay behind much of the emigration from the country with the most industrialized economy in the world at the time.[41]

One could conclude that emigration did not help where help was most needed—in the adaptation to urbanization and new industrial methods. But one must keep in mind that perhaps one-third of English emigrants went to Canada in 1831, and this contingent may well have contained more paupers and more people in real need. Moreover, the example of the Irish—among whom 39 percent of those who managed

[40] See the essay "British Immigrants in the Old Northwest, 1815–1860," above.

[41] Edwin G. Wakefield, *England and America* (London, 1833), pp. 94–95, cited in R. S. Neale, *Class and Ideology in the Nineteenth Century* (London: Routledge and Kegan Paul, 1972), p. 6. See the essay "Agrarian Myths of English Immigrants," above; Stephen Fender, *Sea Changes: British Emigration and American Literature* (Cambridge: Cambridge University Press, 1992), pp. 161–63.

to go directly to the United States, by traveling in smaller groups or as individuals, were laborers—suggests what might have been possible for the English. Were England's laborers poorer, less well informed than the Irish? Or did they prefer to stay at home and take their chances on survival in England by emigrating from the countryside, changing jobs, accepting poor relief, if not by limiting the number of children in their families? From the little bit we do know about internal migration in England during this period, the contrasts with the overseas movement appear striking. Women predominated instead of men; young people moved internally, with not so wide a spread of age groups as in the overseas movement; single people rather than families were the internal migrants; and they moved short distances, unlike those who crossed the then awesome Atlantic Ocean. Internal migration and opportunities helped the increasing agricultural population where it responded; the smaller emigration to Canada included some of the impoverished. The United States attracted those who feared or disliked industrializing Britain and took a dim view of its future, though many of them may have been beneficiaries of its economic growth.

CHAPTER FIVE

Depression Emigrants: Who Went Where from the British Isles in 1841?

The literature on emigration from the British Isles tends to focus on one or another of the nationality groups within the United Kingdom and to describe the movement to one or another overseas destination. Little attempt has ever been made to compare the streams. We still rely on impressionistic generalizations such as Rowland Berthoff's unquantified hunch that industrial workers went to the United States and agricultural laborers to the colonies, or Wilbur Shepperson's view "that the two extremes of society, the lower class labouring groups and the sons of gentry, preferred the North American colonies."[1] In this essay I investigate those differences more carefully insofar as it was possible without research in the former British colonies. It must be regarded as a preliminary step toward describing the flow of emigrants to various destinations. Is it possible to find evidence of an informed rationality on the part of the majority of the emigrants?

The investigation is based on an intensive study of a single year, 1841. Although no one year can be regarded as typical, the experiment nevertheless seemed worthwhile because 1841 was exceptionally interesting in the history of emigration from the British Isles. This was partly for purely fortuitous reasons. The year 1841 was the only one in the century in which the census authorities undertook an actual count of

[1] Rowland Berthoff, *British Immigrants in Industrial America, 1790–1950* (Cambridge: Harvard University Press, 1953), pp. 117, 118; Wilbur Shepperson, *British Emigration to North America: Projects and Opinions in the Early Victorian Era* (Oxford: Basil Blackwell, 1957), p. 32.

emigrants from Britain by county of origin. The fact that it was a census year provides a base for comparing emigrants with the population from which they emerged. These considerations led me to sample the passenger lists for the five leading ports through which immigrants entered the United States.[2] These data provided benchmarks from which some comparisons with emigrants to other destinations could be made by using Parliamentary Papers and manuscripts in the Public Record Office.

Eighteen forty-one commands attention for other reasons as well. It was a year of poor harvest and industrial depression in Britain and of serious food shortages in Ireland. One might have expected emigration to be declining in view of the equally depressed conditions in the United States. Yet more emigrants went overseas than in 1840 and even more in 1842, before the economy had begun to recover. Although the incidence of emigration in relation to population size was still much lower than it was to be during and after the Irish famine or in the 1880s and 1900s, these few years of acute cyclical depression during a longer period of structural change witnessed the peak emigration for the period 1815–47.

This was also a year when prospective emigrants had an exceptional range of choice of destination and of assistance in emigrating. A large increase in the number of free passages offered to Australia explains, at least in part, the doubling of the number of people leaving for Australia and New Zealand, from 15,850 to 32,625, a figure not to be exceeded until 1852, with the gold rush (see Table 5.1). Emigration to North America also increased, though by much less than it did from 1841 to 1842, when assisted passages were no longer offered. In 1842, in spite of depressed conditions in the British Isles, emigration to North America rose substantially as that to Australia shrank. Assisted passages could divert the emigrant stream to some extent, but it was far from staunched without them. The question is, who was diverted?

Three areas received the bulk of the emigrants in 1841. Although small numbers of emigrants from the British Isles arrived in Van

[2] The results of that research were published as "Emigration from the British Isles to the U.S.A. in 1841," Part 1, "Emigration from the British Isles," and Part 2, "Who Were the English Emigrants?" *Population Studies* 43 (1989): 347–67, and 44 (1990): 21–39. Information about the sample and tests for its validity can be found in Charlotte Erickson, "The Uses of Passenger Lists for the Study of British and Irish Emigration," in *Migration across Time and Nations: Population Mobility in Historical Context,* ed. Ira Glazier and Luigi de Rosa (New York: Holmes and Meier, 1986), pp. 318–35. The computer tapes for that study have been deposited in the Economic and Social Research Council's Data Archive at the University of Essex, no. 2179: "British and Irish Emigrants to the USA in 1841."

Table 5.1. Passengers from the British Isles to extra-European destinations, 1838–1843

Year	Total passengers	Australia and New Zealand	British North America	United States	Other
1838	33,222	42.2%	13.8%	43.1%	0.9%
1839	62,207	25.4	20.3	53.9	0.4
1840	90,743	17.5	35.6	44.8	2.1
1841	118,592	27.5	32.2	38.0	2.3
1842	128,344	6.7	42.2	49.8	1.3
1843	57,212	6.1	41.1	49.5	3.3

Source: N. H. Carrier and J. R. Jeffery, *External Migration: A Study of the Available Statistics, 1815–1950*, General Register Office, Studies on Medical and Population Subjects, no. 6 (London: HMSO, 1953), p. 95.

Diemen's Land (now Tasmania, 806), South Australia (856), West Australia (414), New Zealand (2,006), and South Africa (55), New South Wales, from which Victoria and Queensland were later to be carved, attracted an estimated 22,483 arrivals and was far and away the principal overseas destination in the Eastern Hemisphere.[3]

Most of the immigrants to the Canadian provinces arrived in Quebec and Montreal, destined for the recently united Upper and Lower Canada. The British government's emigrant agents in Quebec and Montreal counted 28,086 arrivals from ports in the British Isles. Only 1,831 came to Prince Edward Island, and 2,344 to Nova Scotia. Of the 7,291 who disembarked in New Brunswick, more than half continued their journey almost immediately to the United States,[4] which is one reason why U.S. authorities recorded a larger number of arrivals from the British Isles than did the British of passengers departing thence. According to an estimate made from the sample of one in every five

[3] "Returns of the Emigrants Who Have Embarked from the U.K., 1841," British Parliamentary Papers (hereinafter B.P.P.), 1842 (231), XXXI, p. 3; "Returns for Each Year, from 1837 to 1846, in Regard to Each of the British Colonies in Which Land Revenues Are Applied to the Introduction of Emigrants," B.P.P., 1847–48 (345), XLVII, pp. 652–53, 655–56; "Return of Emigrants on Bounty Who Have Left the U.K. in Time to Arrive in New South Wales within the Year 1841," B.P.P., 1841, 2d sess. (65), III, p. 291; Peter Burroughs, *Britain and Australia, 1831–1855* (Oxford: Clarendon Press, 1967), app. 3; Matel Harris, "British Migration to Western Australia, 1829–1850," Ph.D. diss., London University, 1934, table after p. 91; Gordon Donaldson, *The Scots Overseas* (London: Robert Hale, 1966), p. 186.

[4] "Despatches from the Governor-General of British North America, Transmitting the Annual Reports of the Agents for Emigration in Canada, 1841," B.P.P., 1842 (373), XXXI, p. 11; *Correspondence Relative to Emigration*, B.P.P., 1842 (301), XXXI, p. 325; Frances Morehouse, "Migration from the United Kingdom to North America, 1840–50," Ph.D. diss., University of Manchester, 1926, pp. 427–28, 441, 452.

Table 5.2. Colonial bounty scheme of New South Wales, 1837–1843

Year	Land revenue	Expenditure on migration	Number of immigrants	Average cost per head
1837	£127,963	£ 49,171	2,360	£14/16/3
1838	125,729	157,366	6,115	23/1/0
1839	172,273	155,593	8,339	17/10/1
1840	354,060	111,694	6,675	15/19/11
1841	117,120	323,084	20,103	15/15/1
1842	63,149	110,521	6,823	14/11/10
1843	47,742	9,407	11	—

Source: "Returns for Each Year, from 1837–1846, in Regard to Each of the British Colonies in Which Land Revenues Are Applied to the Introduction of Emigrants," British Parliamentary Papers (hereinafter B.P.P.), 1847–48 (345), XLVII, pp. 650–51.

ships, 53,560 people arrived in the States from the British Isles, very close to the figure of 53,960 published by the State Department. The figures for both immigrants and emigrants to British North America were swollen by perhaps as many as seven to eight thousand by migrants who merely stopped en route, mainly at St. Johns, and proceeded directly to ports in the United States to be recorded there as immigrants from the British Isles.

A comparison of emigrants to New South Wales, to Montreal and Quebec, and to the United States will include a very high proportion of those who arrived at overseas destinations from the United Kingdom in 1841. Before considering the emigrants, a look at some features of these three fields is appropriate. How did they compare with one another as destinations? One cannot assume that all emigrants were in a position to make comparisons, but the historian is able to do so as a basis for judging how well informed the emigrants were in deciding where to go in this particular year. Therefore, I propose to assess in broad outline these fields' respective features as to (1) the nature and amount of assistance available in relation to the cost of the journey, (2) facilities for the protection of emigrants on voyage and reception and distribution on arrival, (3) the availability of land, and (4) sources of information about these areas.

Not the only colony to be offering free passages to the Antipodes, New South Wales was the important one at this time. A sudden increase in land sales in 1840, from which passages were financed, enabled that colony to expand the numbers substantially in 1841 (see Table 5.2). From the time that bounty payments had been introduced in 1831, about a fifth of the immigrants to New South Wales had been self-financed. Now, in 1841, only 685 (or 5 percent) of the arrivals at Sydney and Port Phillip between January and November paid their own passages.[5] In the absence of adequate administrative machinery in the government to undertake the task, bounties were paid to shippers who agreed to select emigrants and fill ships. In 1840 the government service was reorganized with the creation of the three-man Colonial Land and Emigration Commission, which obtained more staff. As the program of assisted emigration expanded very quickly, the commission regretted its inability to keep a tight control on the selection of emigrants.[6] As income from land sales soared in 1840, Lt. Governor Sir George Gipps authorized more and more bounty immigrants, so many that he received a severe reprimand from London for his extravagance.[7] Alarmed by this soaring expenditure as the land boom abated during 1841, the colonial land and emigration commissioners issued new regulations for the bounty system and stated their intention of tightening them further. In April 1841, some of those concerned with receiving bounty payments on behalf of the migrants, led by the London shipper John Marshall, protested that the new regulations would "effectively end the bounty system."[8] Combined with declining land sales and depression in New South Wales, they did just that and brought to an end this particular inducement to emigrate for the rest of the decade.

Bounty emigrants were always supposed to be selected according to the needs of the colony. When he served as government emigrant agent

[5] *Correspondence*, B.P.P., pp. 27–28, 44; "Despatch from the Governor of New South Wales Transmitting a Report of a Committee of the Legislative Council . . . on Emigration," B.P.P., 1841 (241), XVII, p. 258.

[6] R. B. Madgwick, *Immigration into Eastern Australia, 1788–1852* (London: Longmans, Green, 1937), p. 151.

[7] *Correspondence*, B.P.P., 1842 (301), XXXI, pp. 1–5, 14; Burroughs, *Britain and Australia*, p. 262.

[8] *Times* (London), April 6, 1841, p. 6; Fred Hitchins, *The Colonial Land and Emigration Commission* (Philadelphia: University of Pennsylvania Press, 1931), pp. 54–55. The commissioners distrusted John Marshall, who had handled most of this trade on behalf of the government since 1831. At first, Marshall refused to implement the new instructions, which concerned not only outfitting and accommodation on vessels carrying bounty immigrants but also required the immigrants to submit baptismal and marriage certificates and testimonials of good character to enable the commissioners to verify that the personal details by which the Colonial Board would accept them as eligible for bounty payment were correct. "An extensive Emigration has been carried on by Public Funds throughout the whole of the year over which we have had no authority" (Colonial Land and Emigration Commissioners to Vernon Smith, December 16, 1840, and to James Stephen, February 13, 1841, CO 386/58).

in the late thirties, Thomas Frederick Elliot had tried to impose a selective policy on the government's bounty scheme. His efforts were criticized by poor law and private relief agencies in Britain for refusing to countenance assistance to the people most in need, regardless of their qualifications. At the same time, Australian opinion condemned his efforts because too many immigrants were arriving who were without skills and who were from the cities.[9] In vain, Elliot maintained that government assistance was granted not indiscriminately but with regard to colonial preferences and that the relief of distress in Britain was a secondary consideration. Colonial suspicions continued because of the close contacts he had with the poor law commissioners and parochial officers.[10] Because of these suspicions, the land and emigration commissioners ceased intervening directly in the selection of emigrants after 1840. They did, however, retain some control over the bounty system in that after 1840, bounties were not to be paid in the colonies for an immigrant who arrived without a certificate from the commissioners or their agents verifying age and occupation.[11] Nonetheless, criticisms about the quality of the immigrants arriving in 1841 persisted in New South Wales.

Another means of obtaining assistance to emigrate to Australia was to go out indentured, whereby emigrants paid for their passages and outfits by working for three years for the employers who brought them out. This means was one way of getting to Van Diemen's Land in 1841, but as we have seen, few emigrants availed themselves of it. Yet this agency seems to have been preferred by a few crafts workers and

[9] For domestic critics, see Madgwick, *Immigration,* p. 130; David MacMillan, *Scotland and Australia, 1788–1850: Emigration, Commerce, and Investment* (Oxford: Clarendon Press, 1967), pp. 279, 285. For colonial criticism, see Madgwick, *Immigration,* pp. 49, 134, 141, 143; Norman MacDonald, *Canada, 1763–1841: Immigration and Settlement* (London: Longmans, Green, 1939), p. 27.

[10] Madgwick, *Immigration,* pp. 130, 141. Letters to the commissioners from poor law authorities confirm that there was some cooperation with them during the period of the government bounty system in the late thirties (S. Walcott to R. Tournay, Clerk to the Guardians, Ticehurst Union [Sussex], July 8, 1840, to Edwin Chadwick, Poor Law Commissioners, August 21, 1840, and to T. Ticehurst, Clerk to Battle Union [Sussex], July 25 1840, CO 386/25). The commissioners maintained that they were aware of the objections from Sydney and able to take them into consideration. They contended that the selection of emigrants in the British Isles could be "more efficiently executed by our Board" than by bounty agents. In response to inquiries about assisted passages, they did not mention the system being operated by private shippers (Commissioners to Vernon Smith, December 16, 1840, CO 386/58).

[11] F. G. Clarke, *Land of Contrarieties: British Attitudes to the Australian Colonies, 1828–55* (Melbourne: Melbourne University Press, 1977), p. 90; Madgwick, *Immigration,* p. 157; Hitchins, *Colonial Land and Emigration Commission,* p. 205.

servants who hesitated to go to the other side of the world without a job awaiting them at the other end. Some of them regretted having entered indentures when they discovered that they were being paid below the going rate in this colony that was still receiving convicts. Most of those who testified to the Committee on Immigration of the Legislative Council stressed the attraction of the certainty of a job, something not available, except through private or family networks, in any of the other emigrant fields.[12]

Emigration to New South Wales rose steeply in the space of a few months in response to assisted passages, which would seem to suggest a considerable reservoir of potential emigrants seeking the means of fulfilling a longer-term intention. Neither the Canadian provinces nor state or federal governments in the United States offered such assistance. Other types of aid to emigrants were financed in the United Kingdom by poor law authorities, landlords, and charities. In contrast to the Australian programs, which were at least nominally selective in accord with the requests of the colonies, these other sorts of aid clearly went to the poor, those people the colonies and the United States least wanted to receive.

There were not very many of them: the total number assisted to emigrate in 1841 from funds derived from the poor rates in England was only 1,058.[13] In the wake of the Canadian Rebellion of 1837, a small amount of poor law emigration to Australia had been subsidized from 1838 to 1840. Although only 1,662 people were so assisted, that was enough to arouse an outcry in Australia.[14] Some paupers had been sent to the United States during the 1820s and 1830s. The editor of *Niles Weekly Register*, who kept up a barrage of complaint against shoveling out paupers, ceased to mention the issue after 1839.[15] The American states with immigrant ports were beginning to take action to protect themselves, as they saw it. I have come across one case in 1838 (there may

[12] "Van Diemen's Land: Evidence before the Committee of the Legislative Council on Immigration," *Correspondence*, B.P.P., pp. 128, 151–65. "Both Western and Southern Australia cannot be recommended to any emigrants who do not go out without a prior engagement" *Saturday Journal* (London), February 8, 1840, p. 110.

[13] "Number of Emigrants Who Have Embarked from the Various Ports of the U.K.," B.P.P., 1843 (90), XXXIV, p. 1.

[14] Madgwick, *Immigration*, p. 143. On poor law emigration, see also Shepperson, *British Emigration*, p. 43, and Arthur Redford, *Labour Migration in England, 1800–1850*, 2d ed. (Manchester: Manchester University Press, 1964), pp. 108–9.

[15] See, for example, the broadside against England for committing "such putrescent masses of humanity on our shores" (*Niles Weekly Register*, June 10, 1837, p. 226).

have been more) where the consignees of a vessel agreed to take paupers back to Liverpool and to reimburse New York City for its related expenses.[16] By 1841, pauper emigration had come to mean emigration to Canada.[17]

Private donations contributed more to emigration than did parochial funds or the poor rates. For Scots and Irish people, private schemes of aid, mainly from landlords, afforded the only assistance available in 1841, apart from colonial bounty grants to Australia. Prospective emigrants without savings of their own could not take advantage of free passages to New South Wales anyway, unless they were able to obtain a further grant to cover the cost of clothing and outfit and of internal travel to the port of embarkation. Unemployed operatives in Paisley estimated that they needed at least an additional £4 per head, which was nearly enough to send an emigrant to Canada.[18] Thus private funds tended to be directed toward subsidizing colonists to Canada. When landowners wrote to the commissioners asking for some form of government encouragement, chiefly in the form of land grants, Thomas Frederick Elliot always recommended that the petitioners should plan to send their people to Canada.[19] During the spring of 1841, the British government's emigration agent in Quebec, A. C. Buchanan, reported the arrival of 116 immigrants sent by Lord Portman from his estates in Dorset and Kent, of handloom weavers sent by the Carlton Emigration Society, of 45 people assisted by Lord Charlemont to leave his estate in Armagh, and of 48 persons who arrived from Limerick aided by Colonel Wyndham.[20] Scottish landlords sent more than seven hundred

[16] *Niles National Register*, September 15, 1838, p. 46. In 1831, the average size of family among laborers arriving in the United States from England had been higher than for most other occupations. In 1841, it was lower. I interpret this as evidence that such assistance had, in fact, virtually ceased. See also *Massachusetts State Laws*, 1837, Chap. 238, p. 270, cited in United States Immigration Commission, *Reports*, 1911, 21: 692–93. After 1832, immigrant carriers to New York could choose whether to pay a head tax or to be bonded to cover the costs of any immigrants who became public charges (Edwin Guillet, *The Great Migration* [Toronto: Thomas Nelson, 1937], p. 180).

[17] Redford estimated that less than 2 percent of emigrants from the United Kingdom between 1835 and 1846 were financed by poor law authorities (*Labour Migration*, p. 110).

[18] *Times* (London), August 20, 1841, p. 6c, November 20, 1841, p. 6b, and November 15, 1841, p. 6b. The colonial land and emigration commissioners learned that shipowner John Marshall was charging married couples £4 plus £4 for each child, in addition to collecting bounty payments (Colonial Land and Emigration Commissioners to James Stephen, April 21, 1841, CO 386/58).

[19] *Albion* (New York City), March 7, 1840, p. 79; MacMillan, *Scotland and Australia*, p. 283.

[20] *Times* (London), September 3, 1841, p. 5d.

migrants to Canada in 1841.[21] Taken together, poor law and private assistance to the emigration to Canada in 1841 accounted for only 7.9 percent of the immigrants who arrived at Quebec and Montreal that year.[22]

Poor law authorities and landlords preferred to send emigrants to Canada rather than the United States not only because they were under pressure to keep them within the Empire. Although sending emigrants to the United States cost less than passages to Australia, fares to Canada, especially on timber ships, might be as low as £1–3, whereas fares to ports in the United States started at about £5. Emigrants, however, also had to be provisioned, or provision themselves, for a journey that averaged fifty nine days, if they arrived in Quebec during the summer of 1841. Buchanan reported that many passengers arrived that summer "in very destitute circumstances owing to the long voyage," though he did also report some cases in which assisted immigrants had been "well-provided for by the poor law commissioners or a landlord."[23]

If assisted passages played a minor role in the emigration to Canada, in marked contrast to that to New South Wales, immigrants were led to expect more help on arrival than was afforded immigrants at Sydney, Port Phillip, or ports in the United States. As early as 1828, A. C. Buchanan had arrived in Quebec as resident superintendent and agent for emigrants to be succeeded by his nephew of the same name in 1838. A. B. Hawke was appointed to a similar post for Upper Canada in 1831. These men and their staffs were responsible for receiving immigrants when they landed, clothing and feeding the starving, hearing complaints and prosecuting defaulting shipmasters, keeping in touch with those needing jobs, helping newcomers to find their friends, arranging their onward journeys, and providing information about where land was available, roads, distances and costs.[24] New York State

[21] Oliver MacDonagh, *A Pattern of Government Growth, 1800–1860: The Passenger Acts and Their Enforcement* (London: MacGibbon and Kee, 1961), p. 3; Shepperson, *British Emigration,* p. 46.

[22] This percentage represents 2,214 of 28,086 immigrants arriving in Quebec and Montreal between May 6 and October 31, 1841 ("Annual Reports of Agents for Emigration in Canada," *Correspondence,* B.P.P., p. 282). Cf. A. C. Buchanan's weekly returns, *Correspondence,* B.P.P., pp. 250–62. See also *Niles National Register,* May 13, 1843, p. 176.

[23] Buchanan's weekly reports for August 28 and July 24, 1841, *Correspondence,* B.P.P., pp. 251–53, 261; Annual Report for 1841, B.P.P., 1842 (373), XXXI, p. 14.

[24] MacDonald, *Canada,* pp. 20, 487. For criticism of inadequate preparation in Montreal in 1841, see p. 29.

did not begin to try to fulfill such functions until Castle Garden, the old Revolutionary fort at the Battery, was converted for this purpose in 1855.[25]

Many immigrants arrived in Quebec in 1841 expecting to have their transport costs for the further journey to Upper Canada paid for them. Buchanan, on the other hand, was authorized to subsidize only widows, orphans, and others in dire distress. As he commented, "It is much to be regretted that exaggerated accounts . . . have been circulated among (more particularly the Scoth) emigrants this season. They all land with the idea that they are to be forwarded at government expense to whatever section of the province they may fix on."[26] Although the paternalism was not so great as many anticipated, the prospect of such aid may have been another factor attracting poorer emigrants to Canada rather than the United States.

Buchanan did try to provide employment in or near Quebec for those whose resources were exhausted on arrival. He complained that immigrants refused work at 3s. 6d. or 3s. 9d. a day in Quebec and even sold their belongings to reach Upper Canada, where he feared they would become public charges in Montreal or Kingston. Urging "the necessity of providing some immediate employment for the labouring population coming into the province," as well as the importance of transport as such, officials in Upper Canada sought loan guarantees from the British Treasury to finance canal and road building.[27]

Although managing to keep a certain amount of road building going, both Buchanan in Quebec and Lord Sydenham in Montreal asked the colonial land and emigration commissioners to post placards in the outports urging unskilled laborers to take the work offered them on road building in Quebec and Montreal rather than proceed farther

[25] See also the description of poor arrangements for the reception of immigrants in Queensland as late as the 1870s in Helen Woolcock, *Rights of Passage: Emigration to Australia in the Nineteenth Century* (London: Tavistock Publications, 1986), pp. 211–15. New York City did provide a hospital on Staten Island for immigrants detained because of illness and a facility on Ward's Island where they could rest temporarily before emerging into New York City (Guillet, *Great Migration,* pp. 180–81).

[26] *Correspondence,* B.P.P., p. 251; *Times* (London), September 3, 1841, p. 4d; *Report of Colonial Land and Emigration Commissioners,* B.P.P., 1842 (567), XXV, p. 10.

[27] R. B. Sullivan, Presiding Councillor, Executive Council Chamber, Toronto, June 16, 1840, to Sir George Arthur, Lt. Governor, Upper Canada, Great Britain, Colonial Office, *Public Works (Canada),* B.P.P., 1843 (595), XXXII, p. 44. Lt. Governor Sir George Arthur did manage to get loans of £40,000 from banks for such expenditure (MacDonald, *Canada,* p. 494; Roger Dennis Hall, "The Canada Company, 1826–43," Ph.D. diss., Cambridge University, 1973, pp. 369–71).

west, where unskilled labor was in little demand.[28] The public works tended not to be located where the immigrants hoped to acquire land. As one Scotsman, scouting for land in Upper Canada, wrote to his brother, "They say in this country, where they are not in the habit of putting any metal on roads, that you never can have good roads and good land in the same place."[29] The agitation from British officials in Canada finally produced legislation in August and September 1841 to facilitate the negotiation of a loan in England and the establishment of a Board of Public Works for Canada.[30] On the basis of this legislation and encouragement from officials in Canada, the colonial land and emigration commissioners confidently encouraged emigration to Canada in 1842, with the assurance that there would be plenty of work for laborers on canals and roads.[31] Insofar as it enhanced emigration, this governmental activity on both sides of the water sent many to bitter experiences, as the promised jobs failed to materialize. During 1842 hundreds of immigrants wandered from Quebec to Kingston, from Kingston to Niagara, on to Rochester, Utica, and Albany, and finally to New York City, where many turned to begging until they could get passage back to Britain.[32]

Emigrants of this generation, whether from towns or rural areas, whether industrial workers or agricultural laborers, shared a hope of securing land of their own. For a long time, American historians could do nothing but criticize and condemn federal land policies, either for encouraging speculation and retarding settlement, on one hand, or for inducing too many ill-equipped settlers to take it up, on the other hand. Yet, to British officials working in Canada, conscious of direct competition with the United States for emigrants, American land policy appeared as a model to be emulated. Land was easier to acquire and cheaper in the United States than it was in the British colonies.

[28] Despatch from Lt. Governor Sir George Arthur, Government House, Toronto, July 14, 1840, to Lord John Russell, and C. Poulett Thompson (later Lord Sydenham), Governor-General, Government House, Montreal, May 20, 1840, to Sir George Arthur, *Public Works*, B.P.P., p. 43.

[29] Joseph Abbott, *The Emigration to North America;* 2d ed. (Montreal, The Author, 1843), p. 67.

[30] Lord Sydenham, Montreal, February 21, 1841, to Lord John Russell, *Public Works*, pp. 51–52. The various acts were printed in the same volume, pp. 1–11.

[31] Hamilton H. Killary, President of the Board of Works, December 8, 1842, to Rawson W. Rawson, Chief Secretary, in *Public Works*, p. 108.

[32] Frances Morehouse, "Canadian Migration in the Forties," *Canadian Historical Review* 9 (1928): 310–11.

Land policies applied in Canada have also been condemned by its historians as "a complicated and wasteful" system.[33] No single uniform policy was followed in all the provinces, but Upper Canada (Ontario) was the most attractive to prospective farmers in 1841. Of the twenty eight thousand immigrants arriving in Quebec that year, nineteen thousand headed for that district. Complications and confusion arose in part because instructions sent from the Colonial Office, which were continually being modified, were not always followed by the lieutenant governor in office or always interpreted in the same way. The land business itself was conducted by two separate offices, the Surveyor-General and the Crown Commissioner. As a consequence, the process of securing title to land, after application for it, could be a lengthy business.

Not only was the process of acquiring land cumbersome, but it was also riddled with patronage and favoritism. Long before 1841, most of the land had been given away or sold to land companies, individuals, Loyalists during the American Revolution, or reserved for the clergy or other purposes. According to Norman MacDonald, by 1837, of 1.7 million acres surveyed, 450,000 constituted a road reserve and 500,000 were earmarked to satisfy past pledges. Only 700,000 acres of land of inferior quality were available, while 1.1 million acres of Crown land were still unsurveyed.[34] In the United States, 1.1 million acres were sold by the federal government in 1841 alone.

In 1831 the Colonial Office had tried to end the favoritism and jobbing that accompanied free and special grants by insisting on the sale of land by auction. This policy was finally adopted as law by the legislature of Upper Canada in 1837. The governor-in-council, however, retained the power to fix the minimum price and terms and conditions of sale. The price tended to be fixed at ten shillings per acre, nearly twice the minimum price in force in the United States and high enough to protect the price of the lands of the Canada Company and of other large landowners. Land not sold at auction could still be sold by private sale. Nor were free gifts of land entirely abolished, because the law provided that purchasers of fifty acres could have another fifty acres reserved for them as a free grant once their settlement duties had been fulfilled. Credit was finally abolished, something the United States federal government had done in 1820. Nevertheless, the speculative holders of

[33] MacDonald, *Canada*, p. 510. This paragraph is based on that work and on Lillian Gates, *Land Policies of Upper Canada* (Toronto: University of Toronto Press, 1968).

[34] MacDonald, *Canada*, p. 512.

unimproved lands, many of whom were in the colonial legislature, had their titles confirmed. Furthermore, wild lands remained untaxed, whereas in the United States, most land in private ownership, whether improved or not, was taxed.[35]

Under the circumstances, squatting was endemic in Upper Canada, as in other Canadian provinces, but no move had yet been made toward the right of preemption at the minimum price, such as was being introduced in the United States. One provision of a new Land Act passed in 1839 appeared to mark a step in the direction of assisting immigrants without capital to acquire land: free grants of land to actual settlers along colonization roads. Although officials in the Colonial Office thought these grants were to be for immigrants, local officials regarded them as assisting established settlers to acquire land for their children.[36] Because immigrants did not have the franchise until they had acquired land (in the United States, residence of six months usually secured a vote in local elections), the colonial legislation favored established settlers. Thus access to land was neither so cheap nor so straightforward in Canada in 1841 as it was in the United States.[37]

Australian land policy was, if anything, more disadvantageous than that of Canada to the immigrant with little or no capital. Although the ideas of Gibbon Wakefield were never applied so thoroughly as in South Australia, policy in New South Wales was more consciously influenced by him and what historians have liked to call the "armchair theorists" in the Colonial Office than it was in Canada.[38] Policy was directed specifically toward generating funds by selling land at a sufficient price to deter the emigrants assisted by those funds from becoming small farmers, in order to retain their services as wage laborers for large-scale enterprises in sheep farming. Unlike Upper Canada, New South Wales experienced a persistent labor shortage as this activity expanded during

[35] Until 1847, however, state governments were not allowed to tax federal land within their borders until five years after it had been sold (Paul Gates and Lillian Gates, "Canadian and American Land Policy Decisions, 1930," *Western Historical Quarterly* 15 (1984): 290.

[36] Lillian Gates, *Land Policies*, p. 258.

[37] This is not to deny that land speculation was rife in the States, that land office officials were sometimes guilty of showing favoritism, or that the price of land was the only element in farm-making costs.

[38] This discussion is based on Richard Mills, *Colonization of Australia, 1829–42: The Wakefield Experiment in Empire Building* (London: Sidgwick and Jackson, 1915); Madgwick, *Immigration;* Burroughs, *Britain and Australia;* and Clarke, *Land of Contrarieties.* A contemporary statement of the obstacles to acquiring land or pastoral licenses in the Port Phillip district appeared in *Saturday Journal* (London), December 24, 1839, p. 381.

the 1830s. With the decision to end the transport of convicts to New South Wales in 1840, the labor shortage threatened to become acute.

It has rightly been insisted that circumstances in Australia, rather than land policy, dictated such a pattern of large-scale enterprises. In New South Wales there was not, as in Canada, a shortage of unalienated or unreserved lands. The Ripon Regulations of 1831 that ended free grants and introduced an auction system with a minimum price of five shillings an acre were actually very much like Goderich's instructions to Canadian lieutenant governors the same year. The problem in New South Wales was that a minimum price of five shillings per acre was too much to pay for grazing land and sent many graziers to squatting on land outside the nineteen organized counties around Sydney. Thus the demand for labor was being generated primarily from sheep farmers located at long distances from the ports of immigration. They were now about to lose the convict labor on which they had relied.

The obstacles placed in the way of prospective small farmers were enormous. After selecting land, settlers had to wait nine months for a survey to be conducted, after which the land had to be advertised for a month before auction. Meanwhile, supporting themselves and their families, they still risked being outbid at the auction. The Squatting Act of 1836 required applicants for pastoral licenses to obtain certificates of character and good conduct from a justice of the peace or Crown land commissioner. According to Peter Burroughs, the commissioners "showed little sympathy for squatters of lowly social origins."[39] In any case, £500 to £1,000 was needed to begin a successful sheep farm.[40] Then, in August 1838, Lord Glenelg in London raised the minimum price for auctioned land to twelve shillings an acre to generate money for assisting immigration when convict labor ceased to arrive, and granted power to local governors to raise the price even more if the labor shortage persisted. Finally, in May 1840, Lord John Russell announced the Wakefieldian fixed-price system of land sale at £1 per acre to replace auctions in the Port Phillip district. These new regulations also provided that anyone could select a district of eight square miles for survey (eleven thousand acres) and, after the survey, pick out four thousand of the best acres, even in scattered locations, and reject

[39] Burroughs, *Britain and Australia,* p. 127. For contemporary criticism of land regulations in New South Wales and unfavorable comparisons with the United States, see William Mann, *Six Years' Residence in the Australian Provinces* (London, 1839), pp. 163–64, 227, 283, 301.

[40] Burroughs, *Britain and Australia,* p. 128.

the rest. Lord Russell's instructions did not survive more than a year, and Governor Sir George Gipps did exempt three hundred thousand acres in the Sydney district that had already been advertised at five shillings per acre.

Clearly, if they were at all well informed, the bounty emigrants of 1841 could not have been expecting to become landowners in the near future. Some immigrants had surmounted the obstacles during the 1830s to become small farmers—using family labor—but they generally remained fairly poor for want of markets. Australian conditions, reinforced by land policies, meant dim prospects for freehold yeoman farming in New South Wales.

What sources of information were available at this time to prospective emigrants who might want to make a comparison between various fields of emigration before coming to a decision about destination? There were, of course, those placards, notices, and handbills mentioned by contemporaries but not surviving as documentary evidence for historians. The colonial land and emigration commissioners would send out information about any of the colonies to those who applied to them or any of their agents. A prospective emigrant who was literate could also consult newspapers and guidebooks.

An abundance of information about Canada was available in England. Thomas Rolph, who was appointed emigration agent for Canada in 1840, was very active at this time. A second edition of his book *A Descriptive and Statistical Account of Canada* was published in London in 1841, and this guidebook was just one of a number on the market that praised Canada.[41] Chartered in 1826 with a grant of two million acres in Upper Canada, the Canada Company was also actively recruiting.[42] The sharp drop in emigration to Canada in 1838 after the Rebellion led the company in 1840 to begin advertising more widely the terms on which its land might be obtained and to begin offering to provide settlers with work on its transport projects immediately after arrival. Its publicists claimed that settlers "who began *without one farthing of*

[41] On the promotional activities of Thomas Rolph, see Helen I. Cowan, *British Emigration to British North America*, rev. ed. (Toronto: University of Toronto Press, 1961), pp. 123–27; Thomas Rolph, *Canada vs. Australia: Their Relative Merits Considered* (London, 1839); and Rolph, *A Descriptive and Statistical Account of Canada*, 2d ed. (London: Smith Elder, 1841); Hall, "Canada Company," pp. 323–30.

[42] For a discussion of this and other land companies in the Canadian provinces, see MacDonald, *Canada*, pp. 269–309; Cowan, *British Emigration to British North America*, pp. 132–43; and Hall, "Canada Company."

capital" had become successful farmers, and they encouraged "the poor labourer and small farmer who is struggling at home for a bare subsistence" to emigrate to Canada.[43] While thus encouraging the emigration of people without capital, the company counseled the emigrant not to ask for "exorbitant wages on his arrival."[44] As one of its boosters, Joseph Abbott, chided:

> It is not to be supposed that tailors and shoemakers should all at once become expert axe-men and good farmers, and it may be said that the mass of people in Canada, since the manufacturing districts supply the greatest number of emigrants, never held a plough or worked on a farm until after their arrival in Canada, and yet one of these raw hands will spurn lower wages than are paid to experienced labourers.[45]

One might have expected Thomas Rolph and the Canada Company to have advertised in the newspapers of East Anglia; but there was not a single notice or advertisement in the four newspapers in Norfolk and Cambridgeshire searched for 1840 and 1841, although offers of land for sale in New Zealand, South Australia, West Australia, Van Diemen's Land, New Brunswick, and even Texas appeared.[46] Advertisements for passage to Canada, including ships sailing from Hull and Great Yarmouth, also appeared in the East Anglian press.[47]

Historians of assisted emigration to Australia have concluded that neither the private operators of the bounty system nor the agents of the Colonial Land and Emigration Commission actively encouraged emigration. The bounty agents, working in cooperation with agents of the Colonial Board, merely issued notices and placards to the effect that free passages to New South Wales were available. The agents of the colonial land and emigration commissioners, six of them in Ireland and

[43] Abbott, *Emigration to North America,* pp. 86–88, 102; *Albion* (New York City), April 24, 1841, p. 146; Canada Company, *A Statement of the Satisfactory Results Which Have Attended Emigration to Upper Canada* (London: Smith, Elder, 1841), p. 4.

[44] "Texas and California," brochure of Canada Company (London, 1841), inside cover; Canada Company, *Statement,* pp. 20, 48.

[45] Abbott, *Emigration to North America,* p. 88.

[46] *Independent Press* (Cambridge), March 13, 1841, p. 2, col. 3; *Norfolk Chronicle and Norwich Gazette,* September 5, 1840, p. 1, col. 1, September 12, 1840, p. 1, col. 1, June 9, 1840, p. 1, col. 1, and March 6, 1841, p. 3, col. 5; *Mercury* (Norwich), March 14, 1840, p. 4, col. 7, December 5, 1840, p. 1, col. 2, February 20, 1841, p. 4, col. 7, March 6, 1841, p. 1, col. 4, May 15, 1841, p. 1, col. 1, and May 22, 1841, p. 4, col. 5.

[47] *Norfolk Chronicle and Norwich Gazette,* April 4, 1840, p. 3, col. 6, February 20, 1841, p. 3, col. 4, and May 8, 1841, p. 1, col. 2. *Mercury* (Norwich), April 4, 1840, p. 2, col. 1, June 13, 1840, p. 1, col. 1, February 21, 1841, p. 1, col. 3, and May 8, 1841, p. 1, col. 2.

two in both England and Scotland, simply distributed forms and literature to inquirers.[48] Of four newspapers searched for East Anglia, a natural recruiting ground for the agricultural laborers and servants sought for New South Wales, only an urban paper, the Norwich *Mercury*, carried announcements of assisted passages. Advertisements from bounty agents appearing in that paper conformed fully to the regulations that the colonial land and emigration commissioners were seeking to enforce. Notices about ships sailing for New South Wales carried offers of free passages to "labourers, shepherds, carpenters, masons and female domestic or farm servants" but warned that "unexceptional testimonials as to character would be required."[49]

It may be that little control could be maintained over verbal statements. Late in 1840 the commissioners were concerned that bounty agents were making false and exaggerated statements to poor, sometimes illiterate emigrants and that they could do little to counteract "the glowing descriptions which offer to the fancy of the poor the ready acquisition of every worldly good." They noted with alarm that a publication entitled "Twenty Years Experience in Australia," a pamphlet aimed at creating a prejudice against every colony except New South Wales, was being distributed by John Marshall's agents in every direction throughout the country.[50]

Anyone relying on the newspapers in East Anglia for guidance about emigration would find the information provided confined to the colonies and a generally hostile attitude taken to the United States as a field of emigration. With but a couple of exceptions, this was true of all the editorials, offers of pamphlets and journals for sale, and emigrant letters that appeared during 1840 and 1841 in the four newspapers searched.[51] For example, a letter to the editor of the *Norfolk Chronicle*

[48] Robin Haines, "Government-assisted Emigration from the United Kingdom to Australia, 1831–60: Promotion, Recruitment, and the Labouring Poor," Ph.D. diss., Flinders University of South Australia, 1992, pp. 161, 177; MacMillan, *Scotland and Australia*, p. 293.

[49] *Mercury* (Norwich), April 18, 1840, p. 1, col. 1, June 13, 1840, p. 1, col. 1, June 20, 1840, p. 4, col. 6, April 24, 1841, p. 2., col. 5, and May 1, 1841, p. 4, col. 7.

[50] Commissioners to Vernon Smith, December 16, 1840, Commissioners to James Stephen, January 15, and April 29, 1841, CO 386/58.

[51] The exceptions were in the *Independent Press* (Cambridge), which, in an editorial on November 20, 1841 (p. 1, col. 4), urging the government to assist emigration on a large scale to relieve current distress, noted that urban artisans would be useless as peasant farmers in the colonies and would emigrate instead to the United States or the Continent. *The British Mechanics and Labourers Handbook and Guide to the United States*, published by Charles Knight at four shillings, was advertised on August 22, 1840, p. 1, col. 1. For favorable notices of colonial fields, especially New Zealand, see *Chronicle* (Cambridge), August 22,

and Norwich Gazette from "A Friend" stated that "from America being so much nearer than Australia and there being generally a cousin or acquaintance already in a country to which it has long been more customary to emigrate, than to any other; thousands resolve to go there and they sail full of hopes which to their great disappointment are never realized."[52] Although shipping for the United States was advertised in London and Liverpool newspapers and even in the Chartist *Northern Star*, not a single notice of ships bound for ports in the United States or of lands for sale there appeared in these East Anglian papers.

In view of the quantity of information available and the pressures and inducements in Britain for intending emigrants to settle in the colonies, it is remarkable that the United States, which provided no assistance with passages, kept its fares higher by stiffer regulation, and did little to assist immigrants on arrival, received more immigrants from the British Isles in 1841 than either the Canadian provinces or the Australian colonies. The analysis would seem to point to the greater importance of easier access to land among many intending emigrants in this generation. It also reinforces the view that "there being generally a cousin or acquaintance already in a country to which it has long been more customary to emigrate" formed a considerable obstacle to be overcome by those who wished to encourage settlement in the colonies. Information obtained through private letters and visits overrode that supplied in print.

To single out assistance, cost of passage, reception facilities, access to land, and information as variables influencing the choice of destination of emigrants from the British Isles obviously does not cover all possibilities. Nevertheless, it does provide a background for examining, insofar as is possible at the moment, the differences between the flows to these main destinations in this year of hardship for many inhabitants of the United Kingdom.

1840, p. 4, col. 5, October 23, 1841, p. 1, col. 1, August 14, 1841, p. 1, col. 1, September 11, 1841, p. 1, col. 1, and December 4, 1841, p. 4, cols. 4–5. *Norfolk Chronicle and Norwich Gazette,* December 18, 1841, p. 1, col. 3; *Mercury* (Norwich), January 4, 1840, p. 1, cols. 7–8, and May 1, 1841, p. 1, col. 1.

52 *Norfolk Chronicle and Norwich Gazette,* June 6, 1840, p. 3, col. 4. See also in the same issue an advertisement for a pamphlet by Edmund Edmunds, a returned immigrant farmer, "A Word to the Wise," priced at only six pence, which claimed that America "holds out but very poor prospects to the English farmer and is not much better to the English labourer" (p. 1, col. 2).

Table 5.3. Emigrants from the British Isles to selected destinations, 1841, by nativity

Place of Birth	New South Wales[a]		Quebec and Montreal		United States	
	Number	Percent	Number	Percent	Number	Percent
England and Wales	4,563	23.4	5,970	21.4	23,190	43.3
Scotland	1,616	8.3	3,559	12.8	4,005	7.5
Ireland	13,344	68.3	18,317	65.8	26,315	49.2
Total	19,523	100.0	27,846	100.0	53,510	100.0

Sources: Imre Ferenczi and Walter Willcox, eds., *International Migrations* (New York: National Bureau of Economic Research, 1931), 1: 360; "Papers Relating to Emigration," B.P.P., 1843 (90), XXIV, p. 46; sample of one in every five passenger lists from ships of five United States ports (multiplied by 5). Sample based on National Archives, microfilms no. 237, roll 44; no. 255, roll 3; no. 277, rolls 13–15; no. 425, roll 58; and no. 259, rolls 21–22.

[a] Only the bounty immigrants (84 percent of the total) were designated by nativity in the published reports.

First, in what ways and to what extent did the sudden availability of a far greater number of assisted passages to New South Wales modify the pattern of emigration? It was mainly the Irish who responded to the offer of free passages. Nearly 70 percent of the bounty immigrants arriving in New South Wales that year were Irish (see Table 5.3). The number of bounty passengers increased by 13,428 between 1840 and 1841. The Irish, with 13,344 bounty passengers in the latter year accounted for just about all the additional immigrants. This fact is all the more remarkable in that over a longer period in subsequent years—from 1840 to 1862—the English and Scots obtained 68 percent of the bounty passages to Australia.[53] Undeterred by the higher fares, 69 percent of the English and Welsh who emigrated to these three destinations in 1841 arrived in ports in the United States, whereas nearly two-fifths of the Scots and the Irish took advantage of cheaper fares to British North America.

It is more difficult to demonstrate this pattern over time because the figures that the United States published for the natives of the British Isles who were immigrating are useless.[54] The British figures tell us only

[53] "Returns of the Number of Emigrants Sent Out by the Government Emigration Board," B.P.P., 1863 (504), XXXVIII, p. 30.

[54] Donald Akenson's criticism of United States immigration figures for underestimating the numbers of Irish immigrants before 1855 is misplaced. The United States authorities merely assumed that 70 percent of arrivals in American ports from the British Isles were Irish, whereas passenger lists show that estimate to have been much too high for years before the famine (Akenson, *Being Had: Historians, Evidence, and the Irish in North America* [Port Credit, Ontario: P. D. Meany, 1985], pp. 47, 52).

Table 5.4. Location of ports in the British Isles from which passengers left for selected destinations, 1840–1842

Destinations and location of port	1840	1841	Percent change 1840–41	1842	Percent change 1841–42
British North America					
England and Wales	5,305	7,469	41	13,005	79
Scotland	3,053	6,606	116	7,708	17
Ireland	23,935	24,089	< 1	33,410	39
Australasia					
England and Wales	14,495	23,179	60	6,639	-71
Scotland	817	5,026	5	4,420	-12
Ireland	0	4,420		937	-79
United States					
England and Wales	35,309	39,066	11	53,439	37
Scotland	1,246	2,058	65	4,214	104
Ireland	4,087	3,893	-4	6,199	59

Source: N. H. Carrier and J. R. Jeffery, *External Migration: A Study of the Available Statistics, 1815–1950*, General Register Office, Studies on Medical and Population Subjects, no. 6 (London: HMSO, 1953), p. 95.

the ports from which emigrants sailed, and many Irish left from Liverpool or from Plymouth at this time.[55] Table 5.4 does provide a further hint of this redirection of Irish emigration with the offer of free passages. The emigration from Irish ports, predominantly Irish-born people, to North America barely increased at all, whereas that to Australasia rose from zero to 4,420. Emigration from Scottish ports to North American destinations actually rose between 1840 and 1841, and that to Australasia did not show the steep decline (79 percent) evident from Irish ports as the bounty passages disappeared.

Nothing can be gleaned from Table 5.4 about the behavior of the English. We do know that the number of English people taking up assisted passages increased a little, from 3,614 in 1839 to 4,735 in 1841, and the proportion of self-financed emigrants to New South Wales, most of whom were probably English and Scots, actually fell from 24 percent of the immigrants in 1840 to 16 percent of those arriving in Sydney and Port Phillip in 1841.[56] The Scots migrating to the United States, as

[55] I am grateful to Jill Waterhouse for pointing out to me the Dublin—Plymouth route by which several ships of Irish emigrants traveled to Australia that year.

[56] "Emigrants Who Have Embarked," B.P.P., pp. 58–59; MacMillan, *Scotland and Australia*, pp. 293, 298, 300–302. John Marshall had been carrying bounty emigrants to New South Wales since 1831. The commissioners claimed that he had a "virtual monopoly of the business." With the increase in bounty warrants in 1840, however, other shippers

Table 5.5. Number of assisted immigrants arriving in Canada (Quebec) in 1841 and 1842, by national origin

National origin	1841	1842
England	697	1,079
Scotland	771	946
Ireland	656	504

Sources: "Despatch from the Governor-General of British North America, Transmitting the Annual Reports of the Agents for Emigration in Canada, 1841," B.P.P., 1842 (373) XXXI, pp. 6–7; "Copies of Reports . . . by the Emigrant Agents of Canada, New Brunswick, and New South Wales to the Governors and Councils of Those Colonies," B.P.P., 1843 (109), XXXIV, pp. 13, 25.

reflected in departures from Scottish ports, continued to rise through these depressed years of 1840–1842. No distinct shift in the numbers assisted to go to British North America between 1841 and 1842 can explain the increased Irish emigration to Canada in 1842. (see Table 5.5).

People from the poorest part of the United Kingdom responded to free passages. Nearly half of the bounty immigrants (49 percent) were recorded as Roman Catholic. But were bounty immigrants and other assisted emigrants from England being drawn from the poorest parts of that country? We do have details on the county of origin of English emigrants who were being sent to Canada by poor law authorities or taking up free passages to New South Wales. The emigration census of 1841 gives the county of origin of all English emigrants during the first five months of the year. These figures are not representative of the entire migration of that year because many industrial workers tended to leave in the autumn, whereas farm workers clustered in the early months of the year, when the census was taken. Unfortunately, U.S. passenger lists rarely provided details of place of origin within England. In spite of its bias toward agriculturists, the population census estimates by county are firmer. Thus it is possible to compare the origins of assisted emigrants and of all emigrants from England with the distribution by county of the English population. Less is known about the

were entering the trade. At least one of these, Carter and Binns, had previously been engaged in carrying emigrants to Canada (Commissioners to James Stephen, February 19, 1841, CO 386/58).

Table 5.6. Emigrants from England, 1841, by groups of counties from which they came

Type of county	Emigration census		Bounty immigrants, New South Wales		Poor law migrants, April 1840–December 1842		United States ship lists		United Kingdom population ('000's)	
	Number	Percent	Number	Percent	Number	Percent	Number	Percent	Number	Percent
Agricultural low-wage	2,358	25.4	1,156	26.2	588	20.5	65	28.5	4,372	29.4
Agricultural high-wage	2,225	24.0	788	17.9	1,990	69.4	57	25.0	1,882	12.7
Industrial low-wage	1,391	15.0	518	11.7	211	7.4	7	3.1	2,134	14.3
Industrial high-wage	3,311	35.6	1,951	44.2	77	2.7	99	43.4	6,474	43.6
Total	9,285	100.0	4,413	100.0	2,866	100.0	228	100.0	14,862	100.0

Sources: One-in-five sample from United States ship lists (see Table 5.3, above); "Papers Relating to Emigration," B.P.P., 1843 (90), XXXIV, p. 46; "Returns for Each Year from 1836–47 . . . ," B.P.P., 1847–48 (345), XLVII, pp. 14–23; proportion of male labor force in agriculture from N. F. R. Crafts, *British Economic Growth during the Industrial Revolution* (New York: Oxford University Press, 1985), p. 4; wage data as in Table 3.11, above.

Table 5.7. Emigrants from England per 10,000 inhabitants, 1841, by groups of counties

	Emigration census, January 1, 1841–June 4, 1841	Bounty migrants, New South Wales, 1841	Poor law migrants, April 1840–Dececember 1842
Agricultural low-wage	5.4	2.6	1.3
Agricultural high-wage	11.8	4.2	10.6
Industrial low-wage	6.5	2.4	1.0
Industrial high-wage	5.1	3.0	0.1
Average for country	7.1	3.4	2.2

Sources: As given in Table 5.6.
Note: These are not annual rates because the time period covered differs from group to group. The rates are presented for purposes of comparison only.

origins of self-financed emigrants to the United States and the colonies. A summary of the results is set out in Tables 5.6 and 5.7.

The well-publicized offer of free passages to New South Wales did not bring a great response in the English counties ranked as low-wage agricultural. As a group they fell slightly below the average for all English counties in numbers of bounty and poor law emigrants. Only Devon and Somerset in the west country were providing more than their share of bounty emigrants (see Table 5.8). Rather, the group of counties in which more than a third of the male labor force was still in agriculture and where wages were ten shillings a week or more—those distinguished in Table 5.6 as high-wage agricultural counties—were overrepresented both in the emigration census and among assisted emigrants. Kent and Sussex were granting much more poor law assistance than were authorities in any other counties in the country, as well as sending out an above-average share of bounty passengers.[57] People in most of the poorer agricultural counties of England did not rush to take advantage of assisted passages in the way that Irish people did.

The counties classified as industrial, where less than a third of the men worked in agriculture, were represented almost as well as the low-wage agricultural counties. The strength of the low-wage industrial counties was accounted for by the single county of Cornwall, which had

[57] The colonial land and emigration commissioners inherited contacts with the poor law authorities in these counties near London. They noted that in case they became able in future to select government bounty emigrants, "the district around you from which so many emigrants have been supplied before, will be borne in mind" (W. Walcott to R. Tournay, Clerk to the Guardians, Ticehurst Union [Sussex], July 8, 1840, CO 386/25; see also S. Walcott to Edwin Chadwick, August 21, 1840, CO 386/25).

Table 5.8. Counties with above-average rates of emigration per 10,000 population, 1840–1842

	Emigration census, 1841	Poor law, 1840–1842	Bounty, 1841
Agricultural low-wage			
Devon	13.8	.8	6.2
Somerset	15.4	6.6	6.6
Dorset	10.1	.4	2.4
Hereford	9.8	—	3.3
Rate for class	5.4	1.3	2.6
Agricultural high-wage			
Sussex	25.3	29.9	11.6
Kent	11.9	20.0	5.5
Cumberland	20.1	—	3.8
Westmorland	10.8	—	4.3
Rate for class	11.8	10.6	4.2
Industrial low-wage			
Cornwall	23.3	4.4	3.5
Gloucestershire	6.7	1.3	5.1
Rate for class	6.5	1.0	2.4
Industrial high-wage			
Cheshire	8.3	—	2.2
Lancashire	8.2	—	4.8
Yorkshire, W.R.	8.2	.3	3.2
Nottinghamshire	7.0	—	3.2
Rate for class	5.1	.1	3.0

Sources: Census of Great Britain, 1841: Enumeration Abstracts, Pt. 1, *England and Wales,* B.P.P., 1843 (496), XXII, pp. 399, 458; sources for Table 5.6.

Note: These are rates per 10,000 inhabitants, but not on an annual basis. Thus, only the relative rates are significant.

a higher incidence of both poor law and bounty emigrants than the average. Much of the emigration from Cornwall, however, was clearly self-financed, as its assistance rates were far below those of Kent and Sussex. Other low-wage industrial counties in the Midlands—Warwick, Stafford, Worcester, and Leicester—showed fairly low rates of emigration.

The proportion of emigrants from high-wage industrial counties would probably have been higher had the emigration census covered the autumn months, when there was a peak in the immigration of industrial workers to the United States. Very little poor law assistance was given in these industrial counties; but workers in some of them—Lancashire, Yorkshire, and Nottinghamshire—were fully represented among the English bounty emigrants.

Counties in the west of England—Cornwall, Devon, Somerset, Hereford, Westmorland, and Cumberland—were all sending out more than what their proportion of the population of the country would imply. Here, people were responding to the offer of free passages to Australia, though, apart from Somerset, there was not much poor law–assisted emigration. Two counties near London—Kent and Sussex—far exceeded the average density of emigration, with the help of substantially greater shares of both poor law and bounty aid. The lowest rates were in some of the southern and eastern counties, where the poverty of agricultural laborers was most pronounced (see Appendix Table 5.14).

Although these are but indirect inferences about who was leaving England during this year of economic depression, it seems possible that better information about assistance and about emigration fields, rather than unique distress, lies behind the limited English take-up of free passages to Australia. Irish people appear to have been far more alert and responsive to the opportunities.[58]

If the response to free passages was highly selective by county of origin of emigrants, it also tended to be selective of women. This was the result of a deliberate government policy, which set bounties at £15 on young unmarried women but only £10 on men. As can be seen in Table 5.9, women actually exceeded men in the assisted emigration to New South Wales, with a ratio of 1,036 per 1,000 men among the emigrants aged fifteen or over. Among unassisted immigrants the ratio of 506 women to 1,000 men was close to the ratios among English and Scots arrivals in the United States (529 and 551, respectively). Among Scottish bounty emigrants from 1838 to 1842, 773 women per 1,000 males were recorded, exactly the same ratio as was found for immigrants through Quebec and Montreal, among whom were only a small number who had received any kind of assistance.

One reason for the higher proportion of women in the emigration to the Empire was the larger percentage of women among Irish emigrants. Even in the self-financed Irish emigration to the States, 758 women

[58] Possibly of relevance here was the fact that the British government had more official emigrant agents in Ireland than in either Scotland or England from the late 1830s, and some of those agents in Ireland became involved "in a vague and informal fashion" in selecting emigrants for Australia and in organizing local committees of gentlemen, poor law authorities, and clergy to assist (MacDonagh, *Pattern of Government Growth,* p. 123; Gerard O'Brien, "The Establishment of Poor-Law Unions in Ireland, 1838–42," *Irish Economic and Social History* 12 [1985]: 41–42).

Table 5.9. Females per 1,000 males among emigrants from the British Isles to various destinations, 1841

	Among all immigrants	Among adults aged 15 or older
Emigration census, 1841	714	n.a.
Bounty immigrants, New South Wales	1,002	1,036
Unassisted immigrants, New South Wales	553	506
Arrivals in Quebec and Montreal	824	773
English to United States	615	529
Welsh to United States	702	700
Scots to United States	521	551
Irish to United States	805	758

Sources: One-in-five sample of United States passenger lists (see Table 5.3); for Quebec and Montreal, "Despatch from the Governor-General of British North America, Transmitting the Annual Reports of the Agents for Emigration in Canada, 1841," B.P.P., 1842 (373), XXXI, p. 1; for New South Wales, "Number of Emigrants Who Have Embarked from the Various Ports of the United Kingdom, 1842," B.P.P., 1843 (90), XXIV, pp. 46, 49.

arrived for every 1,000 men, a significantly higher proportion than among British immigrants.

A high proportion of women in a particular stream was associated with assisted passages. For families to take their female members overseas with them required means. Yet the Irish emigration was not so much a family migration as was the British. Among the adult bounty immigrants to New South Wales in 1841, fewer than half (45 percent) of the women were married. A number of writers have been studying the reasons for the emigration of single women from Ireland after the famine. Here is evidence that this tradition had begun before that time, probably for the same reasons suggested by Lynn Lees and John Modell. Young Irishwomen stood a better chance of marrying or of finding employment by emigrating than they did by moving to the barely growing Irish towns with their excess female populations.[59] Single women also formed a larger proportion of Irish immigrants to the United States than they did of British immigrants. Among the Irish immigrants to the States who arrived without spouses or children were

[59] Lynn Lees and John Modell, "Irish Countrymen Urbanized," *Journal of Urban History* 3 (1977): 392. The emigration of single women from Ireland after the famine years has been discussed in the literature on the assumption that this was a new phenomenon (Pauline Jackson, "Women in Nineteenth-Century Irish Emigration," *International Migration Review* 18 [1984]: 1004–20, and references cited there; Hasia R. Diner, *Erin's Daughters in America: Irish Immigrant Women in the Nineteenth Century* (Baltimore: Johns Hopkins University Press, 1983], pp. 4, 15–16, 31).

543 females per 1,000 males.[60] Only 188 English- and Welshwomen per 1,000 males emigrated alone, as did 168 Scotswomen. The adverse publicity given to female emigration during the first four years that colonial funds were used for bounties (1832–36) may have had something to do with the hesitation of Englishwomen to go alone. After a few highly publicized scandals about the contamination of respectable women by their associates on shipboard and by New South Wales itself, the government officials involved became persuaded that no respectable woman would apply for assistance. Many applications from country servants were withdrawn in 1834.[61]

The youth of the Irishwomen is particularly notable. The only age group in all the emigration from the British Isles to the United States in 1841 in which there was a significant excess of women was in the age range of fifteen to nineteen among the Irish, 59 percent of whom were women, hardly any of them married.

A search for employment opportunities may have been as important as looking for a husband among young women who went overseas on their own or with siblings or friends. Sex ratios can be obtained by county from the emigration census of 1841 (see Table 5.10). The ratios of women to men in some of the more industrialized counties such as Lancashire and Yorkshire (590/ 1,000 and 614/1,000, respectively), where, presumably, opportunities for women to find work were reasonably good, were strikingly lower than that in Sussex, a more agricultural county, where the ratio of 979/1,000 was actually higher than among Irish immigrants to the United States (805/1,000). Other important counties of emigration that were largely agricultural and rural—Kent, Devon, Somerset, and Cumberland—showed a higher proportion of women among their emigrants (776, 716, 794, and 899 women per 1,000 men, respectively) than did industrial counties or British immigrants to the United States as a whole. These findings are in marked contrast to those of Dudley Baines for the latter part of the century, by which time employment opportunities for women in England were changing.[62]

[60] Cf. Cormac Ó'Gráda, "Across the Briny Ocean," in *Migration across Time,* ed. Glazier and de Rosa, p. 83, where he gives a ratio of 546 women per 1,000 men from a sample of United States passenger lists, from the years 1820–46.

[61] James Hammerton, "Without Natural Protectors: Female Immigration to Australia, 1832–6," *Historical Studies* 16 (1975): 59 and passim. Eighteen forty-one was the year when Caroline Chisholm established the Female Immigrants' Home in Sydney.

[62] Dudley Baines estimated sex ratios in net emigration of 669 women per 1,000 men for all highly urbanized counties, 1861–1901, and 510 women per 1,000 men for all rural counties (*Migration in a Mature Economy: Emigration and Internal Migration in England and*

Table 5.10. Females per 1,000 males among emigrants from English counties with high rates of emigration, January–June 1841

Agricultural low-wage	
Devon	716
Somerset	794
Dorset	654
Hereford	850
Agricultural high-wage	
Sussex	979
Kent	776
Westmorland	1,033
Cumberland	899
Industrial low-wage	
Cornwall	725
Gloucestershire	712
Industrial high-wage	
Nottinghamshire	944
Cheshire	754
Yorkshire, W.R.	614
Lancashire	590
Middlesex	584
Entire country	714

Source: Census of Great Britain 1841, Enumeration Abstracts, Pt. 1, *England and Wales*; B.P.P., 1843 (496), XXII, pp. 399, 458.

Except for the emigration to the United States, I was unable to provide a profile of family groups in the movement. The published information on the migration through Quebec and Montreal and into New South Wales does permit a comparison of the proportion of children under fifteen years old in the different streams and the calculation of dependency ratios—the ratio of adults to children—which are given in Table 5.11. The proportion of children was lower and the dependency ratio more favorable in the migration to New South Wales than among emigrants to Canada and most of those to the United States. At this point, children were not eligible for bounties. Even so, the Irish entering the United States had the highest proportion of adults

Wales, 1861–1900 [Cambridge: Cambridge University Press, 1985], p. 163). It seems possible that these very different findings for net emigration in the late Victorian period reflect changing work opportunities after 1841. The number of females in the labor force recorded in the census was rising much more slowly in the later period than it had been from 1841 to 1851.

Table 5.11. Children and adults among emigrants from the British Isles to various destinations, 1841

	Immigrants aged 14 or younger (percent)	Adults per child aged 14 or younger
Unassisted immigrants to New South Wales	15.6	5.41
Bounty immigrants to New South Wales	24.3	3.12
Scots bounty immigrants to New South Wales, 1838–1842	29.6	2.37
Arrivals in Quebec and Montreal	30.9	2.24
English and Welsh arrivals in United States	29.2	2.45
Scots arrivals in United States	29.0	2.45
Irish arrivals in United States	19.6	4.10

Sources: Figures for Scots bounty immigrants provided from sources in Australia by David MacMillan, *Scotland and Australia, 1788–1850: Emigration, Commerce, and Investment* (Oxford: Clarendon Press, 1967), p. 294; other sources as in Table 5.6.

to children of any group, in spite of the large number of women present. This was to be expected because the Irishwomen were younger than the British, and far more of them were single.

The contrast with the movement into Canada is noteworthy. We know that the Irish predominated in the Canadian immigration, where they constituted nearly as large a proportion (66 percent) as they did of bounty immigrants to New South Wales (68 percent). Yet, among the Canadian immigrants there were only just over two adults per child on average, as compared with a little more than three in the assisted emigration to New South Wales and four in the Irish emigration direct to the United States. Thirty-one percent of immigrants to Upper and Lower Canada were less than fifteen years old—or were reported to have been so young—as compared with only 24 percent of bounty passengers and 20 percent of unassisted Irish immigrants to the United States. Because of difference in the way children were counted under the British and the American Passenger Acts, it was cheaper to transport them to Canada than to the United States. Although children constituted only 20 percent of Irish immigration through American ports, insofar as some of those families going by way of Canada later crossed the border into the United States, the Irish immigration was likely to have been more of a family migration than the United States ship lists suggest. Immigrants to Canada had an interest in lowering the reported age of their teenagers as those to New South Wales had in raising the ages of their children. The Australian colonies wanted young adults. Apparently, they got what they wanted, whereas the less well-off emigrants with families went to Canada.[63]

If some ages were adjusted a little in the records to conform with regulations, the problem is even greater where the reporting of occupations of colonial immigrants is concerned. The occupations given in the United States passenger lists—at least on those ships which reported them in detail and which I used for my sample—are more accurate, as well as more detailed, than the figures available in the Parliamentary Papers for emigrants to Canada and New South Wales. Because no preference was given to particular occupations or any official guidance provided, emigrants to the United States selected themselves, relying primarily on private and family contacts.

Although the colonial land and emigration commissioners were always more concerned with emigration to Australia and New Zealand than to the rest of the Empire, they did collect information "for emigrants of the labouring classes" on other fields. In 1841 they reported that agricultural laborers were needed in all parts of Canada, with the rider that in Upper Canada, "agricultural labourers with some experience" were in demand. All kinds of mechanics were wanted, especially carpenters, blacksmiths, shoemakers, and tailors. For Upper Canada, the additional trades of bricklayers, masons, coopers, millwrights, millers, boatbuilders, tanners, and wheelwrights were mentioned—all trades needed in developing agricultural regions.[64]

The same occupations—agricultural laborers and mechanics—were eligible for bounties in New South Wales. As the immigrants poured in during 1841, the authorities became more explicit in stating that it was shepherds, rather than farm laborers, who were required. In July, the Council in New South Wales sent to the colonial land and emigration commissioners a plea claiming that no special training was necessary for shepherds:

[63] In the atmosphere of labor shortage in New South Wales, the Committee of its Council recommended that older relatives of bounty immigrants be permitted to travel on the same ships if paying their own way. They also suggested that couples in their forties, but not over fifty, be allowed bounty passages for each child over ten whom they brought along with them, up to a maximum of five ("Report of the Committee of the New South Wales Council on Immigration, July 17, 1841," *Correspondence,* B.P.P., p. 40). These suggestions came too late to influence the movement in 1841. They do further underline that selectivity in bounty passages was designed not to relieve distress in the British Isles but to suit the needs of the colonies.

[64] Ibid, June 7, 1842, pp. 217–18.

> The points of attention are . . . so few and simple that they can be mastered by anyone possessing the disposition to observe and learn . . . . It would be advantageous that copies of this paper should be circulated as generally as possible in the manufacturing districts. Many of the inhabitants of the latter, persons accustomed to sedentary habits, who are now at a loss to obtain employment even at a low rate of wages, might be found willing to engage in an occupation neither injurious to health nor requiring laborious exertion.[65]

A circular describing a shepherd's duties stated specifically that "a weaver or buttonmaker after a few months' experience, will generally prove a better shepherd, in New South Wales, than the man brought up as a shepherd in England."[66]

It seems clear from Table 5.12 that New South Wales was not getting many shepherds. Not surprisingly, most of the shepherds appear to have been Scots immigrants. In keeping with the bounty regulations, 72 percent of the immigrants of 1841 were reported as agricultural laborers, though New South Wales agent for immigration F. L. S. Merewether suspected that

> not one-third of the number calling themselves agricultural labourers were really such. In many cases, where men have really been out-door manual labourers, though ignorant of agriculture, and have been so represented originally in their certificates, the bounty agents, aware that such persons were not properly eligible, appear to have supplied the deficiency, by prefixing "Agl" to their more correct description of themselves, given in the general term "labourer."[67]

The bounty regulations, combined with assisted passages, enticed more general laborers than could readily be employed in the colony. Farmers had not the means to employ labor. Although workers were

[65] Ibid, July 27, 1841, p. 41. A contemporary journal, whose advice to emigrants was not biased in favor of any one field, recommended Canada as a field for farmers with capital and for agricultural laborers, but not for urban people of any kind (*Saturday Journal* [London], February 8, 1840, p. 110).

[66] "Report of the Committee of the New South Wales Council," *Correspondence*, B.P.P., p. 49.

[67] "Minutes of Evidence before the Immigration Committee, 25 May 1842," B.P.P., 1843 (90), XXXIV, pp. 97–98. Madgwick misread this quotation in reporting the witness as saying that only a third of the agricultural laborers sent out were really such (*Immigration*, p. 183). An Australian scholar has suggested that such criticism of the immigrants they received was "mandatory for colonial agents" (Haines, "Government-assisted Emigration," p. 92).

Table 5.12. Recorded occupations of male emigrants from the British Isles to various destinations, 1841

	Bounty immigrants arriving in New South Wales		Immigrants arriving in Quebec and Montreal		Immigrants to five ports in the United States[a]	
Occupations	Number	Percent	Number	Percent	Number	Percent
Agricultural workers	5,629	78.4	2,577	24.7	790	17.9
Farmers	—		—		665	
Farm laborers	5,149		2,577		1	
Shepherds	331		—		4	
Gardeners	149		—		35	
Other	—		—		385	
Laborers	—	—	6,868	65.9	1,562	35.3
Servants, etc.	92	1.3	191	1.8	100	2.3
Craftsmen	1,378	19.2	792	7.6	991	22.4
Building trades	889				257	
Miners	8				120	
Food trades	18				119	
Metal trades	312				80	
Clothing trades	49				235	
Woodworking trades	102				55	
Miscellaneous					125	
Industrial workers	3	—	—	—	632	14.3
Modern tertiary workers	—	—	—	—	282	6.4
Unclassified	81	1.1	—	—	62	1.4
Total	7,183	100.0	10,428	100.0	4,419	100.0

Sources: A. C. Buchanan's Quarterly Return of Emigrants, Quebec, July 31, 1841, and October 31, 1841, *Correspondence Relative to Emigration*, B.P.P., 1842 (301), XXXI, pp. 196, 278; "Papers Relating to Emigration," B.P.P., 1843 (90), XXXIV, p. 48; one-in-five sample of ships arriving in New York, Boston, Philadelphia, Baltimore, and New Orleans, 1841 (see Table 5.3).

[a] Figures for the United States are from the one-in-five sample and therefore do not represent numbers for the entire immigration of males as do those for Canada and Australia.

wanted by graziers in the outback, immigrants seemed reluctant to leave the towns. Officials in Canada also complained of too many laborers; and their impressions of the immigrant arrivals may, in part, explain why they reported nearly two-thirds of the immigrants to Quebec and Montreal as general laborers and only a quarter as agricultural laborers. "We receive in Canada quite too large a proportion of mere labourers, that is, persons who can only use the spade and axe [wrote Buchanan of the immigrants of 1841]. . . . [T]here is much less demand for persons of this class in the province than people at home are generally aware of."[68] Most of these general laborers were probably Irish, because the latter formed two-thirds of the immigrants to both Canada and New South Wales. Agricultural and general laborers were also far more numerous among the Scottish bounty immigrants than they were among Scots who arrived in U.S. ports (see Table 5.13). Without access to records in Australia, I cannot postulate what proportion of the smaller number of English bounty immigrants that year were laborers.

Neither Canada nor New South Wales was in a position to absorb so many laborers, as is indicated by the desperate efforts to extend public works to employ them. Some of these laborers crossed over the border, if they had come to Canada. Buchanan maintained that "mere labourers" formed "the principal mass of emigrants who proceed to the United States."[69] This statement was true of the Irish who came down to Boston from New Brunswick that year. Eighty-three percent of the Irishmen arriving in Boston were recorded as laborers, as compared with only 53 percent of those coming to New York, mostly direct from Britain. In a letter admittedly solicited by the lieutenant governor of New Brunswick, the British consul at Boston reported in September that there were more Irish in Boston than the labor market there could absorb: "Those who leave Massachusetts . . . after vain attempts to get employment, invariably remove to the West, through New York state. Numbers are now temporarily engaged on the Western Railroad."[70]

For immigrants without capital or skills, the United States did not offer much haven in 1841 either. For the laborers in New South Wales, there was no means of escaping the engulfing depression, though several hundred immigrant laborers to Sydney in 1841 reemigrated to Valparaiso in South America in 1843.[71]

[68] Cited by Frances Morehouse, "Canadian Migration," p. 396. Donald Akenson, who has criticized historians of Irish emigration for failing to use available quantitative data, himself asserts (without evidence as to occupations) that laborers and subsistence farmers would have been unable to secure the means to emigrate before the famine, and he concludes that emigrants in this period were commercial tenant farmers who sold their last cash crop, pocketed the money instead of paying the rent, and departed (*Being Had,* pp. 132–33). Even bounty emigrants had to have some cash for provisions and outfit and internal travel. Yet, it seems impossible to dismiss this contemporary evidence that laborers were already finding a way of emigrating at this time.

[69] "Annual Reports of the Agents for Emigration in Canada, 1841," B.P.P., p. 8.

[70] British Consul in Boston, September 2, 1841, to Lt. Governor of New Brunswick, B.P.P., 1842 (373), XXXI, p. 230.

[71] Clarke, *Land of Contrarieties,* p. 94; G. J. Abbott, "The Emigration to Valparaiso in 1843," *Labour History* (Canberra) 19 (1970): 2.

Table 5.13. Recorded occupations of Scottish male immigrants to Australia and the United States

Occupations	Bounty immigrants to Australia, April 1838–August 1842		Immigrants to the United States, 1841[a]	
	Number	Percent	Number	Percent
Agricultural workers	628	49.3	62	17.8
Farmers	25		49	
Farm laborers	291		0	
Shepherds	252		2	
Other agriculture	60		11	
Laborers	225	17.7	59	17.0
Servants, etc.	21	1.7	5	1.4
Craftsmen	370	29.1	86	24.7
Building trades	206		27	
Miners/quarriers	4		9	
Food trades	12		7	
Metal trades	86		5	
Clothing trades	22		28	
Woodworking trades	32		2	
Miscellaneous	8		8	
Industrial workers	26	2.0	92	26.5
Textile workers	3		64	
Iron and engineering	20		11	
Miscellaneous	3		17	
Modern tertiary workers	3	.2	44	12.6
Total	1,273	100.0	348	100.0

Sources: One-in-five sample of ships arriving in United States ports, 1841 (see Table 5.3); David MacMillan, *Scotland and Australia, 1788–1850: Emigration, Commerce, and Investment* (Oxford: Clarendon Press, 1967), p. 294; other sources as in Table 5.6.

[a]Figures for the United States are based on a one-in-five sample and therefore should be multiplied by 5 to get an approximation of figures for the entire year.

Farmers who emigrated in 1841 clearly preferred the United states, which attracted about thirty-five hundred of them. Among the unassisted Scots immigrants to New South Wales, there were a few farmers. The availability of land and its low price in the United States, as well as contacts with previous immigrants, were deciding factors among men who did not have to search for assistance or the cheapest fares.[72]

Because mechanics or craftsmen were approved for bounty payments, New South Wales did receive a good complement of preindus-

[72] "Some of the most respectable of the middle class of Scots farmers . . . are about to try their fortunes in the United States" (*Niles National Register,* May 15, 1841, p. 176). See also Shepperson, *British Emigration,* p. 32, as well as Table 5.12, above.

trial craftsmen. The proportion of such workers in the intake to New South Wales was almost as high as among the immigrants to the United States, in spite of the much larger contingent of English immigrants in the latter. It would appear that Canada lost out with respect to craftsmen in 1841, in the face of the opportunity for free passages to Australia.

New South Wales was not obtaining a representative range of preindustrial skills, however. Most of the immigrants were building workers of various kinds and metal workers, particularly blacksmiths.[73] The United States was receiving a much greater array of craft skills. Among the English immigrants, all the categories of craftworkers distinguished in Table 5.12 were arriving in the United States, in roughly the same proportions as they constituted of the English labor force, according to the 1841 census. It seems that Scots masons, carpenters, and blacksmiths were responding to the offer of free passages in a way not evident among the English. Other sorts of craftsmen, who were not in any case officially eligible for bounties, could expect to find more opportunities where the more developed American economy generated a greater demand for crafts workers in a wide variety of consumer goods industries. These preindustrial craftsmen were not suffering from technological unemployment or shrinking job opportunities in Britain.[74] If those applying for free passages did so from a loss of work, it was more likely to have been because of declining village populations in particular places or because of the business depression.

Some of the industrial workers shown in Table 5.11 came from industries that were being transformed by new methods of production and in which some preindustrial skills were becoming obsolescent. Male textile workers were very much overrepresented in the British emigration to the United States in comparison with their share of the British labor force. A quarter of the English textile workers were weavers, many of whom may have been threatened handloom weavers. Such weavers did not qualify for bounty passages to Australia. Although not reported in Buchanan's listing of the occupations of immigrants, some

[73] Although the New South Wales Legislative Council maintained that occupations of artisans were not reported accurately, the reported occupations of bounty immigrants did include some of those trades—like painter, upholsterer, cabinetmaker, and tailor—that supposedly were ineligible for bounties.

[74] E. Anthony Wrigley, "Men on the Land and Men in the Countryside: Employment in Agriculture in Early-Nineteenth-Century England," in *The World We Have Gained: Histories of Population and Social Structure,* ed. Lloyd Bonfield, Richard Smith, and Keith Wrightson (Oxford: Basil Blackwell, 1986), pp. 300–301.

handloom weavers did arrive in Canada that year, when they were described by the government's emigrant agent in Toronto as "the only immigrants this season who appear to have been unsuccessful." Reports came in from from the chief agent at Kingston that "the Scotch weavers and wool-carders are very badly off, as they can neither read nor plough they are very troublesome, daily bringing me letters from their clergy and insisting upon support until employment can be procured for them—many of them state that Government encouraged them to come out and are now letting them starve."[75]

Men from every category of industrial workers in modernizing industries were finding the means to emigrate to the United States during this depression year, in larger numbers than would be predicted by their share in the British labor force: spinners, calico printers, iron- and steelworkers, printers, chemists, paperworkers, and a variety of others. Only engineers and millwrights, instrumentmakers and other metalworkers, and glassworkers fell short of full representation. Conspicuous by their tiny representation were some of the most depressed occupations at this time, such as framework knitters and nailers, ineligible for bounty payments and probably unable to gain the means for self-financed emigration to America. Australia seems to have attracted Scots engineers and millwrights, some of them without assistance. Like the English, however, most Scots from modernizing industries went to the United States.[76] Thus, industrial workers were able to get away in the midst of this depression to the emigration field that cost most to reach. It cannot be irrelevant that the United States was also the place where their skills could be best employed.

Modern tertiary workers—clerical, professional, and commercial people—did not demonstrate this same propensity to emigrate; but, like the preindustrial craftsmen, they were going out to the United States in proportions similar to those they constituted of the English labor force. Because very few commercial and professional people went either to Canada or to Australia, the arrivals in U.S. ports made up the bulk of

[75] "Extracts from Reports of Emigrant Agents for 1841," *Correspondence*, B.P.P., p. 291. See also William A. Carrothers, *Emigration from the British Isles* (London: P. S. King, 1929), p. 71; George Hilton, "The Controversy Concerning the Handloom Weavers," *Explorations in Entrepreneurial History*, 2d ser., 1 (1964): 181. This picture of the handloom weavers, no doubt describing a minority, contrasts with the way in which those of Paisley are depicted by Thomas C. Smout, *A Century of the Scottish People, 1830–1950* (London: Collins, 1985), pp. 24–27, and Smout, "The Strange Intervention of Edward Twistleton: Paisley in Depression," in *The Search for Wealth and Stability*, ed. Thomas C. Smout (London: Macmillan, 1979), pp. 222–23.

[76] MacMillan, *Scotland and Australia*, p. 290.

these emigrants.[77] Unlike the English, Scots tertiary workers, who would not have been eligible for bounty passages, were overrepresented in the emigration to the United States.

The year 1841 was an exceptional one in the history of emigration from the British Isles. The sudden increase in the number of assisted passages on offer brought a response that doubled the outward movement to Australasia—which had stagnated since 1839—after an initial rise in 1838 in the wake of the Canadian Rebellion. The huge shift in the destinations of emigrants from one year to the next during these very economically depressed years signals an awareness on the part of intending emigrants of conditions and opportunities open to them in the various fields of migration. Irish people appear to have been more ready to take up assisted passages than did people in the parts of rural England where wages were lowest and underemployment in agriculture endemic. Similarly, young Irish girls responded, whereas the English and Scottish did not. Some writers would emphasize the settlement laws as a barrier to emigration from, say, East Anglia.[78] Two counties near London—Kent and especially Sussex—did send out an unusually large number of the bounty emigrants from England at this time. But more people actually went from industrial Lancashire on assisted passages to Australia than from Kent and Sussex combined. Although information about the availability of assisted passages was widely distributed, it may be that the networks with poor law authorities developed by government emigration agents in London during the thirties and the proximity of shipping help explain the prominence of Kent and Sussex in both poor law- and colonial-assisted emigration.

Insofar as we can trust the data, the differentials in the occupational mix of the emigrants—with agricultural and general laborers going to New South Wales and Canada and workers in modernizing industries, farmers, and commercial and professional people to the United States—also suggest a high degree of informed decision making as to destination.

Nonetheless, there must be considerable doubt as to whether the overall level of emigration from the British Isles was increased by this

[77] The passenger lists used for the sample made clear whether merchants and professional people were intending to remain in the United States or were simply temporary visitors. Only the former were included in my estimates.

[78] See, for example, Keith D. M. Snell, *Annals of the Labouring Poor: Social Change and Agrarian England, 1660–1900* (Cambridge: Cambridge University Press, 1985), pp. 334, 339.

burst of assistance to New South Wales, which, as we have seen, even with the assisted passages probably cost the emigrant or a patron as much as a passage on a sailing vessel to Quebec. Perhaps the strongest evidence for this is the fact that emigration actually increased again in 1842, from 115,826 to 126,509 outward-bound passengers from the United Kingdom, even as the assisted passage program collapsed and in spite of continued depressed economies in the United States and Canada, as well as in the British Isles.

The bounties of 1841 do appear to have deterred some voluntary, self-financed emigration to Canada and the United States, an argument British government ministers later deployed against using British taxpayers' money to assist emigration. The experience of 1841 put an end in 1842 to agitation for a national emigration scheme, if it had ever had a chance of success. During the Irish famine, Earl Grey argued that if the British government were to assist emigration, remittances from former emigrants would dry up and costs of emigration rise with the resultant pressure on shipping. Emigrants whose passages had been paid by the government would expect it to take responsibility for finding them jobs or land on arrival.

> If passages were provided at the public expense for all who desired to emigrate, these remittances, and the sacrifices now made by so many persons for the purpose of doing so, would cease, and a very large proportion of those who now, by some means or other, find their own way across the Atlantic, would have to be conveyed at the public expense.... The system of voluntary emigration, which is now working so satisfactorily, and upon so large a scale, would be entirely deranged.[79]

This would seem a fairly reasonable conclusion to have drawn from the experience of 1840–42.

[79] Despatch from Earl Grey to Lord Elgin, Downing Street, January 29, 1847, *Papers Relative to Emigration to the British Provinces in North America,* B.P.P., 1847 (777), XXXIX, pp. 53–54, 55. See also Hitchins, *Colonial Land and Emigration Commission,* p. 135.

Appendix

Table 5.14. Emigrants from England, 1840–1842, by county

	Population census, 1841 (000's)	Emigration census, January–June 1841	New South Wales bounty migrants, 1841	Poor law migrants, 1840–1842	United States ship list, 1841
		AGRICULTURAL LOW-WAGE			
Bedford	108	28	5	9	7
Berkshire	161	33	20	27	—
Buckinghamshire	156	n.a.	28	30	2
Cambridgeshire	165	18	23	4	1
Devon	533	736	333	42	3
Dorset	175	177	42	7	3
Essex	345	55	65	—	3
Hampshire	355	90	82	31	20
Hereford	114	111	37	—	3
Hertfordshire	157	42	24	—	—
Huntingdonshire	59	n.a.	10	—	—
Norfolk	413	117	48	8	—
Northamptonshire	199	55	23	46	3
Oxford	162	50	22	—	1
Rutland	21	4	4	—	—
Shropshire	239	14	25	6	—
Somerset	436	671	291	287	—
Suffolk	315	59	12	16	19
Wiltshire	259	98	62	75	—
Total	4,372	2,358	1,156	588	65
		AGRICULTURAL HIGH-WAGE			
Cumberland[a]	178	357	67	—	36
Kent	548	652	300	1,094	16
Lincolnshire	363	82	48	—	5
Sussex	300	758	349	896	—
Westmorland	56	61	24	—	—
Yorkshire, E.R.	195	162	—	—	—
Yorkshire, N.R.	242	153	—	—	—
Total	1,882	2,225	788	1,990	57
		INDUSTRIAL LOW-WAGE			
Cornwall	341	795	120	150	—
Gloucestershire	431	291	219	56	4
Leicestershire	216	45	26	5	—
Staffordshire	511	98	53	—	—
Warwickshire	402	112	60	—	3
Worcestershire	233	50	40	—	—
Total	2,134	1,391	518	211	7

Table 5.14. (Continued)

	Population census, 1841 (000's)	Emigration census, January–June 1841	New South Wales bounty migrants, 1841	Poor law migrants, 1840–1842	United States ship lists, 1841
		INDUSTRIAL HIGH-WAGE			
Cheshire	396	328	86	—	6
Derbyshire	272	84	32	19	—
Durham	324	92	17	—	—
Lancashire	1,667	1,362	802	—	50
Middlesex	1,577	160	413	—	9
Northumberland	250	32	42	—	—
Nottinghamshire	250	175	80	—	6
Surrey	583	134	108	27	4
Yorkshire, W.R.	1,155	944	371	31	24
Total	6,474	3,311	1,951	77	99

Sources: One-in-five sample from United States ship lists (see Table 5.3); "Papers Relating to Emigration," B.P.P., 1847–48 (90), XXXIV, p. 46; "Returns for Each Year from 1836–47 . . . ," B.P.P., 1847–48 (345), XLVII, pp. 14–21; N. F. R. Crafts, *British Economic Growth during the Industrial Revolution* (New York: Oxford University Press, 1985), p. 4; wage data as in Table 3.11, above.

[a]With 34 percent of its male labor force reported in agriculture in 1851, Cumberland was classified as an agricultural county in Table 3.11, above. The 1841 census showed only 30 percent of its labor force in agriculture. Enumerators in that year were instructed to classify indoor farm servants as agricultural laborers, but it was noted that they had not always followed that instruction. Because Cumberland had a relatively large number of indoor farm servants, the error may have been quite pronounced in this case, and for that reason, I have classified it as an agricultural county.

CHAPTER SIX

Was the American West a Safety Valve for Lancashire?

One of the most absorbing questions about English emigration during the nineteenth century is its relationship to the process of industrialization. In most of the European countries whose inhabitants went overseas in large numbers, the heaviest emigration took place before industrial and urban growth provided sufficient alternatives for fast-increasing rural populations. In contrast, England experienced substantial overseas migration—certainly underestimated in the official statistics collected during the period—throughout the 1820s, 1830s, and 1840s, when its towns were growing at their peak rates for the entire century, when steam power and factory manufacture were spreading to new activities, and where employment in traditional crafts was expanding far more rapidly than agricultural employment.[1] Nonetheless, as has been shown in Chapter 3, maturing industrialization did not reduce emigration from Great Britain. Overseas emigration from England and Scotland reached new peaks in the 1850s, in the 1880s, and in the decade after 1900.

The role in the United States of these emigrants from the most advanced industrial economy in the world is no less engaging a question. The first United States census to provide information about the occupations of workers according to nativity—the census of 1870—

[1] E. Anthony Wrigley, "Men on the Land and Men in the Countryside: Employment in Agriculture in Early-Nineteenth-Century England," in *The World We Have Gained: Histories of Population and Social Structure*, ed. Lloyd Bonfield, Richard Smith, and Keith Wrightson (Oxford: Basil Blackwell, 1986), pp. 298–304.

demonstrated that the English-born were heavily concentrated in manufacturing and mining employment.[2] But were English emigrants the means by which new technology was introduced in the United States? Because so much of the new technology rested on empirical skills rather than scientific knowledge, early students of the subject possibly exaggerated the migrants' contribution.[3] Other scholars have wondered whether it was the people most skilled in the newest English industrial practices that emigrated, whether investigating tours of English works by American managers and owners were not more productive, and whether some of those empirical skills were not already available in the native-born work force, especially in New England and the Brandywine district.[4] Possibly it was those people whose skills were becoming outmoded that emigrated in the greatest numbers to the United States.

It has not generally been noticed that, according to the 1870 census, the English were nearly as well represented in agriculture in the United States as was the native-born population. During the preceding half-century, the activities that absorbed the energy and means of most of the native-born population were the westward movement, farm making, and transport building. What contribution, if any, did English immigrants make to these endeavors? From the beginning of the century, were they attracted primarily to the infant industrial sector in America, as was suggested by Rowland Berthoff in his classic study *British Immigrants in Industrial America*?

[2] Edward Hutchinson, *Immigrants and Their Children, 1850–1950* (London: Chapman and Hall, 1956), pp. 81–84.

[3] Rowland Berthoff, *British Immigrants in Industrial America, 1790–1950* (Cambridge: Harvard University Press, 1953); Herbert Heaton, "The Industrial Immigrant in the United States, 1783–1812," *Proceedings of the American Philosophical Society* 95 (1951): 519–27; Frank Thistlethwaite, "The Atlantic Migration of the Pottery Industry," *Economic History Review*, 2d ser., 11 (1958): 264–78.

[4] David Jeremy, *Transatlantic Industrial Revolution: The Diffusion of Textile Technologies between Britain and America, 1790–1830s* (Cambridge, MIT Press, 1981); Richard Margrave, *The Emigration of Silk Workers from England to the United States in the Nineteenth Century, with Special Reference to Coventry, Macclesfield, Paterson, New Jersey, and South Manchester, Connecticut* (New York: Garland, 1986); Geoffrey Tweedale, *Sheffield Steel and America: A Century of Commercial and Technological Interdependence, 1830–1930* (Cambridge: Cambridge University Press, 1987); Andrew Lamb, "A History of the American Pottery Industry: Industrial Growth, Technical and Technological Change, and Diffusion in the General Ware Branch, 1872–1914," Ph.D. diss., University of London, 1985; Oscar Handlin, "International Migration and the Acquisition of New Skills," in *Progress of Underdeveloped Areas*, ed. Bert Hoselitz (Chicago: University of Chicago Press, 1952).

Recent scholarship makes it possible to explore some of these questions a little more than has been done until now. For a start, I propose to examine here some new data on emigrants from England's most industrialized county, Lancashire, in the light of some of the recent work on English emigration as a whole. I will do so through the reconstruction of lifetime careers on both sides of the Atlantic of some Lancashire emigrants, with a focus on their occupations rather than social mobility, a subject that has received so much more attention in the past. Nor will I have anything to say about the role of Lancashire immigrants in the trade union movement, labor politics, and in working-class communities, again subjects to which some labor and social historians in recent years have given prominence to English immigrants.[5] But, first, a summary of what we do now know about emigration from Lancashire in relation to that from the rest of the country is in order.

The analysis of samples from lists of passengers arriving in ports in the United States has given us estimates of the proportions of various occupational groups in the emigration from England to the United States in a few selected years, all of which were high points at the time in the flow of emigrants. These years are 1831, 1841, and 1851, before the American authorities began in 1875 to publish data on the occupations of immigrants by nationality.[6] Although it is rash to generalize about the composition of the emigrant flow from sample

[5] Philip T. Silvia, Jr., "The Position of Workers in a Textile Community: Fall River in the Early 1880s," *Labor History* 16 (1975): 230–48; Donald B. Cole, *Immigrant City: Lawrence, Massachusetts, 1845–1921* (Chapel Hill: University of North Carolina Press, 1963); Dean R. Esslinger, *Immigrants and the City: Ethnicity and Mobility in a Nineteenth-Century Midwestern Community* (Port Washington, N.Y.: Kennikat Press, 1975); Howard M. Gitelman, *Workingmen of Waltham: Mobility in American Industrial Development, 1850–90* (Baltimore: Johns Hopkins University Press, 1974); John T. Cumbler, *Working-Class Community in Industrial America: Work, Leisure, and Struggle in Two Industrial Cities, 1880–1930* (Westport, Conn.: Greenwood Press, 1979), and Cumbler, "Transatlantic Working-Class Institutions," *Journal of Historical Geography* 6 (1980): 275–90; Mary H. Blewett, "Traditions and Customs of Lancashire Popular Radicalism in Late Nineteenth-Century Industrial America," Paper presented at the Third International Labor and Working-Class History/Mouvement Sociale Colloquium, Paris, October 1991, draft kindly provided by the author; Cynthia Shelton, *The Mills of Manyunk: Industrialization and Social Conflict in the Philadelphia Region, 1787–1837* (Baltimore: Johns Hopkins University Press, 1986); Bruce Laurie, *Working People of Philadelphia, 1800–50* (Philadelphia: Temple University Press, 1980), Chaps. 4, 8.

[6] See Chapters 3 and 4 above and also Charlotte Erickson, "Emigration from the British Isles to the U.S.A. in 1841," Part 2, "Who Were the English Emigrants?" *Population Studies* 44 (1990): 21–39; William Van Vugt, "British Emigration during the Early 1850s, with Special Reference to Emigration to the U.S.A.," Ph.D. diss., University of London, 1985.

Table 6.1. Occupations of English and Welsh male immigrants aged 20 or older, 1831–1888

Occupational class	1831	1841	1851	1885–1888[a]
Agricultural workers	24.6%	21.3%	24.4%	9.5%
Laborers	9.5	12.5	23.5	29.5
Servants, etc.	2.1	2.5	3.4	3.2
Preindustrial craftsmen	34.9	31.3	32.7	34.3
Industrial workers	16.5	23.2	8.5	7.8
Modern tertiary workers	12.4	9.2	7.5	15.7
Total	100.0%	100.0%	100.0%	100.0%
Number	1,794	1,750	1,606	8,698

Sources: 1885–88 figures are based on good ship lists (see Table 3.10). Early in my work I did not record details for the English, Scots, and Welsh separately. For 1831, see the five-month sample of ship lists as in Table 4.2. For 1841, see the one-in-five sample of ship lists in sources listed in Table 5.3. For 1851, see the one-in-ten sample of ship lists as in William van Vugt, "British Emigration during the Early 1850s, with Special Reference to the Emigration to the U.S.A.," Ph.D. diss., University of London, 1985, app. E, p. 321. I have adapted his figures to combine the English and Welsh. See also Appendix Table 6.5 for comparisons of emigrant labor force with my estimates based on the British census.

[a] Includes Scots.

years, the findings are at least suggestive of the role of emigration in a "mature economy."

First, emigration did play a limited part in containing and, after 1850, reducing England's agricultural labor force. Those who emigrated appear to have been farmers and their sons, rather than farm laborers. The proportion of emigrants from the farming sector fell from one-fourth of the emigrants in 1831 to less than a tenth in the late 1880s (see Table 6.1). Farming was always underrepresented among English emigrants, and in that sense, emigration could not be said to have played a major role in the adaptation of laborers in agriculture to industrial expansion and free trade (see Appendix Tables 6.4 and 6.5). Farm laborers and their children sought alternative opportunities near at hand, although farmers did go in significantly larger numbers than their share of the labor force would warrant. It is quite probable that more farm laborers went to the Empire than arrived in the United States direct from England.

Second, preindustrial craftworkers, whose occupations and methods of work did not change significantly in the course of the nineteenth century, also showed a tendency, though a weaker one than did farmers, to be overrepresented among English emigrants to the United States in the early part of the century. This emigration included a great variety of craftsmen, but by the 1880s only building trades workers and miners—as adaptable in an industrializing as in a preindustrial economy—were overrepresented. Thus passenger lists suggest that emigration was a genuine option for farmers and for craftsmen in responding to industrial change and population decline in some rural areas, at least until the 1850s.

In 1831 and 1841, industrial workers in the most markedly changing and expanding industries, especially textile workers and those engaged in metallurgical and engineering industries, were also overrepresented, although rather less so than were traditional craftsmen (see Appendix Table 6.5). One of the most telling findings from the sampling of passenger lists was the very steep decline in the proportion of industrial workers from the modern sectors—which were becoming England's staple industries—to emigrate to the United States. This drop was already evident in 1851, when their share was more than halved as compared with the 1841 sample, and it seemed to be confirmed in the sampling of the years 1885–88. In 1831 and 1841, industrial workers of all kinds, craftsmen as well as those in more modern sectors of manufacturing industry, accounted for more than half of the adult male emigrants from England and Wales. In the two post-1850 samples, this figure was only about 40 percent; and the decline was accounted for largely by the reluctance of workers in England's staple industries, apart from mining, to emigrate.

The gap was filled by unskilled laborers, who made up an increasing proportion of each successive sample, from 10 percent in 1831 to 30 percent in the late 1880s after attaining an even higher proportion earlier in that decade. In 1851, laborers already made up 24 percent of the emigrants, two and a half times as many as were leaving industrial jobs in Britain's major industries. Some of these men may have begun life as farm laborers or have been their sons; but the evidence suggests that they were either urban laborers from the outset or had already taken their first jobs off the farm before emigrating. As these occupational shifts took place, English emigration became more and more urban in origin and included an increasing number of temporary migrants and fewer married men with families than had been the case in the migration during the years of discontent from the 1820s to the 1840s. As the scale of emigration increased in both numbers and density, it struck deeper into the unskilled part of the labor force, which even by the 1850s was more overrepresented than were farmers in the movement to America.

As this hypothetical framework emerges, the emigration from particular counties in England can be examined, at least tentatively, in relation to the larger picture. Not only was Lancashire the virtual cradle of the industrial revolution, but that county also probably supplied more emigrants to the United States than any other. Because Lancashire's population was growing more rapidly than that of the country as a whole from 1811 to 1881, it is likely that the county was, on balance, an immigrant receiver in net terms throughout the period, mainly through internal migration. Even during that bumper emigration decade of the 1880s, when the rate of growth of Lancashire's population fell, it still exceeded the national average, but now by only two percentage points.

Some of the passenger lists do provide details on the place of last residence or on place of birth, but not enough to put much confidence in the results, except those for the late 1880s, when full data appear on so many lists. We do, however, have two more comprehensive sources on the county of origin of English emigrants. The 1841 census of emigration has been available for a long time but on its own was not much help. Now, at enormous scholarly labor over a long period of time, Dudley Baines has calculated the place of birth of England's internal and overseas migrants from 1861 to 1900 from the British census data on place of birth of the country's inhabitants.[7]

The 1841 census reported the number of people emigrating from each county during the first five months of the year. Baines's work provides estimates of net emigration by county by decade rather than the actual numbers of people emigrating each year. Some of the passenger lists reveal the complexity of English internal migration, which must make us hesitate to draw too many inferences from these estimates of net emigration. Someone like the fifty-year-old engineer, who emigrated in 1841 from Liverpool but who had been born in Glusburn, West Riding of Yorkshire, would not be counted as an emigrant from Lancashire, though his wife, son, and daughter, born in Blackburn, would be. His younger children, who were nine, eleven, and 13 years old and had been born in Farmington, Gloucestershire, also were not emigrants from Lancashire by this method. A thirty four-year-old carpenter who arrived in New York from Liverpool early in 1849 did, in fact, emigrate from Lancashire, as his three-year-old son had been born there. He himself, however, would have counted as an emigrant from Cumberland, the county in which he was born, although his wife was born in

[7] Dudley Baines, *Migration in a Mature Economy: Emigration and Internal Migration in England and Wales, 1861–1900* (Cambridge: Cambridge University Press, 1985), pp. 283–98.

Northumberland and the older children arrived during migrations in Northumberland, Durham, and the West Riding of Yorkshire over a period of nine years. On the other hand, a man like George Farrell, who was born in Lancashire of Irish parents and returned with them to Northern Ireland at the age of three, would qualify as an emigrant from Lancashire.[8] Moreover, because Baines estimated net emigration, any Lancashire-born emigrant returning from overseas during a particular decade would cancel out an immigrant.[9]

What these sources tell us is that the incidence of emigration from Lancashire, or of Lancashire-born people, tended to be neither much above nor much below the national average. At the same time that the county was attracting migrants from other parts of the United Kingdom, substantial numbers of Lancastrians were departing for destinations overseas. In 1841, when about seven persons per ten thousand population left England during the first five months of the year, departures from Lancashire were eight per ten thousand. It is possible that Lancastrians made up an even higher proportion of the smaller numbers going overseas earlier in the century. The few passenger lists that gave place of last residence on ships arriving in New York between 1827 and 1831 revealed 36 percent of the immigrants from England to have come from Lancashire.

The county did not continue to produce so large a proportion of England's growing number of emigrants later in the century. According to Baines, Lancashire ranked slightly below the national average in net emigration over the period 1861–1900, with an average net loss of 270 males and 150 females per ten thousand population per decade compared with 310 males and 170 females for England and Wales.[10] Lancashire ranked far below Cornwall, the county of heaviest net emigration, with 1,050 male emigrants per ten thousand males, but far above Bedfordshire and Leicestershire at the other extreme, with 130 and 140, respectively. Thus, in spite of its population growth and industrial progress, Lancashire continued to send its sons and daughters

[8] See the ship *Sheffield,* arriving in New Orleans from Liverpool, March 31, 1841, ship no. 149, roll no. 259/21, and the ship *Princeton,* arriving in New York from Liverpool, January 31, 1849, ship no. 71, roll no. 237/71, National Archives, Microfilm. For more on George Farrell, see *Portrait and Biographical Album of Washington, Clay, and Riley Counties, Kansas* (Chicago: Chapman Brothers, 1890), p. 230.

[9] These comments are not meant as criticisms of Baines's most valuable contribution, for he was fully aware of the limitations of net estimates. Indeed, there is no other way of proceeding to get any kind of overall estimates of the counties of origin of English overseas emigrants.

[10] Baines, *Migration in a Mature Economy,* p. 150.

overseas in the last half of the century at respectable rates, in view of the national average. The numbers were smaller—but the outflow from Lancashire proportionately larger—during the years of greater structural change and social discontent earlier in the century.

Men dominated the emigration from Lancashire to an extraordinary degree during the early part of the century, if 1841 is any guide. Only 590 female emigrants were recorded per 1,000 males in the census of emigration taken in 1841, whereas among the emigrants from more agricultural counties, the ratio of females to males was much higher, 979 per 1,000 in Sussex, for example. Although the figures are not strictly comparable, the proportion of women in the net emigration from Lancashire rose a little during the last part of the century to 614 per 1,000, though women still figured less prominently in the emigration from this industrial county than they did in that of the country as a whole.[11] As heavy industry grew more rapidly in the last part of the century and expansion in the cotton industry slowed, women probably found opportunities for employment less encouraging than when new machinery was being introduced in cotton textile manufacture.

The emigration from Lancashire in the early part of the century appears to have been selective not only of males but also of people from principal towns with twenty thousand or more inhabitants. At least this was the case during 1841, a year of industrial depression. It so happens that the census enumerators for Lancashire in 1841 actually commented on the place of origin of the total number of emigrants counted in the emigration census of that year. This information indicates that 68 percent of the emigrants from Lancashire came from principal towns, whereas only 57 percent of the county's population lived in such cities.[12] Over the entire year, it is likely that Lancashire emigrants were even more urban in origin because industrial workers left in larger numbers after June 4, the terminal date of the emigration census. In contrast, none of the emigrants from Sussex—one of the counties with the highest rate of emigration, although smaller numbers of emigrants—came from its only major town, Brighton. By the late 1880s, Lancastrians were

[11] Ibid., p. 163.

[12] British Parliamentary Papers, *1841 Census of Great Britain, Population*, 3 (Shannon: Irish University Press, 1971), pp. 140–49. William Van Vugt has pointed out the possible bias toward urban emigration in passenger lists that gave place of origin. People living in villages near large towns might have been inclined to name the large town ("British Emigration during the Early 1850s," p. 293). This criticism does not apply to these census data, which were reported by enumerators for each place in the county.

emigrating almost entirely from its major towns.[13] On the basis of this limited evidence, one can only suggest that Lancastrians figured more largely among England's emigrants in the first half of the century than they did later and that the emigration from Lancashire was more selective of males and of urban dwellers than was the case with emigrants from more rural and agricultural counties.

From another point of view, that of their overseas destinations, Lancastrians were even more important than they were in the overall movement overseas. Even though emigration rates were not outstanding, because of the size of its population, Lancashire recorded more emigrants in 1841 than did any other county. With 1,362 emigrants recorded during those five months, Lancashire saw its emigration exceed that of the next largest county as a source of emigrants, the West Riding of Yorkshire, which was also industrializing and which yielded 944 emigrants during those months (see Table 5.14 above). In the decades from 1861 to 1900, only London and Middlesex together produced more net emigrants than did Lancashire. During the 1880s, when the margin of the county's rate of population growth narrowed to nearly the national rate, Lancashire-born people accounted for over hundred thousand emigrants—male and female—on a net basis.[14]

The few passenger lists that contain information on occupation by place of last residence tend to agree with the evidence from the census on the importance of industrial workers from towns among Lancashire's adult male emigrants early in the century. As compared with ten farmers, there were thirty nine textile workers, forty three craftsmen, as well as twenty seven laborers on the few good lists from the period 1827–31. The industrial, or secondary sector, not the primary producing sector, was yielding most of the emigrants from this industrializing county just emerging from depression. Some of them were people who may have been facing changing technology with low wages and underemployment; but emigrants with better prospects at home because of their familiarity with new technology—power loom weavers, boilermakers, and machine makers, as well as overseers and managers—also appeared on the lists.

Textile workers from Lancashire were conspicuous among emigrants to the United States during the 1820s and probably continued to be until the cotton industry revived in the mid-1840s. Emigration was an option for some handloom weavers, many of whom lived a precarious existence

[13] See above, Table 3.3.

[14] Baines, *Migration in a Mature Economy,* pp. 285, 293.

long before the expansion in numbers of power looms further undermined their traditional source of livelihood during the 1820s and 1830s. In the passenger lists from the years 1824–31, weavers, about 2,695 of them, not all of whom are known to have come from Lancashire, greatly outnumbered spinners and other textile workers, by more than ten to one.[15] Even if they had all been cotton handloom weavers, this was hardly enough to reduce significantly an estimated quarter of a million such workers in the county. On the few good lists from the period 1827–31, weavers from Lancashire outnumbered spinners by four to one. If these few ship lists are any guide, the weavers who were emigrating in the twenties were not coming from country villages but from the larger towns. Workers from Bury, Blackburn, and Bolton accounted for fifteen of these 23 weavers. Power loom weaving had not yet penetrated these towns in the southern part of northwest Lancashire. Duncan Bythell described Bolton and Burnley as "late starters in acquiring power looms."[16] Only four of the weavers came from Manchester or Rochdale, where new employment opportunities, including those on power looms, were appearing.

In 1841, more weavers were emigrating from those country villages. Weavers still formed the largest group of emigrant textile workers at 41 percent, down from 46 percent in 1831. In this very depressed year for the industrial towns of the north, textile workers managed to emigrate in considerably larger numbers than in 1831. By this time, after the boom of the mid-1830s, towns like Bolton and Preston had introduced power loom weaving. Some of the country villages appeared as places of origin of weavers—Longton, Leyland, Kirkham, and Downham, among others. One suspects that these weavers, like those who emigrated in the late twenties, were handloom weavers, whose opportunities for alternative employment close to home for themselves and their children were less plentiful than they were in the southern part of the county. Nearly all the spinners, on the other hand, though not yet seriously challenged by the introduction of self-acting mules, came from major towns. Weavers were more frequently departing with their families and with larger families than were spinners and other textile workers, or industrial workers in general. This fact indicates not only the finality of their decisions to emigrate but also suggests that those

[15] Jeremy, *Transatlantic Industrial Revolution,* pp. 270–71.

[16] Duncan Bythell, *The Handloom Weavers: A Study in the English Cotton Industry during the Industrial Revolution* (Cambridge: Cambridge University Press, 1969), pp. 51–52, 91–92, 268.

who did could not have been among the most poverty-stricken of their numbers.[17]

By 1851 this mini-exodus of textile workers from Lancashire had ended. Textile workers as a whole, and weavers in particular, constituted a much smaller proportion of the emigrants in that year. William Van Vugt, who analyzed a sample from the 1851 lists, concluded that emigration was still being used as an alternative by handloom weavers on a small scale, as 10 percent of them were in their forties and 14 percent were fifty-five or older.[18] Many of them were going to the Philadelphia area, where handloom weaving survived. During the 1880s, Lancastrian textile workers were emigrating in larger numbers but were very much underrepresented among emigrants when compared with their share in the labor force. By this time nearly all those who gave a place of last residence left from cities and large towns with more than twenty thousand inhabitants.

A second feature that emigrants from Lancashire shared with those of the country as a whole was the relative decline of all sorts of skilled industrial workers—including craftsmen but with the exception of miners and building trades workers—in the emigration of the last part of the century. The ship lists from the late 1880s indicate that Lancashire accounted for more than a third of the adult male emigrants going to the United States, whereas its population was only 13 percent of that of England and Wales at the time. Now unskilled laborers formed the most overrepresented group from Lancashire, as well as from England, in the movement to the United States. Nearly all of them proceeded from towns, at least twenty-two of which were mentioned in the passenger lists in 1885 and 1887. The vast majority boarded the transatlantic steamers without wives or children.

Emigration fever never really struck Lancashire. Emigration remained one option for ambitious or dissatisfied people, and Lancastrians did not lag behind people in the country as a whole in their propensity to emigrate. Over time, people from more and more communities built up links with friends and relatives who had emigrated earlier. Many emigrants with knowledge of conditions in the United States returned to visit or to stay. Furthermore, the relatively literate population of this county had other sources of information available to

[17] Erickson, "Who Were the English Emigrants?" pp. 29–30.

[18] William Van Vugt, "Prosperity and Industrial Emigration from Britain during the Early 1850s," *Journal of Social History* 22 (1988): 344.

them.[19] By the last half of the century, thousands of unskilled laborers were willing to make the plunge in search of greater opportunities, often as a kind of speculation, as skilled workers had done earlier, with the option of returning home if those expectations were not fulfilled.

At the cost of a lot of tedious and time-consuming counting or feeding of computers, one can estimate the number of emigrants leaving a particular English county and some of their main social and demographic characteristics. Following them to the United States and in their subsequent careers or tracing their precise origins in England and their premigration experience present even more obstacles. For such work, emigrant letters sometimes give an in-depth view of the experiences of a few families. Fewer than a dozen really good collections of letters from emigrants from Lancashire have so far been found.[20]

I have been trying another approach that, if nothing else, yields a larger number of careers: the use of the short biographies that appeared in county histories in the United States, commemorative volumes published for the most part between the 1870s and the 1920s. Whether they describe careers more or less typical than those of immigrant letter writers must remain an open question. This is a perennial problem for the historian. On the basis of details provided in these sources, I have attempted to verify and expand the information by going back to birth and marriage certificates and, to a limited extent, parish and nonconformist registers before 1837, as well as to census manuscripts and local directories in England. On occasion, the United States census manuscripts provided clues that opened up the English records on an individual. One could extend this kind of research by means of fuller exploitation of census manuscripts and local sources on both sides of the Atlantic. But limited time, energy, and means force me to draw a line while many biographies are still less full than they might be.

[19] Lawrence Stone, "Literacy and Education in England, 1640–1900," *Past and Present* 42 (1969): 122; Baines, *Migration in a Mature Economy,* pp. 328–31.

[20] Fairly complete transcriptions of the Morris, Bond, and Butterworth letters are to be found in Charlotte Erickson, *Invisible Immmigrants: Adaptation of English and Scottish Immigrants in Nineteenth-Century America* (1972; rpt., Ithaca: Cornell University Press, 1990). Other collections concerned with emigrants from Lancashire include the John T. Hall Diary, 1864, Bentley Historical Library, Ann Arbor, Mich.; Thomas Heywood Journal, 1856–65, Illinois Historical Survey, Urbana; Letters to William Hunter in Lowell, Mass., Private Collection of Roger Haydon; Letters of James Nowland, Huntington Library, San Marino, Calif.; Juan Pattison Letters, Olin Library, Cornell University; William Stockdale Letters, 1866–86, Indiana Historical Society, Indianapolis.

I did try to take a systematic approach to the selection of counties to be included in my sample. The first stage was to identify counties whose histories provided rather full and detailed life stories. From these I selected a number of counties in which the English formed a higher-than-average share of the population, counties in which the English made up a proportion of the foreign-born that was above average, and some in which the English were insignificant on both counts. Within the sample drawn, I made a final selection in such a way as to provide a balance between rural and urban counties and among the various regions of the country. Neither the South nor the mountain states were included because they produced so few county histories.[21]

Passenger lists have distinct limitations in what they reveal about an emigrating population. Most of the lists failed to specify precise places of origin of emigrants. Moreover, like censuses, they provide only a snapshot of the structure of a population at a single point in time. Lifetime careers, built from the biographies in county histories as a starting point, are no doubt selective of moderately successful immigrants, though as we shall see in the case of Lancashire, they did include some failures in an economic sense and did not include any individuals of national fame. Only a few who remained industrial workers or miners for their entire careers found their way into these publications. Nonetheless, social historians have been criticized of late for paying so little attention to the middle class, and that is largely where, at least late in their careers, most of these people fall, by any structural definition. If they were not mostly manual workers all their lives, neither were they part of an elite in wealth or influence. These life stories may tell us something about the ambitions and goals of emigrants, as well as the means by which they sought to attain them.

[21] The counties included in the study are Bristol, Essex, Middlesex, and Norfolk, Mass.; New Haven, Conn.; Bergen, N.J.; King's, Queen's, Monroe, Oneida, and Orange, N.Y.; Allegheny, Delaware, Clearfield, Schulkill, and Westmoreland, Pa.; Fairfield, Perry, Trumbull, and Washington, Ohio; Vanderburgh, Ind.; Bureau, Cook, Hancock, Jackson, Sangamon, and Will, Ill.; Lenawee, Oakland, Houghton, and Saginaw, Mich.; Dane, Grant, LaFayette, Racine, Rock, and Washtenaw, Wis.; Clayton, Clinton, Dubuque, Polk, Pottawattamie, Plymouth, and Woodbury, Iowa; Clay, Kans.; Alameda, Contra Costa, Los Angeles, counties in the Sacramento Valley, Placer, Nevada, and Santa Clara, Calif.; and Seattle, Wash. The microfilm collection "County and Regional Histories," publishd by Research Publications, Woodbridge, Connecticut, is widely available. Other libraries that have wide-ranging collections of county histories include the Huntington Library in San Marino, California, the Suttro Library in San Francisco, the Library of Congress, and also the British Library, which contains a surprising number catalogued under the name of the county. I have not provided precise references to all the subjects of this review because it would overload the footnotes. Particular individuals are noted.

In all, I have collected material on some 1,600 immigrants from England. Of these, 165 were emigrants from Lancashire. Only men and youths who entered the labor force in the United States shortly after their arrival have been included. The county histories provide a fine opportunity to study the second generation, but I have not attempted to do so.

As I suspected, the lives drawn from these county histories tell us little about the mass of textile operatives, ironworkers, and miners who remained manual workers all their lives. Nor do we find representatives of the growing numbers of unskilled laborers who emigrated after the Civil War prepared to take work of any kind. Nevertheless, among these 165 men from Lancashire traced in my sample, there are two cases of men whose farm real estate was valued at a mere $100 in the United States census; others who ended up as industrial workers after trying independent business or farming; two whose attempts at cotton manufacture failed; and a railway engine driver who lost his job, apparently for his trade union activity. The Lancashire sample includes at least ten men who had been laborers in Lancashire and fourteen weavers. The less fortunate and less skilled have not entirely slipped through the net.

One might begin by dividing the emigrants into two broad groups. Throughout the century there continued to be emigrants who aimed at, and succeeded in, getting to the land as farmers. In the entire sample of Lancashire emigrants over the course of the century, only 6 percent, or nine of those whose occupations before emigration have been identified, came from agriculture. At least three of the nine had been farm laborers. By the time their biographies were published, 57 of these 165 immigrants from Lancashire had become farmers or ranchers, and many more had tried to farm at some point during their careers in the States. The attraction of western land was stronger among those who emigrated before the Civil War and thus reflects the increased proportion of English migrants who remained in the East after the war.[22] Fifty-nine percent of the Lancastrians in counties sampled east of the Appalachians emigrated after the Civil War, as compared with less than 10 percent of those sampled in states from Ohio west to Kansas. This stream of migrants into agriculture included, as we shall see, people from an astonishing variety of former occupations (see Table 6.2).

The other group of immigrants sought better opportunities in towns, either in the East or the West. Of the eight post–Civil War emigrants

[22] See above Table 2.1.

Table 6.2. Last occupations (or father's occupation) in England and the United States of Lancashire male immigrants in sample

Occupations	Last occupation in England	Or father's occupation	Last occupation in United States
Farmer	6	2	57
Farm laborer	3		0
Laborer	7		0
Servant, etc.	3		0
Craftsman	29	3	21
	(1 owner)		(7 owners/managers)
Industrial worker	62	4	41
	(3 owners)		(28 owners/managers)
Commercial/professional worker	24		46
Total	134	9	165
Not known[a]	22		
Total	156	9	165

Sources: County histories; U.S. and British census manuscripts; birth and marriage certificates; and passenger lists.

[a]Of the unknowns, 9 were less than 20 years old on emigration. In a few cases where the subject's previous occupation has not been discovered, that of his father is given.

identified in midwestern counties after the Civil War, six were located in Chicago or Springfield, Illinois, in the region's growing urban-industrial sector, rather than in rural areas and agriculture. The immigrants to towns and cities also came from a variety of occupations—from workers in crafts and industry to retail traders, children of manufacturers in business for themselves, and even professional people. The most noticeable gap we find among these modestly successful urban migrants from Lancashire is that none started from agriculture. On this evidence, the conventional generalization that European emigration was predominantly a movement out of agriculture into the urban-industrial sector does not apply, even in small measure, to the emigration from Lancashire.

Against this background, one can examine the careers of these 165 men from the point of view of their occupations when they arrived in the States. I begin with those who had been textile workers, metalworkers, and machine makers, in Lancashire industry. Understandably, these people have received rather more attention from historians than have the others. Rowland Berthoff gave a strong impression that English immigrants contributed in an important way to the transfer of textile technology to the United States. This hypothesis has been tested by David Jeremy, who concluded that the entire emigration of textile workers from England during the 1820s could have filled no more than a quarter of the new demand for male workers in the American cotton and woolen industries, though closer to half of the demand for workers of both sexes and all ages. Already by the 1820s, the experience of Lancashire emigrants was no longer appropriate for the rapidly expanding cotton textile industry of northern Massachusetts. There the need was for power loom weavers and throstle spinners, not the mule spinners and handloom weavers who were arriving from Lancashire. What American cotton manufacturers most wanted were overseers and managers, machine makers, and cotton printers. According to Jeremy, qualified immigrants could have filled no more than 46 percent of the new jobs in cotton management in the 1820s. Men who had supervised three or four handlooms in a weaving shed were not qualified to oversee a room of power looms.[23]

Former textile workers feature prominently in the county history sample. Forty-six of the 165 immigrants had worked in the textile industries of Lancashire before emigration. No other county studied turned up so many immigrants from Lancashire as did Bristol County, Massachusetts, which contained the towns of Fall River and New Bedford, where mule spinning survived well into the second half of the century. In fact, as late as 1890, a higher proportion of Fall River's population was English-born than in any other of the principal cities in the States.[24]

Eight of the fourteen immigrants found in Bristol County histories had worked in some branch of textile manufacture before emigrating. Elsewhere in Massachusetts and in Connecticut, New York, Pennsylvania, and New Jersey, sixteen immigrants with experience in textiles appeared in a total of forty six subjects. None of the men in Massachusetts who had worked in mills in Lancashire as weavers, spinners, warpers, carders, or simply "millworkers," most of whom emigrated after the Civil War, arrived in a county history by way of achieving a managerial position or by going into business for himself as a cotton manufacturer. All but one did seek careers in independent business, though in quite different

[23] Berthoff, *British Immigrants*, pp. 46, 61, 74, 85; Jeremy, *Transatlantic Industrial Revolution*, p. 162.

[24] Charlotte Erickson, "The English," in *Harvard Encyclopedia of American Ethnic Groups*, ed. Stephan Thernstrom (Cambridge: Harvard University Press, Belknap Press, 1980), p. 328.

fields—as real estate dealers, grocery and liquor store owners, a candy peddler and wholesale confectioner, a partner in a firm manufacturing and selling mineral water, and a tobacconist and hardware dealer. Two of them bought farms in Massachusetts, and one remained a mule spinner all his life in Newburyport, Essex County, where he was described as one of the last to use the hand method.[25]

Their careers say something about the aspirations of cotton millworkers who emigrated in the last part of the century. At least eight of them have been found to have left the mills even before they emigrated to enter the same sorts of occupations in Lancashire—as a baker, a farmer, a crofter, a stonecutter, and dairymen—as they seem to have sought in America. For example, Sandy Harrison was born in Padiham, the illegitimate son of an illiterate mother. At the age of nine he was at work as a part-timer in a cotton mill. After marrying the daughter of a journeyman stonemason, he showed his inclination to leave the mills by working as a fishmonger before he and his wife emigrated in 1869, when he was twenty five. After employment for six years in a Fall River cotton mill, Harrison did become overseer in the carding department. Nonetheless, he resigned this position to go into partnership in a real estate and insurance business.[26]

Fewer former weavers or millworkers were traced elsewhere in the East. Again one finds them as hotel owners and in the real estate business. Two very early immigrants in New Jersey, however, did try to remain in textiles. John Bentley, a cotton spinner from Manchester who had emigrated in 1818, earned enough in a country store business retailing smallwares to buy a cotton mill, but he had to relinquish it. John Nightingale, a weaver from near Chorley who arrived in Paterson at eighteen, used earnings made keeping a public house and as tollgate keeper on a New York state turnpike, at the same time weaving on his premises, to buy a cotton mill with a partner, but leased it out to others.[27]

[25] See William Holker, son of John Holker, in *Biographical Review Containing Life Sketches of Leading Citizens of Essex County, Massachusetts* (Boston: Biographical Review Publishing, 1898), pp. 50–51; son's birth certificate, Wigan, December 1845, xxi/790; United States Census Manuscripts, 1850, Essex County, Mass., p. 407.

[26] *Our County and Its People: A Descriptive and Biographical Record of Bristol County, Massachusetts* (Boston: History Company, 1899), p. 292; birth certificate, Burnley, December 1844, xxi/255; marriage certificate, Burnley, March 1866, 8e/324.

[27] See John Bentley, in *History of Bergen and Passaic Counties, New Jersey,* comp. W. Woodford Clayton (Philadelphia: Everts and Peck, 1882), pp. 545–46; John Nightingale, in *Bergen and Passaic Counties,* pp. 533–34; United States Census Manuscripts, 1850, Passaic County, N.J., p. 245. See also John Brewster, a weaver who emigrated from Droylsden but failed as a cotton manufacturer in Pennsylvania (biography of his son Joseph in Samuel T.

If these former operatives and handloom weavers tended to seek careers outside the industry, a few immigrants with experience in textiles did go into textile manufacture for themselves with some success or become managers in textile firms. They were men who had already been in business for themselves in Lancashire, including a sizing manufacturer, a flannel manufacturer, and a woolen manufacturer.

One branch of cotton manufacture did offer opportunities to former operatives sufficient to entice them to stay in the industry. Cotton manufacturers in Massachusetts did rely very heavily on Lancashire men when it came to introducing the colored printing of cotton fabrics, whether by block printing or the newer cylindrical method. Bleachers, dyers, printers, and color mixers achieved managerial positions in Massachusetts firms more frequently than did other sorts of textile operatives, if these samples are any guide. David Jeremy has emphasized the peculiar difficulties associated with the introduction of printing in the late 1820s. Because of the absence of chemical analysis, dyers and color mixers relied on empirical skills handed down by tradition. The first firms to attempt to add printing to cotton manufacture actively recruited Lancashire workmen to assist them: indeed, in this field, all the early recruits came from Lancashire, so far as is known.[28] A few letters have survived that were received by a Lancashire-born color mixer working at the Hamilton Manufacturing Company in Lowell, which had begun introducing color printing in 1829. Thomas Crawshaw, a family friend and former associate in Manchester, was sending William Hunter dye recipes for "fast green," "madder purple," yellow, pink, and blue, as well as offering to send muslin dyes that were "the principal things going here." A reminder that highly skilled Lancashire men could also find opportunities on the Continent of Europe at this time is found in Crawshaw's remark that "my extract of Indigo is not so good has I could wish to send you and the People here buy it already prepard .... I have sent to my acquaintance in france has I know they do it best in the Trade."[29]

Wiley, *Biographical and Historical Cyclopedia of Delaware County, Pennsylvania,* ed. Winfield Garner [New York: Gresham Publishing, 1894]), pp. 258–59). Richard Margrave found three former spinners from Lancashire who eventually owned silk businesses in Paterson, New Jersey (*Emigration of Silk Workers,* pp. 354–57, 361).

[28] Jeremy, *Transatlantic Industrial Revolution,* pp. 106, 111, 115, 116.

[29] Thomas Crawshaw, Manchester, April 1, 1842, to William Hunter in Lowell. The recipes were sent along with a letter dated December 2, 1841. Copies of the Hunter letters were made available to me by Roger Haydon, to whom I am most grateful.

The key role of color mixers, as well as print designers, is illustrated in the case of James Henry, who was apprenticed at fifteen to the old method of block printing in the firm in Clitheroe, where his father had been overseer of calico printing until his death in 1813, when James was eight years old. Emigrating in 1829, Henry began work as a color maker in Springvale, Maine, but after working for periods in Lowell, Massachusetts, and Dover, New Hampshire, arrived in Fall River in 1832 to take charge of the color department at the Globe Print Works. By 1837 he had become manager of the American Print Works and, in addition, superintendent of the Globe Works. When he resigned in 1873, Henry was succeeded in both positions by his son, Robert.[30] That men who were not acquainted with advanced printing machinery were able to find managerial positions is further illustrated in the case of Jonathan Crabtree, a handblock printer, who left for the United States with his wife and eight children in 1846, when new machinery was introduced at the mills in which he worked. Crabtree secured work as a handblock printer on Staten Island and eventually became factory manager.[31]

Such men continued throughout the century to find opportunities for promotion within the industry. Henry Wylde emigrated as late as 1879. Grandson of a day laborer and son of a machine calico printer and a mother who could not sign her name on his birth certificate, Wylde married the daughter of a weaver. Following in his father's footsteps, he started work as a block boy but emigrated at twenty two, within five years of which he became overseer of a coloring department, advancing to superintendent of the entire works in 1896 at the age of forty one.[32] In all, five men in the finishing branches of cotton manufacture appeared in these eastern samples as overseers, managers, or owners in eastern factories.

Obviously, these few cases do not provide any picture of the careers of the mass of weavers and operatives who emigrated from Lancashire and remained in the East. Anthony Wallace has emphasized the very high turnover of textile operatives in the mills of Rockdale, Pennsylvania, in the first half of the nineteenth century. Though many of them moved to other mills in the region, Wallace suggested that the Morris

[30] Duane Hamilton Hurd, ed., *History of Bristol County, Massachusetts, with Biographical Sketches* (Philadelphia: J. W. Lewis Publishing, 1883), pp. 406–7.

[31] See the biography of Jonathan Crabtree's son John in *Biographical Review of Dane County, Wisconsin* (Chicago: Biographical Review Publishing, 1893), pp. 152–53.

[32] Henry Wylde, in *Biographical Review Containing Life Sketches of Leading Citizens of Essex County, Massachusetts* (Boston: Biographical Review Publishing, 1898), 28: 85; father's marriage certificate, June 1851, Oldham, xx/749.

family, handloom weavers who left Rockdale to buy farms in Ohio in 1837, were "typical."[33] A fierce attack on this version of the safety valve was launched by Cynthia Shelton, who concluded that many textile workers in nearby Manyunk remained factory operatives all their lives and that even cheap land could not be bought on eastern textile wages.[34] Biographies from county histories cannot settle the issue, though more lifetime careers are considered here than were accessible to either Shelton or Wallace. The story of John Entwistle does cast doubt on the assertion that it was impossible to save enough to buy land from cotton textile wages. Entwistle was a cotton weaver in Haslingden, son of an illiterate cotton weaver. In 1884 at the age of thirty four, he emigrated with his wife, who had been a cotton beamer at the time of their marriage. After working six years in a Fall River mill, they were able to buy a farm in Massachusetts.[35]

Textile workers who emigrated from Lancashire before the American Civil War were more likely to turn up in midwestern county histories as farmers than they were to appear in county histories in the East. They were not found in the sample of midwestern urban counties. Their careers lend some support to Wallace's emphasis on the Morris family of handloom weavers in Ohio as being typical. Ten of the farmers in midwestern samples in seven different counties in Illinois, Wisconsin, and Kansas came from a background in textiles in Lancashire. They included men in preindustrial crafts such as fuller and wool comber, as well as spinners, weavers, and cotton bleachers and printers. All had emigrated between 1832 and 1857.

Like the Morrises, most of them had worked for a time in the East before going west. One weaver, who emigrated in 1847, had worked in Philadelphia and New Bedford for four years before turning to farming in Macon County, Illinois. Another weaver worked in Philadelphia from 1848 to 1855 before moving to Monroe County, Illinois. A weaver from Blackburn worked with his two sons in Fall River for two years before moving west in 1844 and buying a farm five years later.

Only two of the ten went west straightaway. Marsden Hopwood, a bleacher from Accrington, himself the son of a laborer, emigrated with his father and brother in 1857 to buy a farm in Illinois; and Thomas

[33] Anthony Wallace, *Rockdale: The Growth of an American Village in the Early Industrial Revolution* (New York: Alfred A. Knopf, 1975), pp. 63–65; Erickson, *Invisible Immigrants,* pp. 139–74.

[34] Shelton, *Mills of Manyunk,* pp. 97–98.

[35] John Entwistle, in *Our County and Its People,* p. 281.

Moulding, who had managed a cotton factory in Lancashire, emigrated with ample means to buy a large farm on his arrival in Illinois in 1851.[36] These two cases provide a hint that even the finishers and managers, so much more in demand in the American labor market than textile operatives, were lured by the prospects of land ownership and farming in the second quarter of the century. Even a man such as Joshua Rhodes, hardly highly skilled and experienced on his emigration at the age of eighteen, moved to Illinois in 1839 at the age of thirty nine and in so doing gave up a position as overseer in a woolen factory in Boston. In Kane County, he combined positions as postmaster, merchant, and insurance agent to become the owner of 280 acres.[37]

One former textile worker appeared in midwestern samples in a role other than farmer and landowner. Within two years of his emigration in 1832, John Lyons, a cotton spinner from Manchester, arrived in Potosi in the lead-mining region of Wisconsin at a time when Cornish miners were appearing there in significant numbers. There he was returned in the United States census in 1870 at the age of sixty nine as a lead miner with real estate worth a mere $100 and his three sons as day laborers.[38]

If the county histories are any guide, industrial workers other than textile operatives were not so much drawn to agriculture in the United States. Jeremy stressed that Englishmen who could build textile machinery were much in demand in America. The late Herbert Gutman described the success of a few Lancashire emigrants in establishing their own firms making parts or machinery for the silk industry of Paterson, New Jersey, another city where the English formed an above-average proportion of the population in 1890.[39] The county histories suggest that their success was repeated elsewhere. Eighteen Lancashire-born machine builders, engineers, and metalworkers were located in sample

[36] For Hopwood, see *History of Sangamon County, Illinois* (Chicago: Interstate Publishing, 1881), p. 1016; birth certificate, Haslingden, September 1840, xxi/387. For Moulding, see *The Past and Present of Kane County, Illinois* (Chicago: William le Baron, Jr., 1878), p. 622.

[37] Joshua Rhodes, in *Kane County*, p. 719.

[38] John Lyons, in *Commemorative Biographical Record of the Counties of Rock, Green, Grant, Iowa, and Lafayette, Wisconsin* (Chicago: J. H. Beers, 1901), pp. 848, 979; United States Census Manuscripts, 1870, Grant County, Wis., p. 49.

[39] Jeremy, *Transatlantic Industrial Revolution,* pp. 20, 34–35. Four of the five examples that Herbert Gutman provided of Lancashire-born entrepreneurs in Paterson had experience in Lancashire as machinists and machine makers. Interestingly enough, the other was the son of a cotton printer (*Work, Culture, and Society in Industrial America* [New York: Knopf, 1976], pp. 226–29). Of the eight entrepreneurs in Paterson listed by Margrave who were Lancashire-born, two were former dyers or printers and one a machinist (*Emigration of Silk Workers,* pp. 354, 356, 357, 361).

counties. None of them turned up in the Massachusetts counties sampled. Eight of them were living in Connecticut, New York, and Pennsylvania. Among them was the owner of a large foundry in King's County, New York, who had emigrated early (1829), and the foreman of an ironworks; but a steel rod roller also obtained a biography. A certain restlessness, shared by textile workers, was evident in the careers of at least two of these men: John M. Blake, a steel plate shearman in New Haven County, Connecticut, who chose to become owner of a café; and John Spencer, who began work at eleven in Oldham by assisting his father in firing engines in a colliery and later followed his father into a firm in Neshanock, Pennsylvania, as a pump hand. By the time he was twenty one, Spencer was in the grocery business with an uncle. Ten years later he was off to Cumberland County, Tennessee, where he bought a farm; but after four years he retreated again into merchandising with a partner with whom he returned to Pennsylvania in the same business.[40]

These workers in industries, in which women found fewer opportunities than they did in textiles, were also drawn to the West. But although ten of them turned up in midwestern counties, only two appeared as farmers. James Westerman, a coppersmith from Manchester who emigrated in 1817 at the age of twenty one and worked at his trade for thirteen years in Baltimore, Lowell, and Pittsburgh, eventually turned to farming, first in Pennsylvania and then in 1852 at the age of forty six in Michigan.[41]

Westerman's career, which resembled that of textile workers who went west, was not typical of this small group. Not surprisingly, two blacksmiths and a millwright who emigrated between 1837 and 1840 seem to have found plenty of work at their old trades. Others such as a steam engine fitter, machinists, a boilermaker, and an engineer found work in railway repair shops, in agricultural implement manufacture, or in looking after the machinery in a packing company, three of them in the Chicago area. An indication that some of these people may have found opportunities to use their skills to have outweighed an agrarian

[40] John M. Blake, in *Commemorative Biographical Record of New Haven County, Connecticut* (Chicago: J. H. Beers, 1902), p. 1492; birth certificate, Warrington, March 1854, 8c/128. John Spencer, in J. G. White, *A Twentieth Century History of Mercer County, Pennsylvania* (Chicago: Lewis Publishing, 1909), pp. 571–72; birth certificate, Oldham, March 1856. 8d/502.

[41] James Westerman, in *Portrait and Biographical Album of Lenawee County, Michigan* (Chicago: Chapman Brothers, 1888), pp. 276–77; New York passenger lists, roll 261/100, ship 200, p. 47, National Archives, microfilm.

myth in the family comes from the career of Thomas Faulkner. The son of an engineer in Shaw, he married the illiterate daughter of a railway fireman and described himself as an engineer in the marriage register. Together, they emigrated in 1852, when he was twenty six, to Jackson County, Michigan, where his parents and a brother were already established on a farm. Within a year, Faulkner left farming to work, first, in the repair shops of the Michigan Central Railroad and, then, in succession, as a fireman and an engine driver. Faulkner helped found and headed a local of the Brotherhood of Locomotive Engineers. Whether for this reason or another, he was dismissed by the railroad about 1880, when he was fifty four, and there, so far, I have lost his trail.[42]

Almost 40 percent of the immigrants from Lancashire in this sample from county histories came from these two sectors of English industry, which were to make the country for a time the workshop of the world. The rest of these immigrants might be divided into two broad groups: those who did go into farming in the United States and those who did not.

To begin with those who did not end up on the land, we find that the sample included fifteen Lancashire emigrants in the coal-mining and heavy industry counties of Pennsylvania, another fourteen immigrants in the East, as well as fifteen nonfarmers in the Middle West and nine in California and Washington on the West Coast. A great majority of this other third of the sample remained in, or eventually returned to, occupations identical or very similar to those they reported near the time of their emigration. Among the fourteen who remained in the East were traditional craftsmen: a merchant tailor, three carpenters, a shoemaker, and a hatter, as well as a store clerk and a secondhand clothes dealer. In the Middle West, three former butchers became provision dealers in the Chicago area; a clerk for a wholesale leather association became clerk first to a manufacturing firm and then a railroad company; a woodturner ended up manufacturing cigar boxes in Janesville, Wisconsin; and a surveyor thrived as surveyor for American railroads. Many of these immigrants remained remarkably mobile, migrating from one place to another in America as well as back and forth from employee to employer status, often more than once, and even trying other sorts of jobs. Those who ended up in county histories

[42] Thomas Faulkner, in *Portrait and Biographical Album of Jackson County, Michigan* (Chicago: Chapman Brothers, 1890), pp. 556–57; marriage certificate, Manchester, March 1846, 20/454.

for the most part arrived there in the same line of work as they were in at the time of emigration, though usually in business for themselves in the United States.

Three cases will be cited, not as typical, but as illustrative of the variety of paths followed—both occupationally and geographically—of some of these people. The son of a collier, Charles Beswick also began his career in the mines in Lancashire. He signed the register with his mark when he married in 1845 at the age of twenty. In 1854, Beswick set out for the gold mines in Australia but returned to England to try to go into the grocery business for himself. In 1860 he sold out and emigrated to Pennsylvania, where he immediately bought a farm in Westmoreland County. Unable to scrape a living from it, Beswick worked as a miner for two different firms for fourteen years, meanwhile hiring help to work the farm. At the end of that time he was able to sell the farm and retire, careful investments having gained him a "competency."[43]

Another escape route from industrial work in Lancashire was taken by Abel Howard. The son of a silk weaver, Howard had worked in a textile mill as a boy. He managed to go to night school and even to attend a business college for a term. By the time he emigrated in 1848 at the age of 24, he was employed as a clerk in a wholesale leather store. In Pottsville, Pennsylvania, he went to work as a timekeeper in a machine shop and then taught school for three years before becoming an itinerant Methodist preacher for thirty years in Delaware and Chester counties. At the age of fifty six, Howard retired to devote his time to dealing in real estate. He built 150 stores and homes and by 1894 owned sixty houses, ten tenements, and four stores.[44]

Unlike the poorly educated Charles Beswick, Sutcliffe Baxter, the son of a substantial farmer of four hundred acres in Lancashire, rebelled

[43] Charles Beswick, in J. N. Boucher, *History of Westmoreland County, Pennsylvania* (New York: Lewis Publishing, 1906), 1: 44–45; marriage certificate, Manchester, June 1845, 20/752. The word "competency" was used frequently in county history biographies of English immigrants. It reflected the acquisition of an income sufficient for retirement from active work. Like the word "independence," in an economic sense it may be a key word in describing the goals of emigrants from England, though without a systematic analysis of a large number of such biographies, one cannot conclude that it did not reflect the views of the editors of the histories themselves. Was it used as frequently in biographies of immigrants of other nationalities or of the native-born? I cannot answer this question. It is worth investigating. On the meaning of the word to radical workers in America, see Bruce Laurie, *Working People of Philadelphia,* p. 75; Paul Krause, "Labor Republicanism and 'Za Chlebom': Anglo-American and Slavic Solidarity in Homestead," in *"Struggle a Hard Battle": Essays on Working-Class Immigrants,* ed. Dirk Hoerder (De Kalb: Northern Illinois University Press, 1986), pp. 149, 164n.

[44] Abel Howard, in Wiley, *Cyclopedia of Delaware County,* p. 394.

against a career in agriculture. After attending a national school to the age of fourteen and Tunliffe Academy for a year thereafter, Baxter concluded that he disliked farming. In 1862 at the age of twenty one, he emigrated to the Cariboo goldfields, apparently in search of more than a competency. In six years in Canada, he worked as a gold miner, a foreman building a wagon road, a mail carrier on horseback, and a bookkeeper for an interior merchant. In 1868, at twenty seven, he arrived in San Francisco, where he first found employment as a coal weigher and then as bookkeeper for a coal company, eventually to become treasurer of another coal company.[45]

For many others, it was not contributing to the enrichment of American industrial skills but farming that appeared to be the road to a competency and independence and thus the attraction of the United States. Perhaps the most notable feature of this survey is the very substantial exodus into agriculture of men who had not farmed in Lancashire. Of the 165 cases considered, 51—or nearly a third—appeared in western county histories as farmers. They included eight cattle raisers and fruit farmers in California. Nearly all these men had emigrated before the Civil War, like the textile workers already considered. Of the fifty one, only four are known to have been farmers or sons of farmers before emigration, though a weaver turned dairyman in Bury sired three sons who established a very large cattle business in California.[46]

These few farmers and farmers' sons settled very quickly on farms in the United States. What seems remarkable is how few of them turned up in the county histories. Nine of the midwestern farmers had been general laborers or farm laborers or stated that they arrived without means or with less than five dollars. It took them longer to reach their goal. Three of them worked for a time in the East, one in the lumber trade in Chicago, another mining gold in California, and still another as a shoemaker for three years, though he appears not to have been brought up to the trade.

Craftsmen with work experience in Lancashire were not missing from the ranks of Lancashire farmers in the Middle West, however. In this small sample appeared two shoemakers, a stonemason, two carpenters, and a saddler, all of whom headed west rather soon after arrival, sooner

[45] For Baxter, see Clarence B. Bayley, *History of Seattle, Washington* (Chicago: S. J. Clarke Publishing, 1916), 3: 514–18; birth certificate, Burnley, December 1841, xxi/190.

[46] Henry, John, and William Holt, in W. B. Lardner and M. J. Brock, *History of Placer and Nevada Counties, California* (Los Angeles: Historical Record Company, 1924), pp. 993, 463, 653; John's birth certificate, Bury, September 1839, xxi/283.

than the laborers. Another three of the midwestern farmers had been petty tradesmen—an ale seller, a hawker, and an unspecified dealer. James Neild, who emigrated from Ashton-under-Lyme in 1842 at twenty six, bought 260 acres in Kenosha County, Wisconsin, straightaway but had to go back to his trade as a butcher in the town of Kenosha for eighteen years before he again bought a farm of 117 acres in Racine County in 1860. By this time he had other investments, as well as town property.[47]

No clear line can be drawn as to particular groups of people, at least according to prior occupation, who were attracted to the goal of farming. Among the farmers in the West were found four white-collar workers—a warehouseman, two bookkeepers, and a banker from Rochdale—all of whom went west directly and bought land very soon thereafter. California farmers included a doctor, a merchant, and John Forster, who went to sea from Liverpool very young and married into a Mexican family in California, becoming a truly large-scale rancher and cattleman with 144,000 acres.[48]

Obviously, proportions mean little in this small sample of immigrants drawn from county histories. They do indicate the astonishing range of occupations from which Lancashire people became farmers and landowners in the United States, especially before the Civil War. Among these emigrants who turned to farming were fifteen textile workers, two engineers, a coal miner, two building trades workers, six other craftsmen, nine laborers, four white-collar workers, three petty tradesmen, as well as a merchant, a seaman, and a doctor.

Scholars have investigated the contributions to industrial technology and skills made by immigrants to the United States from the industrial sector in Britain. More recently, they have been exploring the role of such immigrants, especially those from Lancashire, in the American labor movement and the formation of working-class communities in cities such as Lowell, Fall River, and Paterson. I make no claim that the lives to which I have drawn attention are typical. But they add another dimension to the analysis of emigration from industrial England, other than that of bearers of advanced technology or refugees from economic

[47] James Neild, in *The History of Racine and Kenosha, Wisconsin* (Chicago: Western Historical Company, 1879), p. 632; son's birth certificate, Ashton-under-Lyme, December 1837, 20/49.

[48] John Forster, in *An Illustrated History of Los Angeles County, California* (Chicago: Lewis Publishing, 1889), pp. 470–71.

disaster. These lives were probably more representative of emigrant aspirations than they were of the careers of most emigrants from Lancashire to the United States.

Many of the emigrants from Lancashire had migrated within England before they set out for America.[49] Among these cases there is no pattern of emigration from a rural village to a larger town, the conventional model of stage migration. There was more movement from one town to another. Chain, or family, migration does seem evident in many cases, from wives and children reuniting with husbands and fathers to adult emigrants bringing out parents, couples going to join the wife's family, as well as young people going out to uncles.

Just as pronounced as repeated migration among these people was the willingness and ability to change occupation. A few are known to have done this even before they went to the States, again sometimes as a consequence of opportunities afforded by marriage. One such case is that of the weaver who became a stonecutter after his marriage to the daughter of a quarryman. Emigrating soon after his marriage in 1840, James Livesey worked in several states before arriving in Madison, Wisconsin, in 1841. There he was to serve as a contractor for stonework in the building of not only the state capitol but also schools, churches, the courthouse, and bridges.[50]

Whether finally settling in the East or the West, these emigrants from Lancashire were not reluctant to change job or location. Many had done so even before they emigrated. Some American observers of textile workers from Lancashire in Fall River described them as unwilling to move geographically or to change trade, as regarding themselves as having a vested interest in their particular jobs.[51] The county histories provide a different view of other emigrants from Lancashire.

To acquire a farm or a business of one's own in order to achieve independence and a competency, rather than great wealth, seems to have motivated most of these moderately successful Lancastrians. When an emigrant handloom weaver could write to his father, a carpenter,

[49] We have 22 such cases, but references to previous migrations are by no means complete in the data.

[50] James Livesey, in *Dane County*, pp. 453–54; *History of Dane County, Wisconsin* (Chicago: Western Historical Company, 1880), p. 1010. Livesey was the son of a farmer in Withnall. His siblings who remained in Lancashire were all weavers or laborers according to the British Census Manuscripts, 1841, Withnell, HO 525/18, p. 125, marriage certificate, Chorley, December 1840, 21/188.

[51] Blewett, "Lancashire Popular Radicalism," pp. 22–23.

that "you used to say you could like to occupy land of your own," it seems difficult to doubt that the prospect of land ownership was a powerful influence on working-class immigrants as well as on others.[52] It was particularly pronounced among workers in the textile industry. Given the opportunities they found to work for wages in the United States, many did achieve that goal.

Thus this question arises: If so many Lancashire industrial workers managed to get farms in the United States, why have American historians interpreted the safety valve simply as a psychological one at best for the native-born worker? One handloom weaver in Ohio in 1841 provided an almost classic statement of the safety valve: "Times has been rather dull in America for this last 4 years and some macanics have been out of work at their own trades; but their is one advantage in this countrey and that is in such times their are a number of mecanics moves back to the land where their is plenty for them to do and this gives more room for the others."[53]

Having a young family could prove an obstacle to an immigrant who had no land to which to return. In some of our cases where there were older children, father and son (or sons) came west first to make a start. Evidence of both economic mobility within Lancashire and the impediment of a large family is to be found in the case of George Horrocks. Born about 1812, Horrocks was the son of a country weaver in a valley lying between Bolton and Darwen. He moved up the valley after marriage to begin as a cotton spinner and from there to Farnworth, a town with a railway link, where he went into business as a cotton spinner and manufacturer with the husband of one of his sisters. From there he wrote to a brother in America in the 1850s: "If I had no family I should have come before now. I think I should like to have a nice farm upon a rich and fertile piece of land but it appears my lot to be amongst machinery."[54]

A poor farm in the East might prove as much of an obstacle to moving west as low wages. James Nowland was the Liverpool-born son of an Irish quill and feather merchant. On a farm in Maine in the 1850s, Nowland suffered greatly from the harsh winters and short harvests. Left a widower with two young daughters, he longed to move west but

[52] Erickson, *Invisible Immigrants,* p. 154.

[53] William Morris, Barnsville, Ohio, July 14, 1841, to Jonathan, his brother, in ibid., p. 168.

[54] James Horrocks, *My Dear Parents: An Englishman's Letters Home from the American Civil War,* ed. A. S. Lewis (London: Victor Gollancz, 1982), pp. 12–13, 11.

Table 6.3. Lancashire-born people in the county history sample by state, compared with the distribution of English-born in the United States census of 1870

State	Percent of sample born in Lancashire	Percent of population of state born in England and Wales
Massachusetts	31.9	9.7
Connecticut	13.9	3.0
New York	12.2	2.3
New Jersey	31.3	3.1
Pennsylvania	16.3	2.5
Ohio	5.1	1.9
Michigan	5.9	3.0
Indiana	0.0	2.2
Illinois	10.4	2.3
Wisconsin	13.5	3.4
Iowa	3.9	1.6
Kansas	14.3	2.0
Utah	15.4	18.5
California[a]	8.9	3.2
Washington[a]	20.0	2.3
Average	10.1	1.4

Sources: Ninth Census (1870), vol. 1, *The Statistics of the Population of the United States* (Washington, 1872), table 6, p. 340; *Compendium of the Eleventh Census, 1890*, Pt. 2, *Vital and Social Statistics* (Washington, 1894), pp. 600–601.

[a]Comparison made with the 1890 U.S. census.

was unable to sell his farm. After remarrying, he found, with little difficulty, a clerkship in St. Johns, New Brunswick, but opined that he "always felt more independent on a farm until times got so bad that I could not live at all."[55] After serving in the Civil War, Nowland returned to Maine as a farmer in Aristook County, raising livestock rather than potatoes and grain but still struggling for a livelihood.

Although in the sample counties Lancastrians were more numerous among the English-born in Massachusetts and New Jersey, they made a respectable showing in Illinois, Wisconsin, and Kansas as well as in Utah (see Table 6.3). Nora Faires has suggested that Irish and German immigrants who ventured west of the Appalachians may have been somewhat less skilled, though possessing more savings, than the masses

[55] James Nowland, St. Johns, June 22, 1856, to his sister, Mary Ann Reid, in Liverpool, and also his letter of June 7, 1852, Nowland Letters, Huntington Library; Edward Baines, *History, Directory, and Gazeteer of . . . Lancaster* (Liverpool, 1825), 1: 301; British Census Manuscripts, 1851, HO 107/2179, p. 21; United States Census Manuscripts, 1850, Aroostock County, Maine., roll 248, p. 029.

who remained in the East.[56] It is possible that the same generalization might apply to the Lancastrians. Only eight of these immigrants specifically declared that they had served apprenticeships in England. Six of them were located in the East and the other two in Chicago. Many others had learned their trades working with their fathers or other relatives. As has been shown, if those who came west had more savings than others, those savings were very frequently acquired through working in eastern states. It also seemed a reasonable assumption that those who moved west had delayed marriage to be able to accumulate savings for the move. The data do not support such an assumption. Of those for whom marriage details are available, the average age at first marriage of those remaining in the East was 25.9 years and of those who went to the Middle West, 25.6 years. There was no significant difference in the proportions of men marrying at thirty or older between immigrants settled in the East and Middle West. Among the cases that have been verified, no significant difference was found between the proportion emigrating before marriage and those arriving in the United States with families. Slightly more than half of the known cases married after their arrival in the United States, whether they eventually settled in the East or the Middle West.

At least it seems probable that it was not primarily "stout English farmers" who found their way to the cheap lands of the American West from industrial Lancashire. English farmers came from counties other than this industrial leader. For people in Lancashire, emigration was not a means of moving from the agricultural sector into the secondary or tertiary occupations. It was often the reverse. Earnings in industrial work, whether in Lancashire or the United States, did make it possible for some well-motivated and able people to attain their goals of a competence and independence in farming, land ownership, or other businesses of their own. When these opportunities for traditional craftsmen and workers in Lancashire's staple industries began to shrink

[56] Nora Faires, "Occupational Patterns of German Americans in Nineteenth-Century Cities," in *German Workers in Industrial Chicago, 1850–1910*, ed. Hartmut Keil and John Jentz (De Kalb: Northern Illinois University Press, 1983), p. 40; Jo Ellen Vinyard, *The Irish on the Urban Frontier: Nineteenth-Century Detroit, 1850–1880* (New York: Arno, 1976), pp. 2, 39, 52. The daughter of a building trades worker, who had been apprenticed in West Clayton, Yorkshire, and emigrated with his family in 1850, recalled that in Chicago her father had housed and employed newcomers from West Clayton, whether known to him or not. "Belonging to the unskilled class, or rather skilled only as weavers, they were farsighted enough to see that farming offered a better outlook" (Jeanette Hinchcliffe Root, "Early Days in Chicago," as told to her great-niece, typescript, Chicago Historical Society).

after the American Civil War, urban laborers came to constitute a larger proportion of Lancashire's emigrants. When Canada's economy boomed after 1905, disaffected laborers flocked to the Empire rather than compete with southern and eastern Europeans in the American labor market.

Appendix

Table 6.4. Occupations of English and Welsh male immigrants, 1831 and 1841, and of British males, 1851 and 1885–1888, aged 20 or older, compared with British labor force

	English and Welsh			
	1831		1841	
Occupational class	Lists	Census	Lists	Census
Agricultural workers	24.6%	33.8%	21.3%	28.6%
Laborers	11.3	16.7	12.5	8.2
Servants, etc.	2.1	4.0	2.5	8.9
Craftsmen	33.1	21.6	31.3	29.9
Industrial workers	16.5	13.2	23.2	14.9
Modern tertiary workers	12.4	10.7	9.2	9.5
Total	100.0%	100.0%	100.0%	100.0%
Number occupied males	1,794	3,179,729	1,750	3,499,000
	British			
	1851		1885–1888	
Occupational class	Lists	Census	Lists	Census
Agricultural workers	23.0%	27.3%	9.5%	15.6%
Laborers	25.7	6.9	29.5	8.2
Servants, etc.	3.8	9.3	3.2	12.8
Craftsmen	31.1	30.0	34.3	30.3
Industrial workers	9.3	15.8	7.8	17.0
Modern tertiary workers	7.2	10.7	15.7	16.1
Total	100.1%	100.0%	100.0%	100.0%
Number occupied males	2,224	6,618,452	8,698	8,892,985

Sources: Ship lists as in Table 6.1; *Population of Great Britain, 1831, Enumeration Abstracts,* vol. 1, British Parliamentary Papers (hereinafter B.P.P.), 1833 (12), XXXVI, pp. xiii–xiv; *Census of Great Britain, 1841, Enumeration Abstracts,* Pt. 1, *England and Wales,* B.P.P., 1844 (587), XXVII, pp. 27–45; *Census of Great Britain, 1851, Population Tables,* Pt. 2, *Ages, Civil Condition, Occupations, and Birth-places,* vol. 1, *England and Wales,* B.P.P., 1852–53 (1691–1), LXXXVIII, Table 54, pp. cxxviii-cxl, and Table 24, pp. ccxxviii-ccxxl, and ccxviii-ccxxl; *Census of England and Wales, 1881,* vol. 3, *Ages, . . . Marriage, Occupations, and Birth-places of the People,* B.P.P., 1882 (C.3722), LXXVII, Table 5, pp. x-xvi; *Ninth Decennial Census of the Population of Scotland,* vol. 2, B.P.P., 1883 (C.3657), LXXXI, Table 15, pp. 406–13.

Note: The immigrant labor force in 1831 has been classified to conform with data available in the 1831 census: miners are placed with laborers and removed from crafts. For a fuller explanation, see Table 4.12, above. Totals do not always equal 100 percent because of roundings.

Table 6.5. Index of representation in the British population of British male emigrants aged 20 or older, 1831–1888, by occupational class

Occupational class	English and Welsh		British	
	1831	1841	1851	1885–1888
Agricultural workers	73	75	84	61
Laborers	68	52	372	598
Servants, etc.	53	28	41	25
Craftsmen	153	105	104	132
Industrial workers	125	156	59	46
Modern tertiary workers	116	97	67	98

Sources: See those for Table 6.4.

CHAPTER SEVEN

Englishwomen in America in the Nineteenth Century: Expectations and Reality

With the increase in attention paid to women's history during the past two decades, the experiences of women as migrants have been gaining the consideration of historians. This essay is an attempt to add Englishwomen to the story of emigration.

At first sight the sources I have used over the years in the study of English migrants did not bring women into focus. Surviving emigrant letters were not often written by women.[1] The manuscript passenger lists, which I have been exploiting more recently, provide less information about women than about men. County biographical histories in the United States only very occasionally recorded the life story of a woman, usually the widow of a distinguished immigrant. In the wealth of emigrant guides and travel accounts that poured forth from British and European presses in the nineteenth century, few were written by women. Although the works of Harriet Martineau, Frances Trollope, and Fanny Kemble are well known and frequently cited, ordinary immigrant women rarely wrote letters, guides, or memoirs.[2] Such an

[1] Possibly women's letters were less frequently kept by their descendants. A Scots immigrant in Canada in the 1840s explained that he did not write to his wife because "it is well known that the post office folk are no just so precise about women folks' letters as about men's, in respect that they are not supposed to contain matters of such weighty concernment" (Joseph Abbott, *The Emigrant to North America from Memoranda of a Settler in Canada*, 2d ed. [Montreal: Lowell and Gibson, 1843], p. 73).

[2] Women who participated in the overland trail to the West, especially Mormon women, do appear to have recorded their experiences more frequently than most. See LeRoy Hafen and Ann Hafen, *Handcarts to Zion: The Story of a Unique Western Migration, 1856–*

unusual work as *A True Picture of Emigration,* first published anonymously in London in 1848, as a pamphlet, was written by Edward Burlend, who never emigrated, from an oral account his mother Rebecca provided of her early life as an immigrant in Pike County, Illinois, during a visit to her native Yorkshire in 1846.[3]

If one does not want to rely entirely on what men said about women emigrants, the source materials appear to be scant and fragmentary. Nevertheless, in returning to the kinds of sources that I have used before, especially immigrant letters written from America to England in the nineteenth century, I found confirmation for the proposition that historical sources yield answers to the questions one asks of them.

Questions concerning the role of women in the great migration of the nineteenth century have an intrinsic interest. Overseas migration during that century was historically distinctive. In spite of some assisted emigration and attempts at group colonization, its characteristic features, so far as emigration from the United Kingdom to the United States was concerned, were that it was atomistic, based on decisions of families and individuals, voluntary, and self-financed. Indentured servitude, so important in the peopling of the North American colonies, virtually disappeared from the migrations of the North Atlantic. In this sense, to examine what we are able to discover about the women who participated in that remarkably free movement of people—no passports,

---

1860 (Glendale, Calif.: Arthur H. Clarke, 1960); Kenneth Godfrey, Audrey Godfrey, and Jill Mulvay Derr, *Women's Voices: An Untold History of the Latter-Day Saints* (Salt Lake City: Deseret Book Company, 1983); Ruth Moynihan, Susan Armitage, and Christiane Fischer Dichamp, *So Much to Be Done: Women Settlers on the Mining and Ranching Frontier* (Lincoln: University of Nebraska Press, 1990); Kenneth Holmes, ed., *Covered Wagon Women,* vols. 4–6 (Glendale, Calif.: Arthur H. Clark, 1985–86), and vol. 9 (Spokane, Wash.: Arthur H. Clark, 1990); Lillian Schlissel, ed., *Women's Diaries of the Westward Journey* (New York: Schocken Books, 1982); Sandra Myres, ed., *Ho for California!: Women's Overland Diaries from the Huntington Library* (San Marino: Huntington Library, 1988), and Myres, *Westering Women and the Frontier Experience, 1800–1915* (Albuquerque: University of New Mexico Press, 1982).

[3] Milo Milton Quaife, ed., *A True Picture of Emigration* (Chicago: Lakeside Press, 1936). The work was listed anonymously in bibliographies of early American history. The identity of the Burlends was established by the editor of Lakeside Press through descendants of Rebecca Burlend in whose hands the only known copies lay. In the preferatory remarks to the 1848 publication, reprinted in this 1936 edition, the author declared that "the material and facts herein contained were delivered to him *viva voce* by his mother . . . during a late visit to this, her native country" (p. 5). A second edition was published in London in 1856 or 1857 with the brief title *The Wesleyan Emigrants* by Edward Burlend (p. xxvi). For some comments on the authenticity of the work, see Stephen Fender, *Sea Changes: British Emigration & American Literature* (Cambridge: Cambridge University Press, 1992), pp. 282–86.

no visas, no quotas—leads us into their role in a unique historical process.

I have been reconsidering those scant remains which have come to my attention over the years with respect to two main questions: first, the decision to emigrate. What attitude did Englishwomen take toward it, and to what extent were they consulted? In short, what were their expectations? Second, what can be said about their adaptation as immigrants? Did the reality of their new homes conform to expectations, and if not, to what extent were they able to adapt to the differences?

One no more than scratches the surface before one comes across statements about the hesitation of women to emigrate. One might take as an opening theme some of the remarks of the candid, if insensitive, William Cobbett, who had lived twice in the United States as a political refugee before he published his emigrant's guide in 1829. "Women, and especially English women," he warned, "transplant very badly. . . . [T]here are some who are obstinately perverse" in refusing to emigrate. Men must resist this obstinacy, he declared, but if a man could not subdue this perverseness before he emigrated, let him not go, for to "live in a state of petty civil war . . . in clear addition to the ordinary inconveniences of life, is too great a deduction even from the advantages attending a residence in America."[4]

Throughout the nineteenth century, women formed a minority of immigrants from Europe to the United States. After reaching its lowest level for the entire period from 1820 to 1910 of 20 percent in 1824, the proportion of women climbed to just over a third (35.6 percent) in 1831. This figure was almost identical to that of my estimate of the proportion of women among the immigrants entering the United States from England and Wales in that year (35 percent). By 1841, the share of women in both the entire immigration and that from England and Wales had risen to 39 percent. Of course, if one excluded children and people over fifty and included only those migrants in prime working age ranges, the proportion of women was lower. In 1841, only 32 percent of the immigrants from England and Wales aged twenty-five to twenty-nine were women. For the rest of the century, the proportion of women in the total immigration to the United States did not change much from that picture in 1841. As is well known, the migration from parts of southern and eastern Europe after 1900 brought a significant rise in the

[4] William Cobbett, *Emigrant's Guide in 10 Letters Addressed to the Taxpayers of England* (London, 1829), pp. 34–35.

proportion of male immigrants. At the peak in 1902, men constituted 72 percent of the total immigration and 82 percent of the Italian but only 60 percent of the immigrants from England.[5]

From the samples taken of passenger lists, one finds that most of the women who did emigrate from England and Wales traveled with relatives. In 1841, 34 percent of the females were wives traveling with their husbands, and 43 percent were daughters accompanied by their fathers. Only 16 percent of the females aged fifteen or older immigrating in 1841 from England and Wales traveled alone, compared with 84 percent of the men. (In 1831 the proportion was 15 percent.) Those estimates certainly exaggerate the proportion traveling truly on their own, because we cannot identify in-laws or friends in the passenger lists. In 1841, close to another 10 percent of the women were heads of household traveling with children or younger siblings. These estimates are not significantly different from the 28 percent of women setting out without a clear adult male relative identified by William Van Vugt in his sampling of the ship lists for 1851.[6] By the end of the century, the proportion of women among English immigrants had not changed, though a somewhat larger proportion were traveling on their own or with children, rather than with husbands, fathers, or brothers.

Although most Englishwomen throughout the century emigrated with adult male relatives, their role in the decision-making process cannot be assumed to have been negligible, in spite of the long-standing tendency to regard nineteenth-century women as dependents. Those who did set out on their own or with their children, who may have constituted as many as a quarter of the women who emigrated from England and Wales to the United States, clearly had many decisions to make for themselves.

In contrast with the overseas movement, Dudley Baines's estimates of net internal migration across county boundaries confirms the view of

[5] The percentages of women in the total immigration are calculated from statistics provided in *Abstracts of Reports of the Immigration Commission*, 61st Cong., 3d sess., S. Doc. 747, (Washington: GPO, 1911), 1: 57–58, 93. For my estimates of the English- and Welshwomen in 1831 and 1841, see n. 6, below.

[6] See above, Table 4.10, and Charlotte Erickson, "Emigration from the British Isles to the U.S.A. in 1841," Part 1, "Emigration from the British Isles," *Population Studies* 43 (1989): 360–61; William Van Vugt, "Who Were the Immigrant Women from Britain to the United States in the Mid-Nineteenth Century?" in *Immigration and Ethnicity: American Society—"Melting Pot" or "Salad Bowl?"* ed. Michael D'Innocenzo and Josef Sirefman (Westport, Conn.: Greenwood Press, 1992), p. 165. Van Vugt cites some preliminary figures that I supplied him to quote me as saying that only 5 percent of the women traveled alone in 1841. This error was not corrected in the original version of this article.

Table 7.1. Females among passengers from the United Kingdom to various destinations, 1877–1907

	To United States		To Canada		To Australasia	
	English and Welsh	Irish	English and Welsh	Irish	English and Welsh	Irish
1877–1880	33.8%	49.7%	29.6%	37.1%	35.7%	45.3%
1881–1890	35.8	49.8	31.4	40.5	37.2	46.6
1891–1900	38.9	55.2	34.1	41.1	39.8	41.6
1900–1907	39.7	53.7	30.7	33.6	41.1	34.9

Source: Calculated from figures in N. H. Carrier and J. R. Jeffery, *External Migration: A Study of the Available Statistics, 1815–1950*, General Register Office, Studies on Medical and Population Subjects, no. 6 (London: HMSO, 1953), p. 104.

contemporaries that women predominated in internal migration, men in external migration.[7] Much of that internal migration was short-distance, not caught by intercounty estimates, and did not necessarily involve the severing of frequent visits home. Country girls in particular more or less had to leave home between the ages of 12 and 14 to go into service, which normally involved some migration. It was said in Dorset in the 1880s that every girl born into a laborer's family was bound to move.[8] Among women, the unmarried and the young were more likely to be internal migrants and married women to form a larger share of the overseas movement. A succession of charitable ventures combined with assisted passages and specially arranged and supervised voyages never seem to have succeeded in inducing large numbers of single women to undertake the journey to Australia and New Zealand in the nineteenth century (see Table 7.1). The surplus of women in the population of England and Wales continued to rise, in part because of this differential migration. In 1841 there were 359,000 more women than men recorded in the census; by 1901 the surplus had mounted to over a million women (1,070,000).

One might think that this hesitancy of Englishwomen to participate fully in emigration needs no explaining, and one can readily indulge in inventing common-sense explanations. Yet Irishwomen did not demonstrate the same tentativeness about emigrating. According to my

[7] Dudley Baines, *Migration in a Mature Economy: Emigration and Internal Migration in England and Wales, 1861–1900* (Cambridge: Cambridge University Press, 1985), pp. 235–57.

[8] Barbara Kerr, "The Dorset Agricultural Labourer, 1750–1850," *Proceedings of the Dorset Natural History and Archeological Society* 84 (1962): 167. See also Bogusia Wojciechowska, "Brenchley: A Study of Migratory Movements in a Nineteenth-Century Rural Parish," *Local Population Studies*, no. 41 (Autumn 1988): 33.

Table 7.2. Unmarried women among female passengers from the United Kingdom to various destinations, all ages

	To United States		To Canada		To Australasia	
	English and Welsh	Irish	English and Welsh	Irish	English and Welsh	Irish
1877–1880	44.7%	83.1%	43.9%	69.3%	51.8%	83.7%
1881–1890	49.4	85.1	49.7	66.9	52.4	83.0
1891–1900	46.3	90.1	50.7	66.7	51.0	74.3
1900–1907	41.3	87.2	42.3	58.3	44.0	63.3

Source: See those for Table 7.1.

research men outnumbered women in the Irish emigration to the United States in 1831, but by 1841, even before the famine, women were rapidly closing the gap. Eight hundred women left for every thousand men as compared with 633 per thousand among the English and Welsh immigrants that year. In the last quarter of the century, the sexes were just about in balance in the Irish movement into the States. Unmarried Irishwomen went to all the principal destinations of passengers going overseas from the British Isles in larger proportions than did single Englishwomen (see Table 7.2). The surplus of women in the Irish population (124,000 in 1861) was more than halved to a mere 58,700 by the end of the century.

Whereas Irishwomen took readily to emigration, Cobbett clearly had a point in insisting on the reluctance of Englishwomen to make such a move. One can find evidence in reminiscences, letters, and diaries both of resistance to the original decision and of a failure to adapt to new surroundings when reality did not conform to expectations.

It is conventional to regard women in the nineteenth century as having been subservient to their husbands and fathers. In law, they were admittedly nonpersons until the modest legal gains in the last quarter of the century with respect to married women's property and custody and maintenance. Yet an examination of women's status from the intimacy of private letters reinforces a historian's suspicions that the law did not always prescribe what happened in human affairs. One might well take the decision to emigrate—or not—as a test case for family attitudes, historically, in the rapidly growing literature on the history of the family.

The stereotype may be illustrated by the remarks of Rebecca Burlend, wife of a hard-pressed tenant farmer in Yorkshire, who accompanied her husband to Pike County, Illinois, in 1831. As her son reported her attitude, Mrs. Burlend would not have emigrated if obedience to her husband's wishes had left her any alternative. So also Sophia Courtauld, the mature but unmarried daughter of George Courtauld, wrote at the time of her reluctant emigration that she was resolved to stay with her father in accordance with her duty.[9] In 1846, a young woman in Yorkshire wrote to her cousin in Wisconsin that she would not leave family, home, and country unless she saw it as her duty. And as late as 1882, another young Yorkshire woman confided to a cousin in Minneapolis that she agreed with her grandfather that women are like cats, made to stay at home. "I am so afraid of—I dont know what," she wrote. "I think its called the world."[10]

Some wives were not given the option of choosing to join their husbands from a sense of obedience or duty. Emigration was a familiar means of escape from unwanted legal ties. Sometimes the escape appears to have been maneuvered in the other direction. An emigrant about to leave for Australia in May 1839 from Plymouth, where the ship with nearly two hundred passengers was at anchor in the channel awaiting favorable winds, wrote that "we are not allowed to go ashore lest any married should think proper of leaving his wife to continue her journey by herself."[11]

Voluminous letters have survived from the Courtauld family, in which the toing and froing of a decision to emigrate to the United States is traceable in considerable detail. George Courtauld, a man in his fifties, went out to the States in 1818, purchased land, and then wrote to his wife and grown sons and daughters about the prospect of their joining him. His intention, he wrote in December 1818, was

> to give you as full & as fair (I mean *just*) a view of our probable situation as Americans [as he could in order to] assist the Judgmt of all concern'd—whether it be more desirable that they should remove hither, or whether I wind up & return to them. I rather lean to *their* remove; . . . but my opinion shall not—*should not*—be imperative upon

[9] Quaife, *Picture of Emigration,* p. 7. Note by Sophia Courtauld, on board the *Elektra* bound for New York, September 23, 1820, in *Courtauld Family Letters* (Cambridge: Bowes and Bowes, 1916), 2: 738.

[10] Jane Barrett, Hunslet Hall, Yorkshire, January 29, 1835, to Matthew Dinsdale, Dinsdale Papers, Mss HSS/DL, Wisconsin State Historical Society, Madison; Emma Pollard, Nether Hall, Dalton, August 10, 1882 to her niece Lizzy Bell, Scott/Forsyth Papers, Mss P1590, folder 1, Minnesota Historical Society archives, St. Paul.

[11] Frank Crewe, May 18, 1829, "at anchor, Plimouth," to John Crewe, Liston Grove, Marylebone, copy supplied to author by Hugh Brogan from a letter in private possession.

> any of you. . . . I shall be happy to receive you all, . . . or I shall willingly agn prepare to cross the Atlantic should it be the general opinion that 'tis better for you to remain in Engd."[12]

Although, as he wrote to his son Samuel that same month, "it was his decided wish" that all the families should come, "it would be very unreasonable that I should attempt to over rule it by the supposed authority of a husband or a father."[13]

In among passages that expressed sanguine hopes for the future in America, he did warn the women of what might await them, should they decide to come.

> But a perft American wilderness will neither supply (for Love or Money) the many artifical wants which long Habit has render'd important to daily & hourly comfort, nor even a few Neighbours whom my Daughters or Nieces could call pleasant. . . . [Y]e comforts of a convenient House, & some portion of domestic assistance, besides such as their Daughters & Nieces could pleasantly or desirably give, wd probably be found essential to the Ease of *all* Parties.

He wanted the young women in particular to be told what to expect. Society in America was

> unpleasantly mixed. . . . There is less, much less, of what is desirable in mind & manners among the females & still more especially in remote parts, indeed anywhere except in the large towns. This arises from a very inferior education, from the wives & daughters even of persons of considerable property doing almost if not all quite the drudgery of the house; they have frequently no "help" as tis called; servants you shd know are not known; . . .they marry at sixteen, & then have to nurse as well as keep house (& have no chance of improvement or refinement).[14]

In this case, in spite of other passages of romantic hopes for the future, the reluctance of the women to emigrate perhaps needs no further explanation. His daughter, Mrs. P. A. Taylor, was also influenced by reading Henry Bradshaw Fearon's *Sketches of America*. She found his account of the character of the Americans "most disgusting" and hoped

[12] *Courtauld Family Letters,* 2: 453–54.
[13] Ibid., pp. 474–75.
[14] Ibid., pp. 422–23, 483–84.

her father's feelings would change.[15] A few weeks later, she summarized the reactions of the women to their father's proposal: "I cannot tell you dearest Sophy *how* disappointed I felt, on finding that my father had so completely forgotten his (I may say *promise*) not to commit himself to anything specific before his return to us. . . . My Mother I know will not, cannot like it. . . . My dearest Sophy's wishes and feelings, I well know, are not in America." Their sister Eliza was somewhat less definitively against the project: "Really I think it a difficult thing to decide whether to remain in England or go to America. . . when there how are we to live until the farm produces something I know not but. . . Should we remain in Gt. Britain I believe the look forward is not more or indeed so promising," she wrote during the summer of 1819. By autumn she confessed to Sophia that she would not be disappointed should America be given up in view of "the difficulties that would await us there," while Sophia herself was horrified at the plan that she should teach school in Marietta, Ohio—"a rather dismal lookout," she thought.[16] Nevertheless, in spite of his display of unauthoritarian parenthood, George Courtauld's will prevailed with his daughters.

This resistance of women did sometimes succeed, though such cases are less likely to leave a historical trace. Ruth Courtauld did not go with her husband but remained in England to be well supported by her son Samuel's increasing business success in silk manufacture. One other large extended family migration on which we have abundant documentation is that of the Morris family from Chorlton, Lancashire, most of whom were handloom weavers and who emigrated in stages from 1828 to 1831 because they had not the means to go all at the same time as did the Courtaulds. The eldest son, Jonathan, was the only one in this large family to remain in England, and he did so quite clearly because of the resistance of his wife and her family to the undertaking.[17] In-laws also featured in the successful resistance of Mrs. Jonas Booth to emigration. As her husband wrote in 1829 from Oneida County, New York, to his brother, a stuff manufacturer in Bradford: "I wish my children and wife was over, but I have wrote to them but I have got no answer back. I suppose it is that infernal crew that has stopped her from sending, which

[15] Henry Bradshaw Fearon, *Sketches of America* (London, 1818); ibid., p. 512.

[16] *Courtauld Family Letters,* 2: 514, 578, 613, 603.

[17] Charlotte Erickson, *Invisible Immigrants: The Adaptation of English and Scottish Immigrants in Nineteenth-Century America* (1972; rpt., Ithaca: Cornell University Press, 1990), pp. 140–41.

has been the cause of all my trouble. They wished me a thousand miles off but I got four thousand miles from them."[18]

Other cases of the opposition of a wife deterring a willing husband from emigrating turn up in letters written to English immigrants in the United States.[19] Sandra Myres concluded from her examination of diaries and reminiscences of mostly native-born women moving to the American West Coast that 28 percent strongly opposed the move and 32 percent favored it. "A reading of numerous accounts by British and Canadian women suggests similar percentages," she maintained.[20] Although I cannot make quantitative judgments in this respect, I am certain that the percentage opposed would shoot up with the inclusion of women who succeeded in preventing the emigration of their husbands.

Women who resisted emigration but went reluctantly often failed to adapt to the New World. Such failure could end in remigration, if the family could afford to return to England. After sixteen years in the United States, Charles Streater finally had to inform his sister in Hampshire: "I regret to tell you that Mrs. Streater does not like the situation I have chosen for my future residence & she is set against a residence altogether in the Country, so much so that I am apprehensive no circumstances will tend to reconcile to remain."[21]

The letters of the Courtauld daughters—very reluctant immigrants—constituted such a stream of complaint that their mother, who after her marriage in the 1780s had been an emigrant to upper New York State, whence she and her husband had retreated to England in 1794, now remonstrated with her daughters about their attitudes. In September 1821 she wrote to Sophia and Catherine from Bocking, Essex: "I was

[18] Jonas Booth, New Hartford, Oneida County, N. Y., March 20, 1829, to his brother and sister in Bradford, copy in the British Library of Political and Economic Science (cited hereinafter as BLPES).

[19] See statement that Benner would like to emigrate but does not know whether he'll ever get his wife to go, in W. Squier, Pinchbeck, Lincs., June 27, 1851, to his uncle and aunt in Wis.; and that Mr. Barwell hesitates, for the same reason, Henry Squier, January 2, 1854, to his uncle and aunt, both in Kimberley Letters, Wisconsin State Historical Society, Madison, Mss/DV; B. Norton, Bagdon Hall, May 13, 1852, to James Clarke, Albion, Dane County, Wis., Lawrence C. Whittet Papers, Wisconsin State Historical Society, Madison, Whs Mss 27.

[20] Sandra Myres, "Victoria's Daughters: English-Speaking Women on Nineteenth Century Frontiers," in *Western Women: Their Land, Their Lives*, ed. Lillian Schlissel, et al. (Albuquerque: University of New Mexico Press, c.1988), p. 268.

[21] Dr. Charles Streater, Chevy Chase Farm, near Baltimore, December 31, 1838, to his sister in Headley, Hants., papers in private possession, copy made for the author. For another case of return migration, see the letters of Rebecca Butterworth in Erickson, *Invisible Immigrants*, pp. 175–78.

rather surpris'd at your disappointment in finding things so rough on your first arrival. I think I took no small trouble to inform you while you were deliberating & if you only thought of what it was possible for your father & brothers to accomplish in the thick woods in so short a time with so little assistance I think you would be rather astonished at things being so well." In December, a letter to Catherine responded to another sort of complaint from her daughters.

> How very sorry I am to see you indulging a spirit of contemtuous dislike to your new country and its inhabitants. Such a spirit and mode of expressing it is not calculated to bend your own mind to your present situation or to conciliate those among you whom you are likely to spend the remainder of your days . . . to kick and scratch at a new Country because you have not every convenience the moment you come into it, and as someone said, the geese running about ready roasted, beging you to eat them, and the stonish'd inhabitants beging you to condescend to accept their vegetables for which, I suppose, they had in their time labour'd and join you in your ill-judg'd aspersions of a country of which you may well be proud.[22]

She warned them not to marry "until the country about you is a little better settled." It was clear that her married daughter was even more bitter, with a sick husband and children to care for. As Catherine Taylor wrote to her sister Sophia in the summer of 1822, "Oh, dearest Soph, when those flattering pictures of the *backwoods* were sketched, when the small but therefore more endeared circle was pourtrayed by family enjoying after the various occupations of the day 'the feast of reason & the flow of souls,' oh had truth snatched the pencils & shown us that little circle so widely scattered o'er these boundless woods—how would our hearts have sunk within us." And in November, after a third miscarriage, her bitterness overflowed: "In this Country women brought up as we have been & the wives of poor men must labour themselves to their graves sooner or later. If I were unmarried no *poor man* however beautiful & amiable could tempt me." The reality of frontier life was more than these women could bear, not simply the poverty and hard work, but also, as Mrs. Taylor wrote, the want of people of the right sort: "I want Society, not company."[23] One after another, they retreated to England in 1823.

[22] *Courtauld Family Letters*, 2: 848, 865.
[23] Ibid., 2: 917 and 3: 963.

The Courtauld women might be said to epitomize some features of an unsuccessful adaptation.[24] They left England, not primarily for economic reasons but to avoid a feared future loss of status. In America they were disappointed in not finding social refinement and artistic interests among frontier people. These reactions were linked to their idealization of the prospect of being landowners, as well as their inexperience of hard work and want of inclination to try it. This expectation on the part of some women of a life without work was expressed most forcefully by one of Richard Flower's daughters from Albion, Illinois: "Its not a good place to get that small income or to get a comfortable living without one except you go out to labour."[25]

Not all immigrant women were defeated by the clash between expectations and reality. In some we find a tone of resignation. Martha Bottomley's husband was the son of a woolen mill manager near Huddersfield. He had given up a position as pattern designer at that mill to take his wife and family to start out on an unimproved farm in Wisconsin in 1842. Martha confided in a letter to her cousin, Mary Wood, a year later, "As for saying How I like the cuntry all I can Say is I am Happy with a good husband and I know it is my Duty to strive to make him happy also and I say with the words of Ruth wether thou goest I will go and where thou Diest I will Die."[26] When her husband died in 1847, leaving her with a young family, she refused the offer of her in-laws to take them back to England, writing that "I feel it is my

[24] See also Mrs. Joseph Priestley, in Northumberland County, Pa., in 1795, "much pester'd & provok'd from the impossibility of getting or keeping Servants" (Norman Wilkinson, ed., "Mr Davy's Diary," October 3, 1795, *Pennsylvania History* 20 [1953]: 258). Morris Birkbeck's daughters were said to have made themselves thoroughly disliked by other females in Princeton, Indiana, where he stopped for the winter after his arrival in 1817 ("Diaries of David MacDonald, 1824–6," *Indiana Historical Society Publications* 14 [1942]: 279). Or see Prudence, daughter of Morris Birkbeck, writing to her aunt, Mrs. Bush, from Wanborough, Ill. August 14, 1825, after her father had drowned, "We *could not* move now, but I hope many years will not pass over us, in this country, in which I can no longer have any interest whatsoever" (Gladys Thomson, *A Pioneer Family: The Birkbecks in Illinois* [London: Jonathan Cape, 1953], p. 105). Richard Flower's daughters, Martha Pickering and Katherine Ronalds, bemoaned the want of servants and companions (Mary Katherine Ronalds, Albion, Ill., March 7, 1830, to her brother Edward Flower, a brewer in Stratford-on-Avon [a firm that survives to this day], George Flower Collection, Chicago Historical Society, ACCN: 1933 0008).

[25] Martha Pickering, Park House, Albion, Ill., June 16, 1828, to her brother Edward Flower, George Flower Collection, Letters, 1824–46.

[26] Milo Milton Quaife, ed., *An English Settler in Pioneer Wisconsin: The Letter of Edwin Bottomley,* Publications of the State Historical Society of Wisconsin, Collections 25 (1918): 49.

duty to stay hear and strugal with the cares of this world so long as the lord sees fit to spare me."[27]

The importance of a "good husband" to a woman's adaptation is further illustrated in the case of Sarah Knight. Emigrating with her husband in 1821 to the same backwoods of southern Ohio that defeated the Courtaulds, she wrote four years later:

> I am not surprised at your being so much delighted with English scenery, when I only *think* of it, which I often do I am surprised how I so contented as I am here—But I hope that best of earthly comforts will never forsake me for if it shd *even* Eng—with all *its beauties* wd not *satisfy me* . . . . If Mr. K did [not] love the children as well as I do myself it wd render me very uncomfortable. But his heart is a fountain of affection from whence are continually issuing springs of love that dayly adds to my comfort."[28]

That her husband appreciated the contribution of his wife is indicated in a letter he wrote seven years later in 1832:

> Mrs. Knight was once in the enjoyment of all that I have mentioned—she accompanied me to the wilderness—she has borne the fatigues and cares of a new settler with me—she has left the home of her fathers—she has severed herself from all that was dear to her in her native land—she has participated with me in all the toils and perils—the hopes and fears—the joys and sorrows—and *now* nothing would induce her to return.[29]

The writing is flowery and trite, no doubt; but it would seem that the Knights' relationship was a significant factor in Mrs. Knight's successful adaptation.

A variation on the theme of the good husband can be found in a letter that Martha Ingle wrote from southern Indiana in 1820,to her sister in Hertfordshire. John and Martha Ingle had seen better times in England, and she might have been expected to echo the complaints of the Courtauld, Birkbeck, and Flower women, situated as they were on indifferent farming land. Yet it is difficult to doubt her sincerity when she wrote: "Rest assured my dear Mary that if I was not comfortable I should not say I was. I again tell you I was never more comfortable in my life . . . Perhaps the greatest secret of my happiness lies here, when

[27] Ibid., p. 210.
[28] *Courtauld Family Letters*, 3: 1308–9.
[29] Ibid., pp. 1922–23.

in prosperity in England I had an affectionate husband but not a praying Husband, now I possess both."[30]

In 1888 from another frontier, Kansas, Catherine Bond, daughter and wife of agricultural laborers, still somewhat regretted her emigration nineteen years after she had left Lancashire, mainly because of the uncertainties of Kansas farming but also because of loneliness: "I wish we was nearer so that we could see each other some times. I feel lonely many a time so far from you all. We left to better ourselves but Sometimes I thinck we should have done as well if we had stayed . . . . I often tell Jim we should have more pleasure of our life if we lived in Old England even if he only had his days labour for he got payed for it but we work many a month and dont get any pay." Yet four years later, after her eldest son left home saying there was nothing to be made farming, and her daughter, who had been her companion, died at nineteen, Catherine Bond wrote: "I could never go to England to live now after being here in Kansas. The air is so light here." And after her husband's death in 1897, she noted: "I would like to see you, but I shall never leave Kansas. This is my home as long as I am on this earth." Resignation and acceptance came late in life. She too felt that her husband had been "a good father and a kind husband and has left a good home for us."[31]

A far more favorable initial response to emigration is to be found in the letters of Jane Morris, wife of Andrew, a handloom weaver, formerly of Chorley, Lancashire. "Please to tell my father that I should be very glad if I could go over to see him somtime, but I never want to see him in that country. I would much rather he would come and see me . . . . I am well of, for I have good health, a good house and a good husband and am perfectly satisfied with the country."[32] This was an early reaction, within two years of immigration and before the family left for Ohio. After that, all the letters were signed by both Andrew and Jane Morris. Even the early ones may have reflected his views or have been written as much for his eyes as for those of the relatives still in England. If taken at face value,

[30] Martha Ingle, The Refuge, Saundersville, Vanderburgh County, Ind., March 2, 1820, to Miss Mary Sutton, her sister, Buntingsford, Herts., Ingle Correspondence, Indiana Historical Society, Mss M167, folder 3.

[31] Erickson, *Invisible Immigrants*, pp. 221–23, 224.

[32] Ibid., p. 153. See also her words just after their arrival in America, "I find this country much like Andrew often told us. There is plenty of work; plenty of victules, and clothing is nearly as cheap as in England . . . . I am in better health and better spirits and more content than ever I was before but I am sorry when I think that all our relations is in such an oppresst land" (p. 147).

however, this seems to have been a family in which the wife shared her husband's enthusiasm for and hopes from emigration.

In this family, as in most of those referred to where the women's views surface, one finds again attitudes on the part of men that are not altogether in keeping with the stereotype of the nineteenth-century patriarchal household. Andrew's brother Thomas, also a handloom weaver, described three revealing incidents on board the ship *Telegraph* on which he and his wife sailed for Baltimore in May 1830. First, three days out to sea, "at night the ship began to rool rather heavy which made some of the boxes tumble about in the steerige which alarmed the whoman and children. A greate many prayed and wished themselves at Liverpool or at home again." He also recounted, however, that "one man fell down in the steerige and wanted the captain to hold the ship still wile he got up again and placed his boxes."

If there was condescension toward the women in these remarks, the Lancashire men clearly supported their women in an incident two days later, when "before breakfast was ended a sad disaster broke out. Our whoman began to find a live stock of gray horses which had strayed from a few Irish men, so we made them bring out their beds and beding wich we found very throng. 1 of their blankets we put overbord and a bed the steward hung by a rope outside the ship to air . . . . [T]he day was a day of great slaughter among the Irish horse for we made the Irish men examin all their body clothing."

The third incident is even more revealing. It occurred on June 17, when they were nearly a month out of Liverpool. A "man struck his wife. So we called our Comitty to try him and sentence him and his sentence was that there should be 6 whomen chosen and give him 6 slaps each with a handsaw on his backside. So they began and laid him on a barrel. But Mary Fairbrother being the 4th and being inraged gave him 7 slaps which made his friends fly in. So it was agreed to let him go."[33] Apart from their aged mother, the women in the Morris clan were eminently successful migrants in that they positively supported their husbands' decision to emigrate and encouraged others to come after they had settled in America. The support they received in these shipboard incidents from their Lancashire men—among whom were carpenters, a blacksmith, and handloom weavers—is clear. They also shared their husbands' images of America as a land of liberty and equality where taxes did not oppress the poor.

[33] Ibid., pp. 148–49.

Some other English immigrant men expressed a positive belief in the equality of women. Samuel Blackwell, a failed sugar refiner from Bristol, dissenter, and abolitionist, who emigrated in 1832 with his wife and nine children, rejected traditional female roles. His five daughters all had careers and never married, while one of his sons married feminist Lucy Stone and another, Antoinette Brown, an ordained minister.[34] Another Englishman, John S. Webb, wrote in a private letter that he wanted to take the affirmative in a local debate on the view that women "should have all rights and privileges of men—socially, morally, politically." Son of an accountant in Sheffield, Webb was attempting, through keeping a school in Illinois, to establish his family on a farm, unsuccessfully in the end. As the depression of the late 1850s settled on them, his wife's endless attempts to persuade him to return to England finally prevailed.[35]

The English letters also provide some support for the view that gender roles in the West "if separate were permeable."[36] Casualness about women's role is apparent in the diary kept by the Quaker Yorkshireman William Savage, who farmed in Van Buren County, Iowa. "Took corn to the mill, and Anna and I killed two hogs," he recorded on January 4, 1859. A few months later, entries such as "Anna & I went to the spring to wash" and "Mrs Bennett, Mrs Wells, and Mrs Sneath here Got dinner and washed up" were recorded.[37] Struggling against heavy odds to make a farm in Boone County, Nebraska, during the 1870s, John Turner, whose wife was sickly, frequently did the housework with their sons. "This experience in housework was not despised and looked upon as degrading," he wrote later, "nor ought it

[34] Margot Horn, "Sisters Worthy of Respect: Family Dynamics and Women's Roles in the Blackwell Family," *Journal of Family History* 8 (1983): 367–82.

[35] She was daughter of a calico printer in Manchester (Marriage Certificate, March 1855, 8d/218). For the quotation, see J. S. Webb, Dundee, Kane County, Ill., December 28, 1857, in J. Barry Davies, ed., *Letters from America, 1853–60*, (Upton-upon-Severn, Worcs.: Self Publishing Association, 1991), p. 160; for her attempts to persuade him to return, see pp. 125, 144.

[36] Elizabeth Jameson, "Women as Workers, Women as Civilizers: True Womanhood in the American West," *Frontiers: A Journal of Women's Studies* 7 (1984): 3; Sandra Myres, *Westering Women*, p. 272.

[37] Edgar Harlan, ed., "William Savage, Iowa Pioneer, Diarist, and Painter of Birds," *Annals of Iowa*, 3d. ser. 19 (1933–35): 192, 216, 217. Another example is provided by Robert Tate, a bell-hanger from northern England who was trying to farm in Elk Grove, Lee County, Illinois, in the 1840s. Tate recorded in his diary that his wife shared the field work with him (Robert Nicholson Tate Diary, 1835–71, p. 53, microfilm, Illinois State Historical Survey).

to be regarded by any boy, no matter what his social standing may be, though that seems to be too often the case."[38]

Scholars have posited a change in "gender ideology" among textile workers in Lancashire in the mid-nineteenth century in favor of a family breadwinner and home-based wives, even at the price of a reduced standard of living. Mary Blewett traced such a change in attitudes occurring in Fall River, Massachusetts. In contrast, British scholar Richard Margrave, who found silk workers in Paterson insisting that their wives remain at home, concluded that this had been traditional among silk workers in Macclesfield.[39] Many immigrant letter writers revealed no such expectation. Women were too important to the success of the immigrant with modest means, whether on a farm or in a city. In the many families divided for a while during the process of emigration, women of necessity undertook greater responsibilities. Those who did thereby gave evidence of their participation, both in decision making and in carrying out the enterprise.

To make emigration possible, women often had to take charge both of family and of finance in their husbands' absence. Sometimes aided by parents or in-laws, these Englishwomen may have had a lonelier and more exposed existence than did women from some parts of Europe where the tradition of male emigration, seasonally or for a few years, was well established. Jesse Fielding, a fustian weaver in Oldham, Lancashire, agreed to her husband's emigration alone after they had been unable to save during four years of marriage. She helped raise

[38] John Turner, *Pioneers of the West* (Cincinnati: Jennings and Pye, 1903), p. 200. From the same decade, the 1870s, compare the remarks of William B. Brown, Sr.: "Helping wife some at washing[.] [S]he has to work to hard such days so I help what I can." He had been an agricultural laborer before their emigration (Diary of William P. Brown, Sr., March 25, 1878). See also the entries of March 10, 1878, and October 19, 1876, William P. Brown Papers, 1852–1914, Bentley Historical Library, Ann Arbor, Mich., AA2 Mss C000 T80; John Greening Diary, April 8, 1849, in Josie Greening Croft, ed., "A Mazomanie Pioneer of 1847," *Wisconsin Magazine of History* 26 (1942): 217. Of course, one also meets the more expected view in someone like John S. Webb, agent in New York of Sheffield steel firm John Brown. Webb welcomed the fact that his first child was a daughter because she would be able to nurse the children to follow: "She will knit & sew & make porritch when a boy would only be playing marbles" (Davies, *Letters from America*, p. 128).

[39] Mary H. Blewett, "Traditions and Customs of Lancashire Popular Radicalism in Late Nineteenth-Century Industrial America," Paper presented at the Third International Labor and Working-Class History/Mouvement Sociale Colloquium, Paris, October 1991, p. 5, unpublished manuscript kindly given me by the author: p. 5; Richard Margrave, *The Emigration of Silk Workers from England to the United States in the Nineteenth Century, with Special Reference to Country, Macdesfield, Paterson, New Jersey and South Manchester, Connective* (New York: Garland, 1986), p. 265.

£4.10 for his journey, then went to work in a factory, leaving her little boy with a neighbor, and supported them both until she could join her husband in America.[40] Men encouraged their wives to go to work in their absence, when they found themselves unable to send remittances for support of the family.[41] Others left their wives to handle their business affairs, the collection and payment of debts, and the sale of homes and household goods, in addition to the care of children.[42]

The women in the Morris family went to work to assist in the success of the emigration venture and to enable the family to buy land. We have other instances in which still single sisters and daughters, as well as wives, helped their families get a foothold by their work in textile mills.[43] Young John Worrall Williamson found that "our girls" obtained work on power looms more quickly than he could get an apprenticeship as a mechanic in Pittsburgh, and he decided to follow them into the mill where they worked to see if he could get a job as an overlooker.[44] The mother of an English miner in Illinois, Alexander Bradley, was described as "the forceful member of the family. To supplement the income she peddled vegetables from her garden door-to-door and ran a one-room store in the house. A large pipe-smoking woman with a vocabulary of colorful profanity that was easily loosed on anyone in her presence, she was awe-inspiring."[45]

From a more privileged background, orphaned Lucy Rutledge and her sister made their way on their own to an uncle who was a Baptist minister near Davenport, Iowa, in 1848. There they found him living with his wife and several children in a one-room house. "Had we left a

[40] John Regan, *The Emigrants Guide* (Edinburgh: Oliver and Boyd, 1852), p. 209.

[41] William Darnley, New York City, July 20 and August 29, 1858, to his wife, Darnley Family Letters, 1843–84, New York Public Library; "S," Albion, Ill. Spring 1844, to parents, in Grant Foreman, "English Settlers in Illinois," *Illinois Historical Society Journal* 34 (1941): 318. See also a case in which the wife of a silk weaver emigrated first with the children, leaving her husband to follow when he had saved passage money, in ibid. p. 22.

[42] Letters of Mrs. Williams, Poole, Dorset, December 17– February 25, 1889, to her husband, Thomas Williams, in Minneapolis, passim, Charles Garrett Roe Papers, Minnesota Historical Society Archives, Mss A R698–9; William Darnley, Liverpool, June 3, 1857, to his wife, Darnley Family Papers.

[43] John Wilson, Lowell, Mass., April 21 and July 29, 1849, to his father in Halifax, Yorks., BLPES. Wilson expected his wife and sister to go to work in a carpet factory as soon as they arrived. Richard Hails, Lincoln, Mass., July 31, 1841, to his brother George, in North Shields, Northumberland, in Erickson, *Invisible Immigrants,* p. 315.

[44] John Worrall Williamson, Allegheny City, Pa., June 5, 1848, to his sister Charlotte and her husband, Samuel Ashton, private papers, lent to me by the late T. S. Ashton.

[45] John Keiser, "The Union Miners Cemetery at Mt. Olive, Illinois: A Spirit Thread of Labor History," *Journal of the Illinois State Historical Society* 62 (1969): 235.

comfortable home in London and travelled this distance to find ourselves placed in such surroundings!" wrote Lucy Rutledge. Soon marrying into a family from Leeds, she set out to make the overland trek to California with her husband and his family in the spring of 1852. Before setting out, she and her mother-in-law "gave a concert last night borrowed a piano in town. I had the honor of playing duets & singing. [T]he house was crowded it being but small[.] [S]till we cleared $23 so that will pay some ferrages."[46]

Little trace has been found of the minority of Englishwomen who emigrated on their own, not simply in response to the decisions of their husbands or fathers, whether dutifully or enthusiastically. One daughter in the Grayston family in Aughton, Lancashire, appears to have wanted to emigrate in the 1860s because her parents, an agricultural laborer and his wife, as well as others in the community, disapproved of her keeping company with an Irish immigrant who was a Roman Catholic. She could secure neither the means nor family approval until she became pregnant. At that point the family sufficiently overcame their typical Lancastrian prejudice against the Irish to help them leave for America.

Mary Wilson was another young woman assisted to go to Sheffield relatives in the cutlery town of Waterbury, Connecticut, with her illegitimate child. Unlike Ann Grayston, Mary Wilson had no prospective husband to accompany her, and she was miserable in America. As James Roberts wrote in February 1850: "Mary is [working] in our warehouse, but she does not like the country. If she did she might do well." Two months later, however, "something else hapend," he reported.

> but before I tell you I shal let you know of the gloominess of Mary. She had been continually going to England. It was on the carpet every verse end untill I was quite tired & I told her that if she would wait untill the back end of August I would go to England with her & she almoast agread but thought [it] to long to wait. [B]ut since then she has been rather more composed up to the 1st of April when to the great surprize of the whole ville she made a April fool of [us] by marrying Mr. Thomas Bradley that was partner with Thomas Evans.[47]

Another woman's unhappiness in Minneapolis in the 1880s and inability to get on with nieces and nephews—who had enabled her to emigrate

[46] Lucy Rutledge Cooke, in Holmes, *Covered Wagon Women*, 4: 76–77, 230.

[47] For the Grayston family, see Erickson, *Invisible Immigrants*, p. 211; for Mary Wilson, pp. 324–25.

with her thirteen-year-old son—arose from disappointed hopes of marriage. A widow, Harriet Wicks left Manchester dissatisfied with her life, taking in lodgers to supplement her son's earnings of eight shillings a week, determined to be married to a kind but rich husband.[48]

Far from conforming to a stereotype, Englishwomen displayed a range of attitudes, from resistance to resignation to positive agreement or initiative, on the question of immigration. To give another angle on these differences in expectations, we can compare them with the attitudes of native-born American women faced with proposals for long-distance migration within the United States. In recent years, several studies have appeared of women who participated in the overland trek to the Far West, across the plains, deserts, and mountains from the Middle West to the Pacific coast in the 1840s and 1850s before a railway had been built. In many respects the Overland Trail could be compared to the Atlantic crossing: The journey was as physically terrifying and forbidding as crossing the great deep by sail. It also meant breaking up the home, selling all one's earthly belongings not appropriate for the journey, and making a sharp separation from the past, as communication would be slow and visits not far from prohibitive, at least for a while.

John Mack Faragher emphasized the resistance of women to the prospect of the Overland Trail. Women did not want to go and frequently agreed only when they realized that their husbands would otherwise leave them behind. The prospect of desertion, of being left alone to cope with a young family without an independent livelihood, was worse. "The threat of some husbands to go alone was enough to change women's minds," he concluded.[49] On the long journey their diaries reveal that they quietly suppressed their opposition and homesickness, hiding their tears and enduring the hardships. They did not want to be held responsible for a decision to turn back (what could not be done at sea) and often suspected their husbands' own uncertainties were so near the surface on the trail that they would have seized an opportunity to blame their wives for failure and defeat.

I have found other letters of internal migrants, not presented with the daunting decision to go to the Far West but with a lesser trek west, who

[48] Harriet Wicks, Hulme, Manchester, January 16, 1883, to nieces and nephews in Minneapolis, and to Emma Pollard, June 3, 1883, to Maria, December 16, 1883, and to Emma Pollard, February 26, 1884, Scott/Forsyth Papers.

[49] John Mack Faragher, *Women and Men on the Overland Trail* (New Haven: Yale University Press, 1979), pp. 167–68. Also emphasizing the resistance of women to migration is Schlissel, ed., *Women's Diaries of the Westward Journey,* p. 150.

did not want to move. Robert Bowles, an immigrant farmer in Ohio in the 1820s, delighted in his cottage with morning glories around the door, in land ownership, and in low taxes. Nevertheless, he seems to have been at least mildly affected by the itch to seek more land farther west in Indiana but gave up the idea because his wife was "so timid it is quite out of the question." She clearly did not share his delight—or professed delight—with Ohio, though he wrote confidently that "she only wants weaning and she will feel as I do."[50] Or take the remark of New England—born Sarah Kenyon from Plum Creek, Iowa, in August 1856: "Mr. Parsons sold his farm a week ago for 27 hundred and is going farther west about two hundred miles. His wife feels very bad about it. I don't blame her . . . but any of the westers are ready to sell any time to make money."[51]

But, as in the case of overseas migrants, one also finds women who agreed with the decision, such as Fanny Hatch, who wrote to her sister Patty from Rochester, New York, in August 1839:

> You will be surprised to hear that we are going to move to the west. Henry went to Illinois last May his health is much better there and he wishes us to go, Brother Charles likewise wishes us to go, and he will assist the boys, Frederick wants very much to go, there are more Mechanicks in Rochester than can find employment. . . . [S]hould I refuse to go Henry will return for he will not leave us. . . . I can see no inducement to stay here[.] [o]ur Family expences are increasing, my health is not good, all that was dear to me is gone. I have now only to consult the interest of my children. . . . [W]e intend to leave here in about two weeks. . . . [I]t is but a few days since we made up our minds to go."[52]

Mrs Hatch may have felt cornered, but she also felt, as indicated by "we," that she had shared in the decision.

Many Englishwomen displayed feelings of social dependency—loss of status and betrayal of their own values respecting the role of wives and mothers should they refuse to go—that Faragher emphasized as governing the agreement of reluctant women to undertake the overland trek. Nevertheless, the evidence indicates that this is only a part of the

[50] Robert Bowles, Harrison, Hamilton County, Ohio, October 11, 1823, to his brothers, Robert Bowles Letters, Ohio Historical Society, Columbus.

[51] Mildred Throne, ed., "Iowa Farm Letters, 1856–65." *Iowa Journal of History* 58 (1960): 56.

[52] Fanny Hatch, Rochester, N.Y., August 26, 1839, to her sister, Newcomb-Johnson Papers, Huntington Library, San Marino, Calif.

picture. Some wives participated actively in decision making and found their expectations fulfilled in America. Julie Roy Jeffery reached this conclusion in her study of frontier women. Like the English letters, her sources showed a range of response, which made her avoid characterizing all women as reluctant emigrants.[53]

It is possible to explain in part this range of response by summarizing some of the factors that governed the readiness or reluctance of women to emigrate and the quality of their adaptation as migrants. Clearly, I have drawn on letters and diaries that largely concern migrations to the frontier and, more specifically, to the farming frontier. Margaret Walsh has reminded us that for all the generalizations so common about the surplus of males on the frontier, census data for farming regions in the underdeveloped West show that the surplus was small in contrast to mining and lumbering regions.[54] It was exceedingly difficult to run a farm without women, and men who arrived without them began to search for one almost immediately. As Edward Gilley, an immigrant from Northumberland, confessed to his sister in a letter written from Wisconsin in 1845: "I found when I got settled that I could not get on without a housekeeper. So I got me a wife last January, and she, by casting some clothes in the month of June, caught cold and turned to inflammation in the bowels and died in the month of July which causes me to feel very destitute as am liveing alone with a great deal of care."[55] In the English emigration from the 1820s to the 1850s—when the hope of land ownership, if not the reality of farming life in a developing economy, drew so many of the immigrants, even those who knew that they would have to work at other occupations before realizing that dream—the migration was primarily a family movement, and the role of women essential, even if, as we have seen, they were outnumbered by men. Social dependency worked in both directions.

Like the American women on the Overland Trail, these Englishwomen often moved to the frontier, uprooting themselves from established social and familial ties and moving to a less developed economy than that from which they came. I detect among the women who

[53] Julie Roy Jeffery, *Frontier Women: The Trans-Mississippi West, 1840–80* (New York: Hill and Wang, 1979).

[54] Margaret Walsh, *The American Frontier Revisited* (London: Macmillan, 1980), p. 63.

[55] Edward Gilley, Porter, Rock County, Wis., September 28, 1845, to his sister, BLPES. Other examples of the immense difficulties experienced by bachelors or widowers can be found in the Fisher Letters, in Erickson, *Invisible Immigrants,* pp. 119–21, and in James Nowland, Houlston, Maine, June 29 and March 30, 1849, and December 1850, to Mary Ann Reid, his sister, in Liverpool, Nowland Papers, Huntington Library.

embraced migration certain differences in motivation between English migrants and native-born Americans. Thus far, I have found no Englishwomen who brought a consciousness of a civilizing and religious mission to frontier regions. There is no trace of the "pull factor" distinguished by Polly Kaufman in her study of American teachers on the frontier—"their sense of mission, of bringing Protestant evangelical religion and education to the West."[56] Nor have I yet found among English immigrants the broadly developed ideological conception of women's sphere that American historians have detected in the writings of literate, middle-class American women.

In contrast, the enthusiastic emigrants among Englishwomen avowed their faith in social equality and liberty—they do not seem to have had a desire to change or improve the world. In fact, three themes persistently recur among those who adapted successfully: good health, economic success, and religious faith. The women who accepted their situations almost invariably expressed a simple faith that families and friends, separated by migration, would be reunited in heaven and that the trials of this world were to be borne in that hope.

Three further considerations appear to have been sensitive ones for Englishwomen and can be summarized as those of companionship, work, and status. In these spheres, the attitudes Englishwomen brought to America and the women's willingness to modify them in the light of circumstances introduce further dimensions to the possibilities of successful adaptation.

If women came from a background in which they had satisfying primary group relations through family and friends with whom they had continuous social contact, the prospect of life in a thinly populated farming region with isolated homesteads was daunting. Unwillingness to emigrate may have been a function of the strength and warmth of these ties which had to be severed.[57] A single woman working as a

[56] Polly Welts Kaufman, *Women Teachers on the Frontier* (New Haven: Yale University Press, 1984), p. 17. On the other hand, Elizabeth Jameson warned that one should not assume "that western men were mythic rugged individuals whom women went to civilize" and suggested that western women "did not see themselves as passive civilizers or as uniquely oppressed" (Jameson, "Women as Workers," p. 7).

[57] One native-born woman in Lancaster, Pennsylvania, begged the owner of a paper mill to reemploy her husband to enable them to return to western Massachusetts "as I was never away from home and friends before, had no idea how I should feel" (Judith McGaw, *Most Wonderful Machine: Mechanization and Social Change in Berkshire Paper-Making, 1801–85* (Princeton: Princeton University Press, 1987), p. 330. For an ingenious quantitative test for the strength of kin networks as a deterrent to migration in Yorkshire,

governess in a strange household might be more willing to leave the country than a married woman with family nearby. But in their new situation, women were likely to find the work of a farm household—even in a kitchen, dairy, and garden—to be more isolating socially than men's work in the fields, which included contacts with neighbors and in market towns. It was more difficult for a woman to reestablish supportive social ties. A pertinent statement comes from Mrs. M. A. Rochester, wife of a store clerk in Nelsonville, Ohio, in 1825: "You wish to know how we spend the sundays[.] I am sorry to say they are not kept as I could wish[. S]ometimes there is meetings in Nelsonville but I have so many little ones I cannot very easyly well leave them but as they get older I shall not be confined[.] I go out but very little[. O]nce a month is as often as I get to Mr. Knights."[58]

In a town as well, the social isolation of a married woman as an immigrant might be distressing. Tom Martin, a piano maker from London, wrote of his wife's situation in Rochester, New York, soon after their arrival in 1850, "Jane. . . . seems very lonesome as she has no one to speak to from morn to night unless I am at home and that brings no grist to the mill."[59] Wives who went out to work may have avoided such lonely isolation.[60]

An unwillingness to mix with Americans (such as the Courtaulds demonstrated) or unfriendliness on the part of Americans could enhance the isolation if other English people had not settled in the area. Catherine Steel was the daughter of a carpenter who had worked at Buckingham Palace. On the Wisconsin frontier in the 1840s, she married a doctor who was the son of a civil servant in London. "I often think," she wrote to her sister-in-law in 1846, "we may congratulate ourselves upon our seclusion from the world for with the exception of

---

see R. J. Johnston, "Resistance to Migration and the Mover/Stayer Dichotomy: Aspects of Kinship and Population Stability in an English Rural Area," *Geografiska Annaler,* ser. B, Human Geography 53 (1971): 16–26.

[58] *Courtauld Family Letters*, 3: 1316–17.

[59] Thomas Martin, Rochester, N. Y., July 27, 1851, to his uncle in London, Martin Letters, Kent County Record Office, Maidstone. See also Mary Hannah Webb's laments in Newark, New Jersey, that there was no social going out to tea and that she had not had a single meal out of the house, except in New York City, since she arrived (Davies, *Letters from America,* p. 125).

[60] "As my wife and daughter could see nothing in America, that could make them forget England, and felt the more uncomfortable because they had no employment to occupy their minds and fill up their time, they rather urged me to get to a farm; in the hope that when they had a dairy, their thoughts would be diverted" (Edmund Edmunds, *Emigration, or, "A Word to the Wise"* [London: L. & G. Seeley, 1840], p. 4).

one or two english families with whom we occasionally exchange visits we have no society here. There are many traits in the American character I cannot admire. I have been much vexed several times to see the spirit they exhibit towards their transatlantic brethren even females for everybody is a politician."[61] That the situation was irksome to her she confessed later that month: "I do sometimes wish there was a little society here but Thomas does not care much for it."[62] In the following year they finally gave a party for twenty people: "A Mr. Dodson and his 2 sisters a very respectable and amiable family from England 2 years ago—Miss Case and 2 brother Yorkers but rather superior." Parties clearly began to liven Catherine Steel's life and spirits.[63]

On a farm, work was one reason for women's isolation. It was feared by and unfamiliar to women like the Courtaulds and a serious obstacle to their adaptation. It was not simply a question of the want of servants to those accustomed to having them but also the manifold inconveniences of a frontier farm. Catherine Steel proved more willing to work than were the Courtaulds. She was not used to having servants but wished that she could occasionally buy bread in a shop as in London and that the well in their village was finished after five years in Wisconsin. "When I ask myself how people do with two or three children [she had one] and no help I feel determined to try but I am not a first rate hand and there is not the same convenience in this country having to boil a pot on the log fire and no wash houses &c &c." She milked four cows and made eighteen pounds of butter a week, and she worried about feeding the fifty people who would come to raise the roof on their barn in May 1851.[64]

Catherine Steel's life was easy as compared with that of Martha Bottomley and her daughters Hannah and Ruth nearby in Wisconsin in the same decade. Edwin Bottomley had left Huddersfield so that his

[61] Catherine Steel, Genesee, Wis., May 2, 1846, to her sister-in-law, Lilly Steel, in London, Thomas Steel Papers, Wisconsin State Historical Society, Madison, Wis Mss 51 PB, file 4.

[62] Catherine Steel, May 29, 1846, to Lilly Steel, Thomas Steel Papers.

[63] Catherine Steel, April 13, 1848, and July 3, 1851, to Lilly Steel, Thomas Steel Papers, file 6. See also as late as the 1940s the letters of Mrs. Madge Jones in Washington, D.C. She resisted the temptation to transform herself into a "real Yank" longer than did her husband and children "and maintained a 'them' and 'us' attitude while the rest of the family devoted their energies to getting accepted" (Dallas Jones, "Just the Same only a Little Bit Different: A Case Study of an English Family's Assimilation in the United States," *North Staffordshire Journal of Field Studies* 13 [1973]: 62).

[64] Catherine Steel, November 2 and June 7, 1847, and May 15, 1851, to Lilly Steel, Thomas Steel Papers, files 5 and 6.

children would not have to work in a factory. In March 1845 Edwin wrote to his parents that they had sent, Hannah, their eldest daughter, to school for the winter. "But I see as we are situated we cannot well Do It and we have taken her home . . . . Hannah is going as a servant to Mr Nortons in about a fortnight and she is to have 1/2 Dollar a week." The next year he had to confess to his father:

> With Thos being sick it has caused me to be very busy and had it not been for our Hannah and Ruth I do not know how I should have got through so far . . . . [N]ow the girls in your neighbourhood would think it a Disgrace most likely to bee seen driveing oxen and hor[s]es but they were glad they could render their father so much service . . . [N]ow I would not have you think that I make my Girls Do this kind of work nor do I intend to. I only state this to show they are willing to Do anything they can Do."

That autumn, Hannah was still helping.

> When it came a fit day Our Hannah and me begun to Stack them [oats] we got two Loads up and Thos came and help[ed] me . . . . [T]hank god I have been able to get on pretty well for our Hannah said She would Drive for me while I Ploughed and we commenced a fortnight ago last Monday and we Ploughed with my oxen from 12 to 14 acres up to last Saturday night that is in a fortnight I comenced Sowing last monday and our Hannah and Ruth [h]arrow it one with oxen and the other with one horse.

Conscious of possible disapproval from his parents, he explained "my Children Hannah and Ruth are Determined to work what they can in the land and theire are plenty of jobs which will be no Disgrace for them to Do such as helping in the hay and Planting corn and several other little jobs which take time for me to Do which they can Do with propr[i]ety."[65] Four years later, Hannah was married and a mother, and her father was dead of typhoid fever. His widow remained in Wisconsin.

Those who did not worry overmuch about status—or were too poor to do so—were less likely to be particular about what companionship was available and what work, including field work, they had to do, if only in an emergency. Those who could say with Mrs. Hatch that "it is very inconvenient sometimes to be poor but no disgrace" managed better than Sarah Kenyon, who wrote from Iowa to her family in Connecticut

[65] Quaife, *English Settler,* pp. 87, 123–24, 134–35, 143.

in 1860, "We are the poorest folk you ever saw but I would not own it to anybody but you."[66] These were native-born women, but the surviving letters of Englishwomen also support the suggestion that those who stuck it out in western agriculture were people who if they had cared about status had little time to worry about it.

It might seem that the success of women as migrants was simply a function of their social class. Those used to work, indifferent to social rank, and willing to associate with their neighbors did better than women like the Courtaulds. But the latter were only tenuously middle-class, and many poor people failed or never reached the frontier. In general, a well-grounded economic motivation gave a better chance of success than did others. Those like the Courtaulds, who left because of other problems, carried those problems away and home again. Yet, economic motivation and success in their own terms were not enough for these women, evidence of whose adaptation survives. Migration forced the immigrant family to rely on its own human and material resources. Whatever their social origins, those women fortunate enough to have married men who were not only good workers but also had resources for social interaction with their wives and children had a distinct advantage in adapting to their migration. Therein lay one aspect of their social dependency.

One might leave the subject appropriately with the picture of an extending family in Monroe County, Illinois, in May 1856. The very well adapted Ann Whittaker wrote to her brother in Leeds that her husband "Thomas his as busy and has anxius has he was the first day we come. He is fenceing and clearing new ground every year. He looks fresh and well and Grandpappy to death nearly. [H]e hardly ever sits down to eat without one or the other of Elizabeth's children on his knees" "We are out of debt and a shilling to spare, so if we are not has happy as we need to be I know not."[67] It was more a question of the expectations of women than the reality of their situation that governed their adaptation as immigrants.

[66] Fanny Hatch, Farmington, Ill., June 27, 1838, to her nephew, Henry Johnson, in Cleveland, Newcomb-Johnson Papers; Throne, "Iowa Farm Letters," p. 74.

[67] Ann Whittaker, Monroe County, Ill., May 1856 to her brother and sisters, Photostat, B.L.P.E.S.; Erickson, *Invisible Immigrants*, pp. 188, 183.

Index